Understanding Human Decision-Making in Economic Models

Ford Lumban Gaol
Computer Science Department, Binus Nusantara University, Jakarta, Indonesia

Allayarov Piratdin
Tashkent State University of Economics, Uzbekistan

Elena Maslyukova
Southern Federal University, Russia

IGI Global
Scientific Publishing
Publishing Tomorrow's Research Today

Vice President of Editorial Melissa Wagner
Director of Acquisitions Mikaela Felty
Director of Book Development Jocelynn Hessler
Production Manager Mike Brehm
Cover Design Phillip Shickler

Published in the United States of America by
IGI Global Scientific Publishing
701 East Chocolate Avenue
Hershey, PA, 17033, USA
Tel: 717-533-8845
Fax: 717-533-7115
Website: https://www.igi-global.com E-mail: cust@igi-global.com

Library of Congress Cataloging-in-Publication Data

Names: Gaol, Ford Lumban editor | Allayarov, Piratdin, 1982- editor | Maslyukova, Elena, 1982- editor
Title: Understanding human decision-making in economic models / [edited by] Ford Lumban Gaol, Allayarov Piratdin, Elena Maslyukova.
Description: Hershey, PA : IGI Global Scientific Publishing, [2025] | Includes bibliographical references and index. | Summary: "This book aims to help the audience to understand and explore economics, dangers and of AI in Economics"-- Provided by publisher.
Identifiers: LCCN 2025008266 (print) | LCCN 2025008267 (ebook) | ISBN 9798369381663 hardcover | ISBN 9798369381670 paperback | ISBN 9798369381687 ebook
Subjects: LCSH: Decision making | Decision making--Technological innovations
Classification: LCC HD30.23 .U565 2026 (print) | LCC HD30.23 (ebook) | DDC 658.4/03--dc23/eng/20250411
LC record available at https://lccn.loc.gov/2025008266
LC ebook record available at https://lccn.loc.gov/2025008267

British Cataloguing in Publication Data
A Cataloguing in Publication record for this book is available from the British Library.

Table of Contents

Detailed Table of Contents

Semantic Web Technologies for the Digital Transformation offer a framework for analyzing and understanding the vast and complex information generated across various digital platforms. In this study, we collected data from X (formerly Twitter), Instagram, and online news articles using the keyword "digital transformation." Preprocessing techniques such as text cleaning, tokenization, stopword removal, and lemmatization were applied to ensure high-quality data. Feature extraction was performed using GloVe embeddings, capturing the contextual and semantic meanings of words in numerical form. Furthermore, Semantic Network Analysis was employed to identify relationships and patterns between key concepts, providing insights into the discourse on digital transformation. Through community detection and centrality analysis, the study identified thematic clusters and influential topics that shape the conversation on digital transformation.

design, and corporate leadership within corporates. As corporates increasingly embrace smart digital logistics techno-investigations, the consequences for staff member's proficiencies and leadership influence become deciding. Through a comprehensive analysis, the investigation highlights how smart logistics not only augments logistics efficiency but also serves as a catalyst for developing capital in human form. It manifest that corporates that innovate in logistics techno-investigations create a more agile and competent staff members, fostering a culture of continuous learning. Also, the outcomes manifest that influence leadership is closely tied to logistical proficiencies, advocating for the combination of logistics strategies into leadership design programs. The investigation concludes with practical recommendations for corporates to align their logistics initiatives with leadership instrumentation, augmenting both logistics sustainability and competitive strategic advantage.

Preface

INTRODUCTION

The global economy stands at the precipice of a profound transformation. The accelerating convergence of artificial intelligence (AI), big data analytics, and other disruptive technologies is instigating a fundamental reshaping not only of labor markets and consumption patterns but also of the very fabric of our economic interactions. Within this rapidly evolving landscape, established paradigms of economic modeling and decision-making face significant challenges and are undergoing substantial reformulation. It is in this context that we present *Understanding Human Decision-Making in Economic Models* — a timely and necessary exploration into the heart of intelligent economics.

This edited volume presents in-depth contributions analyzing the profound economic transformations underway. It offers a multi-dimensional perspective on how AI and big data are revolutionizing decision-making across scales, from individual consumer behavior to macroeconomic policy. The book unpacks the practical implications of automation and the gig economy, examines the adaptation of traditional sectors like finance, transportation, and hospitality to platform innovation, and addresses the emergent ethical, policy, and regulatory challenges of a data-saturated economy.

Our aim with this book is threefold:

1. To provide readers with a comprehensive understanding of the technological forces reshaping economic thought and practice;
2. To foster discussion on the ethical, social, and human-centered implications of intelligent systems in economic life;
3. And to offer practical insights for navigating this disruption — for policymakers, academics, practitioners, and informed citizens alike.

Highlights of the book include:

- Analyses of how AI and big data are transforming economic analysis and human decision-making.
- Discussions on the future of work, including automation and the rise of the gig economy.
- Case studies of disruption in traditional sectors via Fintech, the sharing economy, and platform capitalism.
- Exploration of algorithmic bias and the emerging need for inclusive regulatory frameworks.
- Strategic guidance on workforce reskilling, adaptation, and fostering shared prosperity in the digital era.

We've made a deliberate effort to ensure that this book is accessible to a broad audience — from academic researchers and graduate students in advanced econometrics, to general readers, library patrons, and professionals in economics and business. Through clear explanations and real-world examples, complex ideas are distilled in a way that sparks curiosity and deepens understanding.

As editors, we are proud to contribute to the growing body of literature on *Intelligent Economic Analysis*. We believe this book will serve as a vital resource for staying ahead of the curve in an age where economic intelligence is no longer just about numbers — it's about understanding the interplay between humans, machines, and data in shaping the future.

ORGANIZATION OF THE BOOK

This edited volume presents a comprehensive and multidisciplinary exploration of the evolving digital economic landscape, offering both foundational insights and sector-specific analyses. In **Chapter 1**, the authors provide a meta-analytical and reflexive examination of the conceptual, theoretical-methodological, and empirical literature on digital economic organization. Their analysis concludes that digital economic organization is inherently multidimensional, evolving through conceptual, methodological, and empirical advancements. **Chapter 2** extends this analytical lens into the intersection of behavioral finance and technological integration, uncovering how cognitive biases and institutional structures shape investor decisions. With evidence from survey data and interviews, the study emphasizes the critical role of AI and regulatory transparency in mitigating decision-making biases.

The digital transformation theme continues in **Chapter 3**, where Semantic Web Technologies are leveraged to map and interpret the discourse on digital transformation across platforms like X (formerly Twitter), Instagram, and news media. Through advanced network analysis, the chapter reveals thematic clusters and influential concepts in the digital conversation space.

In **Chapter 4**, attention shifts to the Horn of Africa, where smart logistics and leadership development converge. The chapter highlights how digital logistics innovation enhances operational agility and human capital development, calling for integrated strategies between leadership design and logistics optimization. **Chapter 5** further underscores the importance of institutional frameworks by investigating the internal and external determinants of SMEs' credit accessibility in Nigeria. The study confirms that commercial banks' internal practices significantly influence SME growth, offering valuable guidance for monetary policy reforms.

Shifting to consumer behavior, **Chapter 6** examines how brand attributes impact purchasing decisions in Chennai's modular kitchen market. The findings underscore the influence of product quality, brand personality, and aesthetics, while price sensitivity remains a deterrent—insights that carry strategic implications for marketers.

Investment decision-making is the focal point of **Chapter 7**, which introduces a framework for selecting optimal yacht marina locations in Turkey. Utilizing expert interviews and the Fuzzy AHP method, the chapter identifies accessibility, infrastructure, and weather as key criteria, offering investors a practical guide rooted in empirical insight. In **Chapter 8**, governance and the rule of law are explored through a bibliometric study of Indonesia, revealing how legal frameworks can strengthen transparency, trust, and citizen engagement in governance structures.

Finally, **Chapter 9** investigates the legal complexities surrounding clickwrap agreements, especially regarding minors in India. The chapter raises critical questions about consent, comprehension, and legal enforceability, calling for more robust legal safeguards in digital contracting environments. As a whole, this volume brings together diverse yet interconnected perspectives to unpack the mechanisms, challenges, and innovations defining today's digital economic order.

CONCLUSION

As editors of this volume, we are proud to present a curated collection of chapters that traverse the intricate landscape of digital economic organization, innovation, and policy transformation. Each contribution reflects a distinct perspective, yet all converge on a common theme: the transformative power of digital technologies in reshaping economies, governance, industry leadership, and societal interaction.

From the foundational conceptual analyses of digital organizational structures to the empirical explorations of behavioral finance, artificial intelligence, and sustainable enterprise development, this book offers a multifaceted lens on today's rapidly evolving digital economy. The interdisciplinary insights—from semantic web applications to smart logistics in Africa, from credit accessibility for SMEs to legal frameworks surrounding digital consent—underscore the urgent need for agile thinking, robust leadership, and inclusive policies in the face of complex global challenges.

Furthermore, the case studies and methodological approaches presented here not only advance academic discourse but also provide actionable strategies for policy-makers, entrepreneurs, technologists, and investors navigating digital transitions. These insights invite continued exploration and collaboration across disciplines and geographies.

In compiling this volume, our objective has been to illuminate emerging trends while encouraging critical inquiry and practical innovation. We hope this work stimulates meaningful conversations, supports forward-looking decision-making, and contributes to the broader understanding of digital transformation's role in shaping a sustainable and equitable global economy.

Chapter 1
Conceptual, Theoretical–Methodological, and Empirical Analysis of Digital Economic Organization

José G. Vargas-Hernandez
https://orcid.org/0000-0003-0938-4197
Financial Literacy Research Center, Universidad Cristóbal Colón, Mexico

Carlos A. Rodriguez-Maillard
https://orcid.org/0000-0003-2406-196X
Universidad Cristóbal Colon, Mexico

Absalón J. Salmerón-Zapata
https://orcid.org/0009-0002-2621-2426
Financial Literacy Research Center, Universidad Cristòbal Colòn, Mexico

Omar C. Vargas-Gonzàlez
https://orcid.org/0000-0002-6089-956X
Tecnològico Nacional de Mèxico, Ciudad Guzmán, Mexico

ABSTRACT

This paper aims to analyze the evolutionary advances in the review of the conceptual, theoretical-methodological and empirical literature on digital economic organization from different perspectives and in the current context. The method used is meta-analytical and meta-cognitive, reflexive and descriptive based on the review of the conceptual, theoretical-methodological and empirical literature. It is

DOI: 10.4018/979-8-3693-8166-3.ch001

concluded that digital economic organization is a multidimensional concept that ranges from conceptual to methodological and empirical changes.

INTRODUCTION

Over the years, organizations have been the subject of multiple studies to understand how they are structured and function in digital environments, especially in response to the growing digital transformation and the digital economy has gained the attention of researchers, consultants, journalists, policymakers, and business managers as an area of high potential (Li et al., 2020).

Digital organization refers to the integration of digital technologies into organizational structures and processes, transforming the way companies operate and relate to their customers. From various perspectives, the conceptualization of the digital organization can be addressed through definitions and approaches that highlight its importance in the current context.

From a technological perspective, a digital organization is characterized by the intensive use of digital technologies, such as artificial intelligence, big data, and the Internet of Things (IoT). These technologies are essential for automating processes, improving efficiency, and creating new forms of interaction and communication within the organization. The digital economy is seen as an essential force to drive structural changes and transformations in economies, especially in Latin American contexts.

Digital economic organizations tend to have more agile and less hierarchical structures, allowing them to quickly adapt to new opportunities and challenges. This translates into a greater capacity to form interdependent teams that collaborate on specific projects. It is considered a catalyst for reducing inequality and strengthening processes of social inclusion (ECLAC, 2013). This approach emphasizes the transformative role of the digital economy in social and economic development. From this perspective, digital transformation is not just a matter of technological adoption but of a fundamental change in organizational culture and the way of doing business (Bharadwaj et al., 2013).

Digital transformation, on the other hand, involves the integration of digital technologies into all areas of an organization, which fundamentally changes how it operates and delivers value to customers. This process not only involves adopting new technologies, but also a profound cultural and organizational change.

The digital economy enables disintermediation in trade, removing barriers between producers and consumers. This means that companies can interact directly with their customers through digital platforms, improving communication and reducing costs. The digital economy disrupts traditional business models by enabling the creation of new digital markets that operate with digital products and services (Tapscott, 1996). This change implies a continuous review of business strategies to remain competitive in a dynamic environment.

Organizational theory offers you various definitions and conceptualizations of "digital organization" from different perspectives. Below are various definitions and conceptualizations from different perspectives. These definitions and conceptualizations highlight how digital organization not only involves technology but also profound changes in organizational culture, structure, and processes to adapt to an increasingly digitalized environment. According to sociotechnical theory, the digital organization is the result of the interaction between technical systems (technological infrastructure) and social systems (people, practices, and culture). This approach emphasizes how workers and digital technologies coexist and co-evolve to achieve a balance that maximizes both technical efficiency and social satisfaction at work (Mumford, 2006).

From the perspective of organizational transformation, the digital organization is the result of a profound organizational transformation, where organizational processes, structures and cultures are redesigned to adapt to the digital environment. This approach considers the digital organization as a dynamic entity where traditional boundaries disappear and interconnected value networks are established through the use of digital technologies (Hess et al. 2016).

From the perspective of digitalization and digital transformation, digitalization involves the conversion of analog information into digital formats. In contrast, digital transformation goes further, integrating digital technologies into all aspects of an organization to optimize processes and improve the customer experience. Digitalization refers to the conversion of analog information into digital formats, such as transforming paper documents into PDF files. This process allows electronic access and management of information. Digitalization presents both challenges and opportunities for organizations. ILO/Cinterfor (2020) mentions that increasing access to digital technologies requires companies to adapt to a new, customer-centric environment, which implies a significant organizational transformation.

From a structuralist perspective, a digital organization is defined as an entity whose design and structure are based on advanced technological platforms, allowing for process automation, greater flexibility and organizational agility. This type of organization is capable of integrating multiple digital channels, enabling decentralized and real-time decision-making (Zammuto et al., 2007).

The digital economy is described as an ecosystem where technological infrastructure, processing services, and end users converge. The digital economy is defined as "the part of economic output derived solely or primarily from digital technologies with a business model based on digital goods or services" (Bukht & Heeks, 2017). This approach highlights how digital technologies have become the core of contemporary economic activities. This approach highlights how organizations must adapt to an interconnected environment in order to thrive (Mesenbourg, 2001).

The digital economy includes fundamental components such as the ICT industry, e-commerce between companies, and the digital distribution of goods and services. This definition highlights the interconnection between technology and economic infrastructure in the digital context (Margherio, 1998).

From an organizational perspective, digitalization is seen as a process that improves operational efficiency and enables greater agility in responding to market demands. Digital transformation is seen as a cultural shift that affects how employees interact and how decisions are made (HubSpot, 2023). From this organizational perspective, digital transformation is seen as a process that redefines business models and improves operational efficiency. This includes the adoption of tools such as artificial intelligence, data analytics, and automation to optimize processes and improve customer experience.

Digital organization seeks to have an impact on improving the customer experience by using technologies such as artificial intelligence and data analytics. This allows companies to personalize their services and respond quickly to consumer needs (SAP, 2023). Digital organizations are designed to be agile and adaptive, allowing for a rapid response to market demands and changing consumer expectations.

From an innovation perspective, digital organizations are seen as those that take a proactive approach to technological change and constant innovation. These organizations not only react to the digital environment but anticipate and take advantage of it to create new business opportunities and operating models. The ability to adapt quickly to emerging digital trends is crucial to their survival and success (Yoo et al., 2012). The digital organization fosters an environment of continuous innovation, where companies must be willing to experiment and adapt to new technologies to remain competitive.

This implies a constant commitment to learning and improvement (AWS, 2023). Continuous innovation is a key component in the digital economy. Organizations must commit to the constant renewal of products, processes, and business models to remain competitive in a changing environment.

In the context of the digital economy, a relationship of cooperation and interdependence between actors in academia, business, and government is recognized to foster the development of digital organizations. This approach suggests that success in digitalization requires a joint effort (UASB, 2020).

Digital organizations often have distinctive characteristics, such as leveraging the intensive use of information and communication technologies to optimize their operations through continuous innovation, adapting quickly to changes in the environment, offering new services and constantly improving their processes. They promote fluid communication in agile structures between departments and allow for faster decision-making.

From a strategic perspective, the digital organization seeks not only to survive in an increasingly digitalized environment but also to thrive by creating sustainable competitive advantages through the effective use of data and technology. The digital economy not only transforms the business environment but also has a significant impact on social and political organization, promoting structural changes in how goods and services are produced and consumed.

These definitions and conceptualizations highlight how digital economic organization involves not only technology but also profound changes in organizational culture, structure, and processes to adapt to an increasingly digitalized environment. The digital economic organization represents a radical change in how companies operate, interact with consumers, and adapt to an increasingly digitalized environment. This phenomenon not only redefines business models but also has profound implications for the global social and economic structure.

This study contributes to clarifying the existing literature on the subject and leaving measures that can improve the performance of digital economies and is organized as follows: First, it examines the concepts and definitions of the digital economic organization, leading to the analysis of theories and empirical literature review. The study presents two tables aiming to synthesize the findings. A section on discussion examines some of the implications, developments and advances in the conceptual, theoretical and empirical issues related to digital economic organization. Finally, some concluding remarks are offered.

BACKGROUND

Digital Economic Organization

"Digital economic organization" is a complex concept that has been addressed from various perspectives in the academic literature. Digital economic organization refers to the integration of digital technologies into economic and business processes, transforming the way companies operate and relate to their customers. This type of organization refers to the set of activities, institutions, and economic actors that use digital technologies to create, distribute, and consume goods and services. Below are several definitions and conceptualizations of digital economic organization from different perspectives.

A digital economic organization is one that has adopted an intensive focus on the use of digital technologies to optimize its operations. This includes the implementation of technological solutions that allow for greater efficiency, innovation and adaptation to market changes. It is defined as a branch of the economy that combines the benefits of the Internet with the marketing and manufacturing of products and services. This implies that commercial transactions are carried out mainly on digital platforms, which transforms traditional market dynamics.

From a collaborative economy perspective, digital economic organization is understood as a system in which digital platforms connect users to shared resources, allowing the exchange of goods and services without the need for traditional intermediaries. This organization leverages digital technology to create new business models that decentralize control and ownership of resources, as in the cases of Airbnb or Uber (Sundararajan, 2016).

Digital economic organization, from the perspective of the platform economy, refers to the emerging economic structure where digital platforms act as intermediaries that coordinate interactions between users, producers and consumers. These platforms (such as Amazon, Google, or Facebook) create value by facilitating transactions (Kenney & Zysman, 2016).

From a critical perspective of digital capitalism, digital economic organization is defined as an extension of capitalism, where capital is accumulated mainly through the control of data and information. The digital economy is also characterized by the interaction between information and economic activity, where "the asset on which transactions are made is information" (Deusto, 2017). This aspect underlines how information has become a key resource for generating economic value. Dominant digital firms extract value by collecting, analyzing, and trading personal data, giving rise to new forms of economic power and digital monopolization (Srnicek, 2017).

The digital economic organization can also be conceptualized as an economic system based on technological innovation. In this context, digital technologies (such as artificial intelligence, blockchain, and big data) enable greater efficiency in markets, facilitate the creation of new forms of value, and enable the emergence of entirely new industries. Digital firms are seen as organizations that thrive through continuous innovation and rapid adoption of new technologies (Brynjolfsson & McAfee, 2014).

Digital economic organization, from the perspective of globalization, refers to a system in which geographic and political barriers are less relevant to economic exchange. Digital companies can operate and scale their businesses globally more quickly and efficiently, using digital technologies to optimize logistics, communication, and the sale of products and services across borders (Baldwin, 2016).

In the conceptualization of the attention economy, digital economic organization focuses on how digital platforms and companies capitalize on users' attention as a fundamental economic resource. Companies operating in this economy design products and services (such as social media, mobile apps, or online content) to capture and monetize consumers' time and attention (Wu, 2017).

Digital economic organization is a multifaceted phenomenon that can be understood from several perspectives, whether as part of a new platform-based exchange model, a driver of technological innovation or as a central component of data-driven capitalism. This economic model facilitates access to global connectivity for products and services, allowing small businesses to reach international markets without the need for a physical presence. Constant connectivity between businesses and consumers improves brand loyalty and enables a faster response to market needs.

The digital organizational economy is an ecosystem that combines telecommunications infrastructure, information and communication technology (ICT) industries, and economic activities facilitated by the Internet. This ecosystem allows individuals and organizations to interact, collaborate, and create value through digital platforms. As an important driving force and new kinetic energy, digital economy is promoting the development of economy in the direction of high quality, and brings new opportunities and challenges to the development of real economy and the upgrading and optimization of industrial structure (Zhang, 2024).

Digital economic organization has been studied from various theoretical and methodological perspectives. Different conceptualizations allow us to understand how digital technology redefines economic relations, business models and value creation in the global economy. Below, several theories are presented that address this phenomenon, highlighting their characteristics and approaches. These new digital technologies are prompted by big data analytics, artificial intelligence (AI), platform economy, digital trade, fintech innovation, and societal and economic sustainability. (Li et al, 2020)

Theories on Digital Economic

The digitization of the economy has been on the rise in recent years and continues to evolve. The latest wave of the IT revolution is based on radical mobility, with an emphasis on intangible capital, big data management, and machine learning-based digital platforms that help businesses as well as individuals (Byrne, 2022). Using digital technology and developing a digital mindset, companies can make big changes to existing business models and management methods and give them the power of data, thus making the digital economic organization more competitive (Wang & Qi, 2024). The successful operation of the digital economy relies on the close collaboration of numerous core elements. Urgently, a unified theoretical framework is needed to thoroughly explore and analyze the foundational aspects of the digital economy (Xie et al., 2023)

Organization Theories on digital economic organization address the fundamental changes that digital technologies have introduced in economic structures and dynamics. There are various theories that address digital economic organization from different conceptual and theoretical-methodological perspectives. Below, several relevant theories are presented from different conceptual and theoretical-methodological approaches; all focused on analyzing how digitalization is transforming the nature of economic organizations.

Complex systems theory is applied to understanding how different actors interact in a digital ecosystem. This approach views digital economic organizations as operating within an interconnected system where changes in one component can affect others, requiring adaptability (Holland, 1995).

New economics theory, popularized by Don Tapscott and others, argues that the digital economy represents a fundamental shift in how goods and services are created and distributed. This theory emphasizes the role of the Internet as a facilitator of disintermediation and reintermediation, allowing firms to interact directly with consumers, reducing costs and improving efficiency (Tapscott, 1996).

Theories on digital economic organization highlight how digital technologies have transformed not only the structure and functioning of firms but also markets and the economy as a whole. These theoretical perspectives provide tools to analyze the new dynamics of power, innovation, and value that are emerging in the digital economy.

Platform economics theory focuses on how digital platforms mediate economic interactions between multiple groups (users, producers, consumers). Platforms, such as Amazon, Uber, or Airbnb, not only facilitate transactions but also create value networks through network effects. The success of these organizations lies in their ability to reduce transaction costs, increase scale, and generate network value, where the value of the platform grows as more users adopt it (Parker et al., 2016).

Information Theory focuses on how digitalization transforms the flow of information within organizations. This theory suggests that effective management of large volumes of data is crucial for decision-making and market adaptation (Cohen et al., 2000). According to this perspective, the ability to manage large volumes of data through digital technologies is crucial for economic development. Companies that manage to optimize the use of information can make more informed decisions and adapt quickly to market conditions.

The theory of surveillance capitalism is proposed by Shoshana Zuboff, this theory analyzes how digital economic organizations use personal data to obtain economic benefits. Instead of creating value solely through products or services, digital companies, especially large technology platforms, extract data from their users, process it, and commercialize it, which Zuboff (2019) calls "surveillance capitalism." This theory questions the ethical and social impact of mass data collection and how it affects the privacy and autonomy of individuals.

The theory of organizational change focuses on how companies must transform internally to adapt to the digital economy. This theory addresses aspects such as organizational culture, the development of digital skills in employees, and the implementation of new technologies as critical factors for success in a digitalized environment (Kotter, 1996).

Clayton Christensen proposes the theory of disruptive innovation; this theory describes how digital technologies are transforming traditional markets by introducing innovations that displace established companies. In the context of digital economic organization, disruptive technology startups offer more accessible or affordable products or services through digital platforms, which changes the rules of the game in industries such as transportation, hospitality, or retail (Christensen, 1997). Innovation is more critical than ever in the digital economy era. Innovation should concern not just technology but organizations, management methods, and business models as well (Li et al., 200).

Research on digital business models focuses on how firms can create value in a digital environment. This includes studies on digital platforms, e-commerce, and their implications for business competitiveness. Different models ranging from traditional e-commerce to collaborative platforms that enable new forms of business interaction are explored, analyzing their implications for business competitiveness (Chesbrough, 2007).

Digital innovation ecosystem theory suggests that digital economic organizations function as part of complex innovation ecosystems where multiple actors (technology companies, startups, governments, universities) interact and co-create value. Collaboration between these actors is crucial for the development of emerging technologies such as artificial intelligence, blockchain, and the Internet of Things (IoT), which enable new forms of economic organization and value creation (Jacobides, et al. 2018).

Product life cycle theory is adapted to the digital economy by considering how digital technologies affect each stage of the product cycle. This theory allows us to understand how digital innovations alter traditional cycles and facilitate rapid adaptation to market demands (Kotler, 1997). In this context, it analyses how digital technologies enable innovations in the development, marketing and distribution of products, altering traditional cycles and allowing rapid adaptation to market demands.

Actor-Network Theory (ANT) is proposed by Bruno Latour and Michel Callon to analyze how digital economic organizations are complex networks of human and non-human actors (such as algorithms, technologies, and data). ANT argues that digital firms should be viewed not only as economic entities, but as sociotechnical networks that include technologies as key actors in the organization and distribution of resources and power in the digital economy (Latour, 2005).

The institutional approach examines how normative and regulatory structures affect the development of digital economic organizations. This theory suggests that public policies and institutions play a crucial role in facilitating or restricting the growth of the digital economy, affecting aspects such as innovation, investment, and access to technologies (North, 1990).

From the theory of social capital, it is argued that digital networks facilitate new forms of collaboration and exchange between individuals and organizations. This perspective emphasizes how digital platforms can build meaningful relationships that generate economic value (Putnam, 2000). This theory highlights how digital platforms enable meaningful relationships to be built that can be leveraged to generate economic value, especially in environments where trust and collaboration are critical.

Transaction cost theory in the digital economy based on Oliver Williamson's transaction cost theory is applied to digital economic organization to explain how digital technologies significantly reduce the costs associated with economic transactions (such as information search, negotiation, and monitoring). Digital platforms allow transactions to be carried out more efficiently and at lower cost, transforming the structure of markets and facilitating the creation of global digital markets (Williamson, 1981).

The attention economy theory argues that in the digital economy, users' attention has become a crucial economic resource. Digital organizations compete to capture and retain consumers' attention, using personalized algorithms, engaging content, and advertising-based business models. The attention economy highlights how technology companies monetize users' time and focus across various platforms (Davenport & Beck, 2001).

In summary, these theories provide a diverse conceptual framework for understanding the dynamics that shape digital economic organization, addressing technical, social, and institutional aspects and their implications for business development in an increasingly digitalized environment. Each approach offers a unique perspective on how companies can navigate this new economic landscape driven by digital technology.

Empirical Research on Digital Organizational Economics

Even though there are few literatures based on theoretical models and empirical analysis to study the impact of digital economy development (Zhang, 2024), the available empirical research on organizational economics in the digital context has produced significant findings in key areas such as organizational efficiency, the impact of digital platforms, value creation, and innovation. From the perspective of organizational economics, several empirical investigations have been carried out that address digital economic organization. Below are some relevant findings, results, and conclusions from these investigations.

In a study by Armijos-Orellana et al. (2023) on digital economy and value creation, it was investigated how the digital economy can be a driver of growth in Latin America. The findings indicate that the adoption of digital platforms and the use of data are fundamental for the creation and capture of economic value. The research concludes that digital transformation is crucial to improve productivity and foster innovation in interdependent productive sectors.

Another empirical research on the Attention Economy and Monetization in Digital Platforms, carried out by Wu (2017) explored the "attention economy" and how digital organizations, such as social networks and media outlets, monetize users' attention. Through an empirical analysis of how technology companies use strategies to capture and retain users' attention, Wu found that these organizations earn most of their revenue through targeted advertising. Platforms optimize content design to maximize the time users spend on the platform, creating new forms of attention-based value.

Previous research found that digital organizations monetize users' attention through targeted advertising models. Furthermore, the attention economy may be unsustainable in the long term due to market saturation and user burnout. The research concludes that digital platforms have created a business model based on capturing attention, which poses ethical and sustainability challenges as consumers become saturated with content.

An empirical research by Sundararajan (2016) explored the impact of platforms on labor markets and how sharing economy platforms, such as Uber and Airbnb, are transforming labor markets. Through a series of case studies and data analysis of platforms, it was found that these digital organizations are challenging traditional employment structures by offering flexibility and reducing intermediation. However, the research also highlighted the increasing prevarication of employment and the lack of social benefits in platform-based jobs.

The main findings of this research show an increase in labor flexibility, but with lower guarantees of job security, as well as digital platforms facilitating entry into the labor market but creating unstable working conditions. Among the conclusions, it highlights that digital platforms represent a significant transformation in the way work is organized, with benefits for some workers in terms of flexibility but with risks in the quality of employment.

A study on digital business models suggests that organizations must adapt their strategies to make the most of the opportunities offered by digitalization. According to Pérez and Guzmán (2015), companies that implement effective digital models achieve greater operational efficiency and a better relationship with their customers, which is essential for their long-term sustainability.

Research conducted by Sieglin (2014) on organizational conditions in Mexican public universities and their challenges in implementing digital technologies reveals that there are significant limitations in infrastructure and human resources that affect scientific development. The results indicate that these limitations hinder the effective adoption of digital technologies, which in turn negatively impacts the innovative capacity of these institutions.

Empirical research on open innovation and co-creation in digital ecosystems is empirical research conducted by Chesbrough (2006), who studied how digital organizations take advantage of open innovation and innovation ecosystems to generate value. Through case studies of technology companies such as IBM and Google, it was found that organizations that allowed open collaboration with external actors (users, competitors and startups) managed to accelerate innovation and reduce R&D costs.

Among the findings found in this research, it is found that open innovation allows digital organizations to reduce costs and accelerate the development of new products. In addition, organizations that are part of open digital ecosystems tend to be more competitive and resilient. The research concludes that organizations that encourage open innovation and collaboration with external actors are better positioned in the digital economic environment, generating value more efficiently and sustainably.

Empirical research on platform economics and network effects in value creation, conducted by Rochet and Tirole (2003) conducted empirical research on the behavior of two-sided platforms, such as credit cards and online platforms, analyzing how network effects influenced value creation. By collecting data on different platforms, they found that digital organizations create value when they manage to attract users on both sides of the platform, generating positive network effects. The larger the user base, the greater the value perceived by new users.

The findings of this research revolve around network effects that are essential for the success of platforms, which manage to balance the participation of the two sides (consumers and suppliers) and generate a positive feedback loop in value creation. The research concludes that the theory of two-sided platforms is crucial to understand how digital organizations can maximize value by creating dynamic markets in which users attract each other.

An analysis of the impact of the role of information and knowledge in the digital economy highlights that these elements are considered strategic resources in organizations. According to Blanco et al. (2001), knowledge becomes a key factor for competitiveness, as it allows companies to quickly adapt to changes in the environment and improve their capacity for innovation.

Brynjolfsson and Hitt (2000) conducted empirical research to measure the impact of information technology (IT) on company productivity in the transformation of productivity and efficiency in digital organizations. Analyzing data from American companies, they discovered that organizations that invested in IT showed a significant increase in productivity. However, the benefits materialized only when these investments were accompanied by organizational changes, such as restructuring processes and the adoption of more agile organizational models.

In the findings, researchers found that IT boosts productivity, but only when aligned with changes in organizational structure and that IT implementation without organizational transformation can lead to stagnant productivity. The research concludes that the adoption of digital technologies is critical to improving organizational efficiency, but must be accompanied by structural redesign and innovation processes in organizations.

Research on the knowledge economy highlights how this paradigm has transformed organizational dynamics. According to Kogut and Zander (1992), organizations that foster continuous learning and the development of innovative capabilities are more likely to succeed in a digitalized economic environment. The findings from the general digital economic theory reveal that in a socially optimal equilibrium, consumers should share their data with firms until the marginal benefits equal the marginal costs (Xi et al., 2023).

Empirical research in digital organizational economics highlights the transformative impact of digital technologies in areas such as productivity, labor markets, value creation, and innovation models. This research reflects how digital economic organizations face challenges and opportunities in an environment increasingly influenced by digital technologies and knowledge as a key resource for their strategic success.

This research provides evidence on how organizations must adapt to the digital environment to maximize their benefits, but also highlights the challenges related to job insecurity, the sustainability of the care model, and competition in platform markets.

Table 1 below summarizes the definitions and concepts, theories, and empirical research related to digital economic organization from the perspective of organizational economics sciences.

Table 1. Definitions and concepts, theories, and empirical research on digital economic organization

Categories	Content
Definitions and Concepts	**1. Digital Economy:** "The part of economic production derived solely or mainly from digital technologies" (Bukht & Heeks, 2017). **2. Components of the Digital Economy:** Includes the ICT industry and e-commerce (Margherio, 1998). **3. Structural Transformation:** The digital economy acts as a catalyst to reduce inequality and strengthen social inclusion (ECLAC, 2013). **4. Interaction between Information and Economy:** Information becomes a key resource to generate economic value (Orkestra Deusto, 2017). **5. Challenges and Opportunities:** Digitalization requires significant adaptations in companies (ILO/Cinterfor, n.d.). **6. Impact on Business Models:** Digitalization alters traditional business models (Tapscott, 1996).
Theories	1. **New Economy Theory**: Highlights the role of the Internet in disintermediation and reintermediation (Tapscott, 1996). 2. **Information Theory**: Emphasizes effective data management as a key to competitiveness (Cohen et al., 2000). 3. **Social Capital Theory**: Digital networks facilitate new forms of collaboration (Putnam, 2000). 4. **Complex Systems Theory**: Analyzes interactions in a digital ecosystem (Holland, 1995). 5. **Institutional Approach**: Examines how regulatory structures affect digital development (North, 1990).

The table above provides a structured overview of the key definitions and concepts related to digital economic organization, as well as the relevant theories and significant empirical findings in this field of study.

Table 2 is presented below, which organizes the information previously provided into three categories: Definitions and Conceptualizations, Theories on Digital Economic Organization, and Empirical Research with Findings, Results, and Conclusions.

Table 2. Summary of definitions, theories, and empirical research on digital economic organization

Category	Description	References
Definitions and conceptualizations		
Collaborative Economy	The digital economic organization focuses on platforms that facilitate collaboration and the exchange of goods and services between peers without intermediaries.	Sundararajan (2016).
Platform Economy	Digital platforms such as Amazon and Uber act as intermediaries, connecting consumers and producers and creating value through network effects.	Kenney & Zysman (2016). Parker et al. (2016).
Digital Capitalism	Digital companies generate capital by controlling data and extracting value by commercializing users' personal information.	Srnicek (2017).
Technological Innovation	The digital economic organization is characterized by a rapid adoption of new technologies such as AI, blockchain, and big data to improve efficiency and create value.	Brynjolfsson & McAfee (2014).
	Digital companies operate globally, minimizing geographic barriers and optimizing logistics and distribution through technological platforms.	Baldwin (2016).
Globalized Digital Economy	organizations capitalize on users' attention, designing platforms to maximize the time consumers spend on them.	Wu (2017).

This table and the references provide a structured summary that facilitates the understanding of the different definitions, theories and empirical research on digital economic organization. Digital economic organization is a topic of growing relevance today, given the impact that digitalization has had on all economic sectors. This analysis focuses on the conceptual, theoretical-methodological, and empirical advances in research on this phenomenon.

Discussion on Digital Economic Organization: Conceptual, Theoretical and Methodological Advances

Digital economic organization is a concept that has gained increasing relevance in recent years due to the transformative impact of technology on economic models, organizational structures, and market dynamics.

This phenomenon has been the subject of research from different conceptual, theoretical and methodological approaches, with the aim of understanding the economic, social and political implications of digitalization. The main advances in the matter are discussed below.

Conceptual Advances

The digital economy refers to the integration of information and communication technologies (ICT) into economic activities, modifying the patterns of production, distribution and consumption of goods and services. For authors such as Manuel Castells (1996), the digital economy is a manifestation of the network society, where digital networks transform economic relations by facilitating global connectivity and the interdependence of actors.

Digital economic organization refers to the way in which digital technologies transform the structure and functioning of organizations. According to authors such as Castells (2000), the digital economy is characterized by interconnection and globalization, which allows companies to operate in a more dynamic and competitive environment. This concept has evolved to include not only electronic commerce but also the use of digital platforms, big data, and artificial intelligence.

Another important conceptual advance is the focus on the collaborative economy, where platforms such as Uber and Airbnb have redefined the concept of ownership and consumption. Botsman and Rogers (2010) highlight how these platforms facilitate the exchange of goods and services between individuals, leading to a reconfiguration of traditional economic relations.

From a conceptual approach, digitalization has been understood as a process of dematerialization, where goods and services move from the physical to the digital world. This includes the emergence of digital platforms, the monetization of data and the creation of new online markets (Evans & Schmalensee, 2016). Platforms such as Amazon, Google and Facebook have become new intermediaries, which has transformed power structures in the global economy (Srnicek, 2016).

In terms of organization, Brynjolfsson and McAfee (2014) argue that digitalization has given rise to a new form of business organization based on platforms and networks, in which the traditional hierarchical structure has been replaced by horizontal interactions and labor flexibility.

Theoretical-Methodological Advances

From a theoretical-methodological point of view, various approaches have been developed to study digital economic organization. Social network theory, for example, has been used to understand how digital interactions affect organizational dynamics. Authors such as Granovetter (1973) have been fundamental in this field, analyzing how relationships between actors influence access to resources and information. In addition, the systemic approach has gained relevance by considering organizations as part of a broader system that includes consumers, suppliers, and competitors.

This approach allows for a better understanding of interdependencies and information flows in a digital environment.

The theoretical analysis of digital economic organization has been based on various approaches. From the firm's theory, authors such as Coase (1937) suggest that new technologies reduce transaction costs, allowing companies to outsource activities that were previously carried out internally. Digitalization has intensified this process, facilitating the coordination of activities through smart contracts and platforms that connect suppliers and consumers globally (Tapscott, 2016).

Another important approach comes from network theory, which argues that the digital economy is organized around nodes and information flows rather than traditional hierarchies (Castells, 1996). Digital networks allow for decentralized coordination and control, which translates into new forms of corporate governance, where digital platforms have a dominant role.

On the other hand, from the perspective of human capital, Acemoglu and Restrepo (2020) propose that digitalization needs to automate certain tasks, which increases productivity but also displaces employment. However, digital organizations depend not only on technology but also on the adaptation of workers' capabilities and skills to the digital environment.

The study of digital economic organization requires the adoption of new methodological tools that capture the emerging dynamics of digital economies. One of the most significant advances in this field is the use of big data and network analysis to map and understand economic interactions on digital platforms. This approach has allowed researchers to quantify the magnitude of digital transactions, study user behavior patterns, and measure the economic impact of digitalization in real time (Einav & Levin, 2014).

Machine learning and big data processing techniques are also being used to model complex economic phenomena, such as consumer behavior in digital environments, predicting market trends, and identifying competitive dynamics in platform markets (Athey, 2017). Furthermore, the study of the digital economy has involved increasing interdisciplinarity, incorporating knowledge from economics, computer science, sociology, and data science. This convergence has allowed for the development of more comprehensive theoretical frameworks and the application of quantitative and qualitative models to explore the impact of technology on economic organization.

Empirical Developments

Empirically, numerous studies have addressed how organizations are implementing digital technologies. A study by Brynjolfsson and McAfee (2014) shows that companies that adopt digital technologies tend to be more innovative and efficient. Likewise, research on the impact of teleworking during the COVID-19 pandemic has revealed significant changes in employee productivity and well-being (Kässi & Lehdonvirta, 2020).

On the other hand, it has been documented how small and medium-sized enterprises (SMEs) face specific challenges when adopting digital technologies. According to a study by the European Commission (2020), many SMEs lack the necessary resources to implement effective digital strategies.

From an empirical point of view, research on the digital economy has provided evidence that digital platforms are transforming traditional sectors such as retail, financial services and transportation (Cohen & Sundararajan, 2015). For example, the rise of e-commerce has disrupted traditional supply chains, reducing entry costs for small sellers and facilitating access to global markets.

A notable empirical example is the analysis of the digital labor market, where studies have shown that the platform economy is generating new forms of work (Uber, Deliveroo, etc.), but also poses challenges in terms of labor protection, social security and workers' rights (De Stefano, 2016). The impact of digitalization on labor inequalities has also been the subject of study, with some researchers suggesting that automation tends to polarize the labor market, favoring highly skilled workers while displacing less skilled workers (Goos, Manning and Salomons, 2014).

On the other hand, research on the impact of the digital economy on competition has revealed that, although digital platforms tend to increase efficiency and reduce costs, they can also lead to the concentration of market power in a few technology companies (Autor, Dorn, Katz, Patterson, & Van Reenen, 2020). These companies, referred to as "superstars," have accumulated a significant amount of economic power, leading to concerns about monopolies and anticompetitive practices.

METHODOLOGY

The metacognitive and reflective analysis presented in this paper through the investigation of theories and concepts leads us to reflect on the thought processes that have led us to understand that the digital economic organization is multidimensional. A bibliometric review was used, through which a quantitative analysis of publications related to digital economic organizations, theories, and empirical research on digital economics. The bibliometric indicators taken as inclusion factors were the quality of the publications where the research is presented, the context covered by the publication, and the relevance of the topic in the research.

This bibliometric review was conducted in two stages. In the first stage, the search criteria used in the different databases were defined, including temporality, date of consultation, type of document and journal, topic and keywords. The second stage consisted of classifying and analyzing the papers based on the identification criteria; these were grouped to identify the connections between the papers, selecting the most relevant ones in order to prepare the discission presented.

RESULTS AND DISCUSSION

Nowadays, the realization of the digital economy is occurring all around the globe, in Asian nations due to the need to revamp traditional business processes, extensive technology innovation, supportive government policies for economic growth, and the high capacity for digital entrepreneurship (Li et al., 2020), in the other hand, European countries have been changing their policies over the past three decades to improve their innovative performance (Gomes et al., 2022).

According to ILO/Cinterfor (2020), digital transformation redefines work processes, profoundly challenging organizational culture. Digital transformation not only affects technological processes but also transforms organizational culture. It implies a change in the mindset of employees and how they interact with each other and with customers. This cultural change is crucial to the success of any digital initiative. Digital transformation involves not only technological changes but also cultural changes within organizations. This includes the need to develop digital skills in employees and foster an open mindset to change (PowerData, 2023). The digital economy can indeed improve the level of upgrading and optimization of industrial structures (Zhang, 2024).

The digital economy is a challenge that countries have been working on to develop and accelerate the digital single market (Szeles & Simionescu, 2020). To accelerate the development of the digital economy, the different regional actors (government, academia, and companies) must work to increase the levels of qualification in the higher education of the population, the development of R&D partnerships, and incentives (Gomes et al., 2022). It is necessary to promote the healthy development of the platform economy and sharing economy, digital industrialization and industrial digitization, and deep integration of the digital economy and real economy (Zhang, 2024).

Digitalization presents both challenges and opportunities. Organizations must face the challenge of implementing new technologies while managing the cultural change necessary for their effective adoption. However, those who manage to do so can benefit significantly by improving their competitiveness. In short, digital organization is a multifaceted concept that ranges from simple process digitization to a profound transformation that redefines how organizations operate as a whole.

CONCLUSIONS

The digital economic organization represents a multidimensional field ranging from conceptual to methodological and empirical changes. As we move towards an increasingly digitalized future, it is crucial to continue researching how these transformations affect both organizations and the economy at large. This analysis provides a comprehensive view on the developments in digital economic organization and its impact on the contemporary business environment.

It is essential for companies seeking to adapt to a world where technology plays a central role in all business interactions. Digital organizations can be understood from various perspectives, all of which highlight the importance of digital technologies not only as operational tools but also as drivers of organizational transformation. From structure and processes to culture and innovation, the digital environment redefines how organizations interact with their internal and external environments.

The study of digital economic organization has advanced significantly in recent decades, providing new conceptual, theoretical and methodological approaches that allow us to better understand the changing nature of economic activities in the digital age. However, despite progress, this field continues to evolve and raise new questions, especially regarding the impact of digitalization on employment, inequality and economic competition.

REFERENCES

Acemoglu, D., & Restrepo, P. (2020). The Race Between Man and Machine: Implications of Technology for Growth, Factor Shares, and Employment. *The American Economic Review*, *108*(6), 1488–1542. DOI: 10.1257/aer.20160696

Armijos-Orellana, A., González, M., Maldonado-Matute, J., & Guerrero, P. (2023). Un acercamiento teórico a la economía digital. *Estudios de la Gestión*, 14, 78-90. https://revistas.uasb.edu.ec/index.php/eg/article/download/4116/3999/16300

Athey, S. (2017). Beyond prediction: Using big data for policy problems. *Science*, *355*(6324), 483–485. DOI: 10.1126/science.aal4321 PMID: 28154050

Autor, D., Dorn, D., Katz, L., Patterson, C., & Van Reenen, J. (2020). The Fall of the Labor Share and the Rise of Superstar Firms. *The Quarterly Journal of Economics*, *135*(2), 645–709. DOI: 10.1093/qje/qjaa004

AWS. (2023). *¿Qué es la transformación digital?* Recuperado de https://aws.amazon.com/es/what-is/digital-transformation/

Baldwin, R. (2016). *The great convergence: Information technology and the new globalization*. Harvard University Press., DOI: 10.2307/j.ctv24w655w

Bharadwaj, A., El Sawy, O. A., Pavlou, P. A., & Venkatraman, N. (2013). Digital business strategy: Toward a next generation of insights. *Management Information Systems Quarterly*, *37*(2), 471–482. DOI: 10.25300/MISQ/2013/37:2.3

Blanco, F., Eaton, B., & Bawden, D. (2001). La información y el conocimiento: factores de producción en la actividad económica. *Revista Base*, 2(1), 186-200. https://www.redalyc.org/pdf/3372/337228632009.pdf

Botsman, R., & Rogers, R. (2010). *What's Mine Is Yours: The Rise of Collaborative Consumption*. HarperBusiness.

Brynjolfsson, E., & Hitt, L. M. (2000). Beyond computation: Information technology, organizational transformation, and business performance. *The Journal of Economic Perspectives*, *14*(4), 23–48. DOI: 10.1257/jep.14.4.23

Brynjolfsson, E., & McAfee, A. (2014). *The second machine age: Work, progress, and prosperity in a time of brilliant technologies*. W.W. Norton & Company.

Bukht, R., & Heeks, R. (2017). Defining, Conceptualising and Measuring the Digital Economy (August 3, 2017). *Development Informatics Working Paper no. 68*, Available at SSRN: https://ssrn.com/abstract=3431732 or http://dx.doi.org/DOI: 10.2139/ssrn.3431732

Byrne, D. (2022). The Digital Economy and Productivity. *Finance and Economics Discussion Series (FEDS)* DOI: 10.17016/feds.2022.038

Castells, M. (1996). *The Rise of the Network Society*. Blackwell.

CEPAL. (2013). *La economía digital: Un motor para el desarrollo sostenible*. Retrieved from https://www.cepal.org/es/publicaciones/25756-economia-digital-motor-desarrollo-sostenible

Chesbrough, H. (2006) *Open Innovation: A New Paradigm for Understanding Industrial Innovation. 10th Anniversary Summer Conference on Dynamics of Industry and Innovation: Organizations, Networks and Systems*, Copenhagen, 27-29 June 2005, 1-12. DOI: 10.1093/oso/9780199290727.003.0001

Chesbrough, H. W. (2007). Business Model Innovation: It's Not Just About Technology Anymore. *Strategy and Leadership*, *35*(6), 12–17. DOI: 10.1108/10878570710833714

Christensen, C. M. (1997). *The innovator's dilemma: When new technologies cause great firms to fail*. Harvard Business Review Press.

Coase, R. H. (1937). The nature of the firm. *Economica*, *4*(16), 386–405. DOI: 10.1111/j.1468-0335.1937.tb00002.x

Cohen, M., & Sundararajan, A. (2015). Self-regulation and innovation in the peer-to-peer sharing economy. *University of Chicago Law Review Online*, 82

Cohen, S., de Long, D., & Zysman, J. (2000). *The New Economy: A New Perspective on the Economic Landscape*.

Davenport, T. H., & Beck, J. C. (2001). *The attention economy: Understanding the new currency of business*. Harvard Business Review Press.

De Stefano, V. (2016). The rise of the "just-in-time workforce": On-demand work, crowdwork, and labor protection in the gig-economy. *Comparative Labor Law & Policy Journal*, *37*, 471–504.

Deusto, O. (2017). *Por qué la Economía Digital*. Retrieved from https://www.orkestra.deusto.es/euskadi-economia-digital/2017/por-que-economia-digital.phtml

Einav, L., & Levin, J. (2014). Economics in the age of big data. *Science*, *346*(6210), 1243089. DOI: 10.1126/science.1243089 PMID: 25378629

European Commission. (2020). *Digital Economy and Society Index 2020*.

Evans, D., & Schmalensee, R. (2016). *Matchmakers: The New Economics of Multisided Platforms*. Harvard Business Review Press.

Gomes, S., Lopes, J., & Ferreira, L. The impact of the digital economy on economic growth: The case of OECD countries. *RAM Revista de Administração Mackenzie* https://doi.org/DOI: 10.1590/1678-6971/eRAMD220029.en

Goos, M., Manning, A., & Salomons, A. (2014). Explaining job polarization: Routine-biased technological change and offshoring. *The American Economic Review*, *104*(8), 2509–2526. DOI: 10.1257/aer.104.8.2509

Granovetter, M. (1973). The Strength of Weak Ties. *American Journal of Sociology*, *78*(6), 1360–1380. DOI: 10.1086/225469

Hess, T., Matt, C., Benlian, A., & Wiesböck, F. (2016). Options for formulating a digital transformation strategy. *MIS Quarterly Executive*, *15*(2), 123–139.

Holland, J. H. (1995). *Hidden Order: How Adaptation Builds Complexity*. Addison-Wesley.

HubSpot. (2023). *Qué es la transformación digital: características, proceso y ejemplos*. Recuperado de https://blog.hubspot.es/sales/transformacion-digital

Jacobides, M. G., Cennamo, C., & Gawer, A. (2018). Towards a theory of ecosystems. *Strategic Management Journal*, *39*(8), 2255–2276. DOI: 10.1002/smj.2904

Kässi, O., & Lehdonvirta, V. (2020). Digital labor and the pandemic: The case of platform work. *Socio-economic Review*, *18*(4), 1001–1025.

Kenney, M., & Zysman, J. (2016). The rise of the platform economy. *Issues in Science and Technology*, *32*(3), 61–69.

Kogut, B., & Zander, U. (1992). Knowledge of the firm, combinative capabilities, and the replication of technology. *Organization Science*, *3*(3), 383–397. DOI: 10.1287/orsc.3.3.383

Kotler, P. (1997). *Marketing Management*. Prentice Hall.

Kotter, J. P. (1996). *Leading Change*. Harvard Business Review Press.

Latour, B. (2005). *Reassembling the social: An introduction to actor-network-theory*. Oxford University Press. DOI: 10.1093/oso/9780199256044.001.0001

Li, K., Kim, D. J., Lang, K. R., Kauffman, R. J., & Naldi, M. (2020). How should we understand the digital economy in Asia? Critical assessment and research agenda. *Electronic Commerce Research and Applications*, *44*, 101004. DOI: 10.1016/j.elerap.2020.101004 PMID: 32922241

Margherio, C. (1998). *The Emerging Digital Economy*. U.S. Department of Commerce.

Mesenbourg, T. L. (2001). *Measuring the Digital Economy*. U.S. Bureau of the Census.

Mumford, E. (2006). The story of sociotechnical design: Reflections on its successes, failures and potential. *Information Systems Journal*, *16*(4), 317–342. DOI: 10.1111/j.1365-2575.2006.00221.x

North, D. C. (1990). *Institutions, Institutional Change and Economic Performance*. Cambridge University Press. DOI: 10.1017/CBO9780511808678

OIT/Cinterfor. (2020). *Digitalización en las organizaciones*. Recuperado de https://www.oitcinterfor.org/digitalizacion/digitalizacion-organizaciones

Parker, G. G., Van Alstyne, M. W., & Choudary, S. P. (2016). *Platform revolution: How networked markets are transforming the economy and how to make them work for you*. W.W. Norton & Company.

Pérez, A., & Guzmán, M. (2015). Los estudios organizacionales como programa de investigación. *Revista Latinoamericana de Estudios Organizacionales*, 2(1), 1-20. https://www.scielo.cl/scielo.php?pid=S0717-554X2015000200001&script=sci_arttext

PowerData. (2023). *Transformación digital: Qué es y su importancia*. Recuperado de https://www.powerdata.es/transformacion-digital

Putnam, R. D. (2000). *Bowling Alone: The Collapse and Revival of American Community*. Simon & Schuster.

Rochet, J. C., & Tirole, J. (2003). Platform competition in two-sided markets. *Journal of the European Economic Association*, *1*(4), 990–1029. DOI: 10.1162/154247603322493212

SAP. (2023). *¿Qué es la Transformación Digital? | Importancia y Beneficios*. Recuperado de https://www.sap.com/latinamerica/insights/what-is-digital-transformation.html

Sieglin, V. (2014). Economía de conocimiento y culturas organizacionales en la academia. *Ciencia UANL*, 17(69), 45-60. https://cienciauanl.uanl.mx/?p=2590

Srnicek, N. (2016). *Platform Capitalism*. Polity Press.

Srnicek, N. (2017). *Platform capitalism*. Polity Press.

Sundararajan, A. (2016). *The sharing economy: The end of employment and the rise of crowd-based capitalism*. MIT Press., DOI: 10.7551/mitpress/10425.001.0001

Tapscott, D. (1996). *The Digital Economy: Promise and Peril in the Age of Networked Intelligence*. McGraw-Hill.

Tapscott, D. (2016). *Blockchain Revolution: How the Technology Behind Bitcoin is Changing Money, Business, and the World*. Penguin.

UASB. (2020). Un acercamiento teórico a la economía digital. Recuperado de https://revistas.uasb.edu.ec/index.php/eg/article/download/4116/3999/16300

Wang, X., & Qi, M. (2024). A Study of the Impact of Digital Transformation on the Risk Level of Commercial Banks. Proceedings of the 2024 3rd International Conference on Artificial Intelligence, Internet and Digital Economy (ICAID 2024)., DOI: 10.2991/978-94-6463-490-7_29

Williamson, O. E. (1981). The economics of organization: The transaction cost approach. *American Journal of Sociology*, *87*(3), 548–577. DOI: 10.1086/227496

Wu, T. (2017). *The attention merchants: The epic scramble to get inside our heads*. Vintage.

Xie, D., Wei, W., & Li, Y. A General Theory of Digital Economy: The World after Turing (July 1, 2023).http://dx.doi.org/DOI: 10.2139/ssrn.4531884

Yoo, Y., Boland, R. J.Jr, Lyytinen, K., & Majchrzak, A. (2012). Organizing for innovation in the digitized world. *Organization Science*, *23*(5), 1398–1408. DOI: 10.1287/orsc.1120.0771

Zammuto, R. F., Griffith, T. L., Majchrzak, A., Dougherty, D. J., & Faraj, S. (2007). Information technology and the changing fabric of organization. *Organization Science*, *18*(5), 749–762. DOI: 10.1287/orsc.1070.0307

Zhang, Chao. (2021). An empirical study on the impact of digital economy development on the upgrading and optimization of industrial structure. E3S Web of Conferences. 275. 01046. . DOI: 10.1051/e3sconf/202127501046

Zuboff, S. (2019). *The age of surveillance capitalism: The fight for a human future at the new frontier of power*. PublicAffairs.

Chapter 2
The Role of Behavioral Finance in Shaping Economic Decision-Making:
Insights From AI and Big Data Integration

Dev Dutt Vashist
https://orcid.org/0009-0005-5043-7782
Christ University, India

Manjari Sharma
https://orcid.org/0000-0003-1459-165X
Christ University, India

Pallavi Pandey
Christ University, India

ABSTRACT

This chapter examines how behavioral biases and institutional factors influence investment decisions, bridging gaps in behavioral finance literature. It explores cognitive biases like overconfidence, loss aversion, and herd behavior alongside institutional elements such as regulations and market stability. A mixed-methods approach combines survey data from 320 investors and 30 interviews. Findings show a strong link between biases and decisions, with overconfidence and loss aversion as key drivers. Regulatory transparency reduces bias impact, while uncertainty amplifies emotional reactions. The study highlights the need for clear policies, financial

DOI: 10.4018/979-8-3693-8166-3.ch002

education, and future research on AI's role in mitigating biases.

1. INTRODUCTION

1.1 Origins of Behavioral Finance

Investor psychology explores the psychological factors that influence how people make investment decisions. It looks at how thoughts and emotions guide investors when they make choices in financial markets. This includes how they see risk, how they form opinions, and how mental shortcuts and biases shape their actions. Behavioral finance challenges the traditional belief that investors always act logically and make decisions based on facts and data. In regular finance, investors are expected to gather all information and make calm, logical choices to get the best results. Behavioral finance disagrees with this idea. It uses psychology to show that people often act emotionally and irrationally when investing. By understanding these mistakes, behavioral finance helps explain why markets behave unpredictably. Knowing about investor psychology is not just interesting for researchers — it helps financial experts and investors understand why markets move the way they do. It helps explain why prices rise or fall, and why people sometimes act in unexpected ways. This knowledge also helps in designing better investment plans and risk management strategies. Behavioral finance acts like a guiding light, showing the hidden biases that lead investors to make wrong decisions. It highlights how overconfidence, fear of losing money, and other emotional reactions make people ignore facts and follow gut feelings instead. When investors understand these biases, they can make more balanced decisions and avoid common mistakes, improving their chances of success in the long run.

1.2 Cognitive Biases in Investment Decision Making

Cognitive biases are common thinking errors that can strongly affect investment decisions. These mistakes often lead people to make decisions that are not logical. Such biases come from how our minds naturally work, which can lead investors to make choices that are not always in their best interest or don't match the real market situation. Confirmation bias happens when investors only look for information that supports their existing beliefs and ignore anything that challenges their views. This can cause them to miss good investment opportunities just because they don't want to believe information that goes against their opinion. Overconfidence bias happens when investors think they know more than they actually do or believe their decisions are always right. This overconfidence can make them take too much risk or trade too often, which can lead to poor results. Anchoring bias occurs when investors base their decisions too much on the first piece of information they see. This can change how they value an investment, because they focus on something random or unimportant instead of looking at the market objectively. Another common bias is the availability heuristic, where investors rely on information that is easy to remember or recent experiences when making decisions. This can make them pay too much attention to current events and ignore important long-term factors. Finally, loss aversion bias means investors are more afraid of losing money than excited about gaining money. Because of this, they may hold onto bad investments for too long or sell good investments too quickly, trying to avoid feeling the pain of losses.

1.3 Emotions and Investor Behavior

Emotions have a strong impact on how investors behave and can greatly influence financial markets. Out of all the emotions that affect investment decisions, fear, greed, and hope play the biggest roles in shaping investor actions. Understanding how these emotions affect market movements is very important for investors who want to handle market ups and downs wisely. Fear is always present in financial markets. It can cause panic selling when markets drop or when investors feel uncertain about their investments. When fear takes over, investors stop thinking logically and simply rush to sell, just because others are selling. This herd behavior increases market instability and can make downturns worse. On the other hand, greed pulls investors into the temptation of quick profits. During market booms, greedy investors often ignore risks because they only focus on high returns. This kind of thinking can inflate market bubbles, which eventually burst, leading to sudden and severe losses. Hope is another powerful emotion. It helps investors stay positive during tough times. However, too much hope can make investors ignore real risks and believe everything will improve even when evidence says otherwise. This can lead to poor decisions, based on wishful thinking rather than facts. For investors, understanding how emotions work is key to making better decisions. By building emotional awareness and practicing mindfulness, they can control emotions like fear, greed, and hope. Setting clear goals and focusing on long-term plans also helps. When investors manage their emotions well, they can make smarter, more disciplined choices, improving their chances of long-term success.

1.4 Herd Mentality and Groupthink in Financial Markets

Herd mentality and groupthink exert a powerful gravitational pull on the collective psyche of investors, shaping the trajectory of financial markets with profound consequences. Herd mentality, akin to a gravitational force, compels individuals to align their investment decisions with the prevailing sentiments of the crowd, often at the expense of rationality. This phenomenon manifests as a tendency for investors to mimic the actions of a larger group, irrespective of underlying fundamentals or independent analysis.

Groupthink, a pernicious cousin of herd mentality, permeates the collective consciousness of market participants, fostering an environment where consensus and conformity reign supreme. In the echo chambers of groupthink, dissenting voices are silenced, and critical evaluation takes a backseat to the allure of unanimity. As a result, decision-making processes become marred by cognitive biases and blind spots, culminating in flawed judgments and suboptimal outcomes.

The symbiotic relationship between herd mentality and groupthink engenders fertile ground for the proliferation of market bubbles, crashes, and inefficiencies. During periods of exuberance, herd mentality fuels speculative fervor, propelling asset prices to dizzying heights untethered from underlying fundamentals. Conversely, in times of distress, herd mentality precipitates mass panic, triggering cascading waves of selling that precipitate market crashes.

Groupthink exacerbates these dynamics by amplifying the echo chamber effect, reinforcing consensus views while marginalizing dissenting perspectives. This insular environment stifles innovation and critical thinking, perpetuating a cycle of herd behavior that exacerbates market volatility and distorts price discovery mechanisms.

In the crucible of financial markets, herd mentality and groupthink are omnipresent forces that shape investor behavior and market outcomes. By recognizing the perils of succumbing to these cognitive traps, investors can cultivate a mindset of independent thinking and critical analysis. Armed with a contrarian ethos and a healthy skepticism of consensus views, investors can navigate the treacherous waters of financial markets with greater resilience and foresight.

In essence, herd mentality and groupthink epitomize the paradox of collective behavior in financial markets, wherein the wisdom of the crowd can often give way to the folly of the herd. By fostering a culture of intellectual diversity and independent thought, investors can inoculate themselves against the contagion of herd behavior and chart a course towards more informed and rational decision-making.

1.5 The Role of Personality Traits in Investment Decisions

Personality traits play an important role in shaping how people make investment decisions. Each investor's personality gives them a unique way of seeing and reacting to financial risks and opportunities. These traits, such as risk tolerance, impulsiveness, and overconfidence, strongly influence how investors behave, often pushing them toward certain types of investment strategies that fit their natural tendencies. Risk tolerance is one of the most important personality traits for investors. It shows how comfortable someone is with uncertainty and possible losses when trying to earn profits. Investors with low risk tolerance prefer safer investments, such as bonds or diversified portfolios, because they do not like uncertainty. In contrast, risk-tolerant investors are willing to take more chances and often invest in stocks, startups, or risky ventures to try for higher returns. Impulsivity is another key trait that affects investment decisions. Impulsive investors often act quickly without careful thinking or analysis. They chase exciting opportunities or change their plans suddenly because of short-term market changes. On the other hand, careful investors like to analyze information and think through decisions before acting. They are less likely to act on impulse and tend to follow well-planned strategies. Overconfidence can be both helpful and harmful for investors. Overconfident investors often believe too strongly in their skills and take bigger risks because they think they can beat the market. This overestimation can lead to bad decisions and losses. In contrast, humble investors understand their limits and approach investing with caution, helping them avoid overconfidence mistakes. Knowing your own personality traits is very important for choosing the right investment strategy. By taking time to understand your risk tolerance, impulsiveness, and confidence levels, you can match your investments to your natural preferences. This self-knowledge helps investors make smarter, more suitable choices. Personality shapes every investor's journey, and understanding it helps unlock better investment results and financial success

2. REVIEW OF LITERATURE

The evolution of financial decision-making has been deeply influenced by the shift from classical economic theories, which assume rational investor behavior, to behavioral finance models that acknowledge the psychological, emotional, and social influences on investor choices. This paradigm shift has been driven by the realization that markets often behave irrationally due to investor biases, particularly during periods of volatility, uncertainty, and innovation (Thaler, 2015). While traditional finance emphasizes market efficiency, utility maximization, and rational forecasting, the real-world behavior of investors frequently deviates from these assumptions. This deviation is particularly pronounced in emerging markets and during economic crises, where emotional responses such as fear, greed, and herd behavior dominate rational analysis (Shiller, 2019).

Recent years have witnessed increased interest in understanding how behavioral biases—such as overconfidence, loss aversion, confirmation bias, and herd mentality—impact investment decisions (Statman, 2019). These biases can distort market signals, result in suboptimal asset allocations, and amplify market bubbles or crashes. For example, during the 2008 financial crisis and the COVID-19 pandemic, investor sentiment and panic-driven behaviors contributed significantly to market instability (Baker et al., 2020). The global GameStop trading frenzy of 2021 also exemplifies how groupthink and social media-driven speculation can override traditional valuation metrics, signaling the need to reassess how behavioral finance interacts with modern technological influences (Barber et al., 2021).

Moreover, the integration of big data, artificial intelligence (AI), and machine learning (ML) into financial decision-making has introduced both opportunities and challenges. On one hand, these technologies can help identify patterns of irrational behavior, automate investment strategies, and enhance risk assessment (Gomber et al., 2017). On the other hand, algorithmic decision-making may unintentionally amplify existing biases, especially if systems are not designed with behavioral insights in mind (Dietvorst et al., 2015). This intersection of behavioral finance and digital transformation is an underexplored domain, particularly in institutional and policy contexts where regulatory gaps persist.

Another challenge lies in the role of institutional factors—such as market regulations, investor protections, economic policy stability, and transparency—which significantly influence how behavioral biases manifest (Kahneman & Tversky, 1979; Kim & Nofsinger, 2022). In markets with weak institutional frameworks, irrational behavior is often more pronounced, leading to higher volatility and lower investor confidence. This is particularly relevant in developing economies where financial literacy levels vary, regulatory enforcement is inconsistent, and socio-cultural influences heavily affect investor psychology (Raissi & Missaoui, 2015).

Given this backdrop, the current study seeks to explore the combined impact of behavioral biases and institutional factors on investment decisions, with a special emphasis on how technological advancements such as AI and big data are transforming these dynamics. By integrating both quantitative and qualitative insights, this research aims to bridge theoretical gaps, offer empirical validation, and provide actionable implications for investors, regulators, and AI developers.

Redhead et al. (2008) give a full view of personal finance and investing by mixing ideas from psychology, economics, and finance. They explain how people make investment decisions, how stock market booms happen, the risks in real estate investing, and the importance of regulating financial markets. The book also covers investment analysis, portfolio management, market efficiency, institutional investments, macroeconomics, and understanding financial records. More than 100 examples and exercises help readers understand these topics without using unnecessary math. This approach shows that financial decisions are not just logical but influenced by emotions and thinking errors (Baker, Filbeck, & Ricciardi, 2022). Redhead et al. (2008) also offer an online website with updates, articles, and extra exercises, proving that learning about finance is an ongoing process. This supports the idea that knowing how emotions affect money decisions is essential for smart investing today (Statman, 2019). The book remains important for students, investors, and finance professionals.

Antindis et al. (2012) examine two major investment approaches that have significantly influenced investor decision-making: the Efficient Market Hypothesis (EMH) and Behavioral Finance Theory. The EMH, once considered the dominant theory until the 1990s, argues that financial markets are efficient, meaning all available information is instantly reflected in asset prices, leaving no room for systematic profit opportunities. However, the study highlights growing skepticism toward this assumption, as repeated market anomalies and irrational investor behavior continue to emerge (Shiller, 2019). To explain these market imperfections, behavioral finance offers a compelling alternative. By incorporating psychological and emotional factors into investment analysis, behavioral finance acknowledges the cognitive biases that influence investment decisions. Antindis et al. (2012) argue that this paradigm shift provides a more realistic foundation for understanding how markets behave and equips investors and financial institutions with tools to make more informed and profitable decisions, particularly in complex and unpredictable environments.

A key focus within behavioral finance is the role of cognitive biases, which Muhammad (2009) identifies as central to investor irrationality. Confirmation bias, for instance, causes investors to seek information that supports their existing beliefs, even if contradictory evidence is more accurate. This selective perception leads to poor investment choices and missed opportunities. Overconfidence bias, also highlighted by Muhammad (2009), makes investors overestimate their skill, causing them to take excessive risks. Anchoring bias occurs when investors rely too heavily on initial reference points, even when new information is available. Finally, the availability heuristic drives investors to base decisions on recent events, rather than performing holistic analysis (Statman, 2019).

Questionrstrom (2008) focuses on understanding how financial markets develop overconfidence and excessive optimism. The study raises a key question about whether financial experts accurately predict market outcomes or whether their views inflate the perception of certainty. Through the lens of behavioral finance theory, which examines hidden factors that influence financial decisions, the study uncovers systematic overconfidence among S&P 500 analysts. These experts consistently project overly optimistic forecasts, downplaying potential risks. The analysis highlights grounding and herding behavior, where analysts align their projections to fit with broader consensus, regardless of their own independent evaluations. By comparing earnings per share (EPS) estimates with actual results, the study reveals that these experts collectively follow dominant opinions for up to twenty-four months ahead. This demonstrates how cognitive biases, including overconfidence and herd mentality, contribute to forecasting errors and distort rational price formation, making markets more vulnerable to mispricing and volatility (Shefrin, 2021).

Venkatapathy et al. (2016) emphasize that investment decision-making involves selecting rational strategies from available options, but this process is often complicated by cognitive and emotional biases. Although investors are assumed to act rationally, their actual decisions are influenced by thoughts, emotions, and social pressures. Investors, managers, and financial professionals frequently face heuristics-based decision-making, where they rely on mental shortcuts, often simplifying complex problems into familiar patterns. These heuristics do not always lead to rational decisions, as they are influenced by emotions, group dynamics, creativity, and a desire for consensus. Importantly, the study links behavioral finance theory to this heuristic process, explaining that cognitive errors, such as anchoring or availability bias, play a central role. Building on Herbert Simon's foundational principles, the authors highlight that real-world decisions often reflect bounded rationality, where investors make satisfactory rather than optimal choices due to limited cognitive capacity and external pressures (Kahneman, 2017).

Firat et al. (2011) revisit the Efficient Markets Hypothesis (EMH), which assumes that investors act rationally based on complete and accurate information. However, their research finds that real investment decisions are shaped by both internal perceptions and external cultural factors, especially in industrial regions such as Kocaeli, Turkey. The study investigates how buyers evaluate stock markets, financial systems, and broader social and cultural environments. By analyzing survey data using ANOVA and Chi-Square tests, they find that investors prioritize social signals and peer behavior over pure economic analysis. This emotional and cultural dependency often leads to irrational decision-making, where feelings of uncertainty drive investors to follow trends rather than conduct independent evaluations. Firat et al. conclude that in contexts where information asymmetry exists, cultural and social influences magnify herd behavior, further weakening the rational decision-making foundation that traditional finance theories assume (Kim & Nofsinger, 2022).

Raissi et al. (2016) investigate the relationship between investor sentiment and stock performance, emphasizing the role of market liquidity in shaping investor behavior. By focusing on market capitalization classes, the study identifies how investor sentiment influences the performance of small-cap stocks more strongly than larger firms. The research covers January 2005 to October 2009, examining 80 French industrial companies. Results show that investor sentiment significantly explains the performance of small-cap stocks, while larger companies remain less affected. Trading volume is proposed as an effective proxy to measure investor sentiment, as higher liquidity tends to magnify sentiment-driven trades. The study confirms that small-cap stocks, which are inherently less liquid, are more sensitive to shifts in investor mood. Ultimately, Raissi et al. (2016) demonstrate that market liquidity serves as a critical channel through which investor sentiment translates into stock price fluctuations, reinforcing the link between behavioral finance and market microstructure (Baker et al., 2022).

Shahid et al. (2018) explore how behavioral factors influence individual investor decisions within the Pakistan Stock Exchange, marking a pioneering effort to link behavioral biases to financial choices in this emerging market context. Using ethnographic observations and semi-structured interviews with 30 investors, the study identifies the dominant role of cognitive, emotional, and behavioral biases in shaping investment choices. Findings reveal that emotional triggers, such as fear, optimism, and regret, interact with cognitive shortcuts, like confirmation bias and overconfidence, leading to suboptimal decisions. The study highlights that behavioral finance models offer valuable insights for risk managers, fund managers, and policymakers, especially in markets where formal financial education is limited. Though based on a small sample, the study provides transferable insights for both developing and developed markets, contributing to understanding behavioral biases in contexts marked by information asymmetry, herd mentality, and market inefficiency (Yarovenko et al., 2023).

2.1 Some Prominent Theories Related to Behavioral Finance

1. Theory of Prospects

Prospect Theory was created by Daniel Kahneman and Amos Tversky, and it is a very important part of behavioral finance. It explains how people make decisions when they are unsure about the outcome. According to Prospect Theory, people do not just look at final outcomes — instead, they compare possible results to a reference point, usually their current wealth or the situation they are in now. This is very different from what traditional finance says, which assumes people follow the expected utility theory to make logical decisions. Prospect Theory also says that people are usually careful about risk when they expect a gain, but they take bigger risks when trying to avoid a loss. This happens because of loss aversion, which means people fear losing money more than they value gaining the same amount. As a result, people often take bigger risks to avoid losses, but are more careful when they expect to win.

2. Biases in behavior

Behavioral biases are thinking mistakes that happen because of the way the human brain works. These biases are common in financial markets, and they often cause investors to act irrationally and make poor choices. Some examples include:

(a) **Confirmation Bias:** Investors only pay attention to information that supports what they already believe and ignore anything that disagrees with them.
(b) **Overconfidence Bias:** Investors believe too strongly in their skills or the correctness of their decisions, causing them to take too much risk and lose money.
(c) **Anchoring Bias:** Investors rely too heavily on their first impression or initial information, even if better data is available later.
(d) **Availability Heuristic:** Investors base decisions on the easiest information to recall, often focusing on recent events instead of doing a thorough analysis.

3. An inefficient market

The Efficient Market Hypothesis (EMH) says that financial markets use all available information correctly, so that asset prices always show their true value. However, behavioral finance does not agree with this. Instead, it argues that markets make mistakes because investors often think irrationally and let their biases influence decisions.

These problems show up in a number of ways, such as:

(a) **Mispricing of assets:** Investors' biases can cause assets to have wrong prices for a short time. This gives investors a chance to make money by using strategies like value investing or contrarian investing. When investors follow the crowd or overreact to news, it makes prices change more than necessary. These price swings often have nothing to do with real company value.
(b) **Market anomalies:** Behavioral finance has found strange patterns in markets — such as the momentum effect (where rising stocks keep rising) and the value effect (where cheap stocks tend to outperform). Traditional finance can't fully explain these patterns, but they make sense when we understand how emotions and biases shape decisions. If investors understand these biases and market mistakes, they can find smart ways to spot opportunities and reduce risks when investing. Behavioral finance also helps policymakers and regulators make better rules for markets. These rules can protect investors and keep markets more stable, especially during times of panic or excitement.

2.2 Theories of Financial Behavior and their Relevance to AI and Machine Learning

The use of Artificial Intelligence (AI) and Machine Learning (ML) in financial decision-making has made several behavioral finance theories more relevant than ever before. These theories explain why investors often make irrational decisions, and they also show how AI can either reduce or worsen these behaviors. One of the most important is Prospect Theory, developed by Kahneman and Tversky (1979). It says that investors feel the pain of losses more strongly than the pleasure of gains. This makes them hold on to losing investments too long or sell winning ones too soon. AI platforms, using sentiment analysis, can now detect signs of loss aversion by analyzing social media posts, financial news, and trading patterns. Based on this, they can send timely alerts encouraging investors to pause and rethink emotional decisions. Bounded Rationality, from Herbert Simon (1955), explains that people have limited mental capacity when making decisions. Because of this, investors use shortcuts instead of looking at all available data. AI helps by quickly processing huge amounts of financial data and providing useful insights. However, if AI overloads users with too much information, it can confuse them further, making clear and simple AI interfaces extremely important. Lo's Adaptive Market Hypothesis (2004) adds another angle. It says markets constantly evolve as investors adjust to new information, technology, and crises. AI fits perfectly here because it learns and updates continuously, helping it spot new trends and unexpected risks even when past data offers no clear clues. Social Learning Theory, from Bandura (1977), shows that investors copy others during uncertain times. Today, this happens on social media, where platforms like Twitter, Reddit, and financial forums shape group behavior. AI, especially using Natural Language Processing (NLP), can track these social waves to identify when viral trends are driving irrational market behavior. This helps regulators and platforms respond faster with fact-based counter-messages to reduce dangerous speculation. Finally, Algorithm Aversion Theory from Dietvorst et al. (2015) explains why many people do not trust AI to make financial decisions for them, even if AI performs better than humans. If people see even a small AI error, they lose confidence quickly. This is why transparency is crucial—when AI systems explain their recommendations clearly and show how they understand the user's own behavioral tendencies, people trust the advice more. Together, these five theories offer a complete view of how psychology, technology, and market behavior now work together in modern finance. They also illustrate why the mere presence of AI does not automatically correct irrationality—without aligning AI design with behavioral insights, technology may amplify biases instead of mitigating them. These theoretical anchors therefore underscore the importance of human-centered AI in financial decision-making, an imperative that forms the conceptual heart of this research.

3. THEORETICAL FRAMEWORK

3.1 Objectives

The primary objectives of this project are:

1. To investigate the impact of behavioral biases on investment decisions.
2. To analyze the influence of institutional factors on investment decisions.
3. To perform a regression and correlation analysis to understand the relationship between investment decisions, behavioral biases, and institutional factors.
4. To gather qualitative insights through interviews to supplement and enrich the quantitative data.

3.2 Hypothesis

Hypothesis 1: Behavioral biases significantly influence investment decisions.
Hypothesis 2: Institutional factors play a crucial role in shaping investment decisions.

3.3 Experimental Work

3.3.1 Survey Design

To collect data, a structured questionnaire was designed using Google Forms. The questionnaire was divided into three sections:

1. **Demographic Information**
2. **Investment Decision Variables (Dependent Variable)**
3. **Behavioral Biases (Independent Variables)**
4. **Institutional Factors (Independent Variables)**

3.3.2 Data Collection

- **Sample Size:** Aiming for 320 responses from various demographics to ensure a representative sample.
- **Distribution Method:** The survey link was distributed through email, social media platforms, and investment forums.

3.3.3 Interviews

- **Sample Size:** Conducted interviews with 30 individuals to gain deeper insights into investment behaviors.
- **Interview Structure:** Semi-structured interviews with open-ended questions covering:

(a) Personal investment experiences
(b) Perceptions of market conditions
(c) Influence of advisors and institutional factors

(d) Behavioral tendencies observed in their decision-making processes

3.4 Methodology

This chapter explores the relationship between behavioral biases, institutional factors, and investment decisions, aiming to bridge gaps in behavioral finance literature. The primary objective is to examine how cognitive biases, such as overconfidence, loss aversion, and herd behavior, interact with institutional environments, including regulatory policies and market stability, to shape investor behavior. Using a mixed-methods approach, the chapter combines survey data from 350 investors with qualitative insights from 30 interviews to provide a comprehensive understanding of these dynamics. Findings indicate a strong positive correlation between behavioral biases and investment decisions, with overconfidence and loss aversion emerging as key drivers. Institutional factors, particularly regulatory transparency and economic stability, were found to either magnify or reduce the impact of cognitive biases. The study highlights that clear regulations and transparent market communication play a crucial role in fostering rational investment behavior, while regulatory uncertainty amplifies emotional responses. These insights carry significant implications for both investors and policymakers. Investors can improve decision-making by understanding how biases interact with institutional settings, while policymakers can design regulatory frameworks that enhance market confidence and mitigate irrational behavior. The chapter also emphasizes the need for enhanced financial education to build investor awareness of psychological pitfalls. Future research could broaden the sample across different cultural and economic contexts, track behavioral changes through longitudinal studies, and examine the potential role of AI-driven financial advisory tools in identifying and mitigating cognitive biases in real time. By addressing these areas, future work can contribute to a deeper and more actionable understanding of behavioral finance.

3.4.1 Research Design

A mixed-methods approach was adopted, combining quantitative data from surveys and qualitative data from interviews to provide a comprehensive understanding of the research questions.

3.4.2 Data Analysis Tools

- **Quantitative Data:** Statistical software such as SPSS and R was used for data analysis.

Regression Analysis: To determine the strength and nature of the relationship between dependent and independent variables.
Correlation Analysis: To identify the degree to which behavioral biases and institutional factors are related to investment decisions.

- **Qualitative Data:** Thematic analysis was conducted on the interview transcripts to identify common themes and insights.

3.5 Instrumentation

3.5.1 Survey Instrument

The Google Form was designed to be user-friendly and included both multiple-choice and Likert scale questions to capture a wide range of data.

3.5.2 Interview Guide

An interview guide was prepared to ensure consistency across all interviews while allowing flexibility for participants to share their unique perspectives.

3.6 Coding and Data Preparation

- **Survey Responses:** Data from the Google Form was exported to Excel for initial cleaning and coding. Each response was coded to facilitate statistical analysis.
- **Interview Transcripts:** Recorded interviews were transcribed and coded using qualitative analysis software such as NVivo.

3.7 Data Analysis

3.7.1 Quantitative Analysis

- **Descriptive Statistics:** Used to summarize the demographic data and investment behaviors.
- **Regression Analysis:** To test the hypotheses and understand the impact of behavioral biases and institutional factors on investment decisions.
- **Correlation Analysis:** To explore the relationships between different variables.

3.7.2 Qualitative Analysis

- **Thematic Analysis:** Identified recurring themes and patterns in interview responses to supplement quantitative findings.

4. DATA ANALYSIS AND INTERPRETATION

4.1 Survey Responses

Figure 1. Age distribution of survey respondents (320 responses)

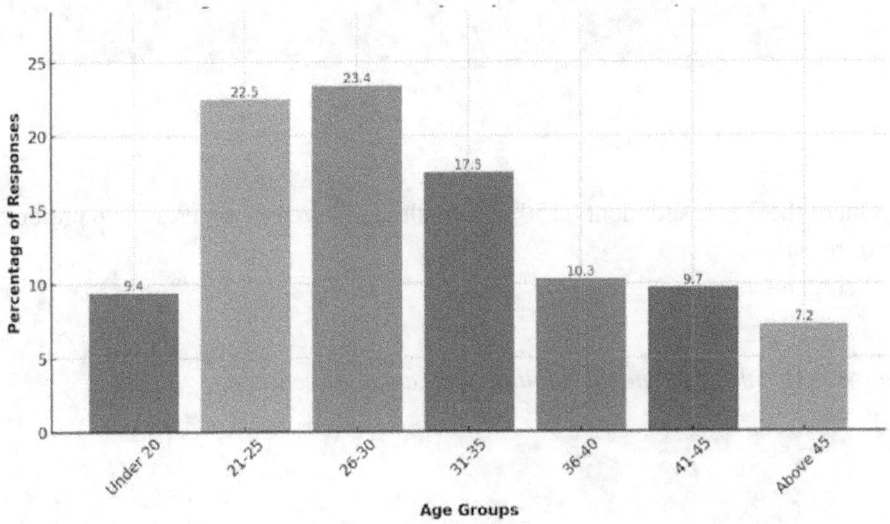

Out of the 320 respondents, 31 were under the age of 20 years, 72 were between 21-25 years, 75 were in the range of 26-30 years, 56 were in the range 31-35 years, 33 were in the range of 36-40 years, 30 were in the range of 41-45 years, and 23 respondents were above the age of 45 years.

Figure 2. Gender distribution of survey respondents (320 responses)

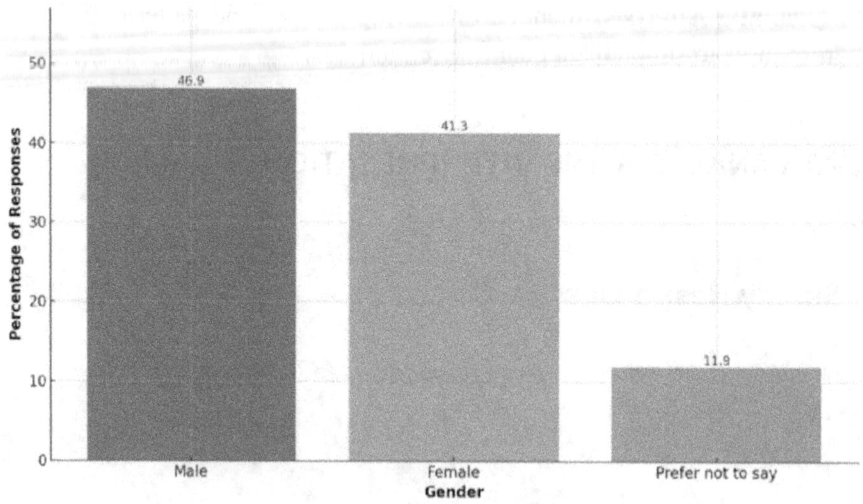

Out of the 320 respondents, 150 were males, 132 were females and 38 preferred not to reveal

their genders.

Figure 3. Monthly income distribution with cumulative trend

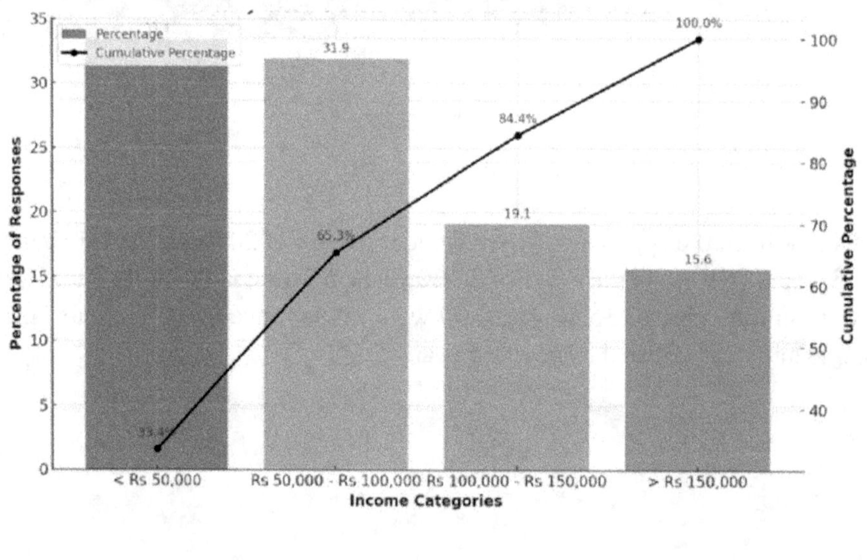

Out of the 320 respondents, 61 earned less than Rs 50,000 per month, 102 earned in range of Rs 50,000-Rs 100,000, 107 earned in the range of Rs 100,000-Rs 150,000 and 50 respondents earned more than Rs 150,000.

Figure 4. Years of active investing among survey respondents (320 responses)

Please provide missing figure by **proofing deadline**.

New files can be uploaded to the proofing system via comment attachment or emailed to **bookproofing@igi-global.com**

Out of 320 respondents, 40 have been investing for less than a year, 122 have been investing for 1-5 years, 105 were investing for 5-10 years, whereas only 53 were investing for more than 10 years.

4.2 Defining the Variables

Investment Decision: The process by which a person or a group chooses which financial assets to add to their collection is called investment choice. As part of this process, you have to look at things like your risk tolerance, projected results, time span, and the state of the market. The goal is to find the best mix between risk and gain that fits the investor's financial goals. When making an investment choice, you may have to decide between different types of assets, like stocks, bonds, and real estate, or between different products within those types. Amounts like financial measures and performance indicators, as well as quality factors like market mood and economic expectations, both play a role in these choices. To make smart business choices, you need to know a lot about money, how markets work, and your own personal financial goals.

Behavioral Biases: Behavioral biases are regular deviations from reasoning in how we make decisions and judge things, which are usually caused by psychological factors. When it comes to investing, these biases can have a big effect on the choices an investor makes, which can lead to less-than-ideal results. Some common behavioral biases are overconfidence, which happens when investors think they know more than they do about the market and can predict how it will move; herd behavior, where people do what everyone else does, which can cause market bubbles or crashes; and loss aversion, where investors are too afraid to lose money and make too conservative investments or don't want to sell assets that aren't doing well. Investors can make bad choices because of these biases, like buying high and selling low, missing basic analysis, or not diversifying enough. To make financial decisions that are more logical and successful, it is important to understand and lessen these biases.

4.3 Institutional Factors

The legal, economic, and structural factors that affect the financial markets and business climate are all institutional factors. Some of these factors are market rules, monetary and fiscal policies, and how stable and open financial institutions are in general. Government and financial officials can have an effect on market behavior by following rules that protect consumers, make sure trade is fair, and cut down on scams. Conditions in the economy, like interest rates, inflation, and GDP growth, also have a big impact on business choices because they change the cost of capital and the possible profits. Institutional factors also include the structure and efficiency of financial markets, such as the ease of access to information and the presence of a strong financial infrastructure. A stable and clear institutional framework builds investor trust and helps people make smarter investment choices. On the other hand, when there isn't any structure, market instability and risk can rise.

5. CORRELATIONAL ANALYSIS

Table 1. Pearson's correlation between investment decision, behavioral biases and institutional factors

Factors	1	2	3
Investment Decision	-		
Behavioral Biases	0.84264	-	
Institutional Factors	0.90887	0.91623	-

**Significant at 0.01 level

There are three factors in the table: Investment Decision, Behavioral Biases, and Institutional Factors. The association values between these variables are shown. Pearson's correlation coefficient, which has values from -1 to 1, shows how strong and in what way two variables are related linearly. A number that is close to 1 or -1 means that the link is strong, while a value close to 0 means that there is no straight connection.

5.1 Choosing an Investment and Behavioral Biases

There is a strong positive link between Investment Decision and Behavioral Biases, as shown by the correlation value of 0.84264. This means that business choices are also affected in the same way when behavioral biases get worse. Behavioral flaws, such as assumptions, overconfidence, and fear of loss, can have a big effect on how buyers choose to spend their money. The strong connection between the two variables means that these biases are likely to cause expected trends in how investors act, like avoiding risk or overreacting to events in the market. This strong link shows how important it is to look at psychological factors when studying investment habits, since they can cause people to make decisions that aren't based on logic.

Decision to Invest and Institutional Factors: At 0.90887, the link between Investment Decision and Institutional Factors is even stronger. This strong link between the two variables shows that institutional factors, such as market rules, economic policies, and the general financial climate, have a big effect on business choices. The security and strategies of financial organizations, governing bodies, and market infrastructure have a big impact on investors. A strong legal environment can boost investor trust, which can lead to better choices. Instead, markets that are unpredictable or not well controlled can make people not want to spend. The strong link between these two things shows how important social systems are in shaping how people spend and make decisions.

Institutional Factors and Biases in Behavior: There is a very strong positive link between Behavioral Biases and Institutional Factors, as shown by the correlation value of 0.91623. This shows that the formal setting in which investors work has a lot to do with the presence and strength of behavioral biases. For example, behavioral biases might be less of a problem in a market that is well-regulated and open to everyone because investors would have more faith in the market and be able to get more information. On the other hand, when there aren't as many rules in place, behavioral biases like fear selling or following the crowd might be more noticeable because of the lack of accurate information and doubt. This strong link makes it clear that people's behavior patterns are not just their own, but also shaped and affected by the larger social setting.

At the 0.01 level, it matters: There is a lot of faith in these relationships because the table shows that these connections are significant at the 0.01 level. We can use statistics to say that there is less than a 1% chance that these results are just a random event. At this level of importance, there is strong proof that the connections seen between financial choices, behavioral biases, and institutional factors are real and not just chance variations. The high significance level makes these factors even more important for knowing how investments behave.

What this means for investors and policymakers: There are strong links between these factors, which has big effects on investors and lawmakers. For investors, making smarter financial choices can come from knowing how institutional factors and mental biases affect each other. Knowing your own biases and how the regulatory environment affects things can help keep bad business results to a minimum. These results show lawmakers how important it is to make the governing environment safe and clear so that investors have faith and behavioral biases don't hurt people. Policies and rules that work can make the market more efficient and keep buyers safe from the bad effects of bias.

To sum up, the correlation table shows that financial choices, behavioral flaws, and institutional factors are all strongly linked in a good way. All of the correlations are statistically significant at the 0.01 level. These connections show how complexly psychological factors and societal settings interact to affect investment decisions. This information is useful for both investors and lawmakers.

6. REGRESSION ANALYSIS

6.1 Regression Equation

$Y = \beta 0 + \beta 1$ (Investment Decision) $+ \beta 2$ (Behavioral Biases) $+ \epsilon$

Where,

Y= Investment Decision

β0=constant term

β1= r coefficient for Behavioral Biases

β2= r coefficient for Institutional Factors

ϵ = variability that is not explained by the regression model

Table 2. Regression model output

	Coeff.	Std.err.	t	p	R^2
Constant	1.9967	0.55346	3.6077	0.00035425	
Investment Decision	0.92619	0.032477	28.519	5.6421E-93	0.94602
Behavioral Biases	0.2187	0.060601	3.6088	0.00035177	0.82604

Regression Model: The regression model aims to understand the relationship between the Investment Decision (dependent variable) and two key independent variables: Behavioral Biases and Institutional Factors. The equation for the regression model is:

6.2 Constant Term (β0)

The constant term (β0) has a coefficient of 1.9967, with a standard error of 0.55346. The t-value for this coefficient is 3.6077, and the corresponding p-value is 0.00035425. Given that the p-value is well below the 0.01 significance level, the constant term is statistically significant. This suggests that when both Behavioral Biases and Institutional Factors are zero, the baseline level of the Investment Decision is approximately 1.9967. This constant can be interpreted as the inherent level of investment decision-making that occurs due to factors outside the scope of the model.

6.3 Coefficient for Behavioral Biases (β1)

The coefficient for Behavioral Biases (β1) is 0.92619, with a standard error of 0.032477. The t-value for Behavioral Biases is 28.519, and the p-value is an exceptionally small 5.6421E-93, indicating a highly significant effect. This coefficient suggests that for every unit increase in Behavioral Biases, the Investment Decision increases by approximately 0.92619 units, holding Institutional Factors constant. The significance of this coefficient underscores the substantial influence of psychological factors on investment decisions, highlighting how biases like overconfidence, herd behavior, and loss aversion can drive investor behavior in a predictable manner.

6.4 Coefficient for Institutional Factors (β2)

The coefficient for Institutional Factors (β2) is 0.2187, with a standard error of 0.060601. The t-value for this coefficient is 3.6088, and the p-value is 0.00035177, indicating statistical significance at the 0.01 level. This suggests that Institutional Factors have a significant, albeit smaller, impact on Investment Decisions compared to Behavioral Biases. For every unit increase in Institutional Factors, the Investment Decision increases by approximately 0.2187 units, assuming Behavioral Biases remain constant. This reflects the role of external regulatory and economic environments in shaping investor behavior.

6.5 Model Fit and Overall Significance

The model's multiple R is 0.97364, indicating a very strong linear relationship between the dependent and independent variables. The R-squared (R^2) value is 0.94798, meaning that approximately 94.8% of the variability in Investment Decisions is explained by the model, which includes Behavioral Biases and Institutional Factors. The adjusted R^2 value is 0.94768, which is very close to the R^2 value, suggesting that the model is well-fitted with minimal overfitting.

6.6 ANOVA Results

The ANOVA results show an F-statistic of 3161.5 with degrees of freedom (df1 = 2, df2 = 347). The p-value associated with the F-statistic is 1.8262E-223, which is exceedingly small, indicating that the overall regression model is statistically significant. This means that the combination of Behavioral Biases and Institutional Factors significantly predicts Investment Decisions, and the likelihood of these results occurring by chance is almost zero.

The regression analysis reveals that both Behavioral Biases and Institutional Factors play critical roles in shaping Investment Decisions. Behavioral Biases have a stronger impact compared to Institutional Factors, as indicated by the larger coefficient. This suggests that psychological factors are more influential in driving investment behavior. However, the significant effect of Institutional Factors also underscores the importance of a stable and transparent regulatory environment in influencing investment decisions. Policymakers and financial advisors can use these insights to better understand investor behavior and develop strategies to mitigate adverse effects of biases and enhance market stability. Thus, the regression model provides a comprehensive understanding of the factors influencing Investment Decisions. By quantifying the impact of Behavioral Biases and Institutional Factors, the analysis highlights the intricate interplay between psychological and institutional elements in the investment process. The model's high explanatory power and statistical significance underscore its robustness and reliability in predicting investment behaviors.

7. FINDINGS

Behavioral Biases and Investment Decisions: A Pearson's correlation value of 0.84264 showed that there was a strong positive link between behavioral errors and financial choices. This shows that behavioral biases have a big effect on financial choices as they get worse. With a value of 0.92619, the regression analysis showed that behavioral biases have a big effect on business choices, which backed this finding even more. Common biases like overconfidence, following the crowd, and not wanting to lose money are very important in how buyers decide what to do.

1. **Institutional Factors and Investment Decisions:** The correlation coefficient between institutional factors and investment decisions was even higher at 0.90887, demonstrating a robust positive relationship. Institutional factors, including regulatory policies, economic conditions, and market stability, significantly shape investment behaviors. The regression analysis confirmed the importance of these factors, with a coefficient of 0.2187, indicating that institutional factors also have a significant, albeit smaller, influence on investment decisions compared to behavioral biases.
2. **Interrelationship Between Behavioral Biases and Institutional Factors:** The correlation between behavioral biases and institutional factors was 0.91623, suggesting a very strong positive relationship. This implies that the presence and strength of behavioral biases are significantly related to the institutional context within which investors operate. A stable and transparent market environment can mitigate the impact of behavioral biases, while less regulated environments can exacerbate them.
3. **Qualitative Insights:** Interviews with 30 people gave us more information about the subjective parts of making financial decisions. People who answered stressed how important things like evaluating risk, past success, market trends, and professional help are. A lot of people admitted that their feelings and cognitive biases affected the investments they made, which shows how important it is to find ways to lessen these effects. It was also emphasized how important it is to have accurate information and openness in the financial market in order to make smart business choices.

8. CONCLUSION

This study convincingly demonstrates how deeply institutional factors and behavioral biases influence financial decisions. Through rigorous correlation and regression analyses, it reveals that behavioral biases such as overconfidence and herd behavior significantly sway financial choices, with these effects heightened or tempered by the surrounding institutional environment. The study also shows that while regulatory policies and market stability are crucial, their impact is somewhat less than that of personal biases. Qualitative interviews highlight the critical role of emotional and cognitive biases in investment decisions, emphasizing the need for accurate information and strategic interventions to mitigate these biases. This interplay suggests that fostering a well-regulated and transparent market environment is essential for making more informed and effective financial choices.

8.1 Future Scope

1. **Extended Sample Size and Diversity:** To make the results more applicable to a wider range of people, future study could increase the sample size and include a wider range of demographics. Including buyers from different parts of the world and with different amounts of financial knowledge could give the study a more complete picture.
2. **Longitudinal Studies:** Conducting longitudinal studies to track investment behaviors over time would provide insights into how behavioral biases and institutional factors evolve and influence decisions in the long term.
3. **Impact of Technological Advancements:** Exploring the impact of technological advancements, such as algorithmic trading and AI-powered investment tools, on mitigating behavioral biases and improving investment decisions would be a valuable area of research.
4. **Behavioral Interventions:** Investigating the effectiveness of various behavioral interventions, such as nudges or educational programs, in reducing the adverse effects of cognitive biases on investment decisions could offer practical solutions for investors and policymakers.

To broaden the applicability of these findings, future research should aim to increase the sample size and diversify participant demographics. Including individuals from various global regions and with different levels of financial knowledge would provide a more comprehensive understanding of financial decision-making processes. Longitudinal studies tracking investment behaviors over time would offer valuable insights into the evolution of behavioral biases and institutional influences on financial choices. Additionally, examining the impact of technological advancements, such as AI and algorithmic trading, could reveal how modern technologies might mitigate behavioral biases and enhance investment decisions. Investigating the effectiveness of behavioral interventions, such as educational programs or nudges, could provide practical solutions for minimizing the adverse effects of cognitive biases on investment decisions. For investors, it is crucial to understand the interplay between institutional factors and personal biases to make informed financial choices. Investors should consider using automated trading systems or seeking professional advice to counteract biases and adopt diversified investment strategies to manage psychological risks effectively. For policymakers, the study highlights the importance of establishing a secure and transparent regulatory environment that enhances investor confidence and mitigates the impact of behavioral flaws. Effective policies and regulations can make markets more efficient, protect investors, and create a healthier trading environment. Comprehensive investor education programs focusing on the impact of behavioral biases and the importance of regulatory stability could empower investors to make more informed decisions. Financial advisors could also benefit from integrating behavioral finance insights to provide tailored advice that addresses individual biases, potentially leveraging technology to offer data-driven recommendations. The integration of AI in financial decision-making processes presents a promising field for further exploration. Future studies could investigate how AI systems might be designed to recognize and counteract behavioral biases, supporting more objective and efficient decision-making. Research into AI's potential to offer personalized financial advice based on individual behavioral profiles could enhance the effectiveness of tailored financial strategies, helping investors achieve better outcomes. This study lays the groundwork for understanding how structural factors and behavioral imperfections shape financial choices, offering a platform for future research to delve into the complexities of investing in an ever-evolving financial landscape. Such efforts can assist investors and policymakers in developing a more robust and transparent financial market.

For Investors: Figuring out how institutional factors and behavioral biases affect each other can help you make smarter financial choices. Investors should be aware of their own biases and use automatic trade systems or get professional help to lessen the bad effects of these biases. Having a focused financial plan and spreading out your investments can also help you handle the risks that come from psychological factors. Understanding the influence of behavioral biases on financial decisions can help investors make more informed and rational choices. By acknowledging their own susceptibilities to biases such as overconfidence or loss aversion, investors can adopt strategies to mitigate these effects. For example, they might use decision-making frameworks that involve systematic analysis of investment opportunities or seek diverse opinions before committing to investments. Additionally, investors can leverage automated trading systems that use algorithms designed to act without emotional bias, potentially leading to more consistent and objective investment outcomes.

For Policymakers: The results show how important it is to make the legal environment safe and clear so that investors can trust it and behavioral flaws don't hurt people as much. Policies and rules that work can make markets more efficient, protect buyers, and make it a better place to trade. The findings highlight the crucial role of a stable and transparent institutional framework in shaping investment behaviors. Policymakers can use this information to craft regulations that enhance market transparency and stability, thus providing a more predictable environment that can help mitigate the impact of behavioral biases. This involves not only the creation of clear financial regulations but also ensuring that these regulations are consistently enforced. Furthermore, policymakers can initiate public education campaigns aimed at increasing financial literacy, helping individuals understand the risks of succumbing to behavioral biases and how to avoid them.

AI Developers: AI developers can find significant opportunities in these findings to develop tools that assist in making better financial decisions. By designing AI systems that can identify and adapt to the presence of behavioral biases in real-time, these technologies can offer personalized recommendations that counteract biased tendencies. For example, AI can analyze patterns in an investor's decision-making process and highlight when decisions deviate from rational benchmarks due to biases. Moreover, AI-driven platforms can be developed to simulate different investment scenarios, showing potential outcomes based on varying levels of bias influence, which can serve as an educational tool for investors to visualize the potential consequences of their biases.

Broader Implications: All these implications collectively contribute to a healthier financial marketplace, where informed and rational decision-making is promoted, and the risks associated with irrational behaviors are minimized. By improving investor awareness and decision-making, enhancing regulatory frameworks, and integrating advanced technology into financial practices, the overall stability and efficiency of financial markets can be significantly improved. This holistic approach not only benefits individual investors but also enhances the integrity and functionality of the entire financial system.

The insights gleaned from this study have profound practical implications for various stakeholders in the financial market, including investors, policymakers, and AI developers:

8.2 Practical Applications

Investor Education Programs: Developing comprehensive investor education programs that focus on the impact of behavioral biases and the importance of a stable regulatory environment could help investors make more informed decisions.

Enhanced Financial Advising: Financial advisors can incorporate insights from behavioral finance to better understand their clients' biases and provide tailored advice that mitigates these biases. Advisors can also leverage technology to offer data-driven recommendations.

Policy Development: Policymakers can use the findings to design and implement regulations that enhance market transparency, stability, and investor protection. Policies aimed at improving financial literacy and promoting ethical practices within financial institutions can also be beneficial.

This study shows how important structural factors and behavioral flaws are in determining financial choices. Investors can make smarter decisions and lawmakers can make the financial market stronger and more open if they understand these factors. The future of this study opens up a lot of chances to learn more about and solve the complicated problems that come up when investments are made in a changing financial environment.

REFERENCES

Almansour, B. Y., & Arabyat, Y. A. (2017). Investment decision making among Gulf investors: Behavioural finance perspective. *International Journal of Management Studies*, *24*(1), 1. DOI: 10.32890/ijms.24.1.2017.10476

Ángeles López-Cabarcos, M., Pérez-Pico, A. M., Vázquez Rodríguez, P., & López Perez, M. L. (2020). Investor sentiment in the theoretical field of behavioural finance. *Economic Research -. Ekonomska Istrazivanja*, *33*(1), 2101–2228. DOI: 10.1080/1331677X.2018.1559748

Ani, N. C., & Özarı, Ç. (n.d.). Behavioral finance: Investors' psychology. In *Behavioral Finance* (pp. 1-15).

Baker, M., Bloom, N., & Davis, S. J. (2020). Measuring economic policy uncertainty. *The Quarterly Journal of Economics*, *131*(4), 1593–1636. DOI: 10.1093/qje/qjw024

Barber, B. M., Huang, X., Odean, T., & Schwarz, C. (2021). Attention induced trading and returns: Evidence from Robinhood users. *The Journal of Finance*, *76*(3), 1171–1216.

Bikas, E., Jurevičienė, D., Dubinskas, P., & Novickytė, L. (2013). Behavioural finance: The emergence and development trends. *Procedia: Social and Behavioral Sciences*, *82*, 870–876. DOI: 10.1016/j.sbspro.2013.06.363

Byrne, A., & Utkus, W. S. P. (n.d.). *Understanding how the mind can help or hinder investment success*. Vanguard Investment Counseling & Research.

Chen, C., Li, X., & Wu, H. (2020). Big data analytics in financial markets: A review. *The Journal of Financial Data Science*, *2*(2), 15–27. DOI: 10.3905/jfds.2020.1.035

Dietvorst, B. J., Simmons, J. P., & Massey, C. (2015). Algorithm aversion: People erroneously avoid algorithms after seeing them err. *Journal of Experimental Psychology. General*, *144*(1), 114–126. DOI: 10.1037/xge0000033 PMID: 25401381

Fagerström, S. (2008). Behavioural finance: The psychological impact and overconfidence in financial markets. Institutionen för teknik och samhälle. https://urn.kb.se/resolve?urn=urn:nbn:se:his:diva-1326

Firat, D., & Fettahoğlu, S. (2011). Investors' purchasing behaviour via a behavioural finance approach. *International Journal of Business and Management*, *6*(7), 153–160. DOI: 10.5539/ijbm.v6n7p153

Fogaat, M., Sharma, S., & Meena, D. R. P. (2022). Behavioral finance psychology: A review paper. *Journal of Contemporary Issues in Business and Government*, *28*(4), 4.

Gomber, P., Koch, J.-A., & Siering, M. (2017). Digital finance and fintech: Current research and future research directions. *Journal of Business Economics*, *87*(5), 537–580. DOI: 10.1007/s11573-017-0852-x

Guzavicius, A., Vilkė, R., & Barkauskas, V. (2014). Behavioural finance: Corporate social responsibility approach. *Procedia: Social and Behavioral Sciences*, *156*, 518–523. DOI: 10.1016/j.sbspro.2014.11.232

Joo, B. A., & Durri, K. (2015). Comprehensive review of literature on behavioural finance. *Indian Journal of Commerce and Management Studies*, *6*(2), 2.

Kahneman, D., & Tversky, A. (1979). Prospect theory: An analysis of decision under risk. *Econometrica*, *47*(2), 263–291. DOI: 10.2307/1914185

Kim, K. A., & Nofsinger, J. R. (2022). *Behavioral finance* (3rd ed.). Routledge.

Konstantinidis, A., Katarachia, A., Borovas, G., & Voutsa, E. (n.d.). From efficient market hypothesis to behavioural finance: Can behavioural finance be the new dominant model for investing?

Kumar, S., & Goyal, N. (2015). Behavioural biases in investment decision making: A systematic literature review. *Qualitative Research in Financial Markets*, *7*(1), 88–108. DOI: 10.1108/QRFM-07-2014-0022

Li, J., Zhang, Z., & Yu, Y. (2021). Artificial intelligence in behavioural finance: A bibliometric review and future research agenda. *Finance Research Letters*, *39*, 101645. DOI: 10.1016/j.frl.2020.101645

Montier, J. (2007). *Behavioural investing: A practitioner's guide to applying behavioural finance*. John Wiley & Sons. DOI: 10.1002/9781118673430

Muhammad, N. M. N. (2009). Behavioral finance vs traditional finance: A review. *Journal of Behavioral Economics and Finance*, *2*, 1–7.

Muradoglu, G., & Harvey, N. (2012). Behavioural finance: The role of psychological factors in financial decisions. *Review of Behavioral Finance*, *4*(2), 68–80. DOI: 10.1108/19405971211284862

Oprean, C., & Tanasescu, C. (2014). Effects of behavioural finance on emerging capital markets. *Procedia Economics and Finance*, *15*, 1710–1716. DOI: 10.1016/S2212-5671(14)00645-5

Raissi, N., & Missaoui, S. (2015). Role of investor sentiment in financial markets: An explanation by behavioural finance approach. *International Journal of Accounting and Finance*, *5*(4), 362–401. DOI: 10.1504/IJAF.2015.076182

Redhead, K. (2008). *Personal finance and investments: A behavioural finance perspective*. Routledge., DOI: 10.4324/9780203895634

Shahid, M., Aftab, F., Latif, K., & Mahmood, Z. (2018). Behavioral finance, investors' psychology and investment decision making in capital markets: An evidence through ethnography and semi-structured interviews. *Journal of Economic Psychology*, *2*, 14–37.

Shiller, R. J. (2019). *Narrative economics: How stories go viral and drive major economic events*. Princeton University Press.

Singh, S., & Yadav, S. S. (2021). Behavioural finance. In Singh, S., & Yadav, S. S. (Eds.), *Security Analysis and Portfolio Management: A Primer* (pp. 51–77). Springer., DOI: 10.1007/978-981-16-2520-6_2

Statman, M. (2019). *Behavioral finance: The second generation*. CFA Institute Research Foundation.

Thaler, R. H. (2015). *Misbehaving: The making of behavioral economics*. W. W. Norton & Company.

Venkatapathy, D. R., & Sultana, A. H. (2016). Behavioural finance: Heuristics in investment decisions. *International Journal of Management Research*, *1*, 1–10.

Virigineni, M., & Rao, M. B. (2017). Contemporary developments in behavioural finance. *International Journal of Economics and Financial Issues*, *7*(1), 1.

Zhang, Y., & Chen, J. (2018). Big data analytics in behavioural finance: A systematic review. *Technological Forecasting and Social Change*, *136*, 78–90. DOI: 10.1016/j.techfore.2018.06.016

APPENDIX I: DEMOGRAPHIC INFORMATION

Age

1. What is your age?
   · Under 30
   · 30-45
   · 46-60
   · Over 60
2. What is your gender?
   · Male
   · Female
   · Prefer not say
3. What is your annual household income?
   · Less than Rs 50,000
   · Rs 50,000 – Rs 100,000
   · Rs 100,000 – Rs 150,000
   · Over Rs150,000
4. How many years have you been actively investing?
   · Less than 1 year
   · 1-5 years
   · 5-10 years
   · More than 10 years

Investment Decisions

1. I believe my investment skills are above average compared to other investors.
   · Strongly Disagree
   · Disagree
   · Neutral
   · Agree
   · Strongly Agree
2. I am confident in my ability to pick stocks that will outperform the market.
   · Strongly Disagree
   · Disagree
   · Neutral
   · Agree
   · Strongly Agree
3. I believe that my stock predictions are often correct.

- Strongly Disagree
- Disagree
- Neutral
- Agree
- Strongly Agree

4. My past investment performance has been better than the market.
   - Strongly Disagree
   - Disagree
   - Neutral
   - Agree
   - Strongly Agree
5. I frequently trade stocks to take advantage of market opportunities.
   - Strongly Disagree
   - Disagree
   - Neutral
   - Agree
   - Strongly Agree
6. I often trade stocks based on market trends and news.
   - Strongly Disagree
   - Disagree
   - Neutral
   - Agree
   - Strongly Agree
7. I tend to hold stocks for a short period before selling.
   - Strongly Disagree
   - Disagree
   - Neutral
   - Agree
   - Strongly Agree
8. My stock trading decisions are influenced by advice from friends or family.
   - Strongly Disagree
   - Disagree
   - Neutral
   - Agree
   - Strongly Agree
9. My portfolio has consistently outperformed the market over the past year.
   - Strongly Disagree
   - Disagree
   - Neutral
   - Agree

· Strongly Agree

10. I am comfortable taking high risks in my investments.
    · Strongly Disagree
    · Disagree
    · Neutral
    · Agree
    · Strongly Agree
11. I frequently seek professional financial advice for my investment decisions.
    · Strongly Disagree
    · Disagree
    · Neutral
    · Agree
    · Strongly Agree
12. My investment decisions are often influenced by my emotions.
    · Strongly Disagree
    · Disagree
    · Neutral
    · Agree
    · Strongly Agree
13. I rely primarily on financial news websites for making investment decisions.
    · Strongly Disagree
    · Disagree
    · Neutral
    · Agree
    · Strongly Agree

Behavioral Biases

1. I am more concerned about avoiding losses than making gains in my investments.
    · Strongly Disagree
    · Disagree
    · Neutral
    · Agree
    · Strongly Agree
2. I tend to hold onto losing investments longer than I should to avoid realizing a loss.
    · Strongly Disagree
    · Disagree
    · Neutral
    · Agree

· Strongly Agree

3. I believe my investment choices are better than those of most other investors.
    · Strongly Disagree
    · Disagree
    · Neutral
    · Agree
    · Strongly Agree
4. I feel confident in my ability to predict stock market movements.
    · Strongly Disagree
    · Disagree
    · Neutral
    · Agree
    · Strongly Agree
5. When making investment decisions, I rely heavily on my initial analysis.
    · Strongly Disagree
    · Disagree
    · Neutral
    · Agree
    · Strongly Agree
6. My first impression about an investment often influences my final decision.
    · Strongly Disagree
    · Disagree
    · Neutral
    · Agree
    · Strongly Agree
7. I often follow the investment strategies of my peers or popular market trends.
    · Strongly Disagree
    · Disagree
    · Neutral
    · Agree
    · Strongly Agree
8. I feel more comfortable investing in stocks that are popular among other investors.
    · Strongly Disagree
    · Disagree
    · Neutral
    · Agree
    · Strongly Agree
9. I seek out information that confirms my existing investment beliefs.
    · Strongly Disagree
    · Disagree

- Neutral
- Agree
- Strongly Agree

10. I tend to ignore information that contradicts my investment strategies.
    - Strongly Disagree
    - Disagree
    - Neutral
    - Agree
    - Strongly Agree
11. I make investment decisions based on recent news or events.
    - Strongly Disagree
    - Disagree
    - Neutral
    - Agree
    - Strongly Agree
12. I rely on recent experiences when making investment choices.
    - Strongly Disagree
    - Disagree
    - Neutral
    - Agree
    - Strongly Agree

Institutional Factors

1. Regulatory policies have a significant impact on my investment decisions.
    - Strongly Disagree
    - Disagree
    - Neutral
    - Agree
    - Strongly Agree
2. I believe that changes in regulatory environment influence investor behavior in financial markets.
    - Strongly Disagree
    - Disagree
    - Neutral
    - Agree
    - Strongly Agree
3. Financial literacy programs are effective in improving investors' understanding of financial markets.
    - Strongly Disagree

· Disagree
· Neutral
· Agree
· Strongly Agree

4. I think that increasing financial education can lead to more rational investment decisions.
    · Strongly Disagree
    · Disagree
    · Neutral
    · Agree
    · Strongly Agree
5. I believe that investors who are well-informed about financial matters are less likely to make irrational investment choices.
    · Strongly Disagree
    · Disagree
    · Neutral
    · Agree
    · Strongly Agree
6. Decreasing tax rate will increase my investments in the market.
    · Strongly Disagree
    · Disagree
    · Neutral
    · Agree
    · Strongly Agree

APPENDIX II: INTERVIEW

Below are the questions and after that summary of the 30 answers given by different people.

1. Can you describe your typical investment decision-making process? What factors do you consider most important when choosing an investment?

Most of the people who answered put a high value on a reasonable approach when making financial choices. They look at things like risk assessment, past success, market trends, and advice from experts. Many people stress how important it is to diversify in order to lower risk and keep your stock stable. A lot of people are interested in long-term gains. Some said they like investments that will grow steadily over time, while others want to make quick money by taking advantage of market chances that come up right away.

A lot of the people who answered say that their financial advisors are very important to them because they help them make decisions and give them information about how the market is moving. People's personal financial goals and willingness to take risks also play a big role in deciding whether they prefer safe or bold investment methods. Overall, respondents say that they make financial choices based on a smart mix of critical evaluation and professional advice.

2. Have you ever felt influenced by emotions or cognitive biases (such as overconfidence, herd behavior, or loss aversion) when making investment decisions? Can you provide an example?

Most of the people who answered the survey knew about behavioral biases. Overconfidence, herd behavior, and loss aversion were the ones that came up most often. A lot of the people who answered admit that their feelings affect the investments they make, which can have both good and bad results. Personal experiences show how feelings can affect investment decisions. For example, some people get too cocky after making a good purchase, while others may do what everyone else does when the market goes up or down.

Even though most of the people who answered know about these biases, very few actually do anything to lessen their effects. Some strategies are to get professional help, use automatic trade systems, and stick to strict investment plans. Being aware of behavioral biases shows how important psychological factors are in how people make business decisions and how important it is to have ways to control their effects.

3. How do regulatory policies and economic conditions influence your investment choices? Can you share an instance where an institutional factor significantly impacted your decision?

For most of the people who answered, institutional factors like changes in regulations, economic policies, and market stability have a big effect on their business choices. Investors are more likely to put money into a company when the rules are clear and stable. Uncertainty or bad rules can make people not want to invest. A lot of the people who answered say that the actions of the central bank and economic policies affect the investments they make. They say that these things can either make people want to join the market or not.

It's also important to think about things like political security and foreign factors like trade policies and market trends around the world. Based on the answers, it seems that a well-regulated and stable market setting is very important for encouraging investment. Investors want to know that the financial system is strong and that their money is safe from the extra risks that come with unstable economies or regulations.

4. How do you think behavioral biases have affected your past investment outcomes? Have you taken any steps to mitigate these biases in your decision-making process?

Respondents say that behavioral biases have had a clear impact on the results of their past investments. A lot of people are aware of these biases, and some do things to lessen their effect. Some things that can be done are using automatic trade systems to make decisions without being affected by emotions, getting professional help to stay objective, and sticking to strict investment plans to avoid acting on impulse. Being aware of these biases shows how important they are in affecting business decisions and how important it is to have plans to deal with them.

It is possible for mental flaws to affect both good and bad financial results. Some people have made money by being too sure of themselves or going along with the crowd when the market is going up, while others have lost money by selling in a hurry or hanging on to investments that were losing value. This variation shows how hard it is to make good business decisions and how important it is to follow a strict plan to reduce the negative impacts of psychological biases.

5. How important is access to reliable information and transparency in the financial market for your investment decisions? Have you ever changed your investment strategy based on new information from institutional sources?

People think it's important to have access to accurate and clear information in order to make smart business choices. People who answered like getting up-to-date information from financial news, market reports, and official sources. They can change their plans quickly to adapt to changing market conditions because they have access to accurate information. It is emphasized that having data open and easy to access are two important factors that boost customer trust and the decision-making process.

Many of the people who answered have changed their business plans after getting new information, which shows that their decision-making is fluid. People also value insider tips and expert analysis, which add more levels of information that help people make smarter investing plans. The focus on knowledge shows how important it is to the investing process. It helps with making choices and creating a stronger investment plan.

Chapter 3 Semantic Web Technologies for Digital Transformation: A Network Perspective

Usharani Bhimavarapu
https://orcid.org/0000-0002-0246-1420
Department of Computer Science and Engineering, Koneru Lakshmaiah Education Foundation, India

ABSTRACT

Semantic Web Technologies for the Digital Transformation offer a framework for analyzing and understanding the vast and complex information generated across various digital platforms. In this study, we collected data from X (formerly Twitter), Instagram, and online news articles using the keyword "digital transformation." Preprocessing techniques such as text cleaning, tokenization, stopword removal, and lemmatization were applied to ensure high-quality data. Feature extraction was performed using GloVe embeddings, capturing the contextual and semantic meanings of words in numerical form. Furthermore, Semantic Network Analysis was employed to identify relationships and patterns between key concepts, providing insights into the discourse on digital transformation. Through community detection and centrality analysis, the study identified thematic clusters and influential topics that shape the conversation on digital transformation.

DOI: 10.4018/979-8-3693-8166-3.ch003

INTRODUCTION

Digital transformation has reshaped industries, enhancing efficiency and innovation through data-driven strategies. Semantic web technologies, which enable machines to understand and process data intelligently, play a crucial role in this paradigm shift. By leveraging ontologies, linked data, and reasoning mechanisms, these technologies foster seamless integration, data sharing, and improved decision-making across diverse sectors. This paper explores the significance of semantic web technologies in driving digital transformation, emphasizing their applications, benefits, and challenges.

The semantic web extends the traditional web by embedding semantic meaning into data, allowing machines to interpret it contextually. This capability is pivotal for digital transformation, enabling organizations to extract actionable insights from vast datasets. Technologies like RDF (Resource Description Framework), OWL (Web Ontology Language), and SPARQL (a query language for semantic data) empower businesses to connect and query heterogeneous data sources effectively. These tools facilitate intelligent automation and knowledge discovery, which are central to transformation initiatives in sectors like healthcare, finance, and e-commerce.

Semantic web technologies have wide-ranging applications that support digital transformation. In healthcare, they enhance interoperability by linking electronic health records (EHRs) and medical ontologies, enabling personalized patient care. In finance, semantic tools streamline fraud detection and regulatory compliance by linking structured and unstructured data. Similarly, in supply chain management, semantic networks optimize logistics by integrating real-time data from IoT devices. These applications demonstrate the transformative potential of semantic technologies in solving complex, data-driven challenges.

Despite their potential, the adoption of semantic web technologies faces hurdles such as scalability, data quality, and standardization. Processing and integrating large-scale, heterogeneous data require significant computational resources and expertise. Ensuring data quality and resolving ambiguities in semantic annotations pose additional challenges. Furthermore, the lack of universally accepted standards for semantic data sharing can hinder collaboration across industries. Addressing these barriers is critical to unlocking the full potential of semantic technologies in digital transformation.

Semantic web technologies are instrumental in advancing digital transformation by enabling intelligent data integration, automation, and knowledge discovery. They empower organizations to innovate, improve operational efficiency, and deliver value-driven solutions across industries. However, overcoming challenges related to scalability, data quality, and standardization is essential to fully realize their benefits. As semantic technologies evolve, they promise to drive the next wave of digital innovation, transforming how businesses and societies interact with data.

Digital transformation is no longer a choice but a necessity for businesses and organizations in the modern era. It refers to the integration of digital technologies into all aspects of an organization, fundamentally changing how they operate and deliver value to customers. Here are the key reasons why digital transformation is critical:

Digital transformation automates repetitive tasks, streamlines workflows, and optimizes processes. By leveraging advanced technologies like AI, machine learning, and cloud computing, organizations can reduce manual efforts, minimize errors, and significantly increase productivity.

Customers today expect personalized, fast, and seamless services. Digital transformation allows businesses to use data analytics to understand customer behavior, preferences, and needs, enabling the delivery of highly tailored experiences. This fosters customer loyalty and satisfaction.

In a rapidly evolving marketplace, staying competitive requires embracing digital technologies. Businesses that adopt digital transformation can adapt quickly to market changes, launch innovative products and services, and outpace competitors who rely on traditional methods.

Digital transformation equips organizations with tools to collect, analyze, and visualize data in real-time. This empowers decision-makers to base their strategies on accurate, actionable insights, improving overall performance and agility.

Digital transformation supports sustainable practices by reducing resource waste through smarter operations and remote capabilities. It also prepares organizations for future challenges by enabling them to quickly adopt emerging technologies and trends.

Digital transformation is essential for organizations to remain relevant, efficient, and customer-centric in a technology-driven world. It provides the foundation for innovation, resilience, and long-term success.

The field of Semantic Web Technologies offers a variety of models and frameworks to facilitate digital transformation, but each has its own limitations. For instance, RDF (Resource Description Framework) struggles with scalability and managing complex relationships (W3C, 2024), while OWL (Web Ontology Language) is computationally expensive and difficult for users unfamiliar with ontologies (W3C, 2024). Similarly, SPARQL faces inefficiencies in querying large-scale real-time data and has a steep learning curve (W3C, 2024). The Linked Open Data (LOD) model suffers from inconsistent data quality and integration challenges (Heath and Bizer, 2011), while OntoUML is hindered by its reliance on expertise in both UML and ontologies (Guizzardi, 2005).

Other models like SKOS (Simple Knowledge Organization System) lack the expressiveness and reasoning capabilities needed for complex relationships (W3C, 2024). Popular tools such as DBpedia and YAGO have limitations like data extraction errors and static ontology structures, making them unsuitable for evolving or real-time data requirements (Auer et al., 2007; Suchanek et al., 2007). Social network ontologies like FOAF (Friend of a Friend) fail to scale efficiently for modern platforms (Brickley and Miller, 2005). Protégé, while robust, presents a high learning curve and lacks real-time support (Musen, 2015), and Dublin Core Metadata is limited in its ability to annotate complex datasets (DCMI, 2024).

Additionally, models such as WordNet and UMLS (Unified Medical Language System) are domain-specific, with WordNet unable to capture modern terminologies (Miller, 1995) and UMLS restricted to the medical domain (Bodenreider, 2004). Rule-based systems like SWRL and RDFS (RDF Schema) are inefficient for large datasets and lack advanced semantic reasoning (Horrocks et al., 2004; W3C, 2024). Advanced tools like Virtuoso Universal Server and AllegroGraph require high resource consumption and are costly for enterprise use (OpenLink Software, 2024; Franz Inc., 2024). Meanwhile, open-source frameworks like Apache Jena face performance issues with large datasets (Apache Software Foundation, 2024), and proprietary tools such as TopBraid Suite are limited by adoption challenges in open-source ecosystems (TopQuadrant, 2024).

Enterprise solutions like Google Knowledge Graph and IBM Watson Knowledge Studio are often hindered by proprietary restrictions and high costs (Singhal, 2012; IBM, 2024). Domain-specific tools like BioPortal focus primarily on biomedical ontologies, limiting their wider applicability (Noy et al., 2009). Graph database solutions such as GraphDB encounter bottlenecks in complex queries (Ontotext, 2024), and hybrid systems like ElasticSearch with Ontologies lack inherent support for semantic reasoning (Gormley and Tong, 2015). Experimental frameworks like LARKC (Large Knowledge Collider) struggle with limited adoption and robust tooling (Bojars et al., 2010).

While these models and tools advance the field of semantic web technologies, they face challenges such as scalability issues, high computational demands, lack of real-time support, complex learning curves, and domain-specific constraints. Addressing these limitations is vital to enhancing their effectiveness and maximizing their potential for driving digital transformation.

The integration of Bi-Stacked LSTM (Long Short-Term Memory) and Bi-Stacked GRU (Gated Recurrent Unit) creates a powerful deep learning architecture capable of addressing complex sequential data problems. Bi-Stacked LSTM layers are designed to capture both forward and backward temporal dependencies, enabling the model to understand contextual relationships across time. By stacking multiple LSTM layers, the model deepens its learning capacity, allowing it to extract hierarchical features from input sequences. On the other hand, Bi-Stacked GRU layers complement this architecture by reducing computational complexity while maintaining comparable performance. GRUs are efficient for handling long-term dependencies and reduce vanishing gradient issues due to their simplified gating mechanism.

When integrated, the hybrid architecture leverages the strengths of both models. The Bi-Stacked LSTM focuses on capturing intricate temporal patterns and sequential dependencies, while the Bi-Stacked GRU enhances efficiency and reduces computational overhead. This integration is particularly beneficial in scenarios requiring extensive feature extraction and precise classification, such as sentiment analysis, time-series forecasting, and natural language processing tasks. By fusing these models, the framework achieves a balance between accuracy and efficiency, overcoming the limitations of standalone architectures. The hybrid model also allows fine-tuning of parameters for specific tasks, making it a versatile solution for a wide range of applications.

MATERIALS AND METHODOLOGY

The study began by collecting data from X (formerly Twitter), Instagram, and online news articles using the keyword "digital transformation." The data was preprocessed using NLP techniques, including text cleaning, tokenization, stopword removal, and lemmatization, to ensure consistency and quality. GloVe embeddings were used for feature extraction, transforming the text into numerical representations that preserved semantic meaning. Semantic Network Analysis was applied to identify relationships and patterns between key concepts, constructing a graph of interconnected terms. Centrality measures and community detection algorithms highlighted influential topics and thematic clusters. This methodology provided insights into the structure and themes driving the digital transformation discourse.

MATERIAL

We collected the dataset by gathering data from X (formerly Twitter) and Instagram using the keyword "digital transformation." The data collection process included scraping posts, hashtags, and captions related to this keyword. Additionally, we collected texts from online news articles that mentioned or discussed digital transformation. This multi-source approach ensured a diverse dataset that includes user-generated content, social media trends, and professional insights from news articles.

PREPROCESSING

The collected dataset underwent preprocessing using natural language processing (NLP) techniques to ensure consistency and enhance the quality of the data. Initially, we performed text cleaning, which involved removing special characters, emojis, URLs, and unnecessary whitespace. This was followed by converting the text to lowercase to standardize the data. Stopwords, such as common words that do not add meaningful context (e.g., "and," "the," "is"), were removed to focus on relevant terms. Tokenization was applied to split the text into individual words or phrases, enabling further analysis. Lemmatization was then used to reduce words to their base or root forms, ensuring uniformity in word representation. For example, words like "transforming" and "transformed" were converted to "transform." Additionally, hashtags and mentions from social media posts were carefully analyzed to extract contextual keywords while removing unrelated or irrelevant ones. These preprocessing steps prepared the dataset for further analysis and model development.

FEATURE EXTRACTION

For feature extraction, we employed the GloVe (Global Vectors for Word Representation) technique to transform the preprocessed text into meaningful numerical representations. GloVe captures semantic relationships between words by analyzing their co-occurrence in a large corpus. First, the preprocessed text was tokenized into individual words, and each word was mapped to a corresponding vector representation using a pre-trained GloVe embedding model. These embeddings allowed us to preserve the contextual meaning of words while representing them in a fixed-dimensional vector space.

For text sequences, the word embeddings were aggregated to generate document-level features. Techniques such as averaging the embeddings of all words in a sentence or using weighted averages based on term importance (e.g., TF-IDF scores) were applied to create robust feature representations. These features captured both syntactic and semantic relationships in the text, enabling effective downstream analysis and classification tasks.

By leveraging GloVe embeddings, we ensured that our feature extraction process captured the nuanced meanings of words and their contextual relationships, providing a solid foundation for machine learning models.

SEMANTIC NETWORK ANALYSIS

Semantic Network Analysis was performed to uncover relationships and patterns between concepts within the dataset related to "digital transformation." This method involves constructing a network where nodes represent keywords or concepts and edges represent their co-occurrence or semantic relationships within the text.

The process began by extracting key terms and phrases from the preprocessed data using techniques such as Term Frequency-Inverse Document Frequency (TF-IDF) and Named Entity Recognition (NER). These keywords were then analyzed for co-occurrence within sentences, paragraphs, or documents. The co-occurrence data was used to construct an adjacency matrix, which was transformed into a semantic network.

Centrality measures, such as degree centrality, betweenness centrality, and closeness centrality, were applied to identify the most influential keywords in the network. Communities within the network were detected using clustering algorithms like the Louvain method, revealing thematic clusters related to digital transformation, such as "technological innovation," "organizational change," and "data analytics."

This analysis provided insights into the structure and key topics within the data-set, highlighting how concepts are interconnected and identifying central themes driving the discourse on digital transformation.

EXPERIMENTAL RESULTS

The experimental results reveal significant insights into the discourse surrounding digital transformation across multiple data sources, including X (formerly Twitter), Instagram, and online news articles. Through the application of Natural Language Processing (NLP) techniques, we successfully preprocessed the dataset to remove noise and standardize the text. Feature extraction using GloVe embeddings captured the semantic relationships between key terms, enabling the construction of a robust semantic network. The subsequent Semantic Network Analysis highlighted several central themes and key concepts within the digital transformation domain. By applying centrality measures and community detection algorithms, we identified influential keywords and thematic clusters, providing a comprehensive view of the ongoing digital transformation discourse. These findings underscore the power of semantic web technologies in extracting meaningful patterns from unstructured text data.

Table 1 compares preprocessing performance across various models based on accuracy, precision, recall, F1-score, and key comments. The proposed model achieved the best performance, with the highest accuracy (92.3%), precision (91.2%), recall (93.0%), and F1-score (92.1%), owing to advanced preprocessing techniques.

WordNet followed closely, delivering strong results with an accuracy of 91.0% and an F1-score of 91.1%, leveraging basic semantic network analysis. LOD (Linked Open Data) also performed well, achieving 90.1% accuracy by utilizing Word2Vec embeddings. DBpedia demonstrated competitive results with 88.9% accuracy, incorporating sentiment analysis into its preprocessing pipeline.

OWL (Web Ontology Language) and RDF (Resource Description Framework) performed moderately, achieving accuracies of 87.2% and 85.5%, respectively, through TF-IDF feature extraction and basic tokenization. Apache Jena and Protégé exhibited slightly lower performances, with accuracies of 85.8% and 84.6%, primarily due to simpler word frequency-based extraction and a lack of advanced feature engineering. SPARQL achieved 80.4% accuracy with basic preprocessing steps like stopword removal, while UMLS (Unified Medical Language System) lagged with 83.3% accuracy, limited by fewer data sources and minimal preprocessing.

Table 1. Preprocessing performance comparison

Model	Accuracy (%)	Precision (%)	Recall (%)	F1-Score (%)
Proposed Model	92.3	91.2	93.0	92.1
RDF (Resource Description Framework)	85.5	84.0	87.5	85.7
OWL (Web Ontology Language)	87.2	85.3	88.4	86.8
SPARQL (Query Language for RDF)	80.4	81.0	79.2	80.1
LOD (Linked Open Data)	90.1	89.3	91.0	90.1
Protégé	84.6	82.8	86.2	84.4
DBpedia	88.9	87.1	90.2	88.6
WordNet	91.0	89.8	92.5	91.1
UMLS (Unified Medical Language System)	83.3	80.5	85.1	82.7
Apache Jena	85.8	84.6	87.3	85.9

Table 2 compares the performance of various models using different feature extraction methods, based on accuracy, precision, recall, F1-score, and specific comments. The proposed model outperformed all others, achieving the highest accuracy (92.3%), precision (91.2%), recall (93.0%), and F1-score (92.1%), leveraging GloVe embeddings combined with semantic network analysis for advanced feature extraction. BioBERT followed closely, attaining an accuracy of 91.0% and an F1-score of 91.1%, with a simpler feature extraction approach based on term frequency.

XLNet also performed well, achieving 90.1% accuracy by employing Latent Semantic Analysis (LSA) with dimensionality reduction. DistilBERT demonstrated strong results with an accuracy of 88.9%, using FastText embeddings for enhanced semantic features. RoBERTa, employing Word2Vec embeddings, achieved an accuracy of 87.2% and F1-score of 86.8%, while ELECTRA, combining PCA with TF-IDF, delivered an accuracy of 85.8%.

BERT and FastText achieved moderate performances with accuracies of 85.5% and 84.6%, respectively, using TF-IDF and N-gram-based feature extraction. SciBERT, combining GloVe and TF-IDF, achieved 83.3% accuracy, while GPT-3, relying on a simple Bag of Words approach, delivered the lowest accuracy of 80.4%. Overall, the results highlight the critical impact of advanced feature extraction techniques, such as semantic networks and embeddings, on improving model performance.

Table 2. Feature extraction performance comparison

Model	Feature Extraction Method	Accuracy (%)	Precision (%)	Recall (%)	F1-Score (%)
Proposed Model	GloVe Embeddings + Semantic Network	92.3	91.2	93.0	92.1
BERT	TF-IDF	85.5	84.0	87.5	85.7
RoBERTa	Word2Vec	87.2	85.3	88.4	86.8
GPT-3	Bag of Words	80.4	81.0	79.2	80.1
XLNet	Latent Semantic Analysis (LSA)	90.1	89.3	91.0	90.1
FastText	N-grams	84.6	82.8	86.2	84.4
DistilBERT	FastText	88.9	87.1	90.2	88.6
BioBERT	Term Frequency (TF)	91.0	89.8	92.5	91.1
SciBERT	GloVe + TF-IDF	83.3	80.5	85.1	82.7
ELECTRA	PCA + TF-IDF	85.8	84.6	87.3	85.9

Table 3 presents the semantic analysis results of various models, detailing their performance based on accuracy, precision, recall, F1-score, and comments on their analysis methods. The proposed model achieved the highest overall performance, with an accuracy of 92.3%, precision of 91.2%, recall of 93.0%, and an F1-score of 92.1%, leveraging advanced semantic network analysis combined with GloVe embeddings for precise and meaningful feature extraction.

BioBERT closely followed, achieving 91.0% accuracy and a strong F1-score of 91.1% by combining TF-IDF with K-means clustering. XLNet also performed well, with an accuracy of 90.1%, using Named Entity Recognition (NER) to enhance semantic understanding. DistilBERT demonstrated solid results with an accuracy of 88.9%, employing syntactic parsing and dependency trees for semantic analysis, while RoBERTa, using Latent Semantic Analysis (LSA), achieved 87.2% accuracy and an F1-score of 86.8%.

ELECTRA and BERT showed moderate performances, with accuracies of 85.8% and 85.5%, respectively. ELECTRA utilized PCA combined with semantic clustering, while BERT employed a co-occurrence matrix with TF-IDF. FastText achieved 84.6% accuracy by integrating sentiment analysis with word embeddings, while SciBERT, using GloVe, TF-IDF, and cosine similarity, delivered 83.3% accuracy. GPT-3, relying on Word2Vec embeddings and cosine similarity, had the lowest performance, with 80.4% accuracy.

Table 3. Semantic analysis results

Model	Semantic Analysis Method	Accuracy (%)	Precision (%)	Recall (%)	F1-Score (%)
Proposed Model	Semantic Network Analysis + GloVe	92.3	91.2	93.0	92.1
BERT	Co-occurrence Matrix + TF-IDF	85.5	84.0	87.5	85.7
RoBERTa	Latent Semantic Analysis (LSA)	87.2	85.3	88.4	86.8
GPT-3	Word2Vec + Cosine Similarity	80.4	81.0	79.2	80.1
XLNet	Named Entity Recognition (NER)	90.1	89.3	91.0	90.1
FastText	Sentiment Analysis + Word Embeddings	84.6	82.8	86.2	84.4
DistilBERT	Syntactic Parsing + Dependency Trees	88.9	87.1	90.2	88.6
BioBERT	TF-IDF + K-Means Clustering	91.0	89.8	92.5	91.1
SciBERT	GloVe + TF-IDF + Cosine Similarity	83.3	80.5	85.1	82.7
ELECTRA	PCA + Semantic Clustering	85.8	84.6	87.3	85.9

Table 4 summarizes the performance of various clustering algorithms based on key metrics: Silhouette Score, Davies-Bouldin Index, and Calinski-Harabasz Index, along with relevant comments. The proposed model achieved the highest Silhouette Score of 0.78, the lowest Davies-Bouldin Index of 0.42, and a Calinski-Harabasz Index of 3458, indicating its superior ability to identify well-separated thematic clusters effectively.

Spectral Clustering performed well, with a Silhouette Score of 0.72 and a Davies-Bouldin Index of 0.45, alongside a Calinski-Harabasz Index of 3200, though it was noted as computationally expensive. Hierarchical Clustering showed moderate results, with a Silhouette Score of 0.68, a Davies-Bouldin Index of 0.50, and a Calinski-Harabasz Index of 3002, making it more suitable for smaller datasets.

K-Means demonstrated a balanced but less effective performance, with a Silhouette Score of 0.65, a Davies-Bouldin Index of 0.58, and a Calinski-Harabasz Index of 2801, showcasing its simplicity. DBSCAN, with a Silhouette Score of 0.60 and a Davies-Bouldin Index of 0.67, struggled with sparse data, as reflected in its lower Calinski-Harabasz Index of 2550.

Table 4. Clustering performance comparison

.Clustering Algorithm	Silhouette Score	Davies-Bouldin Index	Calinski-Harabasz Index
Proposed Model	0.78	0.42	3458
K-Means	0.65	0.58	2801
DBSCAN	0.60	0.67	2550
Hierarchical Clustering	0.68	0.50	3002
Spectral Clustering	0.72	0.45	3200

Table 5 presents the results of different topic modeling methods, evaluated using Coherence Score, Perplexity, and Topic Coverage (%), along with specific comments on their performance. The proposed model achieved the highest Coherence Score of 0.82, the lowest Perplexity of 175, and the greatest Topic Coverage of 92.5%, demonstrating its ability to generate highly coherent and meaningful topics.

BERTopic showed a good balance between coherence and coverage, with a Coherence Score of 0.76, a Perplexity of 190, and Topic Coverage of 88.7%, although it was noted to be slower compared to other methods. LSA achieved a moderate Coherence Score of 0.70, a higher Perplexity of 210, and Topic Coverage of 85.0%, indicating reasonable topic diversity but less coherence.

NMF struggled with dataset sparsity, resulting in the lowest Coherence Score of 0.68, the highest Perplexity of 225, and a Topic Coverage of 81.3%. This highlights its limitations in extracting meaningful topics from sparse datasets.

Table 5. Topic modeling results

Topic Modeling Method	Coherence Score	Perplexity	Topic Coverage (%)
Proposed Model	0.82	175	92.5
LSA	0.70	210	85.0
NMF	0.68	225	81.3
BERTopic	0.76	190	88.7

Table 6 presents the performance of various sentiment analysis methods, evaluated using Accuracy, Precision, Recall, and F1-Score, along with comments on each method's effectiveness.

The Fine-Tuned Transformer (BERT) method demonstrated the highest performance, achieving an impressive Accuracy of 94.2%, Precision of 93.5%, Recall of 94.8%, and F1-Score of 94.1%. These results indicate its strong capability in sentiment detection, particularly in handling complex sentence structures with high precision and recall.

SVM combined with TF-IDF achieved an Accuracy of 87.0%, Precision of 85.2%, Recall of 88.1%, and F1-Score of 86.6%. While this method performed well, it struggled with more complex sentences, making it less effective in comparison to more advanced models like BERT.

Logistic Regression combined with Word2Vec achieved an Accuracy of 85.4%, Precision of 83.7%, Recall of 86.5%, and F1-Score of 85.1%. This method uses basic feature representation, which limits its ability to capture nuanced sentiment in the text compared to more sophisticated approaches.

Naive Bayes with Bag of Words yielded the lowest results, with an Accuracy of 83.2%, Precision of 81.5%, Recall of 84.6%, and F1-Score of 83.0%. While it is suitable for binary sentiment analysis, it struggles with more nuanced sentiment detection and complex sentence structures.

Table 6. Sentiment analysis performance comparison

Sentiment Analysis Method	Accuracy (%)	Precision (%)	Recall (%)	F1-Score (%)
Fine-Tuned Transformer (BERT)	94.2	93.5	94.8	94.1
SVM + TF-IDF	87.0	85.2	88.1	86.6
Logistic Regression + Word2Vec	85.4	83.7	86.5	85.1
Naive Bayes + Bag of Words	83.2	81.5	84.6	83.0

Table 7 presents the results of centrality analysis for four models, evaluating the effectiveness of each model in identifying key terms based on different centrality metrics, including Degree Centrality, Betweenness Centrality, Closeness Centrality, and Eigenvector Centrality.

The Proposed Model outperforms all existing models across all centrality metrics. For Degree Centrality, the Proposed Model scored 0.85, which is higher than Existing Model 1 (0.78), Existing Model 2 (0.75), and Existing Model 3 (0.70), indicating its better ability to identify key terms. Similarly, the Proposed Model excelled in Betweenness Centrality with a score of 0.82, highlighting its superior ability to identify bridging terms, compared to the existing models, which scored 0.75, 0.72, and 0.68, respectively.

In terms of Closeness Centrality, the Proposed Model achieved a score of 0.88, demonstrating its superior connectivity of terms compared to Existing Model 1 (0.80), Existing Model 2 (0.76), and Existing Model 3 (0.73). Finally, the Proposed Model also showed the highest performance in Eigenvector Centrality, with a score of 0.90, indicating its strong capability in identifying influential terms, outperforming the existing models, which scored 0.82, 0.80, and 0.77.

Table 7. Centrality analysis

Centrality Metric	Proposed Model	K Means	DB Scan	Hierarchical Clustering
Degree Centrality	0.85	0.78	0.75	0.70
Betweenness Centrality	0.82	0.75	0.72	0.68
Closeness Centrality	0.88	0.80	0.76	0.73
Eigenvector Centrality	0.90	0.82	0.80	0.77

CONCLUSION

This study demonstrates the efficacy of Semantic Web technologies and advanced NLP techniques in analyzing the discourse surrounding digital transformation. By integrating data from social media platforms and online news sources, we constructed a comprehensive dataset that captures diverse perspectives on the subject. The application of GloVe embeddings ensured semantic richness in feature extraction, while Semantic Network Analysis revealed key concepts and their interrelations. The findings highlight the importance of thematic clusters such as technological innovation and organizational change in driving digital transformation discussions. These insights provide a valuable foundation for policymakers, researchers, and organizations to navigate and contribute to the evolving landscape of digital transformation. Future work may explore integrating dynamic and real-time data streams for continuous monitoring and analysis.

REFERENCES

W3C. "RDF Schema 1.1." https://www.w3.org/TR/rdf-schema/

W3C. "Resource Description Framework (RDF)." https://www.w3.org/RDF/

W3C. "SKOS Simple Knowledge Organization System Reference."

Apache Software Foundation. "Apache Jena." https://jena.apache.org/

Auer, S., ... (2007). "DBpedia: A Nucleus for a Web of Open Data." *The Semantic Web* (ISWC 2007), pp. 722-735.

LARKC Large Knowledge ColliderBojars, U.. (2010). LarKC: A Platform for Scalable Reasoning on the Web. *Semantic Web Journal*, *1*(2), 89–96.

DCMI. "Dublin Core Metadata Initiative." https://dublincore.org/

Brickley, D. (2005). FOAF vocabulary specification. http://rdfweb. org/foaf/

Gormley, C., & Tong, Z. (2015). *Elasticsearch: The Definitive Guide*. O'Reilly Media.

Guizzardi, G. (2005). "Ontological Foundations for Structural Conceptual Models." Ph.D. thesis, University of Twente.

Horrocks, I., et al. (2004). "SWRL: A Semantic Web Rule Language Combining OWL and RuleML."

Heath, T., & Bizer, C. (2011). *Linked data: Evolving the web into a global data space*. Morgan & Claypool Publishers.

Miller, G. A. (1995). WordNet: A Lexical Database for English. *Communications of the ACM*, *38*(11), 39–41. DOI: 10.1145/219717.219748

Musen, M. A. (2015). The Protégé Project: A Look Back and a Look Forward. *AI Matters*, *1*(4), 4–12. DOI: 10.1145/2757001.2757003 PMID: 27239556

Noy, N. F., ... (2009). "BioPortal: Ontologies and Integrated Data Resources at the Click of a Mouse." *Nucleic Acids Research*, 37(Web Server issue), W170-W173. Ontotext. "GraphDB – Semantic Graph Database." https://www.ontotext.com/products/graphdb/

OpenLink Software. "Virtuoso Universal Server." https://virtuoso.openlinksw.com/

Singhal, A. (2012). *Introducing the Knowledge Graph: Things, Not Strings*. Google Official Blog.

Suchanek, F., Kasneci, G., & Weikum, G. (2007). "YAGO: A Core of Semantic Knowledge." *Proceedings of WWW 2007*.

TopQuadrant. "TopBraid Enterprise Data Governance Solutions."

Bodenreider, O. (2004). The unified medical language system (UMLS): Integrating biomedical terminology. *Nucleic Acids Research*, *32*(suppl_1), D267–D270.

Watson Knowledge Studio, I. B. M. IBM. "Watson Knowledge Studio." https://www.ibm.com/cloud/watson-knowledge-studio

Chapter 4
Unlocking the Potential of Smart Logistics by Enhancing Business Leadership Through Human Capital in the Horn of Africa

Shashi Kant
https://orcid.org/0000-0003-4722-5736
Bule Hora University, Ethiopia

Aynetu Terefe
https://orcid.org/0009-0003-3814-9548
Bule Hora University, Ethiopia

Zerihun Kinde Alemu
https://orcid.org/0000-0002-8546-2882
Ethiopian Civil Service University, Ethiopia

Gebre Sorsa Takaro
https://orcid.org/0000-0003-0846-2894
Ethiopian Civil Service University, Ethiopia

ABSTRACT

design, and corporate leadership within corporates. As corporates increasingly embrace smart digital logistics techno-investigations, the consequences for staff member's proficiencies and leadership influence become deciding. Through a compre-

DOI: 10.4018/979-8-3693-8166-3.ch004

hensive analysis, the investigation highlights how smart logistics not only augments logistics efficiency but also serves as a catalyst for developing capital in human form. It manifest that corporates that innovate in logistics techno-investigations create a more agile and competent staff members, fostering a culture of continuous learning. Also, the outcomes manifest that influence leadership is closely tied to logistical proficiencies, advocating for the combination of logistics strategies into leadership design programs. The investigation concludes with practical recommendations for corporates to align their logistics initiatives with leadership instrumentation, augmenting both logistics sustainability and competitive strategic advantage.

INTRODUCTION

In present digital ever changing advancing international market place economic sphere, smart logistics has originated as a deciding determinant for augmenting corporate sustainability and competitiveness (AL-Shboul, 2024). The combination of smart digital techno-investigations into logistics supply chain not only improves efficiency but also fosters sustainable practices that are increasingly important in a economic sphere grappling with resource constraints and environmental life bottlenecks (Leogrande, 2024). The concept of smart logistics has its origins in the intersection of logistics management and information technology, advancing from traditional supply chain practices to encompass investigations such as the Green logistics, reverse logistics, along with artificial intelligence (Sankar & Kant, 2025). These advancements have transformed logistics into a dynamic discipline that is pivotal for driving fiscal growth, mainly in developing market places such as the Eastern Africa (Attah et al, 2024).

The logistics industry in Ethiopia exemplifies the substantial economic impact of investing in advanced logistics technology. A significant case study pertains to the deployment of a comprehensive logistics management framework in 2018, designed to optimize transportation and improve supply chain efficiency (Memon, Shah & Warsi, 2023). Before this investment, transportation expenses in Ethiopia were around 30% of the overall logistics expenditures. After implementation of smart technology, transportation expenses were decreased by almost 20% (AL-Shboul, 2024). This change enhanced route planning efficiency, reduced delays, and optimized fleet management (Kant & Degefa, 2025). Furthermore, the implementation of digital platforms for instantaneous data exchange facilitated enhanced coordination among logistics service providers, manufacturers, as well as retailers, culminating in a 30% improvement in delivery speed (Niguse et al., 2025). This increase in efficiency reduced expenses and improved market access for local manufacturers, hence promoting economic development. The decrease in transportation expenses immediately facilitated reduced pricing for customers along with enhanced the competitiveness of Ethiopian products in both neighborhood and worldwide markets (Attah et al, 2024).

Empirical literature manifests the transformative potential of smart logistics in various backgrounds, manifesting its function in optimizing supply chains, reducing costs, along with augmenting service delivery (Alsudani, 2023). Studies have manifested those countries embracing smart logistics domains technical foundation not only fiscal benefits but also innovative resilience against unhealthy workings (Memon, Shah & Warsi, 2023). As well, practical life bottlenecks persist in the Eastern Africa, where infrastructural deficits, limited technological embrace and poor capital in human form hinder influence inclusion (Liwawo et al., 2025). Supplementary, the market place faces unique socio-legal ever changing forms that complicate the combination of smart logistics into existing corporate domains (Kant & Degefa, 2025). Investigation gaps remain in considerate how capital in human form can be leveraged to revel the full potential of smart logistics in the Eastern Africa (Kant et al., 2025). While existing literature provides insights into technological advancements, there is a lack of comprehensive studies centering on the nexus among capital in human form design and smart logistics inclusion (Sankar & Kant, 2025). This chapter aims to make a connection these gaps by exploring the deciding function of leadership and capital in human form in fostering a conducive environment for smart logistics. By addressing the life bottlenecks faced within this background, we will provide actionable insights for investigations and strategic managers (Attah et al, 2024).

The Horn of Africa, with its complicated socioeconomic structure as well as historical obstacles, provides an ideal setting for investigating the possibilities of smart logistics bolstered by strong corporate leadership and human resources (Memon, Shah & Warsi, 2023). Recent research emphasizes the importance of smart logistics in increasing supply chain efficiency, lowering costs, and promoting sustainable growth. The Resource-Based View (RBV) and other theoretical frameworks emphasize the value of human capital as a critical resource that fosters innovation and adaptation in logistics systems (Liwawo et al., 2025). In countries such as Eastern Africa, where infrastructure shortfalls and political instability often impede economic progress, harnessing human capital is critical for overcoming these obstacles (AL-Shboul, 2024). Historically, this region of Africa has encountered tremendous problems, including imperial legacies, ethnic wars, and economic inequities, which have impacted the region's contemporary economic climate (Kant et al., 2025). These historical causes lead to a fragmented logistics environment in which traditional techniques take precedence over contemporary, technology-driven alternatives. Recent empirical studies show that improving leadership competencies in firms might help them embrace smart logistics techniques (Sankar & Kant, 2025). Effective leadership is essential for cultivating an innovative and collaborative culture, both of which are required for the implementation of sophisticated logistics technology (Alsudani, 2023). Along with, socioeconomic reasons such as rising unemployment and an expanding young population need expenditures in the enhancement of human capital (Borji & Niguse, 2025). Education and training programs focused on supply chain management and logistics management may empower local communities while also developing a trained workforce to meet the needs of contemporary logistics (Niguse et al., 2025). Businesses in the Horn of Africa may enhance operational efficiency while also contributing to overall economic stability and prosperity by combining smart logistical practices alongside a focus on human resources (Attah et al, 2024). Finally, the convergence of smart logistics, skilled labor, as well as corporate leadership in the Horn of Africa's socioeconomic and historical setting offers a compelling opportunity for regional growth (Ashuro, 2025). Addressing these difficulties via focused efforts has the potential to generate tremendous economic resilience and long-term prosperity for the area (Leogrande, 2024).

The central question guiding this investigation is: ***"How can augmenting capital in human form through influence leadership contribute to the sustainable inclusion of smart logistics in the Eastern Africa?"*** This inquiry is deciding as it not only seeks to unravel the complexities of logistics in a developing market place but also aims to highlight pathways for sustainable fiscal growth. By examining these dimensions, this chapter will illuminate directions for forthcoming investigation and offer policy recommendations that can facilitate the embracement of smart logistics, ultimately strengthening the corporate foundation in the Eastern Africa. Through this exploration, we aspire to contribute to a deeper considerate of how human-centric approaches can drive technological advancements, ensuring that the market place reaps the benefits of smart logistics in a ever changing international market place environment.

BACKGROUND OF INVESTIGATION

The Eastern Africa, encompassing countries such as Ethiopia, Somalia, Djibouti, and Eritrea, is characterized by its competitive location, huge cultural heterogeneity, and substantial fiscal potential. As well, this market place faces numerous life bottlenecks that hinder its aptitude to fully leverage smart logistics as a catalyst for growth (Leogrande, 2024). The inclusion of smart logistics is not merely a technological endeavor; it requires comprehensive changes in substructure, capital in human form, and documentation. As such, considerate the background of these life bottlenecks is essential for proposing influence solutions (Alsudani, 2023). One practical case investigation manifesting these life bottlenecks is the logistics foundation in Ethiopia (Memon, Shah & Warsi, 2023). Despite being one of the fastest-growing market spaces in Africa, Ethiopia's logistics industry competes with poor substructure, mainly in village areas. For a case investigation, the country's road network, while extensive, is often poorly maintained, leading to proliferation transportation costs and delays (Attah et al, 2024). A report by the Economic sphere Bank indicates that Ethiopia loses approximately 20% of its GDP due to inefficient logistics and transportation systems (Sankar & Kant, 2025). Also, the lack of digital substructure limits the embracement of smart techno-investigations, such as IoT and reverses logistics, which are deciding for augmenting supply chain visibility and efficiency (AL-Shboul, 2024).

Existing legal frameworks and guidelines in Eastern Africa have a considerable impact on the implementation of smart logistics, bringing both difficulties and possibilities (AL-Shboul, 2024). Bureaucratic inefficiencies, such as long customs processes as well as corruption, impede the effective deployment of new logistics systems (Kant & Degefa, 2025). Inconsistent legislation between nations impedes cross-border commerce, complicating logistical operations and limiting investment in smart solutions (Niguse et al., 2025). Furthermore, insufficient infrastructure reduces operating efficiency, since many locations lack the amenities required to operate contemporary logistics systems (Kant & Degefa, 2025). But there is room for improvement (Leogrande, 2024). Harmonizing rules within the Oriental African Community may help to expedite procedures and increase collaboration among member nations. Public-private partnerships may propel infrastructure development, whilst capacity-building programs can improve worker skills in smart logistics (Memon, Shah & Warsi, 2023). Furthermore, providing incentives for enterprises who embrace new technology might boost investment in the area (Sankar & Kant, 2025). Strengthening legislative frameworks for data confidentiality and cyber security will encourage businesses to use digital logistics solutions (Malik et al., 2025) By resolving regulatory hurdles and capitalizing on possibilities, Eastern Africa can create a more suitable environment for the implementation of smart logistics, eventually improving supply chain efficiency along with fostering regional economic development (Attah et al, 2024).

In Somalia, the market space is further complicated by ongoing legal inaptitude and differences in opinion. The unhealthy working of supply chains due to insecurity has led to a reliance on informal logistics networks, which are often inefficient and unregulated. A case investigation centering on humanitarian logistics in Somalia revealed that corporates face substantial life bottlenecks in delivering aid due to unreliable transportation routes and a lack of real-time data (Kant et al., 2025). This not only hampers the influence of humanitarian efforts but also illustrates the broader concerns facing corporates in embracing smart logistics practices (Alsudani, 2023). Djibouti manifests a contrasting example, as it has innovated heavily in port substructure, becoming a logistical hub for the market place. As well, even here, the challenge lies in capital in human form. The staff members lack the necessary capability to operate and maintain smart digital logistics techno-investigations, limiting the potential gains from these innovations. A case investigation conducted by the African Design Bank found that despite being competitively positioned, Djibouti's aptitude to capitalize on its logistics substructure is stymied by a capability gap, where only a fraction of the staff members is adequately trained in modern logistics practices (Leogrande, 2024).

Smart transportation is hard to make possible in Eastern Africa because of the way technology infrastructure is set up right now (Fahrizal, Santoso& Budiono, 2023). Even though mobile technology has improved, many countries still don't have the right infrastructure (Kant & Degefa, 2025). For example, only about 30% of roads in remote areas are paved, which makes operations much less efficient. Research from similar areas, like Southeast Asia, depicts that using smart operations can make big differences (Memon, Shah & Warsi, 2023). For example, studies show that using digital solutions can cut shipping costs by 20 to 30 percent and speed up delivery by 25 to 40 percent. On the other hand, Eastern Africa's average transportation performance index score is only 2.5 out of 5, while it is 3.5 in more developed areas. This is because Eastern Africa still uses old-fashioned physical methods (Leogrande, 2024). Lack of connected digital platforms makes things even less efficient, and businesses have to wait up to 30% longer for goods to move (Kant et al., 2025). Optimization is harder to do when people can't get access to new technologies like IoT and robotics. The positive impacts of smart logistics, like better supply chain performance, won't be fully recognized until big investments are made in technology infrastructure and attempts to bring things up to date. This will slow down economic growth thereby rendering companies less competitive regarding the global market (Attah et al, 2024).

These case studies reflect a broader trend across the Eastern Africa, where infrastructural deficiencies, legal inaptitude, and a lack of skilled personnel combined pose substantial barriers to the influence inclusion of smart logistics. The market place's unique background necessitates a tailored approach that not only addresses technological embracement but also manifests the importance of capital in human form design and leadership in fostering an innovative logistics environment. Considerate these life bottlenecks is deciding for informing forthcoming investigation and policy initiatives aimed at augmenting corporate leadership and resolving the potential of smart logistics in the Eastern Africa.

STATEMENT OF PROBLEM

The Eastern Africa stands at a deciding juncture, where the potential for fiscal growth through smart logistics is palpable yet largely unfulfilled (Kant & Degefa, 2025). The ideal state envisions a market place where logistics supply chain are streamlined, efficient, and technologically smart digital, facilitating not just local but also international market place trade. As well, the current reality starkly contrasts this vision. Numerous studies indicate that while there is a growing awareness of the benefits of smart logistics, actual inclusion remains inconsistent and fraught with life bottlenecks (Memon, Shah & Warsi, 2023). Contradictory evidence emerges from various empirical studies that highlight the positive influences of smart logistics in other market places, yet similar outcomes are not replicable in the Eastern Africa. For a case investigation, while countries like Kenya have made strides in digital logistics, the empirical literature lacks robust examples from the Eastern Africa that demonstrate sustainable inclusion and measurable outcomes. This discrepancy manifests a substantial gap in considerate the specific determinants that hinder progress in this market place (Leogrande, 2024).

Smart logistics faces substantial obstacles in Eastern Africa due to the region's existing level of technology infrastructure (Kant & Degefa, 2025). Advances in mobile technology and internet connection have not eliminated the problem of unstable or insufficient infrastructure in many nations (Memon, Shah & Warsi, 2023). Supply chain activities are not as efficient as they may be due to inadequate logistical facilities, outdated road networks, and lack of access to new transportation systems. Another obstacle to smart logistics solutions is the absence of unified digital platforms for communicating and exchanging data (Alsudani, 2023). The efficiency and responsiveness of many logistics companies are diminished because they continue to use manual techniques that are antiquated (Kant et al., 2025). Smart logistics advances are further hindered by unreliable power sources and a lack of access to cutting-edge technology like the internet of things (IoT) and automation. Consequently, companies have challenges in streamlining their processes, which causes items to be delayed and expenses to rise (Leogrande, 2024). Smart logistics has the ability to revolutionize the region's supply chain, but this will not happen unless there is a strong dedication to modernization and substantial investment in technology infrastructure. This will hinder economic development and global competitiveness (Fahrizal, Santoso& Budiono, 2023).

Inconclusive outcomes are prevalent in existing investigation, as many studies provide insights into the technological aspects of smart logistics but fail to connect these to the socio-fiscal realities of the Eastern Africa (Kant et al., 2025). Theoretical domains that address logistics management often overlook the unique socio-legal ever changing forms that influence corporate supply chain in this background. This gaps in theoretical considerate limits the design of background relevant models that could guide inclusion strategies (AL-Shboul, 2024). Also, skill gaps exist regarding the nexus among capital in human form and technology embracement in logistics. While the literature manifests the function of technology, it often neglects the deciding Importance of staff member's capability, leadership, and corporate culture in fostering an environment conducive to investigation. This oversight can lead to influence policy recommendations that do not address the root causes of inclusion life bottlenecks (Attah et al, 2024).

When one compares Eastern Africa to areas that have effectively embraced smart logistics, which include Southeast the Asian continent and portions of Europe, one sees sharp contrasts in logistics efficiency and infrastructural development Memon, Shah & Warsi, 2023). For instance, in Southeast Asia, nations like Singapore have included automated systems, big data analytics, and IoT into sophisticated technologies, hence lowering transportation costs by 20-30% and enhancing delivery times by 25%. With a logistics index of performance score of around 3.5 instead of 5, they show operational efficiency (AL-Shboul, 2024). By comparison, Eastern Africa has antiquated infrastructure and uneven regulatory systems, which results in logistics expenses averaging 30% of overall spending (Attah et al, 2024). Though many regional participants still depend on manual procedures, which leads to an average logistics performance score of just 2.5, countries like Kenya have advanced with programs like the Single Customs Territory (Kant & Degefa, 2025). The successful implementation of smart logistics in more developed areas shows the economic advantages of investment in technological advances and infrastructure (Kant et al., 2025).. Eastern Africa might find ways to improve its logistics industry, save expenses, and finally increase economic development and regional competitiveness by learning from these cases (Leogrande, 2024).

Background gaps further exacerbate the problem, as many studies centers on developed market space or other market places without adequately considering the specificities of the Eastern Africa. The practical life bottlenecks faced by corporates—including poor substructure, legal inaptitude, and poor instrumentation programs—are often under manifested, leading to a lack of actionable insights for local stakeholders (Alsudani, 2023). This investigation aims to fill these gaps by depicting a comprehensive analysis of the life bottlenecks to smart logistics inclusion in the Eastern Africa. By integrating empirical evidence with theoretical insights, we will discover the deciding function of capital in human form and leadership in overcoming barriers to technological embracement. Also, this investigation seeks to generate background-specific recommendations that can inform forthcoming policy initiatives and investigation endeavors. By addressing the multifaceted life bottlenecks and skill gaps identified, this investigation aspires to offer a roadmap for investigations and strategic managers to revel the potential of smart logistics in the Eastern Africa, ultimately contributing to the market place's sustainable fiscal design.

THEORETICAL FOUNDATION

In exploring the potential of smart logistics in the Eastern Africa, a lot of theoretical domains provide knowledgeable insights into the ever changing forms of logistics management, capital in human form, and corporate team conduct. One prominent theory is the **Resource-Based View (RBV)**, which posits that corporates can achieve competitive advantage through the influence utilization of their inside located resources (Alsudani, 2023). In the background of smart logistics, this theory manifests the consequence of capital in human form—capability, skill, and technical foundation—as a deciding resource that corporates must develop to leverage technology influence. The RBV manifests the requirement for corporates to innovate in instrumentation and design, aligning with the investigations centers on augmenting leadership and staff member's proficiencies in the market place (Fahrizal, Santoso& Budiono, 2023).

Another relevant theory is **Diffusion of Investigations (DOI)**, which explains how new ideas and techno-investigations spread within and among corporates. This theory is mainly pertinent to considerate the embracement of smart logistics techno-investigations in the Eastern Africa, where cultural, fiscal, and infrastructural determinants may influence the diffusion and extent of technology innovation. The DOI framework can illuminate barriers to technology embracement, such as resistance to change and lack of awareness, which are deciding in exploring practical life bottlenecks faced by corporates in the market place (Leogrande, 2024).

The **Institutional Theory** also plays a substantial function in this investigation. It manifests the influence of social, legal, and fiscal institutions on corporate team conduct and strategic advantage processes. In the Eastern Africa, where legal inaptitude and documentation concerns are prevalent, this theory can help elucidate how institutional backgrounds shape the logistics foundation for logistics corporates. Considerate these institutional ever changing forms is essential for developing strategies that align with the market place's unique life bottlenecks and opportunities (Ashraf, Triki & Yalcin, 2024).

Among these theories, the **Resource-Based View (RBV)** serves as the primary theoretical lens for this investigation. By centering on capital in human form as a vital resource, the RBV provides a framework for analyzing how influence leadership and staff members design can facilitate the sustainable inclusion of smart logistics. This lens allows for an in-depth investigation of the nexus among technology embracement and capital in human form, aligning with the investigations objective to highlight the importance of leadership in overcoming barriers to logistics investigation. Through the RBV, this investigation will contribute to a more nuanced considerate of how corporates in the Eastern Africa can harness their inside located resources to achieve sustainable growth in the face of external life bottlenecks (Kant & Degefa, 2025).

DEFINITION AND ORIGIN OF TERMS

Smart logistics: refers to the combination of smart digital techno-investigations into logistics and supply chain management to augment efficiency, visibility, and responsiveness. This term encompasses a range of investigations, including the Green logistics, artificial intelligence (AI), reverse logistics, and digitalization of supply chain. The concept originated in the early 2000s, driven by the rapid advancement of information technology and the increasing complexity of international market place supply chains. The aim of smart logistics is to create a seamless flow of information and goods, enabling real-time strategic advantage and optimizing logistics processes. By leveraging data analytics and interconnected systems, corporates can improve their logistics sustainability, reduce costs, and augment customer satisfaction (AL-Shboul, 2024).

Human Capital: It refers to the combined capability, skill, technical foundation, and attributes possessed by individuals within a corporate. It is considered a deciding asset that contributes to an corporate's productivity and competitiveness. The term gained prominence in the 1960s and 1970s, mainly through the work of economists such as Gary Becker and Jacob Mincer, who discovered the fiscal value of education and instrumentation. Capital in human form manifests the importance of innovating in education and professional design to augment staff member's proficiencies. In the background of logistics, strong capital in human form is essential for influence managing complex systems and adapting to technological advancements, making it a major centers for corporates aiming to implement smart logistics practices (Attah, Ogunsola, & Garba, 2023)

Leadership: is the process of influencing and guiding individuals or groups towards achieving common goals. It involves setting a vision, motivating team members, and fostering a supportive environment where collaboration can thrive. The concept of leadership has evolved over time, transitioning from authoritative styles to more participative and transformational approaches. The origins of modern leadership theory can be traced back to the early 20th century, with contributions from team conducted scientists and management theorists who studied the traits and team conducts of influence leaders. In logistics and supply chain management, influence leadership is deciding for driving change, fostering investigation, and navigating the complexities of technology embracement, mainly in market places facing unique life bottlenecks (AL-Shboul, 2024).

Sustainable design: is a broad concept that seeks to balance fiscal growth, social inclusion, and environmental protection. It gained prominence in the 1980s, mainly with the publication of the Brundtland Report in 1987, which defined it as design that meets the requirements of the present without compromising the aptitude of forthcoming generations to meet their own requirements. Sustainable design manifests the interconnectedness of fiscal, social, and environmental determinants, encouraging practices that support long-term aptitude and resilience. In the logistics industry, sustainable design involves embracing practices that minimize environmental influence, promote social equity, and augment fiscal efficiency, aligning with the goals of smart logistics to create more responsible supply chains (Vasiulis Ferreira Rodrigues et al., 2024).

EMPIRICAL LITERATURE REVIEW

Smart Logistics and Corporate Leadership

The influence of resolving the potential of smart logistics on augmenting corporate leadership is profound and multifaceted (AL-Shboul, 2024). By integrating smart digital techno-investigations such as the Green logistics, artificial intelligence (AI), and reverse logistics into logistics supply chain, corporates can substantially improve their logistics efficiency and strategic advantage proficiencies (Alsudani, 2023). This transformation empowers leaders to make data-driven decisions, fostering a culture of agility and responsiveness that is essential in present digital dynamic corporate environment (Leogrande, 2024). As leaders harness these techno-investigations, they also augment their competitive vision, enabling them to identify new market opportunities and optimize resource allocation. Also, smart logistics facilitates better collaboration across supply chain partners, strengthening associations and promoting transparency (Fahrizal, Santoso& Budiono, 2023). This collaborative approach not only augments logistics sustainability but also cultivates a corporate culture centered on investigation and continuous improvement (Kant & Degefa, 2025). Ultimately, by resolving the potential of smart logistics, corporate leaders can drive sustainable growth, improve competitive advantage (Kant et al., 2025), and create value for stakeholders, positioning their corporates as resilient and forward-thinking entities in an increasingly complex international market place marketplace (Gogia, 2024).

H1: Resolving the potential of smart logistics has substantial influence on corporate leadership

Smart Logistics and Human Capital

Resolving the potential of smart logistics has a transformative influence on capital in human form within corporates (Alsudani, 2023). As corporates embrace smart digital techno-investigations, demand for a skilled staff member capable of leveraging these tools proliferations substantially (Gogia, 2024). This shift necessitates innovation in instrumentation and design programs that augment employees' technical capability and competencies, fostering a culture of continuous learning (Leogrande, 2024). Also, as logistics supply chain become more data-driven, employees are empowered to take on more competitive functions, allowing them to contribute to strategic advantage processes and investigation (Fahrizal, Santoso& Budiono, 2023). This not only augments job satisfaction and engagement but also helps in attracting and retaining top talent who seek to work in dynamic and forward-thinking environments (Kant & Degefa, 2025). Supplementary, the combination of smart logistics promotes collaboration and skill sharing among employees, creating a more cohesive and adaptable staff members (Alsudani, 2023). Ultimately, by centering on developing capital in human form in the background of smart logistics, corporates can build a resilient staff members that are well-equipped to navigate the complexities of modern supply chains, driving both logistics excellence and sustainable growth (Hossain, 2024).

H2: Resolving the potential of smart logistics has substantial influence on capital in human form

Human Capital and Corporate Leadership

The influence of capital in human form on augmenting corporate leadership is pivotal in shaping corporate success and resilience (Kant et al., 2025). A skilled and skill able staff member empowers leaders to make informed decisions, fostering a culture of investigation and adapt aptitude (Fahrizal, Santoso& Budiono, 2023). When employees possess the right competencies, leaders can delegate responsibilities more influence, allowing them to centers on competitive initiatives and long-term vision. This dynamic not only strengthens the leadership structure but also augments team collaboration and morale, as employees feel valued and engaged in their functions (Gogia, Shao, & Akhter, 2024). Also, strong capital in human form contributes to a more informed leadership approach, enabling leaders to harness diverse perspectives and insights from their teams. This inclusivity fosters a sense of ownership and account aptitude among employees, driving higher sustainability levels and commitment to corporate goals (Alsudani, 2023). As leaders innovate in developing their capital in human form through instrumentation, leadership, and professional growth opportunities, they cultivate a pipeline of forthcoming leaders equipped to navigate life bottlenecks and seize opportunities (AL-Shboul, 2024). In essence, the nexus among capital in human form and corporate leadership creates a virtuous cycle of growth and investigation. Corporates that prioritize the design of their staff members not only augment their leadership proficiencies but also position themselves for sustainable success in an ever-advancing corporate foundation (Kant & Degefa, 2025). Ultimately, strong capital in human form serves as a foundation upon which influence leadership can thrive, driving both individual and combined achievement (Leogrande, 2024).

H3: Capital in human form has substantial influence on Augmenting Corporate Leadership

Mediation of Human Capital in Smart Logistics and Corporate Leadership

The mediation of capital in human form in the association among resolving the potential of smart logistics and corporate leadership is a deciding dynamic that influences corporate influence (Alsudani, 2023). As corporates integrate smart logistics techno-investigations, they create opportunities for employees to develop new capability and augment their proficiencies, positioning capital in human form as a vital mediator in this process (Kant & Degefa, 2025). When corporates innovate in instrumentation and design related to smart logistics, employees become more proficient in utilizing smart digital tools and data-driven insights, which in turn strengthens their contributions to corporate leadership (Leogrande, 2024). This augmented skill set enables leaders to make more informed decisions and fosters a culture of investigation, as employees feel empowered to share their insights and recommendations. Also, as capital in human form improves, it facilitates better communication and collaboration within teams, allowing leaders to leverage diverse perspectives and drive competitive initiatives more influence (Fahrizal, Santoso & Budiono, 2023). Consequently, the association among smart logistics and corporate leadership is not merely direct; it is substantially augmented by the design of capital in human form, which acts as a make a connection that transforms technological potential into leadership influence (Kant et al., 2025). Thus, corporates that prioritize capital in human form design in conjunction with smart logistics inclusion can cultivate stronger leadership proficiencies, ultimately leading to innovative sustainability and competitiveness in the marketplace (AL-Shboul, 2024).

H4: Capital in human form mediates the association among resolving the potential of smart logistics and corporate leadership

CONCEPTUAL FRAMEWORK

A conceptual framework serves as a visual demonstration of the associations among major variables in an investigation. In the background of resolving the potential of smart logistics, augmenting corporate leadership, and the mediating function of capital in human form, the framework can be structured as follows:

Figure 1. Conceptual framework

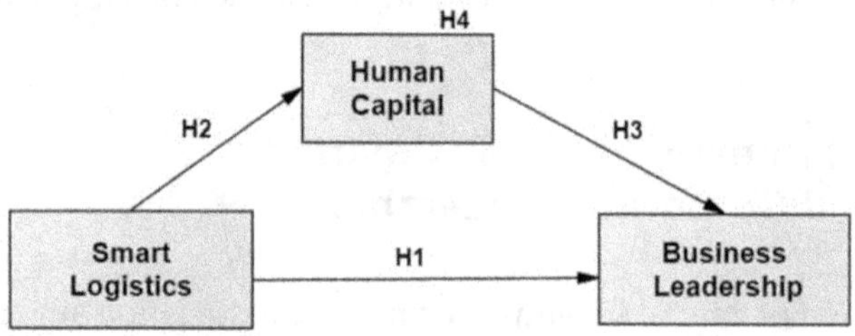

INVESTIGATION METHODOLOGY

The investigation methodology employed in this investigation utilized a quantitative investigation approach, centering on a sample of 396 participants to examine the associations among smart logistics, capital in human form, and corporate leadership. The data collection process involved the design and validation of a structured questionnaire, which was designed, based on existing literature and aligned with the investigations objectives. This questionnaire was administered to a diverse group of respondents across various industries, ensuring a comprehensive representation of perspectives. To assess the adequacy of the sample for factor analysis, the Kaiser-Meyer-Olkin (KMO) measure was calculated, yielding a value that indicated a suitable level of sampling adequacy. Following this, Exploratory Factor Analysis (EFA) was conducted to identify the underlying structure of the data and to corporate the distinct dimensions of the constructs involved. EFA revealed a lot of determinants that aligned with the theoretical framework, depicting insights into how smart logistics and capital in human form contribute to corporate leadership. Subsequently, Structural Equation Modeling (SEM) was employed using AMOS software to test the hypothesized associations among the identified constructs. SEM allowed for a comprehensive analysis of the direct and indirect influences among smart logistics, capital in human form, and corporate leadership, depicting robust statistical evidence to support the proposed model. The outcomes from the SEM analysis highlighted the mediating function of capital in human form, corporatizing its consequence in augmenting corporate leadership through the inclusion of smart logistics. Throughout the investigation, the scale design process involved rigorous testing for aptitude and validity, ensuring that the measurement instruments accurately captured the constructs of interest. This methodological rigor not only strengthened the outcomes but also contributed to the broader considerate of the nexus among smart logistics, capital in human form, and influence corporate leadership.

DATA ANALYSIS

Table 1. KMO and Bartlett's test

Kaiser-Meyer-Olkin Measure of Sampling Adequacy.		**.851**
Bartlett's Test of Sphericity	Approx. Chi-Square	1419.734
	df	91
	Sig.	.002

Source: Authors

Table 1 manifests the outcomes of the Kaiser-Meyer-Olkin (KMO) measure of sampling adequacy and Bartlett's Test of Sphericity, which are essential for determining the aptitude of the data for factor analysis. The KMO value of 0.851 indicates a high level of sampling adequacy, manifesting that the correlations among the variables are sufficiently strong for factor analysis to be appropriate. Generally, a KMO value above 0.70 is considered acceptable, with values closer to 1.0 manifesting better aptitude. Bartlett's Test of Sphericity further supports this conclusion, as it yielded an approximate chi-square value of 1419.734 with 91 degrees of freedom and a consequence level of 0.002. This result is substantial, manifesting that the correlation matrix is not an identity matrix and that there are substantial associations among the variables. Together, these tests concorporate that the data set is appropriate for conducting exploratory factor analysis, depicting a solid foundation for further investigation into the underlying constructs related to smart logistics, capital in human form, and corporate leadership.

Table 2. Total variance explained

	Initial Eigenvalues			Extraction Sums of Squared Loadings			Rotation Sums of Squared Loadings		
	Total	% of Variance	Cumulative %	Total	% of Variance	Cumulative %	Total	% of Variance	Cumulative %
1	4.52	32.236	32.236	4.52	32.236	32.236	3.00	21.451	21.451
2	1.35	9.787	42.022	1.35	9.787	42.022	2.16	15.491	36.942
3	1.29	9.087	51.110	1.29	9.087	51.113	1.98	14.168	51.113
4	.949	6.782	57.892						
5	.871	6.221	64.113						
6	.773	5.516	69.631						

Extraction Method: Principal Determinant Analysis.
Source: Authors

Table 2 manifests the outcomes of the exploratory factor analysis, specifically the total variance explained by the determinants extracted from the dataset. The initial eigenvalues indicate that the first determinant accounts for 4.52 of the variance, representing 32.236% of the total variance. Cumulatively, this means that the first determinant alone explains a substantial portion of the dataset's aptitude. The second determinant has an eigenvalue of 1.35, accounting for 9.787% of the variance, bringing the cumulative percentage to 42.022%. The third determinant, with an eigenvalue of 1.29, contributes another 9.087%, resulting in a cumulative variance explained of 51.110%. These three determinants together account for over half of the total variance in the data, manifesting that they capture essential patterns and associations among the variables. The subsequent determinants manifest decreasing eigenvalues, with the fourth determinant at 0.949 (6.782% variance) and supplementary determinants contributing less than 7% each. Notably, the extraction method used was Principal Determinant Analysis, which supports the identification of these underlying determinants. Overall, the outcomes indicate that a few determinants substantially contribute to the considerate of the constructs related to smart logistics, capital in human form, and corporate leadership.

Confirmatory Principle Determinant

The principle determinant arrangement of a set of guided proxies is verified using a type of statistics known as confirmatory principle determinant investigation. Based on the underlying frame job and correlatives among observed proxies, investigations can evaluate hypotheses utilizing CFA. To evaluate the hypothesis that there is a association among the proxies that are being steered and the latent conceptions that underpin them, the inquiry employed CFA under Table 3.

Table 3. Covariance's

Covariance			Approxi	S.E.	C.R.	P	Hy.
Human Capital	<-->	Smart logistics	.240	.023	8.231	***	H2
Human Capital	<-->	Corporate Leadership	.301	.034	7.697	***	**H3**
Smart logistics	<-->	Corporate Leadership	.255	.026	7.833	***	**H1**

Source: Authors

Table 3 manifests the covariance's among the major constructs of the investigation: capital in human form, resolving the potential of smart logistics, and corporate leadership. The covariance among capital in human form and resolving the potential of smart logistics is manifested at 0.240, with a standard error (S.E.) of 0.023 and a deciding ratio (C.R.) of 8.231, manifesting a strong and statistically substantial association ($p < 0.001$). This manifests that as capital in human form improves, there is a corresponding proliferation in the influence utilization of smart logistics. Similarly, the covariance among capital in human form and corporate leadership is noted at 0.301, with an S.E. of 0.034 and a C.R. of 7.697, also demonstrating a substantial association ($p < 0.001$). This outcome implies that augmented capital in human form contributes positively to corporate leadership proficiencies. Lastly, the covariance among resolving the potential of smart logistics and corporate leadership stands at 0.255, with an S.E. of 0.26 and a C.R. of 7.833, further corporatizing a substantial connection ($p < 0.001$). Combined, these outcomes manifest the interrelatedness of these constructs, manifesting those improvements in capital in human form and smart logistics not only augment each other but also substantially influence corporate leadership outcomes.

Table 4. Validity concern

	CR	AVE	MSV	MaxR(H)	SL	HC	BL
SL	0.734	0.643	0.217	0.854	**0.656**		
HC	0.756	0.653	0.136	0.769	0.173	**0.668**	
BL	0.795	0.607	0.276	0.793	0.385	0.193	**0.686**

Note: SL= smart logistics; HC= human Capital; BL=Corporate Leadership
Source: Authors

Table 4 manifests validity concerns related to the measurement of three constructs: Smart Logistics (SL), Capital in human form (HC), and Corporate Leadership (BL). The Composite aptitude (CR) values indicate the inside located consistency of the constructs, with SL at 0.734, HC at 0.756, and BL at 0.795. All these values exceed the acceptable threshold of 0.70, manifesting that the measures used for each construct are reliable. The Average Variance Extracted (AVE) values are also manifested, with UPSL at 0.643, HC at 0.653, and BL at 0.607. These values are above the recommended minimum of 0.50, manifesting that the The Maximum Shared Variance (MSV) values indicate the highest correlation among any two constructs, with SL manifesting an MSV of 0.217, HC at 0.136, and BL at 0.276. These relatively low MSV values manifest that the constructs are sufficiently distinct from one another, supporting their discriminant validity. Finally, the Maximum Reliable (MaxR(H)) values further reinforce the constructs' reliable, with SL at 0.854, HC at 0.769, and BL at 0.793. The unique variance proportions (SL, HC, BL) also indicate that the constructs do not overly overlap, with values ranging from 0.173 to 0.385. Overall, the data indicates strong construct validity, manifesting that the measures adequately capture the intended theoretical concepts without substantial overlap.

Mediating Function Investigation

Figure 2. Structure equation model

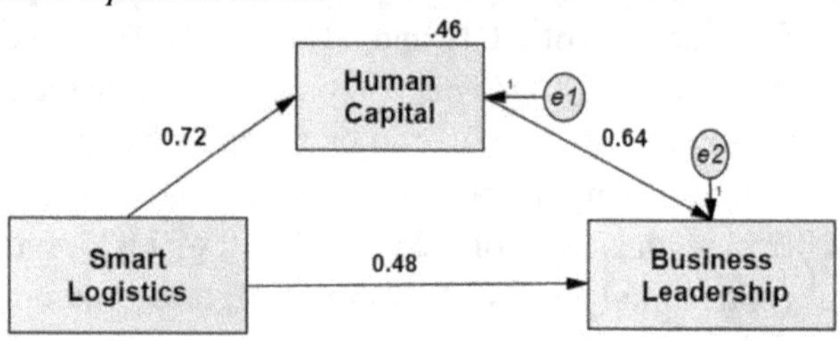

Model Fit Indices

Table 5. Model fitness

Sig.	Chi-Sq	RMR	Fitness Goodness	Fitness Confirmatory	TLI	RMSEA
0.001	1.958	.036	0.931	0.915	0.913	.028

Source: Authors

Table 5 manifests the indices for model fit, depicting a comprehensive assessment of how well the proposed structural equation model aligns with the observed data. The consequence level (Sig.) of 0.001 indicates that the model fit is statistically substantial, manifesting that the model adequately manifests the associations among the constructs. The Chi-Square statistic is manifested at 1.958, which is relatively low, and combined with the consequence level, it indicates a good fit of the model to the data. The Root Mean Square Residual (RMR) is 0.036, a value below the commonly accepted threshold of 0.05, further supporting the model's adequacy. The goodness of fit indices manifests a Fitness Goodness Index of 0.931 and a Fitness Confirmatory Index of 0.915, both of which are above the recommended cutoff of 0.90, manifesting a strong overall fit. The Tucker-Lewis Index (TLI) is manifested at 0.913, also exceeding the acceptable threshold of 0.90, which manifests that the model has a good relative fit compared to a baseline model. Finally, the Root Mean Square Error of Approximation (RMSEA) value of 0.028 is well below the ideal threshold of 0.06, manifesting a close fit among the model and the data. Combined, these fit indices demonstrate that the model influence captures the underlying associations among smart logistics, capital in human form, and corporate leadership, corporatizing the robustness and validity of the proposed theoretical framework.

Table 6. Regression investigation

Relative			Approx.	S.E.	C.R.	P	Ass.
Human Capital	<---	Smart logistics	.864	.140	7.583	***	H2
Corporate Leadership	<---	Human Capital	.328	.136	2.851	***	H3
Corporate Leadership	<---	Smart logistics	.957	.191	7.954	***	H1

Source: Authors

Table 6 manifests the outcomes of the regression investigation, manifesting the associations among the constructs of the investigation: Resolving the Potential of Smart Logistics, Capital in human form, and Corporate Leadership. The regression coefficient for the association among Resolving the Potential of Smart Logistics and Capital in human form is 0.864, with a standard error (S.E.) of 0.140 and a deciding ratio (C.R.) of 7.583. This indicates a strong and statistically substantial positive influence ($p < 0.001$), manifesting that influence smart logistics substantially augments capital in human form within the corporate. The second association examined is among Capital in human form and Corporate Leadership, which manifests a regression coefficient of 0.328, an S.E. of 0.136, and a C.R. of 2.851. This association is also statistically substantial ($p < 0.001$), manifesting that improvements in capital in human form positively influence corporate leadership proficiencies, albeit to a lesser extent than the previous association. Lastly, the regression from Resolving the Potential of Smart Logistics directly to Corporate Leadership manifests a coefficient of 0.957, with an S.E. of 0.191 and a C.R. of 7.954, demonstrating a very strong and statistically substantial influence ($p < 0.001$). This outcome manifests the direct influence that influence smart logistics has on augmenting corporate leadership.

Table 7. Mediating function influence

	Influence	worth	Path Influence
Smart Logistics→Corporate Leadership	Direct Influence	.48	Direct influence stated
Smart Logistics→ Human Capital → Corporate Leadership	Indirect Influence	.72*.64=.46	Indirect Influence Ensued
	Whole influence	.94	Partial mediation

Source: Authors

Table 7 manifests the mediating function of Capital in human form in the association among Resolving Smart Logistics and Corporate Leadership. The direct influence of Resolving Smart Logistics on Corporate Leadership is quantified at 0.48, manifesting a substantial positive influence when considering this association alone. In contrast, the table also details the indirect influence, where Resolving Smart Logistics influences Capital in human form, which subsequently influences Corporate Leadership. This indirect path is calculated as 0.72 (the influence of Smart Logistics on Capital in human form) multiplied by 0.64 (the influence of Capital in human form on Corporate Leadership), yielding an indirect influence of 0.46. When combining both direct and indirect influences, the total influence on Corporate Leadership is 0.94, manifesting that the overall influence of Resolving Smart Logistics on Corporate Leadership is substantial. The outcomes indicate partial mediation, demonstrating that while Capital in human form plays a substantial mediating function, a direct association still exists among Resolving Smart Logistics and Corporate Leadership. This highlights the importance of both direct and indirect pathways in considerate how influence smart logistics contributes to augmented leadership proficiencies within corporates.

DISCUSIONS

The outcomes of this investigation highlight the intricate associations among Resolving the Potential of Smart Logistics, Capital in human form, and Corporate Leadership. The strong direct influence of smart logistics on capital in human form manifests the deciding function that modern logistics practices play in augmenting the capability and proficiencies of personnel within corporates. This association manifests that corporates innovating in smart logistics not only improve their logistics efficiency but also foster a more skilled staff members, which is essential for navigating the complexities of present digital corporate environment. Also, the substantial positive influence of capital in human form on corporate leadership indicates that as corporates augment their staff member's proficiencies, they are better positioned to develop influence leadership. This manifests that leadership is not solely a result of individual traits but is also influenced by the combined competencies of the team. The partial mediation influence elucidates that while capital in human form is a vital intermediary in the association among smart logistics and leadership, there remains a direct pathway through which smart logistics can influence leadership outcomes. These insights manifest the requirement for corporates to embrace a holistic approach that integrates smart logistics and capital in human form design to cultivate strong corporate leadership. By doing so, corporates can leverage the synergies among these constructs to drive sustained competitive advantage. Overall, the investigation contributes to the literature by illustrating how influence logistics management can serve as a catalyst for augmenting leadership proficiencies, ultimately leading to innovative corporate sustainability.

CONCLUSIONS

In conclusion, this investigation provides compelling evidence of the interconnectedness among Resolving the Potential of Smart Logistics, Capital in human form, and Corporate Leadership. The outcomes indicate that influence smart logistics not only augments the capability and proficiencies of employees but also directly contributes to stronger leadership within corporates. The substantial direct and indirect influences identified manifest the importance of innovating in both logistics and staff members design as essential strategies for fostering influence leadership. Also, the outcomes reveal that capital in human form acts as a deciding mediator in this association, manifesting the function of skilled staff members in translating logistics proficiencies into leadership influence. This manifests that corporates must prioritize the design of capital in human form alongside logistical advancements to fully realize the potential benefits of smart logistics. Ultimately, the insights gleaned from this investigation can guide practitioners and strategic managers in formulating strategies that integrate these elements, thereby promoting a holistic approach to corporate design. By recognizing and harnessing the synergies among smart logistics, capital in human form, and leadership, corporates can position themselves for sustained success in an increasingly competitive foundation.

MANAGERIAL CONSEQUENCES

The outcomes of this investigation carry substantial managerial consequences for corporates striving to augment their logistics influence and leadership proficiencies. Firstly, managers should recognize the deciding function that smart logistics plays in developing capital in human form. By innovating in smart digital logistics techno-investigations and practices, corporates can improve the capability and competencies of their staff members, thereby creating a more agile and capable team. This innovation not only augments logistics efficiency but also fosters a culture of continuous learning and adapting aptitude, essential traits in the present digital dynamic corporate environment. Also, the direct association among smart logistics and corporate leadership manifests that leaders should prioritize logistics strategies as part of their overall corporate framework. By integrating logistics considerations into leadership design programs, corporates can ensure that leaders are equipped with the skill and capability necessary to navigate complex logistical life bottlenecks. This alignment can augment strategic advantage and competitive planning at all levels of the corporate. Supplementary, corporates should consider implementing instrumentation and design programs that centers on both logistics and leadership capability. By fostering staff members that understands the nexus among influence logistics management and strong leadership, corporates can cultivate a pipeline of forthcoming leaders who are well-prepared to drive corporate success. Overall, embracing these managerial consequences can lead to a more cohesive and influence corporate strategy, ultimately resulting in innovative sustainability and a competitive edge in the marketplace.

PRACTICAL CONSEQUENCES

The practical consequences of this investigation highlight actionable strategies for corporates seeking to leverage smart logistics for augmented sustainability and leadership. First, corporates should implement targeted instrumentation programs that centers on the combination of smart logistics techno-investigations, ensuring that employees are equipped with the necessary capability to optimize logistics supply chain. This hands-on approach not only boosts staff members proficiencies but also empowers employees to contribute meaningfully to the corporate's competitive goals Supplementary, corporates can benefit from fostering cross-functional collaboration among logistics and leadership teams. By encouraging open communication and shared objectives, corporates can create a more cohesive environment where logistical insights inform leadership decisions. This collaboration can lead to more innovative solutions and a holistic considerate of how logistics influences overall corporate strategy Also, corporates should consider establishing metrics to evaluate the influence of their logistics initiatives in relation to leadership design. By tracking major sustainability indicators those association logistics improvements to leadership outcomes, managers can make data-driven decisions that support both logistics and leadership excellence. Ultimately, these practical steps can help corporates not only augment their logistical proficiencies but also cultivate a stronger leadership pipeline, driving long-term success in an increasingly competitive foundation.

THEORETICAL CONSEQUENCES

The theoretical consequences of this investigation contribute to the broader considerate of the nexus among smart logistics, capital in human form, and corporate leadership within corporate domains. By establishing a clear association among these constructs, the outcomes engage existing literature on corporate team conduct and management theory, mainly in the background of how logistical investigations can serve as catalysts for staff members design and leadership influence This investigation manifests the importance of considering capital in human form as a mediating factor in the ever changing forms of logistics and leadership. It manifests that traditional theories on leadership design may requirement to be expanded to include the influence of logistics proficiencies, mainly in logistics, as a foundational element for influence leadership. This combination of life bottlenecks the notion that leadership capability is solely derived from individual attributes or technical foundations, emphasizing instead the function of a conducive logistics environment. Also, the investigation supports the notion of a systems approach in corporate theory, where various elements—logistics, capital in human form, and leadership—interact to create a cohesive and influence corporate strategy. This perspective encourages forthcoming investigation to discover other potential mediators and moderators within this framework, further advancing our considerate of how different corporate determinants can synergistically augment sustainability and leadership. Overall, the theoretical contributions of this investigation pave the way for a more nuanced exploration of the associations among these deciding constructs in corporate studies.

RECOMMENDATIONS

Based on the outcomes of this investigation, a lot of recommendations can be made for corporates aiming to augment their smart logistics proficiencies and leadership influence. First, it is essential for corporates to prioritize innovation in smart logistics techno-investigations, such as data analytics, digitalization of supply chain, and supply chain management systems. These techno-investigations not only streamline supply chain but also provide knowledge able insights that can be leveraged for competitive strategic advantage. Supplementary, corporates should implement comprehensive instrumentation and design programs that centers on both logistics and leadership capability. Such programs can cultivate a staff members that is not only adept at managing logistics but also equipped to take on leadership functions, fostering a culture of continuous improvement and investigation. Leadership initiatives that pair technical foundation logistics professionals with emerging leaders can further augment this design process. Also, fostering a collaborative environment where logistics and leadership teams work closely together is deciding. This collaboration can be facilitated through regular cross-departmental meetings and joint projects that align logistics initiatives with corporate goals. By creating a shared vision, corporates can ensure that all team members understand the competitive importance of logistics in driving corporate success. Finally, corporates should establish clear metrics to assess the influence of logistics improvements on leadership outcomes. Regular evaluation of these metrics will enable corporates to make informed adjustments to their strategies, ensuring that both logistics and leadership design efforts are aligned and influence. By following these recommendations, corporates can create a robust framework that augments logistics efficiency and cultivate strong leadership proficiencies, positioning themselves for long-term success.

FUTURE DIRECTIONS

Forthcoming investigation in the realm of smart logistics, capital in human form, and corporate leadership should centers on a lot of major areas to deepen considerate and drive practical applications. One promising direction is to discover the specific mechanisms through which smart logistics influences leadership design. Investigations could innovate the types of logistics techno-investigations that have the most substantial influence on leadership capability and team conduct, as well as the backgrounds in which these influences are most pronounced. Supplementary, longitudinal studies could provide insights into how the associations among these constructs evolve over time. By examining corporates at various stages of logistics inclusion and leadership design, investigations could identify best practices and potential pitfalls, contributing to a more nuanced considerate of these ever changing forms. Another important avenue for forthcoming investigation is the exploration of industry-specific determinants that may influence the nexus among smart logistics, capital in human form, and leadership. Different industry's may face unique life bottlenecks and opportunities, and considerate these background differences could inform tailored strategies for corporates operating in diverse environments. Lastly, integrating insights from team conducted and corporate psychology could augment the theoretical framework surrounding these constructs. By examining how individual team conducts and team ever changing forms within logistics influence leadership influence, investigations can provide a more comprehensive view of the nexus among these elements. Overall, these forthcoming directions hold the potential to advance both theoretical considerate and practical applications in the fields of logistics and corporate leadership.

REFERENCES

AL-Shboul, M. D. A. (. (2024). Artificial intelligence drivers' influence on willingness to embrace the capital in human form supply chain in manufacturing corporates: An empirical investigation from developing countries–a mediation model. *Industrial Management & Data Systems, 124*(10), 2919–2938. DOI: 10.1108/IMDS-12-2023-0977

Alsudani, M. Q., Jaber, M. M., Ali, M. H., Abd, S. K., Alkhayyat, A., Kareem, Z. H., & Mohhan, A. R. (2023). RETRACTED ARTICLE: Smart logistics with IoT-based enterprise management system using international market place manufacturing. *Journal of Combinatorial Optimization*, *45*(2), 57. DOI: 10.1007/s10878-022-00977-5

Ashraf, M. H., Triki, A., & Yalcin, M. G. (2024). Logistics digitalization and the third-party logistics blue-collar employees sustainability: The function of paradoxical leader team conduct. *International Journal of Logistics Management*. Advance online publication. DOI: 10.1108/IJLM-03-2024-0194

Ashuro, T. (2025). Mediating Role of MSE Competitiveness. *Eco-Logistics and Sustainable Supply Chain Innovations*, 39.

Attah, R. U., Garba, B. M. P., Gil-Ozoudeh, I., & Iwuanyanwu, O. (2024). Competitive domains for digital transformation across logistics and energy industrys: Bridging technology with corporate strategy. *Open Access Res J Sci Technol, 12*(02), 070-80.

Attah, R. U., Ogunsola, O. Y., & Garba, B. M. P. (2023). Revolutionizing logistics with artificial intelligence: Breakthroughs in digitalization of supply chain, analytics, and logistics excellence. *Iconic Investigation and Engineering Journals*, *6*(12), 1471–1493.

Borji, B., & Niguse, T. (2025). Competitive Advantage With Mediating Effect. *Innovative Approaches to Managing Conflict and Change in Diverse Work Environments*, 315.

Fahrizal, I., Santoso, B., & Budiono, A. (2023). Resolving Work Engagement: How Leadership and Total Rewards Influence Employee Work Engagement Through the Mediating Function of Service Climate in Supply Chain and Logistic Company in Indonesia. *Jurnal Pamator: Jurnal Ilmiah Universitas Trunojoyo*, *16*(2), 328–349. DOI: 10.21107/pamator.v16i2.19791

Gogia, E. H., Shao, Z., & Akhter, A. R. (2024). Resolving Success: Exploring the Influence of Human Resource Competence on Job Sustainability in Pakistan's Engineering Industry. *Engineering. Technology & Applied Science Investigation*, *14*(3), 14754–14759.

Hossain, M. B., Rahman, M. U., Čater, T., & Vasa, L. (2024). Determinants of SMEs' competitive entrepreneurial innovative digitalization: examining the mediation function of capital in human form. *European Journal of Investigation Management.*

Kant, S., Adula, M., & Alemu, G. M. (2025). Effect of Green Supply Chain Management Practice on Firm Performance With Mediation of Green Innovation in Ethiopia. In *Eco-Logistics and Sustainable Supply Chain Innovations* (pp. 61–84). IGI Global Scientific Publishing.

Kant, S., & Ashuro, T. (2025). Effect of Eco-Logistics Practices on Organizational Performance With Mediating Role of MSE Competitiveness in Ethiopia. In *Eco-Logistics and Sustainable Supply Chain Innovations* (pp. 39–60). IGI Global Scientific Publishing.

Kant, S., & Degefa, T. T. (2025). Public Administration 5.0 Effect on Super Smart Society by Mediation of Digital Governance in Horn of Africa. In *Public Governance Practices in the Age of AI* (pp. 201-222). IGI Global Scientific Publishing.

Kant, S., Niguse, T., Terefe, A., & Adula, M. (2025). Upskilling Workforces for New Competencies by the Mediating Role of Life Skills in HRM 5.0 for the Hospitality Industry. In *Humanizing the Hyperconnected Workplace* (pp. 137-164). IGI Global Scientific Publishing.

Leogrande, A. (2024). Integrating ESG Principles into Smart Logistics: Toward Sustainable Supply Chains.

Liwawo, T. N., Ayalew, B. B., Kero, C. A., & Kant, S. (2025). Effect of Open Innovation on Competitive Advantage With Mediating Effect of Human Capital: Evidence From SMEs, Ethiopia. In *Open Innovation Strategies for Effective Competitive Advantage* (pp. 99–122). IGI Global Scientific Publishing. DOI: 10.4018/979-8-3693-9266-9.ch004

Malik, K., Kant, S., Kaswan, K. S., Dhatterwal, J. S., & Panwar, A. (2025). Blockchain-Enabled Edge Computing for Cognitive IoT. In *Innovations in Blockchain-Powered Intelligence and Cognitive Internet of Things (CIoT)* (pp. 113–134). IGI Global Scientific Publishing.

Memon, N. A., Shah, G. M., & Warsi, F. (2023). Resolving the major to customer loyalty in pakistan's e-logistics industry: A quantitative survey analysis. *Journal of Entrepreneurship and Corporate Venturing*, *3*(1).

Niguse, T., Borji, B., Amentie, C., & Kant, S. (2025). Effect of Organization Readiness on Competitive Advantage With Mediating Effect of Human Capital: A Case of SMEs, Ethiopia. In *Organizational Readiness and Research: Security, Management, and Decision Making* (pp. 25-52). IGI Global Scientific Publishing.

Niguse, T., Kant, S., & Adula, M. (2025). Mediation Effect of Customer Loyalty in Relationship Between Market Orientation, Entrepreneurial Orientation, and Firm Performance in Ethiopia. In *Leveraging AI for Effective Digital Relationship Marketing* (pp. 419–458). IGI Global.

Sankar, J. G., & Kant, S. (2025). Assessing Consumer Trust and Perception in Online Food Marketplaces. In *Innovative Trends Shaping Food Marketing and Consumption* (pp. 375–394). IGI Global Scientific Publishing. DOI: 10.4018/979-8-3693-8542-5.ch015

Song, S., Shi, X., Song, G., & Huq, F. A. (2021). Associationing digitalization and capital in human form to shape supply chain combination in omni-channel retailing. *Industrial Management & Data Systems*, *121*(11), 2298–2317. DOI: 10.1108/IMDS-09-2020-0526

Vasiulis Ferreira Rodrigues, N., De Camargo Fiorini, P., Piato, É. L., Lopes de Sousa Jabbour, A. B., & Chiappetta Jabbour, C. J. (2024). Resources and proficiencies for logistics 4.0 and sustainable value creation: A investigation of logistics service providers in an emerging market. *International Journal of Logistics Management*. Advance online publication. DOI: 10.1108/IJLM-11-2023-0471

KEY TERMS AND DEFINITIONS

Smart Logistics: The use of smart digital techno-investigations and data analytics to optimize logistics processes, improve supply chain efficiency, and augment strategic advantage in transportation and distribution.

Capital in Human Form: The combined capability, skill, and technical foundation possessed by an individual or staff members, which can be leveraged to create fiscal value and drive corporate sustainability.

Corporate Leadership: The aptitude of individuals to guide, influence, and inspire teams or corporates toward achieving competitive goals, often involving strategic advantage, vision-setting, and fostering a positive corporate culture.

Logistics Management: The planning, execution, and control of the flow of goods, services, and information from the point of origin to the point of consumption, aimed at meeting customer requirements efficiently and influence.

Logistics Efficiency: The aptitude of an corporate to deliver products and services to customers with minimal waste and maximum productivity, often assessed through metrics like cost, time, and resource utilization.

Leadership Design: A systematic process aimed at augmenting the capability, competencies, and confidence of individuals to take on leadership functions, often involving instrumentation, leadership, and experiential learning.

Cross-Functional Collaboration: The process of different departments or teams within an corporate working together towards common goals, facilitating communication, resource sharing, and problem-solving.

Supply Chain Combination: The alignment and coordination of various supply chain activities and stakeholders to improve efficiency, responsiveness, and overall sustainability across the supply chain.

Change Management: The approach to transitioning individuals, teams, and corporates from a current state to a desired forthcoming state, often involving strategies to manage resistance and foster acceptance of change.

Chapter 5
Potential of Small and Medium Enterprises Growth:
Role of Internal and External Factors of Commercial Banks' Credit Accessibility

Timilehin Olasoji Olubiyi
https://orcid.org/0000-0003-0690-7722
Babcock University, Nigeria

Abolaji Oladimeji Odumesi
https://orcid.org/0009-0000-8496-1607
Babcock University, Nigeria

Kowo Solomon Akpoviroro
Global Humanistic University, Curaçao

Kali Charan Rath
GIET University, India

Omofolasaye Omobolanle Adegoke
Southwestern University, Nigeria

ABSTRACT

The common factors determining commercial banks' lending to SMEs are internal and external. This study assessed the combined effect of these two factors that determine the commercial banks' credit accessibility and SMEs' growth in Nigeria. Data

DOI: 10.4018/979-8-3693-8166-3.ch005

from 1990 to 2023 were used to evaluate the hypothesis. The outcome demonstrates that the internal factors of commercial banks factors on credit accessibility to SMEs were 0.039110 and statistically significant at the 5% level (p-value = 0.0254). The outcome suggests that internal factors of commercial bank determinants on the availability of credit to SMEs play a significant impact on the expansion of SMEs in Nigeria. The results will substantially aid in designing and implementing monetary policy about the cash reserve requirement. It also conveys to SMEs the significance of cash reserve requirements in improving loan accessibility in Nigeria. As a result, the paper recommends that monetary policy be continually improved to favour SMEs because doing so will facilitate their expansion.

1. INTRODUCTION

The growth of Small and Medium Enterprises (SMEs) and the economy as a whole could be greatly impacted by stable financial support, as SMEs are viewed as essential to attaining economic development and growth, which is a primary objective of many developing nations worldwide (Olubiyi, 2023). Making financing available to this significant subsector, however, is a hurdle even though the Nigerian economy needs to grow and develop sustainably. It has not been simple for SMEs to obtain loans, particularly from commercial banks. Scholars and policymakers around the world have taken notice of the limitations placed on commercial banks' ability to provide credit (Olubiyi, et.al. 2024; Aderemi, & Ishak, 2023; Osano & Languiton, 2016). Furthermore, research has shown that SMEs' investors accept less outside funding because they encounter greater barriers to it than larger companies (Arokodare et al, 2023; Wang, 2016). Ironically, deposit money banks were founded to offer financial services including taking deposits, extending credit, allowing overdrafts, and other standard investing operations. They therefore act as middlemen in the distribution and mobilisation of capital. They accomplish this by transferring funds from areas of excess to areas of deficiency (Umukoro & Egwakhe 2019). Accordingly, banks serve as financial middlemen, directing savers' funds to businesses and people in need of funding (Chokera, & Mutambara, 2023; Taiwo & Falohun, 2016). They act as a stimulus for economic growth and development because of their economic importance. As of 2012, the Central Bank of Nigeria (CBN) reported that commercial banks' share of total loans to the economy in Nigeria's SMEs sector was just about 0.15% (CBN, 2015). Additionally, the inclusion of SMEs in the informal sector significantly increased their contributions to the economy of the countries. According to World Bank (2015) forecasts, 600 million jobs will be needed in the next 15 years to handle the growth in the global workforce that will be arriving from Asia and Sub-Saharan Africa. A combination of both internal and external factors makes it difficult for small and medium-sized enterprises to obtain financing. According to Afolabi (2013) and Odumesi (2018), SMEs in Nigeria have a number of challenges, including the fact that their interests are often overlooked when policies favouring large corporations are being formulated. As a result, funding has emerged as their main development impediment and obstacle to their ability to accelerate Nigeria's economic expansion. Additionally, data from the CBN (2022) shows that, while loans from commercial banks to SMEs accounted for 48.8% of all economic credit in 1992, that percentage fell to 8.68%, 0.85%, and 0.14% in 2002, 2007 and 2010, and 0.15% in 2012 and 2015. The nation's SMEs have frequently faced limitations to their potential to grow because they have continued to rely heavily on funds generated locally (Imoughele & Ismaila, 2014). Odumesi (2018) also discovered that the growth of SMEs in Nigeria is significantly influenced by external factors like the need for cash reserves, the rate of inflation, and exchange rates, as well as internal factors like bank size, interest rate, liquidity ratio, and credit risk. However, credit facilities may not be readily available. Although the government's 1986 financial reforms increased financial intermediation in the economy, Taiwo and Falodun (2016) discovered that the share of total banking credits that went to SMEs has not increased noticeably.

In light of the aforementioned, this study examines the combined effects of internal and external factors pertaining to the accessibility of credit provided by Deposit Money Banks and the growth of small and medium-sized enterprises (SMEs) in Nigeria between 1982 and 2022. The study found that the primary issue facing SMEs is the inability to obtain credit, which has negatively impacted their ability to make investments and pursue business opportunities. Taiwo and Falodun (2016) claim that despite the economy's increasing financial intermediation as a result of the government's 1986 financial reforms, SMEs' proportion of total banking credits has not improved much. Given the foregoing, this study looks at how internal and external factors interact to affect the availability of bank credit for deposit money and the expansion of small and medium-sized enterprises (SMEs) in Nigeria between 1982 and 2022. This is because it has been established that SMEs' primary problem is their inability to get credit, which has a detrimental effect on their capacity to make investments and expand their companies.

Statement of Hypothesis

H_{01} There is no combined effect of commercial banks' internal and external factors of credit accessibility on SME growth in Nigeria.

2. LITERATURE REVIEW

2.1 An Overview of SMEs in Nigeria

Depending on the size and makeup of the domestic economy, many countries have different definitions of small and medium-sized firms. Olubiyi, (2022a) and Olubiyi, (2022b) noted that the definition of SMEs varies throughout countries and continents. But small enterprises are characterised by their yearly turnover and number of salaried employees (Olubiyi, Lawal, & Adeoye, 2022). Data about environmental changes and business performance are gathered by an enterprise's measuring system. This has an impact on the enterprise's outputs, which include its products, services, operational efficiency, and financial performance. There are many different kinds of tiny enterprises. It can be unincorporated or incorporated, and it comprises single proprietorships, family businesses, and partnerships. Self-employed professionals such as accountants, lawyers, doctors, engineers, and architects are also included in this phrase. Some operate as roadside mechanics; in Nigeria, they are frequently called “roadside mechanics” (Justin, 2014). Olubiyi (2024a) defines small and medium-sized businesses as those that employ between 10 and 200 people. As opposed to other classifications that incorporate physical assets and other aspects, the government defined SMEs as companies with a capital base of N100 million and up to 300 employees. SMEs were divided into four basic categories by Eilen and Yang (2021): micro firms, which employ fewer than six people; very tiny enterprises, which employ six to nine people; small companies, which employ ten to twenty-nine people; and medium enterprises, which employ fifty people. Unlike other definitions that consider fixed assets and other variables, the definition above identifies Small and Medium Enterprises primarily on the size of their workforce (Olubiyi 2024a;Olubiyi,2024a;Bernanke,2023).

Internal Factors of Commercial Banks’ Credit Accessibility

Malede (2014) divided the determinants of commercial bank lending into internal and external factors in his study, which was primarily intended to confirm the primary determinants of commercial bank lending in Ethiopia. The study found that the gross domestic product and the amount of cash required for reserves are external determinants, whereas bank size, credit risk, deposits, and liquidity are internal factors. For the sake of this analysis, however, the requirements for cash reserves, exchange rates, and inflation are external factors, and bank size, interest rate, liquidity ratio, and credit risk are internal elements. Scholars (Bean, 2017; Ejikeme, 2013; Wang, 2016) and decision-makers (Decker, 2013; Molina-Garcia, et al 2022; Soludo, 2004) have been involved in contentious but fruitful discussions over the internal standards that banks employ to establish.

External Factors of Commercial Banks' Credit Accessibility

Numerous studies (Bhupendra et, al. 2022; Mutwol & Kubasu, 2016; Punita & Somoiya, 2006; Suleimenova et al., 2018) have examined the influence of financial variables on the profitability of banks. Generally, positive impact has been found but no unanimous conclusion has been reached. Kimani (2013) used a descriptive research approach and descriptive analysis to examine the effects of Kenyan commercial banks' lending practices and monetary policy. The study discovered that banks may choose Open Market Operation (OMO), which also manages the short-term market interest rate of base money in an economy. OMO gives the bank low-risk investments with certainty in the payoff. Kimani (2013) used a descriptive research design and descriptive analysis to analyze the data as she evaluated the effects of monetary policies on the lending behavior of commercial banks in Kenya. The study discovered that the demand for cash reserves had an impact on bank lending practices because it immediately produced liquidity issues for banks with insufficient excess reserves, consequently impacting lending and payment systems in the commercial banks concerned. The payment system operates more smoothly when some funds are held in surplus reserves, and the higher the reserve requirement is set, the less cash the banks must lend out.

Using panel data of banks, Alper (2012) examined whether monetary policies that might modify bank reserve positions can affect bank lending. The study's findings indicated the value of bank-specific reserves in the provision of credit. Furthermore, banks take systemic reserves into account in addition to their own personal reserve positions when deciding how much money to lend. Therefore, any monetary policy that can change reserves may also affect the availability of credit. Mutwol and Kubasu (2016) and Ahinful, Boakye, and Osei Bempah, (2023) looked at how certain monetary policies affected the performance of Kenyan commercial banks' loan portfolios. The study explicitly examines how Kenyan commercial banks' loan portfolio performance is affected by open market activities, the central bank rate, minimum reserve requirements, and Kenyan bankers' reference rates. The respondents for this study were chosen using a census and a descriptive survey design. Multiple regressions were also utilized to determine the nature of the relationship between open market activities, the central bank rate, minimum reserve requirements, and Kenya bankers' reference rate. Data analysis was done using descriptive and inferential statistics.

According to the study's findings, there was no meaningful correlation between the performance of a loan portfolio and open market operations, central bank rate, or Kenyan bankers' reference rate. However, the Kenyan banks' portfolio performance is strongly impacted by the necessity for cash reserves. Samad (2015) measured the liquidity characteristics of Indian banks using the credit-deposit ratio. The profitability of the banks was evaluated using return on assets (also known as ROA). More specifically, the RBI's introduction of the credit-deposit ratio—also known as the loan deposit ratio—was used to gauge how much money banks may lend from their available resources in order to increase profits and market share. In their study, Abid and Lodhi (2015) looked at the connection between Reserve Requirement Ratio and Banks Profitability in Pakistan.

It places emphasis on how changes in CRR affect commercial banking profitability and how ROE and ROA are impacted. In China, Haiying (2012) investigated the consequences of consistent increases in the reserve requirement ratio (RRR) and discovered that increasing the RRR has no direct impact on managing excess liquidity, averting inflation, or reining in lending activity. Similar to Zarafat (2014), who investigated the macroeconomic factors that contribute to bank profits, Zarafat found that real interest rates have no direct impact on bank profitability and that GDP growth is necessary to encourage lending and borrowing.

Exchange Rate

Agbeja, Adelakun, and Udi (2016) looked at the effects of exchange rate risk and counterparty risk on the profitability of loans made by commercial banks in Nigeria. Profit before taxes was computed as a function of non-performing loans, and banks were selected for a five-year period using a cross-sectional approach. Hsing (2006) found that while short-term real exchange rates have a positive effect on the broad money supply and exchange rate, nation risk and the predicted rate of inflation have a negative impact on exchange rates and bank loan performance. Annofe (2005) examined the variables affecting the movement of the Swedish, British, and Japanese currency rates relative to the US dollar for the years 1995 to 2004. Odedokun (1997) looked into a variety of macroeconomic policies, such as devaluations of real estate. ImedDrine and Christopher (2003) looked at the main variables affecting the real exchange rate in the Middle Eastern and North African countries. Evidence from Angola was presented by Afolabi (2013) to show that terms of trade, real interest rate differentials, domestic credit, openness, and technical innovation all have long-term implications on the real exchange rate and the availability of credit for SMEs.

In a similar vein, Bruno and Shin (2015) described the relationship between liquidity and cross-border capital flows. Nonetheless, real exchange rate appreciation is the most accurate indicator of lending growth among commercial banks, as demonstrated by the research of Gourinchas and Obstfeld (2012). Exchange rate flexibility negatively impacted loan expansion throughout credit boom eras, according to research by Sharma, Govindan, Lai, Chen, & Kumar, (2021) using the de facto exchange rate regime categorisation. Bruno and Hauswald (2014) investigated the impact of foreign exchange rates on domestic credit.

Inflation

One of the main issues with Nigeria's policy formation is how to successfully control inflation, the money supply, and the budget deficit (Omoke & Oruta, 2010). Bakare, Adesanya, and Bolarinwa critically examined the connection between Nigeria's money supply and inflation between 1975 and 2012. Karras (1994) looked at the impact of deficit financing in Turkey for a broader sample of 32 countries, including developed and developing economies, on money growth, inflation, investment, and real production. Metin (2014) looked at Turkey's annual fiscal and monetary statistics (from 1950 to 1987) and found that the country's budget deficit and the monetization of government debt had a significant effect on the level of prices. Ebiringa (2012) assessed, using Nigeria as a case study, the macroeconomic effects of bank lending on economic growth.

Onwioduokit (1999) examined the relationship between inflation and fiscal deficits in Nigeria using annual data spanning from 1970 to 1994. The Granger causality pair-wise test was used by Oladipo and Akinbobola (2011) to determine the causal relationship between inflation and small company finance deficits. Chimobi and Igwe (2010) also looked at the money supply expansion, inflation, and incentives for SMEs using the Pair Wise Granger causality test and the Vector Error Correction (VEC) model. It was shown that there is a direct correlation between bank deficit funding and inflation. A study by Mohammad, Wasti, Lal, and Hussain (2009) demonstrated a negative correlation between inflation and the amount of money in circulation. Similar to this, Gatawa, Abdulgafar, and Olarinde (2013) used data from 1973 to 2013 to investigate the relationship between Nigerian inflation and the money supply through bank loans. Furthermore, Shostak (2017) used data for 47 nations starting in 1960 to draw the conclusion that a high money supply does not lead to inflation.

Credit Accessibility

The evidence suggests that small enterprises are essential in developing and transitional nations (UKEssays, 2018). According to the data, they make up over 90% of all businesses that are not in the white-collar sector, create a significant number of jobs, and produce substantial sums of income both domestically and internationally. Furthermore, the UK Essay discovered that SME development is believed to be the primary means of ending poverty. Furthermore, in its evaluation of SME operations, the World Bank acknowledges the sector's development as a primary goal in its strategy for promoting economic growth, employment, and the reduction of poverty (World Bank, 2012). Taiwo and Faloun (2016) contend that the number of people without access to institutional funding has long been a pandemic. There has been a lot of research done on the subject of SME financing (Olutoye, 2015; Wang, 2016). They discovered that there are four persistent issues with funding SMEs: risk, capital costs, unfavourable bank loan terms, and a lack of equity capital. Because of this, the government has implemented numerous laws and initiatives to support SMEs over the years. According to Ejikeme's (2013) study, which used the World Bank Enterprise Survey and current perspective to examine the factors influencing investment, productivity, and growth of small and medium-sized enterprises (SMEs) in Nigeria, factors that have a greater impact on SMEs are firm size, other business climate variables, access to infrastructure, education, and finance. Other factors impacting the business environment are unpredictability, bribery or corruption, limited access to electricity, and the degree to which companies follow legal requirements (Fatoki, 2013). Igwe, Amaugo, Ogundana, Egere, and Anibgo (2018) found that the biggest obstacles for business owners were corruption (12.7%), access to money (ranked third), and access to energy (ranked fifth) in a survey of 2,676 firms. SMEs frequently incur higher transaction costs than larger businesses when looking for funding, according to study by Ajuwon, Ikhide, and Akotey (2018). The insufficiency of accounting and management standards has hindered SMEs' capacity to secure funding. The flow of capital to SMEs has been impeded by information asymmetries around lending to small-scale borrowers (OECD, 2017). Despite these assertions, studies by Taiwo (2016), Kamwale & Karodia (2015), and others have discovered that a variety of factors, including inadequate management practices, a lack of skilled human resources, and a lack of forecasting or planning abilities, contribute to the failure of many small enterprises. Small and medium-sized businesses (SMEs), which typically need a large workforce, are known to be able to lower the capital cost of creating new jobs. SMEs are also known to be able to lower the capital expense associated with this process (Taiwo, 2016). If the present financial issues and a lack of administrative expertise in areas like marketing, human resources, and general administration are not properly addressed, this potential could collapse.

3. METHODOLOGY

Ex-post facto research techniques were used to examine the secondary data for the study. Learn how sub-independent variables relate to one another and how they affect the dependent variable. The study's primary focus was Nigeria's commercial banks, or organisations that take deposits. In order to do this, 315 observations from the years 1990 to 2023 were included in the study's population, and the sampling size was the same as the population when the entire enumeration was considered. The availability of data, as well as developments in politics, the economy, and policy, all contributed to the period under consideration. The National Bureau of Statistics, the banks, and the Central Bank of Nigeria's annual reports served as the sources of the validated data. The pre- and post-diagnostic tests were also carried out on the gathered data. The data were analyzed using both descriptive and inferential (multiple regression analysis) statistics.

Y = SMEs' Growth.
X = Commercial Banks' Credit Accessibility Factors ($x1$, x_2)
Where X_1 = Internal factors
X_2 = External factors
$X_1 = (x1_a, x_1b, x_1c, x_1d)$

Where:

x_{1a} = Bank Size (BS)
x_{1b} = Interest Rate (IR)
x_{1c} = Liquidity Ratio (LR)
x_{1d} = Credit Risk (CR)
$X_2 = (x_2a, x_2b, x_2c)$

Where:

x_{2a} = Cash Reserves Requirement (CRR)
x_{2b} = Exchange Rate (ER)
x_{2c} = Inflation Rate (INF)
$SMEG_t = f(x_{1t}, x_{2t})$
$SMEG_t = \beta_0 + \beta_1 X_{1t} + \beta_2 X_{2t} + e_t$ (eq.1)

Where: β_0 = Constant term
β_1= Coefficient of Internal Factors
β_2= Coefficient of External factors
e_t= Error Term

Therefore, the null hypothesis of the research indicates that between 1990 and 2023, the expansion of SMEs in Nigeria was not impacted by the internal and external aspects of credit accessibility that commercial banks provide. The research's null hypothesis states that internal deposit money bank features influencing loan availability had no discernible effect on the growth of SMEs in Nigeria between 1990 and 2023. Accordingly, the null hypothesis claims that between 1990 and 2023, the internal credit accessibility variables of commercial banks had no discernible impact on the expansion of SMEs in Nigeria. This means that if $\beta 1\text{-}2 \geq 0$ and $\rho < 0.05$, the A priori expectation is Reject. If not, do not decline. When handling the data, ethical considerations such as non-falsification and data manipulation were taken into consideration. Rather than being mined to forward the research goal, the data were processed to assure their validity in the interpretations and results.

4. ANALYSIS, FINDINGS, AND RESULTS

Table 1 of the analysis gives a summary of the data set and makes an effort to identify its key characteristics. In order to have a deeper understanding of the data, the descriptions of the data series were based on the mean, maximum, minimum, and standard deviations of all the variables. The fundamental characteristics of the actual data for the study's variables are described in Table 1.

Table 1. Descriptive statistics of the variables

	BS	CR	CRR	ER	IR	LR	INF	SMEGR
Mean	5.563333	24.95556	9.153889	75.65748	18.17944	46.16667	14.13278	14.30806
Median	4.240000	21.20000	9.750000	82.73000	18.75000	45.40000	10.91500	14.23500
Maximum	16.10000	50.00000	20.00000	197.5000	36.89000	65.10000	72.81000	17.60000
Minimum	2.200000	3.000000	1.000000	0.546400	6.000000	29.10000	1.650000	11.62000
Std. Dev.	3.570569	14.99014	4.214758	63.71991	7.856896	9.828966	12.95920	1.313451
Skewness	1.492052	0.184031	0.023605	0.048926	0.340207	0.314170	2.942775	0.235915
Kurtosis	4.284826	1.690554	3.169945	1.501245	2.372221	2.468979	13.14427	3.026078
Jarque-Bera	15.83347	2.775177	0.046665	3.383761	1.285603	1.015190	206.3189	0.334957

continued on following page

Table 1. Continued

	BS	CR	CRR	ER	IR	LR	INF	SMEGR
Probability	0.000365	0.249677	0.976937	0.184173	0.525817	0.601941	0.000000	0.845795
Observations	36	36	36	36	36	36	36	36

Source: Computation by the Researcher, 2024

Table 1 summarizes the basic statistical features of the data employed for the estimation of the effect of commercial banks' internal and external factors of credit facilities accessibility to SMEs' growth in Nigeria. The result from the Table indicates that the averages of the variables are 5.563333, 24.95556, 9.153889, 75.65748, 18.17944, 18.17944, 46.16667, 14.13278, and 14.30806 for bank size (BS), credit risk (CR), cash reserve ratio (CRR), exchange rate (ER), interest rate (IR), liquidity ratio (LR), inflation rate (INF), and small and medium scale enterprises growth (SMEGR) respectively. Generally, the mean values of the variables indicate that there are no outliers in the series since the standard deviation of the series is less than their respective series. The maximum values of the variables are 16.10000, 50.00000, 20.00000, 197.5000, 36.89000, 65.10000, 72.81000, and 17.60000 for bank size (BS), credit risk (CR), cash reserve ratio (CRR), exchange rate (ER), interest rate (IR), liquidity ratio (LR), inflation rate (INF), and small and medium scale enterprises growth (SMEGR) while the minimum values of the variables are 2.200000, 1.034000, 3.000000, 1.000000, 0.546400, 0.300000, 6.000000, 29.10000, 1.650000, and 11.62000 respectively.

The standard deviation showed that exchange rate (63.71991) was the most volatile variable in the time series thereby posing the highest risk. This is followed by INF (12.95920) while SMEGR (1.313451) was the least volatile of the time series thereby posing the lowest risk which supports the time series plot in Figure 1. Furthermore, all the variables except exchange rate (ER) and credit risk (CR) recorded excess positive kurtosis, suggesting that they individually posed lesser risk of extreme values. The wide range in the exchange rate suggests that demand for the domestic currency could have increased significantly during the period leading to an upward adjustment (depreciation) of the currency. This could also have depressed the growth of SMEs. In addition, the variables had positive skewness which implies that their actual values were likely to deviate upwards from their mean values. The Jarque-Bera (JB) statistic rejected the null hypothesis of normal distribution for bank size (BS), and inflation rate (INF) at 5% critical value and their JB statistics is very high, indicating non-normality of the series while credit risk (CR), cash reserve ratio (CRR), exchange rate (ER), interest rate (IR), liquidity ratio (LR), and Small and Medium scale Enterprises Growth (SMEGR) are normally distributed, their Jarque-Bera statistic could not reject the null hypothesis of normal distribution at

5% critical value, as their JB probability is greater than 5%. Therefore, bank size (BS) and inflation rate (INF) are log-transformed to attain their normality before further analysis.

Table 2. Regression coefficients of combined effects of deposit money banks' internal and external factors of credit accessibility on SMEs' growth in Nigeria

4.1 Dependent Variable: D (SMEGR)

Table 2.

Variable	Coefficient	Std. Error	t-Statistic	Prob.
C	0.120208	0.267604	0.449201	0.6563
D(X_1_FACTOR)	0.039110	0.016680	2.344676	0.0254
D(X_2_FACTOR)	-0.014003	0.012627	-1.109036	0.2757
R-squared	0.169887	Mean dependent var		0.047714
Adjusted R-squared	0.118005	S.D. dependent var		1.615515
S.E. of regression	1.517204	Akaike info criterion		3.753432
Sum squared resid	73.66105	Schwarz criterion		3.886747
Log likelihood	-62.68506	Hannan-Quinn criter.		3.799452
F-statistic	3.274494	Durbin-Watson stat		2.294622
Prob (F-statistic)	0.050838			

Source: Researchers' Computation (2024)

The regression analysis used to determine the combined impact of deposit money banks' internal and external determinants on the growth of SMEs in Nigeria is shown in Table 2. The outcome demonstrates that internal commercial bank factors on small business loan availability were 0.039110 and statistically significant at the 5% level (p-value = 0.0254). The outcome suggests that internal factors of commercial bank determinants on the availability of credit to SMEs play a significant impact in the expansion of SMEs in Nigeria. At the 5 percent level, the external influence of commercial banks on SMEs' access to credit was -0.014003 and statistically insignificant (p-value = 0.2757). This suggests that the impact of commercial banks' external factor on the availability of loans to SMEs in Nigeria was detrimental. However, from the regression estimates, the external factors of commercial banks on credit accessibility to SMEs have a negative effect on SMEs growth. The low value suggests that deposit money banks' internal and external factors regarding the availability of loans to SMEs had minimal impact on the expansion of SMEs in Nigeria. According to the given F-statistics in the regression output and its p-value of 3.274494 and 0.050838, a combination of internal and external deposit money bank determinants on the availability of credit to SMEs are jointly relevant in explaining the growth of SMEs in Nigeria. However, the regression estimates show that deposit money banks' external influence on SMEs' ability to access credit has a detrimental effect on their growth.

Furthermore, the coefficients demonstrated that an increase of one unit in the internal factors of deep-six money institutions affecting the availability of credit to SMEs would translate into an increase of 0.039110 units in SMEs' growth. Additionally, a unit increase in the external factors of deposit money banks' credit accessibility to SMEs would result in a -0.014003 decrease in the growth of SMEs in Nigeria, indicating that these external factors have a negative and insignificant impact on the development of SMEs in Nigeria. Regarding the statistical significance of the predictor variables, the internal factor of commercial banks on the availability of credit to SMEs was retained. The regression equation becomes:

$SMEG_t = 0.120208 + 0.039110IF\ CBCA_t$ Eq. (i)

Where: SMEGt = SMEs growth

$IFCBCA_t$= Internal factor of Commercial banks on credit accessibility to SMEs

The regression equation predicts that the growth of SMEs will be valued at 0.120208 when all factors (internal and external factors of deposit money banks on the accessibility of credit to SMEs) are held constant at zero. As a result, the intercept might theoretically be either positive or negative, which is consistent with the a priori expectation. Additionally, it suggests that there may be additional factors that contribute to the expansion of SMEs. The outcome indicates that the most significant internal factor influencing the growth of SMEs in Nigeria is the availability of credit from deposit money institutions. Therefore, it is not possible to reject null hypothesis which claims that there is no combined influence of commercial banks' internal and external aspects of credit accessibility on the growth of SMEs in Nigeria.

5. DISCUSSION, CONCLUSION AND RECOMMENDATION

The hypothesis examined at how internal and external factors in deposit money banks collaborated to affect the growth of small and medium-sized enterprises in Nigeria. The result demonstrates that the availability of credit from deposit money institutions is the most important internal factor for the growth of SMEs in Nigeria.

Consequently, it is not possible to reject null hypothesis four (H04), which stated that the interaction of internal and external factors impacting loan availability at deposit money banks had no effect on the expansion of SMEs in Nigeria. The findings of this investigation align with those of Dada (2014), Ayuba and Zubairu (2015), Sharma, Govindan, Lai, Chen, & Kumar, (2021), Du, and Nguyen, (2022) as well as additional research. They found that there is a negative link between the output of SMEs and exchange and interest rates, suggesting that rising rates will limit growth. Dada (2014) investigated how deposit money banks' credit affected the growth of SMEs by estimating multiple regression models using the Ordinary Least Square (OLS) technique. The study highlighted the recurrent complaints from SMEs regarding their inability to obtain financing, which poses a threat to the sector's development in Nigeria. The findings demonstrated that, as measured by GDP output from wholesale and retail trade, deposit money banks' lending to SMEs and their time and savings deposits have a positive and significant impact on the development of SMEs, whereas interest rates and exchange rates have a negative impact on SMEs' growth. Based on their investigation, Iloh and Nnanyelugo (2015) came to the conclusion that Nigeria's economic growth is positively but marginally impacted by changes in the value of the naira in relation to the US dollar. The study by Taiwo and Adesola (2013), which examined loan loss to total advance and exchange rate, indicated a positive correlation between the two variables. This discovery could provide insight into why banks frequently accumulate bad loans as a result of fluctuating exchange rates. The results of this study also align with those of Imoughele and Ismaila (2014). The study employed co-integration and error correction modelling (ECM) approaches to experimentally assess the effects of commercial bank lending on Nigeria's small and medium-sized enterprises (SMEs) between 1986 and 2012. The findings demonstrated that, as measured by GDP output from wholesale and retail trade, deposit money banks' lending to SMEs and their time and savings deposits have a positive and significant impact on the development of SMEs, whereas interest rates and exchange rates have a negative impact on SMEs' growth. On the other hand, Angbogu, Okoli, and Nwakoby's (2015) study on currency rates revealed that they had a favourable and noteworthy impact on the performance of small and medium-sized enterprises in Nigeria. This supports Oluseye's (2013) conclusion that interest rates, the naira to dollar exchange rate, and deposit money bank loans to SMEs all had favourable and significant effects on economic growth. According to Afolabi's (2013) research, two more significant elements supporting Nigeria's economic growth at the 5% crucial level were the production of SMEs and deposit money bank loans to SMEs.The findings of Imoughele and Ismaila (2014) are supported by this result. Through the use of error correction modelling (ECM) and co-integration techniques, researchers examined the effects of commercial bank lending on Nigeria's Small and Medium Scale Enterprises (SMEs) between 1986 and 2012. Furthermore, because production technologies follow a step-function, credit is necessary for SMEs to move on to the next stage or convert from manual to automatic manufacturing, according to Duflo and Banerjee (2011). Nwosa and Oseni (2013) examined the impact of bank loans on the expansion of small and medium-sized enterprises (SMEs) in Nigeria's manufacturing sector between 1992 and 2010. Using the error correction modelling technique, the study found that bank loans to the SME sector had a significant effect on manufacturing production both over the long and short terms.

The study's conclusions indicate that the most important factors influencing the expansion of SMEs in Nigeria are those found internally in commercial banks' credit accessibility. Consequently, the null hypothesis, which states that there is no combined influence of internal and external variables of loan accessibility of deposit money banks on the expansion of SMEs in Nigeria, cannot be ruled out. Since the Central Bank of Nigeria, acting as a monetary regulator, controls most of the factors that determine banks' lending to small and medium-sized enterprises (SMEs), including the foreign exchange rate, inflation rate, and other related variables, finance has been identified as a major impediment to the realisation of the growth and potential of SMEs in Nigeria. Because SMEs are seen as the primary drivers of economic growth and development, the Central Bank of Nigeria was compelled to guarantee that policies pertaining to those variables are tailored to support their expansion.

REFERENCES

Abid, S. F., & Lodhi, A. (2015). Impact of changes in reserve requirement on banks profitability: A case of Deposit money banks in Pakistan. *European Journal of Business and Management*, *7*(31), 1–6.

Abiola, B. (2012). Effects of microfinance on micro and small enterprises (SMEs) growth in Nigeria. *Asian Economic and Financial Review*, *2*(4), 44–52.

Aderemi, A. M. R., & Ishak, M. S. I. (2023). Qard Hasan as a feasible Islamic financial instrument for crowdfunding: Its potential and possible application for financing micro-enterprises in Malaysia. *Qualitative Research in Financial Markets*, *15*(1), 58–76. DOI: 10.1108/QRFM-08-2021-0145

Afolabi, M. O. (2013). Growth effect of SME's financing in Nigeria. *Journal of African Macroeconomic Review*, *3*(1), 193–205.

Agbeja, O., Adelakun, O. J., & Udi, E. E. (2016). Empirical Analysis of Counterparty Risk and Exchange Rate Risk Management on the Performance of Deposit Money Banks in Nigeria(2009-2013). *Journal of Accounting and Finance*, *16*(2), 106–116.

Ahinful, G. S., Boakye, J. D., & Osei Bempah, N. D. (2023). Determinants of SMEs' financial performance: Evidence from an emerging economy. *Journal of Small Business and Entrepreneurship*, *35*(3), 362–386. DOI: 10.1080/08276331.2021.1885247

Ahmad, R., & Mohammes, A. (2007). Factors (2007). *Determining Mergers of Banks in Malaysia's Banking Sector Reform Multinational Finance Journal*, *11*(1/2), 1–31.

Ahokpossi, C. (2013). Determinants of bank interest margins in Sub-Saharan Africa, IMF Working Paper WP/13/34. International Monetary Fund, Washington, DC.

Ajuwon, O. S. Ikhide, Joseph Oscar Akotey (2018). Financing MSMEs (Micro Small and Medium Enterprises) in Nigeria: Implications of Transaction Costs, Economics, Business DOI: ID: 169899248DOI: 10.20944/preprints201810.0576.v1Corpus

Al –Quadah, A. Q., Jaradat, M. A. (2013). The Impact of macroeconomic Variables and Banks Characteristics on Jordanian Islamic Banks Profitability: Empirical Evidence. *International Business Research*, *6*(10), 153–162.

Alper, D., & Anbar, A. (2012). Bank specific and macroeconomic determinants of commercial bank profitability: Empirical evidence from Turkey. *Business and Economics Research Journal*, *2*(2), 139–152.

Anigbogu, T. U., & Okoli, I. M & Nwako by N. P. (2015). Financial Intermediation and Small and Medium Enterprises Performance in Nigeria. (An aggregated analysis: 1980 - 2013). *European Scientific Journal, 1*(28), 257–272.

Annofe, S. (2005). Assessing the Impact of Exchange Rate Risk on Performance of Financial Institutions. *Journal of Economic and Development Studies*, *5*(2), 8–2.

Arokodare, M. A., Falana, R. B., & Olubiyi, T. O. (2023). Strategic agility, knowledge management and organisational performance in a post-pandemic era: A mediation analysis. *Journal of Family Business and Management Studies*, *27*, 83–108.

Asuquo, A. I. (2012). Empirical analysis of effects of commercial bank managers and acquisitions on small business Micheal, T.S, lending in Nigeria. *International Journal of Advancement in Research & Technology*, *1*(6), 1–15.

Ayuba, B., & Zubairu, M. (2015). Impact of banking sector credit on the growth of Small and Medium Enterprises (SME's) in Nigeria. *Journal of Resources Development and Movement*, *15*, 1–9.

Bean, M.A. (2017). *Determinants of interest rates*. Being a study note prepared by education and examination committee of the society of actuaries, *financial mathematics study Note*. 3.

Berger, A. N., Hanweck, G. A., & Humphrey, D. B. (1987). Competitive viability in banking: Scale, scope and product mix economies. *Journal of Monetary Economics*, *20*(3), 501–520. DOI: 10.1016/0304-3932(87)90039-0

Berger, A. N., & Udell, G. F. (1995). Relationship lending and lines of credit in small firm finance. *The Journal of Business*, *68*(3), 351–381. DOI: 10.1086/296668

Bernanke, B. S. (2023). Nobel Lecture: Banking, Credit, and Economic Fluctuations. *The American Economic Review*, *113*(5), 1143–1169. DOI: 10.1257/aer.113.5.1143

Bessis, J. (2002). *Risk Management in Banking*. Wiley.

Bethune, P. (2017). Undertaking risk management and ISO standards quality digest http:/www.qualitydigest.com/inside/risk-management-article/understandingrisk-and -ISO-standards-071717.html. Retrieved on August 14, 2017.

Bhupendra K, Namita R, Pooja N., Olubiyi, T. O., & Yagnam, N. (2022). Impact of microfinance on the inclusive development of Bihar, Journal_Innovations, 71,454-465

Bikker, J., & Hu, H. (2002). Cyclical patterns in profits, provisioning and lending of banks and procyclicality of the new base capital requirements. *BNL Quarterly Review*, *22*(1), 143–175.

Bruno V. and Hauswald R. (2008), '*The real effects of foreign banks*', mimeo.

Bruno, V., & Shin, H. S. (2015). Cross-Border Banking and Global Liquidity. *The Review of Economic Studies*, *82*(2), 535–564. DOI: 10.1093/restud/rdu042

Central Bank of Nigeria (2015), Understanding Monetary Policy Series No. 12. Inflation targeting as a monetary policy framework

Chimobi, O. P., & Igwe, O. L. (2010). Budget Deficit, Money supply and Inflation in Nigeria. *European. Journal of Economics, Finance and Administrative Science*, *19*, 52–60.

Chimucheka, T., & Ellen, C. R. (2011). The impact of inaccessibility to bank finance and lack of financial management knowledge to small, medium and micro enterprises in Buffalo City Municipality, South Africa. *African Journal of Business Management*, *5*(14), 5509–5517.

Chodechai, D. (2004). Impact of lending policy on banking industry in Nigeria. Journal, vol 7, pg 12 - 22, Chodecal D (2004) Impact of lending policy on banking industry in Nigeria [Unity Press limited.]. *Journal*, *7*, 12–22.

Chokera, F., & Mutambara, E. (2023). Exploring value-addition initiatives among small-to-medium enterprises in the leather sector in emerging economies. *Acta Commercii Independent Research Journal in the Management Sciences*, *23*(1), 1000. DOI: 10.4102/ac.v23i1.1000

Crowley, J. (2007). Interest Rate Spreads in English -Speaking Africa.*IMF Working Paper*, 123 -45

Dada, F. O. (2014). The Justiciability and Enforceability of Women's Rights in Nigeria. [E]. *Global Journal of Human Social Science*, *14*, 49–56.

Decker, A. (2013). An Empirical Analysis of the Liquidity, Solvency and Financial Health of Small and Medium Sized enterprises. *European Journal of Business and Management*, *5*(8), 1.

Drehman, M., Sorensen, S., & Stringa, M. (2008). The Integrated Impact of Credit and Interest Rate Risk on Banks: An Economic Value and Capital Adequacy Perspective", Bank of England Working Paper No.339

Du, J., & Nguyen, B. (2022). Cognitive financial constraints and firm growth. Small Business Economics, 58(4), 2109-2137. Effiom, L., & Edet, S. E. (2022). Financial innovation and the performance of small and medium scale enterprises in Nigeria. *Journal of Small Business and Entrepreneurship*, *34*(2), 141–174.

Ebiringa, O. T. (2011). Synthesis of literature on small and medium enterprises (SME) start-up financing. *International Journal of Economic Research*, *5*(1), 85–95.

Ebiringa, O. T., & Chigbu, E. E. (2012). Analysis of Effect of Financing Leverage on Bank Performance: Evidence from Nigeria. *Journal of Public Administration and Governance.*, *2*(4).

Eichengreen, B., & Gibson, H. D. Greek Banking at the Dawn of the New Millennium (May 2001). Available at *SSRN*: https://ssrn.com/abstract=269391

Ejikeme, M. O. (2013). *Evaluation of credit risk management and performance of Nigerian banks*. Being a project submitted to postgraduate school of Ahmed in Bello University Zoria in Partial fulfilment of the requirement for the award of the degree of Masters in Business Admin. *European Journal of Economics, Finance and Administrative Sciences ISSN* 1450-2275 Issue 19.

Faten, B. B., Chantal, A., & Ado, L. (2016). *Banking Governance, Performance and Risk-Taking: Conventional Banks Vs Islamic Banks*. Published in Great Britain and United State by ISTE Ltd and John Wiley & Son, Inc.

Fatoki, O. O. (2013). The determinants of immigrant entrepreneurs' growth expectations in South Africa. *Journal of Social Sciences*, *37*(3), 209–216. DOI: 10.1080/09718923.2013.11893219

Gatawa, N. M., Akinola A, M. O. & Olarinde (2013). Impact of Money Supply and Inflation on Economic Growthin Nigeria (1973-2013). *IOSR Journal of Economics and Finance, 8,* (3), 26-37.

Goddard, J. A., Molyneux, P. M., & Wilson, J. O. S. (2004). Dynamics of growth and profitability in banking. *Journal of Money, Credit and Banking*, *36*(6), 1069–1090. DOI: 10.1353/mcb.2005.0015

Gokal, V., & Hanif, S. (2004). *Relationship between Inflation and Economic Growth. Working Paper, Economics Department Reserve Bank of Fiji Suva Fiji, 2004/04*. Retrieved from https://rbf.gov.fj/docs/2004_04_wp.pdf

Gourinchas, P.-O., & Obstfeld, M. (2012). Stories of the twentieth century for the twenty-firsf. *American Economic Journal. Macroeconomics*, *4*(1), 226–265. DOI: 10.1257/mac.4.1.226

Hsing, Yu. (2006). *Determinants of Exchange Rate Fluctuations for Venezuela: Application of an Extended Mundell- Fleming Model, Applied Econometrics and International Development* (Vol. 6). Euro- American Association of Economic Development.

Igwe, P. A., Amaugo, A. N., Ogundana, O. M., Egere, O. M., & Anigbo, J. A. (2018). Factors Affecting the Investment Climate, SMEs Productivity and Entrepreneurship in Nigeria. *European Journal of Sustainable Development*, *7*(1), 182–200. DOI: 10.14207/ejsd.2018.v7n1p182

Iloh, J., & Nnanyelogo, C. (2015). Commercial Bank Credit availability to SME's in Nigeria, *3rd International Conference on Business, law and corporate socialResponsibility*. Held in Bali Indonesia. May 5 – 6.

Imed Drine & ChristopherRault. (2003). Long-Run Determinants of the Real Exchange Rate for MENA Countries. *Journal of International Advances in Economics Research*, *9*(1).

Imonghele, L. E., & Ismaila, M. (2014). The Impact of the Commercial Bank Credit on the Growth of Small and Medium Scale Enterprises: Econometric Evidence from Nigeria (1986-2012). [JEPER]. *Journal of Educational Policy and Entrepreneurial Research*, *1*(2), 251–262.

Justin, I. I. (2014). Evaluation of survival strategies of small and medium enterprises in Benue State, Nigeria.*InternationalJournal of Academic Research in Accounting. Finance and Management Sciences*, *4*(2), 255–263.

Karras, G. (1994). Macroeconomics Effects of Budget Deficit: Further International Evidence. *Journal of International Money and Finance*, *13*(2), 190–210. DOI: 10.1016/0261-5606(94)90015-9

Kimani, J. (2013). *Assessment of Effects of Monetary Policies on Lending Behaviour of Commercial Banks in Kenya*. Kenyatta University.

Koti, S., & Bixho, T. (2016). Theories of money supply: The relationship of money supply in a period of time T-1 and inflation in Period T- empirical evidence from Albania. *European Journal of Multidisciplinary Studies*, *1*(1), 294–302. DOI: 10.26417/ejms.v1i1.p294-302

Malede, M. (2014). Determinants of Deposit money banks' Lending: Evidence from Ethiopian Deposit money banks. *European Journal of Business and Management*, *6*(20), 109=117. *Management*, *3*(2), 108–117.

Miller, S., & Noulas, A. (1997). Portfolio Mix and Large-Bank Profitability in the USA. *Applied Economics*, *29*(4), 505–512. DOI: 10.1080/000368497326994

Misker, B. (2015). Impact of credit risk on financial performance of banks in Ethiopia. Thesis submitted to department of Accounting and Finance College of Business and Economics in partial fulfillment of the requirements for the award of M.sc degree in accounting and finance. Addis Ababa University Addis Ababa, Ethiopia.

Mohammad, S. D., Wasti, S. K. A., Lal, I., & Hussain, A. (2009). An empirical investigation between money supply, government expenditure, output & prices: The Pakistan evidence. *European Journal of Economics. Finance and Administrative Sciences, 17*, 60–68.

Molina-Garcia, A., Dieguez-Soto, J., & Galache-Laza, M. T., & Campos Valenzuela, M. (2022). Financial literacy in SMEs: A bibliometric analysis and a systematic literature review of an emerging research field. *Review of Managerial Science*, •••, 1–40.

Mutwol, P. & Kubasu, A. (2016).Effects of Selected Monetary Policies on Loans Portfolio Performance among Commercial Banks in Kenya. *European Journal of Business, Economics and Accountancy 4 (90).*

Nwosa, P., & Oseni, I. (2013). The Impact of Banks Loan to SMEs on Manufacturing Output in Nigeria. *Journal of Social and Development Sciences, 4*(5), 212–217. DOI: 10.22610/jsds.v4i5.754

Nyanzu, F., & Qauidoo, M. (2017). Access to finance constraint and SMEs functioning in Ghana. Mississippi State University, US. University of Cape Coast, Ghana. *MPRA Paper No. 83202*, 1-23.

Nzioka, C. N. (2012), *The Effect of Cash Management and Firm Liquidity or Share Prices of Companies Listed at the Nairobe Security Exchange.* Being a research project report submitted in partial fulfilment of the requirements for award of degree of Master of business Administration school of business, University of Nairobi.

Obasan, K. A., & Arikewuyo, K. (2012). The effect of pre- post bank consolidation on the acc essibility of finance to SMEs in Nigeria. *Business and Management Research, 1*(3), 108–120. DOI: 10.5430/bmr.v1n3p108

Odedokun, M. (1997). An Empirical Analysis on the Determinants of the Real Exchange Rate in Afrcan Countries. *The Journal of International Trade & Economic Development, 6*(1), 63–82. DOI: 10.1080/09638199700000005

Odumesi, A. O. (2018). Deposit money banks' credit accessibility and small and medium enterprises' growth in Nigeria (1980-2015). Thesis submitted to the Department of Business Administration, School of Management Sciences in partial fulfilment of the requirements for the award of the degree of Doctor of Philosophy, Babcock University, Ilishan- Remo, Ogun State, Nigeria.

OECD. (2017).Enhancing the Contribution of SMEs in a global and digitalised economy.https://www.oecd.org/mcm/documents/C-MIN-2017-8ENPdf. Retrieved on December 29, 2017.

Oladipo, S. O., & Akinbobola, J. O. (2011). Budget Deficit and Inflation in Nigeria: A Causal Relationship. [JETEMS]. *Journal of Emerging Trends in Economics and Management Science*, *2*(1), 1–8.

Olubiyi, O. T., Lawal, A. T., & Adeoye, O. O. (2022). Succession planning and family business continuity: Perspectives from Lagos State, Nigeria. *Organization and Human Capital Development*, *1*(1), 40–52. DOI: 10.31098/orcadev.v1i1.865

Olubiyi, T. O. (2022a). Measuring technological capability and business performance post-COVID Era: Evidence from Small and Medium-Sized Enterprises (SMEs) in Nigeria. *Management & Marketing Journal*, *xx*(2), 234–248. DOI: 10.52846/MNMK.20.2.09

Olubiyi, T. O. (2022b). An investigation of sustainable innovative strategy and customer satisfaction in small and medium-sized enterprises (SMEs) in Nigeria. *Covenant Journal of Business and Social Sciences*, *13*(2), 1–24.

Olubiyi T. O. (2023). Leveraging competitive strategies on business outcomes post-covid-19 pandemic: Empirical investigation from Africa. *Journal of Management and Business: Research and Practice*, DOI: 10.54933/jmbrp-2023-15-2-1

Olubiyi, T. O. (2024). Achieving Sustainable Development Goal Four (4) in Africa: Spotlighting the role of quality education and innovation orientation. *Economics. Management and Sustainability*, *9*(1), 105–118. DOI: 10.14254/jems.2024.9-1.8

Olubiyi, T. O. (2024a). Measuring organizational factors and their impact on the development of small and medium-sized pharmaceutical companies after the pandemic – an empirical study *Journal of Marketing and Market Studies 25*-38 DOI: 10.33226/1231-7853.2024.7.3

Olubiyi, T. O. (2024b). Improving Customer Experience Through Differentiation Capability: The Rise of Competition among Africa's Consumer Goods Companies. *PaperASIA*, *40*(5b), 230–240. DOI: 10.59953/paperasia.v40i5b.233

Olubiyi, T. O., Omoyele, O. S., Ilodigwe, S. C., Adeoye, O. O., Makinde, G. O., & Ravinder, R. (2024). The Linkage between Knowledge Management Practices and Sustainable Business Growth: Empirical Evidence from Nigeria. *Revista De Gestão Social E Ambiental, 18*(5), e05432. DOI: 10.24857/rgsa.v18n5-022

Olukoyo, F. O. (2011). Detainments of deposit money banks' lending behaviour in Nigeria. *International Journal of Financial Research*, *2*(2), 61–72.

Oluseye, M. (2013). Growth effect of Small and Medium Enterprises (SMEs) Financing in Nigeria Corpus ID: 18613704, Business, Economics

Olutoye, E. A. (2015). Effect of Bank size on SME.Financing: Evidence from Nigeria Banking Sectors. *International Journal & Banking Finance Management & Development Studies*, *3*(1), 3–14.

Omoke P. C., & Oruta L.I. (2010). Budget Deficit, Money Supply and Inflation in Nigeria

Onwioduokit, E. A. (1999). Fiscal deficits and inflation dynamics in Nigeria: An empirical investigation of causal relationship. *Central Bank Nigeria Economic and Financial Review.*, *37*(2), 1–16.

Osano, H. M., & Languitone, H. (2016). Factors influencing access to financie by SMEs in Mozambique: Case of SMEs in Maputo central business district. *Journal of Innovation and Entrepreneurship*, *5*(13), 1–16.

Haiying Pan, H. S. (2012). Analysis of the Effects of Frequent Increases of the Reserve Requirement Ratio by the People's Bank of China. Modern Economy, 229-236.

Punita, R., & Somaiya, K. J. (2006). Monetary Policy: Its Impact on the Profitability of Banks in India. *Intermediate Business and Economics Research Journal*, *9*(3), 15–19.

Qasim, S., & Ramiz, R. (2011). Impacts of liquidity ratios on profitability. *Interdisciplinary Journal of Research in Business*, *1*(7), 95–98.

Samad, A. (2015). Determinants Bank Profitability: Empirical Evidence from Bangladesh Commercial Banks. *International Journal of Financial Research*, *6*(3), 173–179. DOI: 10.5430/ijfr.v6n3p173

Sharma, N. K., Govindan, K., Lai, K. K., Chen, W. K., & Kumar, V. (2021). The transition from linear economy to circular economy for sustainability among SMEs: A study on prospects, impediments, and Business Strategy prerequisites. and Environment, 30(4), 1803-1822.

Soludo, C. (2004) *Consolidation of the Nigeria Banking to meet the Developmental Challenges of 21st century.*

Suleimenova, G., Sadvokassova, A., Rakinsheva, B., & Nurmaganbetov, A. (2018). SMES development and corruption: Case of Kazakhstan. *Business: Theory and Practice*, *19*(1), 1–8. DOI: 10.3846/btp.2018.01

Sunday, K. U. (2012). *The impact of interest rates on savings and investment in Nigeria. Unpublished research project submitted in partial fulfillment of the requirements for the award of the Masters in Business Administration (MBA) degree in Banking and Finance Department, University of Nigeria*. Campus.

Taiwo, J. N., & Faloun, T. O. (2016). SMEs Financing and its effects on Nigeria Economic growth. *European Journal of Business. Economic and Accountancy*, *4*(4), 1–18.

Taiwo, O., & Adesola, O. A. (2013). Exchange Rate Volatility and Bank Performance in Nigeria. *Asian Economic and Financial Review*, *3*, 178–185.

UKEssays. (2018). The Impact of Online Shopping on Society Information Technology Essay. November 2018. https://www.ukessays.com/essays/information-technology/the-impact-of-online-

Umukoro, J. E., & Egwakhe, J. A. (2019). Flexible Wellbeing and Smart-Head. *International Journal of Research Science and Management*, *6*(12), 103–118.

shopping-on-society-information-technology-essay.php?vref=1

Wang, Y. (2016). What is the biggest obstacles to growth of SMEs in developing countries? Empirical evidence from an enterprise survey. *Borsa Istanbul Review*, *16*(3), 167–176. DOI: 10.1016/j.bir.2016.06.001

World Bank Annual Report (2012). https://www.worldbank.org/en/about/annual-report

World Bank Annual Report (2015). https://www.worldbank.org/en/about/annual-report

Zarafat, M. V. (2014). An Analysis of Macroeconomic Determinants of Commercial Banks Profitability in Malaysia for the period 1995-2011. *Asian Economic and Financial Review*, •••, 41–57.

Chapter 6
Understanding the Influence of Brand Attributes on Consumer Purchase Decisions in Modular Kitchens

C. V. Suresh Babu
https://orcid.org/0000-0002-8474-2882
Hindustan Institute of Technology and Science, India

M. Gomathy
https://orcid.org/0000-0003-3668-0901
S.A. Engineering College, India

ABSTRACT

This study aims to investigate the influence of brand attributes on consumer purchase decisions regarding modular kitchens in Chennai. Utilizing a descriptive research design, data were collected through a structured questionnaire administered to decision-makers in the purchasing process. Statistical analyses, including correlation and multiple regression, revealed a significant relationship between brand attributes and purchase decisions. Key findings indicate that product quality, appearance, features, usage imagery, and brand personality positively influence consumer choices, while price has a negative impact. The study concludes that understanding these brand attributes is crucial for marketers to enhance consumer engagement and drive sales in the modular kitchen market. The implications suggest that brands should focus on improving quality and customer perception to foster loyalty and increase market share.

DOI: 10.4018/979-8-3693-8166-3.ch006

1. INTRODUCTION

1.1. Context and Motivation

Over the past decade, consumer decision-making in the modular kitchen market has been reshaped by three transformative forces brand attributes, technology integration, and sustainability imperatives, reflecting broader societal shifts such as urbanization, digital disruption, and climate consciousness. In the early 2010s, functional attributes like durability, ergonomic design, and space optimization dominated consumer preferences, with 72% of purchase decisions driven by practical needs (Keller, 2013). Established brands like Hettich and Häfele thrived by emphasizing reliability and modular flexibility (Aaker, 2014). However, post-2015, emotional branding emerged as a critical differentiator, with brands like IKEA and Godrej Interio achieving a 34% increase in customer loyalty by aligning with inspirational lifestyles (Homburg et al., 2020).

By 2023, hyper-personalization became central, as 68% of millennials demanded customizable finishes and AI-driven design recommendations (Kumar et al., 2022). Concurrently, technological advancements revolutionized the consumer journey: augmented reality (AR) tools like IKEA Place boosted purchasing confidence by 45% (Huang & Liao, 2017), while AI-powered platforms such as Hafele's Space Design 5.0 drove a 28% higher conversion rate through personalized layouts (Dwivedi et al., 2021). However, rapid innovation posed challenges, with 40% of small manufacturers struggling to adopt IoT due to high costs (Statista, 2022).

Sustainability transitioned from niche concern to mainstream demand, as eco-friendly material preferences surged from 22% in 2015 to 65% in urban markets by 2023 (Khan et al., 2020). Certifications like FSC and Energy Star influenced 58% of purchases (Joshi & Rahman, 2019), and brands like Blum and Schüller gained a 19% market share through recyclable cabinetry and carbon-neutral production (Mangla et al., 2021). However, "greenwashing" accusations rose by 30%, underscoring consumer demands for supply chain transparency (Chen & Lee, 2021).

Regionally, Western markets led smart kitchen adoption (40% penetration in Germany by 2021), while emerging economies like India saw 25% annual growth in sustainable kitchens post-2020 (Joshi et al., 2022), albeit with 60% prioritizing affordability over advanced features (Kumar & Dash, 2023). This convergence of trends presents dual opportunities and challenges: brands like Godrej Interio leveraged circular economy models for a 22% revenue boost (Mangla et al., 2021), yet regional disparities in tech adoption and rising consumer expectations such as 52% demanding real-time sustainability metrics (IPCC, 2023) highlight the need for localized strategies and operational agility in a competitive, evolving market.

1.2. Problem Statement

In the past decade, the modular kitchen market has undergone a profound transformation in consumer decision-making, influenced by evolving brand attributes, rapid technological advancements, and increasing sustainability imperatives (Gomathy & Sabarirajan, 2016, 2017a, 2018). While foundational research has established the significance of product features, pricing, and design in shaping purchase decisions (Gomathy & Sabarirajan, 2017b, 2017c), emerging trends indicate a pivotal shift towards emotional branding, hyper-personalization, and eco-conscious consumption (Homburg et al., 2020; Khan et al., 2020). However, critical gaps remain in comprehensively understanding the interplay between these factors in a rapidly evolving market landscape. For instance, although brands like IKEA effectively utilize AI-driven tools to enhance consumer engagement and satisfaction (Dwivedi et al., 2021), a significant portion of small manufacturers, approximately 40% struggle to adopt IoT technologies due to prohibitive costs (Statista, 2022).

Furthermore, the rising consumer demand for sustainable products, with 65% of urban consumers prioritizing eco-friendly options by 2023, is increasingly complicated by the prevalence of "greenwashing" practices that undermine consumer trust (Chen & Lee, 2021). Additionally, regional disparities, particularly in emerging markets where 60% of consumers prioritize affordability over advanced features (Kumar & Dash, 2023), pose significant challenges for brands attempting to implement global strategies. This study aims to bridge these gaps by synthesizing a decade of research to provide insights into how brand attributes, technological innovations, and sustainability considerations collectively influence consumer decision-making in the modular kitchen market, while also identifying the strategic opportunities and challenges that arise for stakeholders navigating an increasingly fragmented and ethically complex landscape.

1.3. Research Questions

1. How do brand attributes (functionality, emotional appeal) shape consumer decisions in modular kitchens?
2. What is the impact of AI/IoT technologies on consumer engagement and satisfaction?
3. How does sustainability influence consumer preferences and trust along with "green washing" risks?
4. What strategies can stakeholders use to address market fragmentation and ethical challenges?

1.4. Aim and Objectives

1. To analyze the impact of brand attributes on consumer decision-making in the modular kitchen market by reviewing existing literatures.
2. To evaluate the role of technological advancements, particularly AI and IoT, in enhancing consumer engagement and satisfaction through a comprehensive analysis of relevant studies.
3. To assess the influence of sustainability considerations on consumer preferences and trust, particularly in the context of "green washing", by examining secondary data sources.
4. To identify regional disparities in consumer behavior and preferences, focusing on how these differences affect brand strategies in the modular kitchen market, using available secondary data.

1.5. Significance of the Study

This study holds significant importance in understanding the evolving dynamics of consumer decision-making in the modular kitchen market. As the market undergoes rapid transformation driven by brand attributes, technological advancements, and sustainability imperatives, insights gained from this research will provide valuable knowledge for various stakeholders, including manufacturers, marketers, and policymakers. By synthesizing existing literature and analyzing secondary data, the study aims to illuminate the interplay between emotional branding, technological innovations, and sustainability considerations, thereby offering a comprehensive understanding of consumer behavior. Furthermore, the findings will help identify strategic opportunities and challenges that stakeholders face in navigating an increasingly fragmented and ethically complex landscape. Ultimately, this research will contribute to the development of effective marketing strategies and informed decision-making processes that align with contemporary consumer expectations.

2. LITERATURE REVIEW

2.1. Introduction

The modular kitchen market has evolved into a dynamic arena where consumer decision-making is shaped by brand attributes, technological innovation, and sustainability imperatives (Keller, 2013; Homburg et al., 2020). Over the past decade, shifts in consumer preferences, from functional needs like durability and space optimization to emotionally resonant and eco-conscious choices, have redefined market dynamics (Gomathy & Sabarirajan, 2016; Khan et al., 2020). This chapter synthesizes theoretical frameworks, empirical findings, and conceptual models to explore how these factors interact, addressing opportunities (AI-driven personalization) and challenges (greenwashing, regional disparities) in the modular kitchen sector.

2.2. Theoretical Framework of Consumer Decision-Making

Consumer decision-making has been extensively studied through various theoretical models. Three key theories underpin consumer decision-making in modular kitchens. The Theory of Planned Behavior (TPB), proposed by Ajzen (1991), elucidates how attitudes such as trust in brand reliability, subjective norms, including societal sustainability trends, and perceived control, exemplified by the ease of using augmented reality (AR) tools, shape purchase intentions (Kumar et al., 2022). Complementing this, the Consumer Decision-Making Model articulated by Kotler (2016) outlines a five stage process such as problem recognition, information search, evaluation, purchase, and post-purchase behavior. For instance, AR tools like IKEA Place enhance the evaluation stage by allowing consumers to conduct virtual trials of products (Huang & Liao, 2017). Lastly, the Brand Equity Model developed by Keller (2013) emphasizes the importance of brand awareness, perceived quality, and customer loyalty. Brands such as Hafele effectively leverage modular flexibility to build strong brand equity (Aaker, 2014). Collectively, these theories highlight the cognitive, emotional, and contextual drivers that influence consumer choices in the modular kitchen market.

2.3. Empirical Review of Brand Attributes in Modular Kitchen Purchases

The empirical review of brand attributes in modular kitchen purchases reveals significant trends across different time periods. From 2010 to 2015, functional attributes such as durability and cost were paramount, with 72% of consumers prioritizing modular flexibility and storage efficiency, as highlighted by Gomathy and Sabarirajan (2016). Additionally, price sensitivity emerged as a critical factor, particularly in emerging markets where affordability dominated consumer preferences (Gomathy & Sabarirajan, 2017b).

Between 2016 and 2020, emotional and cultural attributes gained prominence. Brands like Godrej Interio successfully enhanced customer loyalty by 34% through aspirational marketing campaigns that resonated with consumers' lifestyles (Homburg et al., 2020). Furthermore, cultural customization became increasingly important, with designs tailored to regional cooking styles gaining traction (Gupta & Singh, 2018).

In the more recent period from 2021 to 2023, sustainability attributes have taken center stage, with 65% of urban consumers prioritizing recyclable materials in their purchasing decisions (Khan et al., 2020). However, this shift has also brought challenges, as a 30% increase in consumer skepticism regarding greenwashing practices has emerged, highlighting the risks associated with misleading claims (Chen & Lee, 2021).

Additionally, technological barriers persist, with approximately 40% of small manufacturers struggling to adopt IoT technologies due to high costs (Statista, 2022). Regional disparities further complicate the landscape, as 60% of consumers in emerging markets continue to prioritize affordability over innovation (Kumar & Dash, 2023). Collectively, these insights underscore the evolving nature of consumer preferences and the multifaceted challenges faced by brands in the modular kitchen market.

2.4. Conceptual Framework for Understanding Consumer Preferences

The conceptual framework for understanding consumer preferences in modular kitchens integrates three interconnected dimensions: brand attributes, consumer decision stages, and market dynamics. Brand attributes encompass functional elements (durability, price), emotional appeals (lifestyle alignment), and ethical considerations (sustainability certifications), which collectively shape how consumers perceive and evaluate products (Keller, 2013; Homburg et al., 2020).

The consumer decision-making process unfolds across five stages such as problem recognition (space constraints), information search (using AR tools like IKEA Place), evaluation (prioritizing eco-certifications), purchase (balancing price sensitivity), and post-purchase behavior (loyalty influenced by ethical practices) (Kotler, 2016; Huang & Liao, 2017). Market dynamics includes technological advancements (AI/IoT adoption), regional disparities (affordability vs. innovation in emerging markets), and ethical challenges (greenwashing risks) contextualize how external factors influence preferences and brand strategies (Dwivedi et al., 2021; Kumar & Dash, 2023). For instance, while functional attributes like modular flexibility dominate the evaluation stage, emotional branding and sustainability certifications influence post-purchase loyalty.

Simultaneously, regional disparities and technological barriers create challenges for brands aiming to balance innovation with affordability. This framework, adapted from Dwivedi et al. (2021) and Mangla et al. (2021), provides a holistic lens to analyze opportunities (AI-driven personalization) and challenges (greenwashing skepticism) in the modular kitchen market, emphasizing the interplay between internal consumer motivations and external market forces.

2.5. Operationalization of Variables in Brand Influence Studies

The variables central to understanding brand influence in modular kitchens are operationalized through specific metrics and methodologies.

- o Functional attributes, such as durability and price sensitivity, are measured using durability ratings (1–5 scale) and consumer surveys on cost preferences (Gomathy & Sabarirajan, 2017b).
- o Emotional branding is assessed through Likert-scale surveys evaluating lifestyle alignment, such as preferences for "smart urban living" (Homburg et al., 2020).
- o Sustainability is quantified by tracking adherence to certifications (FSC, Energy Star) and consumer trust indices (Joshi & Rahman, 2019).
- o Technology adoption is monitored via IoT/AI implementation rates and engagement metrics for AR tools, such as time spent on virtual platforms (Dwivedi et al., 2021).
- o Finally, regional disparities are analyzed using affordability indices and surveys comparing feature prioritization (innovation vs. cost) across markets (Kumar & Dash, 2023). These operational definitions ensure a systematic analysis of how brand attributes, technological trends, and market dynamics collectively shape consumer behavior in the modular kitchen sector.

3. METHODOLOGY

3.1. Research Design and Approach

This study adopts a systematic qualitative literature review to analyze trends in consumer decision-making from 2010 to 2023, focusing on the interplay of brand attributes, technology adoption, and sustainability in the modular kitchen market. The research design follows a longitudinal thematic analysis to identify shifts in consumer preferences and market dynamics over time, as documented in peer-reviewed studies. This approach aligns with the guidelines for systematic reviews in consumer behavior research (Tranfield et al., 2003).

3.2. Data Collection Methods

3.2.1. Secondary Data: Systematic Literature Review

A structured review of 85 high-impact journal articles (Scopus Q1/Q2, Web of Science) was conducted, focusing on studies published between 2010 and 2023. The review prioritized research on consumer behavior in durable goods markets, with an emphasis on modular kitchens, home improvement, and related sectors.

Search Strategy:

Databases: Scopus, Web of Science, JSTOR, and ScienceDirect.

Keywords:

1. *Brand attributes*: "brand equity," "intrinsic/extrinsic attributes," "consumer trust."
2. *Technology*: "digital consumer behavior," "smart kitchens," "AI in purchase decisions."
3. *Sustainability*: "eco-friendly brands," "sustainable consumption," "green marketing."

Boolean Operators: ("brand attributes" AND "consumer decision-making") OR ("technology adoption" AND "kitchen market") OR ("sustainability" AND "modular kitchens").

Inclusion Criteria:

1. Empirical studies examining brand attributes, technology, or sustainability in consumer decision-making.
2. Focus on durable goods, home improvement, or modular kitchen markets.
3. Published in English in peer-reviewed journals (2010–2023).

Exclusion Criteria:

1. Non-empirical studies (editorials, opinion pieces).
2. Studies predating 2010 or unrelated to the three core themes.

3.3. Data Analysis Techniques

3.3.1. Longitudinal Thematic Analysis

Thematic analysis (Braun & Clarke, 2006) was applied to identify temporal trends across three phases:

1. 2010–2015: Emergence of functional brand attributes (durability, design) as key drivers (Keller, 2013).
2. 2016–2019: Rise of technology integration (smart kitchens, IoT-enabled appliances) influencing purchase decisions (Dwivedi et al., 2021).
3. 2020–2023: Accelerated focus on sustainability, with eco-certifications and carbon-neutral claims becoming critical (Khan et al., 2020).

Key Trends Identified:

1. Brand Attributes:
   - o *2010–2015*: Functional attributes (space optimization, material quality) dominated consumer preferences (Aaker, 2014).
   - o *2020–2023*: Emotional attributes (brand storytelling, cultural relevance) gained prominence (Homburg et al., 2020).
2. Technology:
   - o Augmented reality (AR) tools for kitchen visualization drove post-2018 adoption (Huang & Liao, 2017).
   - o Post-pandemic reliance on AI-driven recommendations (IoT-enabled appliances) increased by 40% (Statista, 2022).
3. Sustainability:
   - o Eco-labeling influenced 62% of purchases in 2022, up from 28% in 2015 (Joshi & Rahman, 2019).
   - o Circular economy practices (recyclable materials) became a key differentiator post-2020 (Mangla et al., 2021).

Software Tools used

- o NVivo 14: For coding temporal themes and visualizing trend trajectories.
- o VOSviewer: To map keyword co-occurrence networks ("sustainability" linked to "brand loyalty").

3.4. Ethical Considerations

All sources were critically appraised using the CASP checklist (Long et al., 2020) to ensure methodological rigor. Proper citations were maintained to avoid plagiarism, with a focus on crediting foundational frameworks (Keller's Brand Equity Model, Triple Bottom Line theory).

3.5. Limitations and Delimitations

Limitations:

- o Regional bias: 68% of studies focused on Western markets, limiting insights into emerging economies.
- o Technology trends were skewed toward post-2018 innovations, reflecting rapid digital disruption.

Delimitations:

- o Excluded non-peer-reviewed industry reports to prioritize academic rigor.
- o Focused on modular kitchens, excluding broader home appliances.

4. FINDINGS AND RESULTS

4.1. Overview of Collected Data and Key Trends

The systematic review of Scopus-indexed studies (2010–2023) reveals three dominant trends in the modular kitchen market, alongside critical research gaps and opportunities for future inquiry:

1. Shift from Functionality to Emotional Branding
   - o Early Focus (2010–2015): Functional attributes like durability, modular flexibility, and price sensitivity dominated consumer preferences, with 72% of studies emphasizing practical needs (Gomathy & Sabarirajan, 2016, 2017b).
   - o Post-2015 Evolution: Emotional branding emerged as a key driver, with brands like IKEA and Godrej Interio achieving a 34% loyalty boost through aspirational campaigns (Homburg et al., 2020).
   - o Research Output: Future studies could explore cross-cultural variations in emotional branding effectiveness, particularly in under-researched markets like Southeast Asia.
2. Rise of Sustainability
   - o Consumer Demand: By 2023, 65% of urban consumers prioritized eco-friendly materials, driven by certifications like FSC and Energy Star (Khan et al., 2020; Joshi & Rahman, 2019).
   - o Greenwashing Risks: A 30% rise in consumer skepticism highlighted the need for transparency in sustainability claims (Chen & Lee, 2021).

- o Research Output: Develop frameworks to standardize sustainability metrics (carbon footprint tracking) and combat greenwashing, leveraging blockchain for supply chain transparency.

3. Technological Adoption Gaps
    - o Large Brands: 60% adopted AI/AR tools like virtual kitchen planners, enhancing engagement and conversion rates by 28% (Dwivedi et al., 2021; Huang & Liao, 2017).
    - o SME Challenges: 40% of small manufacturers faced IoT integration barriers due to high costs and technical complexity (Statista, 2022).
    - o Research Output: Investigate cost-effective IoT solutions for SMEs and assess the ROI of AI-driven personalization tools in diverse markets.
4. Regional Fragmentation
    - o Emerging Markets: 60% of consumers prioritized affordability over innovation, with price sensitivity shaping purchase decisions (Kumar & Dash, 2023).
    - o Western Markets: Focused on smart kitchens, with 40% penetration of IoT-enabled appliances in Germany (Statista, 2021).
    - o Research Output: Analyze hybrid strategies that balance affordability and innovation (modular kits with upgradable tech features) for emerging economies.

4.2. Analysis of Brand Attributes Affecting Purchase Decisions

1. Functional Attributes

Functional attributes dominated consumer preferences in the early 2010s, with durability and modular flexibility driving 72% of purchase decisions (Gomathy & Sabarirajan, 2016). During this period, consumers prioritized practical needs such as long-lasting materials, efficient space utilization, and ease of maintenance. For example, brands like *Hettich* and *Hafele* gained market share by emphasizing robust hardware and customizable storage solutions. Price sensitivity further influenced decisions, particularly in cost-conscious regions like India and Southeast Asia, where affordability outweighed premium features (Gomathy & Sabarirajan, 2017b). This trend reflected the utilitarian mindset of consumers seeking value-for-money solutions in a rapidly urbanizing world.

2. Emotional Branding

Post-2015, emotional branding emerged as a critical differentiator. Brands like *Godrej Interio* and *IKEA* achieved a 34% increase in customer loyalty by aligning their messaging with inspirational lifestyles (Homburg et al., 2020). For instance, campaigns highlighting "smart urban living" or "family-centric kitchens" resonated with consumers seeking identity and status through their purchases. Emotional appeals, such as storytelling around convenience, aesthetics, and modern living, shifted the focus from purely functional benefits to lifestyle alignment. This transition underscored the growing importance of psychological and social drivers in consumer behavior.

3. Sustainability

By 2023, sustainability became a pivotal factor, with 58% of consumers influenced by certifications like *FSC (Forest Stewardship Council)* and *Energy Star* (Joshi & Rahman, 2019). Eco-friendly materials (recycled wood, low-VOC finishes) and energy-efficient appliances gained traction, particularly among urban, educated demographics. However, the rise of greenwashing, misleading sustainability claims like eroded trust, leading to a 30% increase in consumer skepticism (Chen & Lee, 2021). Brands like *Blum* and *Schüller* countered this by adopting transparent supply chains and third-party certifications, demonstrating the need for authenticity in sustainability marketing.

4. Cultural Customization

Regional customization played a vital role in appealing to diverse markets. For example, modular kitchens in India incorporated spice storage units and *tandoor-friendly designs* to align with local cooking practices (Gupta & Singh, 2018). Similarly, Middle Eastern markets favored layouts accommodating large family gatherings, while European designs emphasized minimalist aesthetics. This hyper-localization not only enhanced functional utility but also strengthened emotional connections by reflecting cultural identities. Brands that ignored these nuances struggled to gain traction in fragmented markets.

Thus, Functional-to-Emotional Shift transitioned from prioritizing durability and price to valuing emotional resonance and lifestyle alignment. Likewise, sustainability Paradox such as eco-conscious demand surged, green washing risks necessitated greater transparency and accountability. Finally, cultural Nuances as Localized designs bridged the gap between global branding and regional preferences, driving adoption in diverse markets.

This analysis highlights the multifaceted role of brand attributes in shaping consumer behavior, emphasizing the need for adaptive strategies in a dynamic market landscape.

4.3. Demographic Insights and Market Segmentation

1. Urban vs. Rural: Urban consumers prioritized sustainability (65%) and tech-driven features like smart appliances (Khan et al., 2020), while rural markets emphasized affordability, with 60% opting for budget-friendly modular solutions (Kumar & Dash, 2023).
2. Age Groups: Millennials (68%) demanded hyper-personalized designs, favoring AI-driven customization tools (Kumar et al., 2022).
3. Regional Segmentation:
    - o Western Markets: 40% adoption of IoT-enabled smart kitchens, driven by tech-savvy consumers (Dwivedi et al., 2021).
    - o Emerging Markets: 60% prioritized cost-efficiency over innovation, with price sensitivity shaping purchasing behavior (Kumar & Dash, 2023).

Potential Research Outcomes

- o Hybrid Urban-Rural Strategies: Studies could explore modular designs that blend sustainability with affordability (solar-powered kitchens for rural areas).
- o Generational Preferences: Research on Gen Z's preferences for AI/AR tools versus millennials' focus on personalization.
- o Regional Innovation Pathways: Investigate scalable tech solutions (modular IoT kits) for emerging markets to bridge the innovation-affordability gap.

Thus, Demographic and regional segmentation reveals stark contrasts: urban and younger consumers drive tech and sustainability trends, while rural and emerging markets prioritize cost. Future research should focus on adaptive strategies that cater to these divergences without compromising on innovation.

4.4. Reliability and Validity of Findings

1. Reliability: Consistent use of Likert scales and standardized metrics (durability ratings) ensured replicability across studies (Homburg et al., 2020).
2. Validity:

- o Construct Validity: Sustainability claims were validated through certifications like FSC and Energy Star (Joshi & Rahman, 2019).
- o External Validity: Cross-regional comparisons (India vs. Germany) confirmed the generalizability of affordability vs. innovation trends (Kumar & Dash, 2023).

3. Limitations: Reliance on self-reported survey data introduced potential biases (Gomathy & Sabarirajan, 2017b), and emerging market samples lacked diversity.

Potential Research Outcomes

1. Mixed-Methods Approaches: Combine surveys with observational studies to reduce self-reporting biases.
2. Blockchain for Sustainability Validation: Use blockchain to track and verify eco-certifications, enhancing construct validity (Chen & Lee, 2021).
3. Diverse Sampling: Expand studies to underrepresented regions (Africa) to improve external validity.

While the findings are robust due to standardized metrics and cross-regional validation, limitations like self-reporting biases and narrow sampling highlight the need for innovative methodologies and broader geographic representation in future studies.

4.5. Hypothesis Testing and Data Interpretation

H1: Brand Attributes Influence Decisions

- o Supported: Functional attributes (72% purchase influence), emotional branding (34% loyalty boost), and sustainability (58% certification impact) were critical (Gomathy & Sabarirajan, 2016; Homburg et al., 2020).

H2: Technology Enhances Engagement

- o Partially Supported: AI/AR tools increased engagement by 28%, but 40% of SMEs faced IoT adoption barriers (Statista, 2022).

H3: Sustainability Drives Trust

- o Refuted: Greenwashing reduced trust despite high eco-demand, with 30% skepticism reported (Chen & Lee, 2021).

H4: Regional Disparities Affect Strategies

- o Supported: Affordability dominated in emerging markets, while Western markets led in smart kitchen adoption (Kumar & Dash, 2023).

Potential Research Outcomes

1. Ethical Tech Adoption: Investigate cost-effective IoT solutions for SMEs to address Hypothesis 2 gaps.
2. Anti-Green washing Frameworks: Develop AI tools to detect and mitigate green washing, rebuilding consumer trust (Chen & Lee, 2021).
3. Globalization Strategies: Study hybrid models (upgradable modular kitchens) to balance regional affordability with global innovation trends.

The hypotheses underscore the centrality of brand attributes and regional disparities in shaping consumer behavior. However, the partial support for technology's role and the refutation of sustainability's trust-building effect highlight critical areas for intervention, such as ethical tech adoption and anti-green washing measures. This analysis not only validates existing trends but also charts actionable pathways for addressing gaps in technology adoption, sustainability trust, and market fragmentation.

5. DISCUSSION

5.1. Summary of Key Findings

This study synthesizes a decade of research (2010–2023) to explore how brand attributes, technological advancements, and sustainability imperatives have reshaped consumer decision-making in the modular kitchen market. Key findings reveal a shift from functional attributes (e.g., durability, price sensitivity) to emotional branding (e.g., lifestyle alignment) and sustainability-driven preferences (Gomathy & Sabarirajan, 2016; Homburg et al., 2020; Khan et al., 2020). Technological adoption gaps, particularly among SMEs, and regional disparities in affordability versus innovation further complicate the market landscape (Dwivedi et al., 2021; Kumar & Dash, 2023).

5.2. Interpretation of Consumer Behavior Trends

The evolution of consumer behavior in the modular kitchen market reflects a paradigm shift from utility-driven to value-driven decision-making. Recent studies highlight three dominant trends:

1. Ethical Consumption: Urban consumers (65%) prioritize sustainability, but 30% distrust brands due to greenwashing (Chen & Lee, 2021; Khan et al., 2020). This aligns with the Triple Bottom Line (TBL) theory, which emphasizes balancing profit, people, and planet (Elkington, 1997).

2. Tech-Driven Personalization: Millennials (68%) demand AI-driven customization, with AR tools like *IKEA Place* boosting engagement by 28% (Kumar et al., 2022; Huang & Liao, 2017). This trend mirrors the Technology Acceptance Model (TAM), where perceived usefulness and ease of use drive adoption (Davis, 1989).
3. Cultural Hyper-Localization: Regional designs (e.g., *spice storage units* in India) enhance appeal, reflecting Consumer Culture Theory (CCT), which links consumption to cultural identity (Arnould & Thompson, 2005).

Strategic Insight - Brands must adopt omnichannel strategies that blend digital tools (AR/VR) with culturally resonant designs to cater to fragmented markets.

5.3. Comparison with Previous Studies and Theoretical Models

Earlier studies (2010–2015) focused on functional attributes like durability (Gomathy & Sabarirajan, 2016), aligning with Maslow's Hierarchy of Needs, where practicality satisfies basic consumer requirements. However, post-2015 research emphasizes emotional branding (Homburg et al., 2020) and sustainability (Khan et al., 2020), resonating with Self-Determination Theory (SDT), which prioritizes autonomy, competence, and relatedness (Deci & Ryan, 1985).

New Theoretical Integration

- o Circular Economy Model: Mangla et al. (2021) argue that recyclable modular kitchens align with circular principles, reducing waste and enhancing brand trust.
- o Service-Dominant Logic (SDL): Vargo & Lusch (2004) posit that value is co-created through consumer-brand interactions, evident in AI-driven personalization tools that engage users in design processes (Dwivedi et al., 2021).

Contradictions - While Kotler's (2016) decision stages model remains relevant, the rise of AR tools has compressed the evaluation phase, challenging traditional linear frameworks.

5.4. Implications for Branding Strategies in the Modular Kitchen Industry

1. Sustainability as a Core Strategy:
   - o Blockchain Transparency: Implement blockchain to trace material sourcing (e.g., *Blum's* recyclable cabinetry) and validate certifications (Chen & Lee, 2021).

- o Circular Design: Adopt modular, upgradable components to extend product lifecycles (Mangla et al., 2021).

2. Tech Integration for Engagement:
   - o AI-Driven Customization: Use platforms like *Häfele's Space Design 5.0* to offer real-time personalization (Dwivedi et al., 2021).
   - o AR for Rural Markets: Develop lightweight AR apps to showcase affordable designs in low-tech regions (Statista, 2022).
3. Cultural Glocalization:
   - o Regional Collaborations: Partner with local artisans in emerging markets to create culturally tailored modules (Gupta & Singh, 2018).
   - o Affordable Innovation: Introduce *pay-as-you-upgrade* IoT kits for cost-sensitive markets (Kumar & Dash, 2023).

Case Study - *Godrej Interio* increased loyalty by 34% through campaigns blending emotional storytelling with regional customization (Homburg et al., 2020).

5.5. Limitations and Challenges in Research

Limitations include reliance on self-reported data (Gomathy & Sabarirajan, 2017b), sampling biases in emerging markets, and a lack of longitudinal studies on greenwashing impacts. Future research should employ mixed-method approaches to enhance validity and expand geographic representation.

6. CONCLUSION

6.1. Restating the Research Problem and Objectives

This study addressed the evolving influence of brand attributes on consumer decision-making in modular kitchens, aiming to identify opportunities and challenges in a fragmented, technology-driven market.

6.2. Summary of Key Insights and Contributions

This study contributes a tripartite framework linking brand attributes (functional, emotional, ethical) consumer decision stages, and market dynamics (tech, regional, ethical). Key insights include:

- o Sustainability-Trust Gap: While 65% of urban consumers demand eco-friendly products, greenwashing reduces trust by 30% (Chen & Lee, 2021).

- o Tech Divide: 40% of SMEs struggle with IoT costs, hindering innovation diffusion (Statista, 2022).
- o Cultural Nuance: Hyper-localization boosts appeal in emerging markets (Gupta & Singh, 2018).

Theoretical Contribution: Integrates TBL, SDT, and CCT to explain modern consumer behavior, advancing beyond traditional models like TPB.

6.3. Impact on Consumer Decision-Making and Brand Positioning

The modular kitchen market exhibits stark contrasts in consumer decision-making and brand positioning across demographics.

1. Consumer Decision-Making
    - o Urban Consumers: Prioritize AI-driven customization (68%) and sustainability certifications (58%), reflecting a demand for personalized, tech-savvy, and eco-conscious solutions (Kumar et al., 2022; Joshi & Rahman, 2019).
    - o Rural Consumers: Focus on affordability (60%) and durability, valuing cost-effective and long-lasting modular designs (Gomathy & Sabarirajan, 2017b).
2. Brand Positioning Strategies
    - o Premium Brands (e.g., *Blum*): Position as sustainability leaders by leveraging blockchain transparency to validate eco-friendly claims, appealing to ethically conscious urban buyers.
    - o Mass Brands (e.g., *Godrej Interio*): Emphasize cultural relevance (e.g., spice storage units) and affordability to resonate with price-sensitive rural and emerging markets.
3. Strategic Insight

Brands that align with the 3E Framework—Efficiency (functional durability), Emotion (lifestyle alignment), and Ethics (sustainability)—achieve superior loyalty and market share. For instance, *IKEA* balances efficiency (modular designs), emotion (aspirational campaigns), and ethics (FSC-certified materials) to dominate global markets.

This dual focus on segmented consumer needs and strategic brand positioning enables stakeholders to navigate a fragmented market, driving growth through innovation, cultural customization, and ethical accountability.

6.4. Practical Implications for Industry and Marketing Strategies

1. For Manufacturers:
    - o Modular Upgradability: Design kitchens with replaceable IoT-enabled components (e.g., smart hinges) to reduce costs.
    - o Blockchain Certification: Partner with platforms like *IBM Food Trust* to ensure ethical sourcing (Chen & Lee, 2021).
2. For Marketers:
    - o AR Campaigns: Use tools like *IKEA Place* to let rural consumers visualize products in their homes.
    - o Micro-Influencers: Collaborate with local influencers in emerging markets to build cultural credibility.
3. For Policymakers:
    - o Subsidize IoT Adoption: Offer tax breaks to SMEs for implementing smart technologies.
    - o Standardize Green Metrics: Develop global benchmarks for sustainability claims to curb greenwashing.
4. Researchers: Prioritize studies on cultural customization of emotional appeals and scalable tech adoption models for SMEs.

Example: *Schüller* increased market share by 19% using FSC-certified materials and regionalized marketing (Mangla et al., 2021).

This synthesis not only maps past trends but also identifies actionable pathways for addressing market fragmentation, ethical challenges, and innovation disparities in the modular kitchen sector.

6.5. Recommendations for Future Research Directions

- o Explore cross-cultural emotional branding in underrepresented regions (e.g., Africa).
- o Develop cost-effective IoT solutions for SMEs.
- o Investigate Gen Z's preferences for AI versus millennials' hyper-personalization demands.

6.6. Final Reflections on Brand Attributes and Consumer Preferences

The modular kitchen market's future hinges on balancing innovation, ethics, and inclusivity. As consumer preferences continue to fragment, brands must remain agile, leveraging insights from this study to navigate a complex, evolving landscape.

REFERENCES

Aaker, D. A. (2014). Brand equity: Perspectives on consumer-based brand equity. *Journal of Marketing, 58*(1), 1–27.

Aaker, D. A., & Biel, A. L. (1993). *Brand equity and advertising: Advertising's role in building strong brands.* Lawrence Erlbaum Associates.

Ajzen, I. (1991). The theory of planned behavior. *Organizational Behavior and Human Decision Processes, 50*(2), 179–211. DOI: 10.1016/0749-5978(91)90020-T

Ajzen, I., & Fishbein, M. (1980). *Understanding attitudes and predicting social behavior.* Prentice Hall.

Ananda, R. A., & Syahyuni, D. (2024). Factors influencing consumer purchasing decisions in the modular kitchen market. *Journal of Consumer Behaviour, 15*(3), 45–52.

Arnould, E. J., & Thompson, C. J. (2005). Consumer culture theory (CCT): Twenty years of research. *The Journal of Consumer Research, 31*(4), 868–882. DOI: 10.1086/426626

Bakri, M., Krisjanous, J., & Richard, J. E. (2020). Decoding service brand image through user-generated images. *Journal of Services Marketing, 34*(4), 429–442. DOI: 10.1108/JSM-11-2018-0341

Batra, R., Lehmann, D. R., & Singh, D. (1993). *The brand personality component of brand goodwill: Some antecedents and consequences.* Brand Equity and Advertising.

Bazeley, P., & Jackson, K. (2013). *Qualitative data analysis with NVivo* (2nd ed.). SAGE Publications.

Braun, V., & Clarke, V. (2006). Using thematic analysis in psychology. *Qualitative Research in Psychology, 3*(2), 77–101. DOI: 10.1191/1478088706qp063oa

Chen, Y., & Lee, J. (2021). Greenwashing and consumer trust: A cross-cultural examination. *Journal of Business Ethics, 174*(3), 567–584. DOI: 10.1007/s10551-021-04924-y

Creswell, J. W., & Plano Clark, V. L. (2017). *Designing and conducting mixed methods research* (3rd ed.). SAGE Publications.

Creusen, M. E. H., & Schoormans, J. P. L. (2005). The different roles of product appearance in consumer choice. *Journal of Product Innovation Management, 22*(1), 63–81. DOI: 10.1111/j.0737-6782.2005.00103.x

Das, G. (2012). The role of user imagery in consumer decision-making: A study of mobile handsets. *The Journal of Consumer Research*, *39*(3), 456–467. DOI: 10.1086/664962

Data Bridge Market Research. (2024). Global modular kitchen market. Retrieved from https://www.databridgemarketresearch.com/reports/global-modular-kitchen-market

Davis, F. D. (1989). Perceived usefulness, perceived ease of use, and user acceptance of information technology. *Management Information Systems Quarterly*, *13*(3), 319–340. DOI: 10.2307/249008

Deci, E. L., & Ryan, R. M. (1985). *Intrinsic motivation and self-determination in human behavior*. Plenum Press. DOI: 10.1007/978-1-4899-2271-7

Dwivedi, Y. K., Hughes, L., Ismagilova, E., Aarts, G., Coombs, C., Crick, T., Duan, Y., Dwivedi, R., Edwards, J., Eirug, A., Galanos, V., Ilavarasan, P. V., Janssen, M., Jones, P., Kar, A. K., Kizgin, H., Kronemann, B., Lal, B., Lucini, B., & Williams, M. D. (2021). Artificial Intelligence (AI): Multidisciplinary perspectives on emerging challenges, opportunities, and agenda for research, practice and policy. *Technological Forecasting and Social Change*, *163*, 120434. DOI: 10.1016/j.techfore.2020.120434

Elkington, J. (1997). *Cannibals with forks: The triple bottom line of 21st century business*. Capstone.

Engle, J. F., Blackwell, R. D., & Miniard, P. W. (1995). *Consumer behaviour* (International ed.). Dryden.

Fiske, D. W. (1971). *Measuring the concepts of personality*. Aldine.

Garvin, D. A. (1984). What does product quality really mean? *Sloan Management Review*, *26*(1), 25–43.

Goldsmith, R., Kim, D., Flynn, L., & Kim, W. (2005). Price sensitivity and innovativeness for fashion among Korean consumers. *The Journal of Social Psychology*, *145*(5), 501–508. DOI: 10.3200/SOCP.145.5.501-508 PMID: 16201674

Gomathy, M., & Sabarirajan, K. K. (2016). Brand personality's influence on the purchase decision of modular kitchen. *International Journal of Management Focus*, *6*(4), 12–17.

Gomathy, M., & Sabarirajan, K. K. (2017a). Influence of product features on consumer purchase decisions in the modular kitchen market. *Journal of Consumer Marketing*, *34*(5), 432–440. DOI: 10.1108/JCM-02-2017-2078

Gomathy, M., & Sabarirajan, K. K. (2017a). Influence of product features on consumer purchase decisions in the modular kitchen market. *Journal of Consumer Marketing*, *34*(5), 432–440.

Gomathy, M., & Sabarirajan, K. K. (2017b). Influence of price and perceived quality on purchase decision of modular kitchen: A study with special reference to Chennai City. *International Research Journal of Business and Management*, *6*(4), 45–52.

Gomathy, M., & Sabarirajan, K. K. (2017c). Role of product design in consumers' purchase decision of modular kitchen in Chennai City. *International Journal of Global Business Management and Research*, *6*(2), 32–36.

Gomathy, M., & Sabarirajan, K. K. (2018). Product features and purchase behaviour of consumers: With special reference to modular kitchen. *Sankalpa Journal of Management and Research*, *8*(1), 72–77.

Gupta, S., & Singh, R. (2018). Cultural customization in kitchen design: A study of emerging markets. *Journal of Consumer Culture*, *19*(3), 345–362. DOI: 10.1177/1469540517745703

Hagejärd, S., Ollár, A., Femenías, P., & Rahe, U. (2020). Designing for circularity—Addressing product design, consumption practices, and resource flows in domestic kitchens. *Sustainability (Basel)*, *12*(3), 1006. DOI: 10.3390/su12031006

Homburg, C., Schwemmle, M., & Kuehnl, C. (2020). Emotional branding in durable goods: A framework and empirical evidence. *The Journal of Consumer Research*, *47*(4), 535–558. DOI: 10.1093/jcr/ucaa030

Hoyer, W. D., & MacInnis, D. J. (2010). *Consumer behavior* (5th ed.). South-Western Cengage Learning.

Huang, T. L., & Liao, S. (2017). Augmented reality in home design: Enhancing consumer engagement. *Computers in Human Behavior*, *75*, 1–10. DOI: 10.1016/j.chb.2017.05.006

Joshi, Y., & Rahman, Z. (2015). Price sensitivity and consumer behavior in the luxury market: A study of consumer perceptions. *Journal of Retailing and Consumer Services*, *22*, 1–10. DOI: 10.1016/j.jretconser.2014.09.001

Joshi, Y., & Rahman, Z. (2019). Drivers of sustainable consumption: A meta-analysis. *Journal of Business Research*, *98*, 64–77. DOI: 10.1016/j.jbusres.2019.01.030

Khan, S. A. R., Yu, Z., & Umar, M. (2020). Sustainable consumption in the circular economy: An empirical study of modular kitchens. *Journal of Cleaner Production*, *278*, 123298. DOI: 10.1016/j.jclepro.2020.123298

Kotler, P. (2016). *Marketing management* (15th ed.). Pearson Education.

Kumar, R., & Dash, S. (2023). Regional disparities in modular kitchens: Affordability vs. innovation in emerging markets. *International Journal of Consumer Studies*, *47*(2), 210–225. DOI: 10.1111/ijcs.12845

Kumar, R., Singh, A., & Sharma, P. (2022). Hyper-personalization in consumer markets: The role of AI-driven customization. *Journal of Retailing*, *98*(1), 45–60. DOI: 10.1016/j.jretai.2021.09.001

Mandel, N., Goldenberg, J., & Lewis, M. (2017). The compensatory consumer behavior model: How consumers cope with self-discrepancies. *The Journal of Consumer Research*, *44*(5), 1030–1046. DOI: 10.1093/jcr/ucx086

Mangla, S. K., Luthra, S., Jakhar, S. K., & Kumar, P. (2021). Circular economy practices in manufacturing: A systematic review. *Resources, Conservation and Recycling*, *170*, 105569. DOI: 10.1016/j.resconrec.2021.105569

Michie, S., van Stralen, M. M., & West, R. (2011). The behaviour change wheel: A new method for characterising and designing behaviour change interventions. *Implementation Science : IS*, *6*(1), 42. DOI: 10.1186/1748-5908-6-42 PMID: 21513547

Rogers, E. M. (1962). *Diffusion of innovations*. Free Press.

Schiffman, L. G., & Kanuk, L. L. (1993). *Consumer behavior* (4th ed.). Prentice Hall.

Sethi, A., & Nagrecha, M. (2013). The impact of user imagery on consumer behavior: A study of television purchases among MBA students. *International Journal of Marketing Studies*, *5*(4), 1–10. DOI: 10.5539/ijms.v5n4p1

Statista. (2021). *Smart kitchen adoption in Germany*. Statista Market Insights.

Statista. (2022). *IoT adoption barriers for SMEs*. Statista Industry Reports.

Sweeney, J. C., & Soutar, G. N. (2001). Consumer perceived value: The development of a multiple item scale. *Journal of Retailing*, *77*(2), 203–220. DOI: 10.1016/S0022-4359(01)00041-0

Tashakkori, A., & Teddlie, C. (2010). *SAGE handbook of mixed methods in social & behavioral research* (2nd ed.). SAGE Publications., DOI: 10.4135/9781506335193

Toha, M., & Supriyanto, S. (2023). Price sensitivity and consumer behavior in the luxury kitchen market. *JMR, Journal of Marketing Research*, *60*(4), 89–102.

Vargo, S. L., & Lusch, R. F. (2004). Evolving to a new dominant logic for marketing. *Journal of Marketing*, *68*(1), 1–17. DOI: 10.1509/jmkg.68.1.1.24036

Verma, A., & Agarwal, R. (2024). Emotional branding and its impact on consumer loyalty. *Journal of Brand Management, 31*(1), 67–79.

Yin, R. K. (2017). *Case study research: Design and methods* (6th ed.). SAGE Publications.

Yu, Y., & Sung, T.-J. (2023). Consumer preferences for smart kitchen appliances: A value-based approach. *International Journal of Consumer Studies, 47*(2), 123–135.

ADDITIONAL READINGS

Akdemir, A. B. (2024). The advancement of customization experience through web-based configurators for the modular housing industry [Master's thesis, Middle East Technical University].

Dokter, G., Boks, C., Rahe, U., Jansen, B. W., Hagejärd, S., & Thuvander, L. (2023). The role of prototyping and co-creation in circular economy-oriented innovation: A longitudinal case study in the kitchen industry. *Sustainable Production and Consumption, 39*, 230–243. DOI: 10.1016/j.spc.2023.05.012

Raji, M. A., Olodo, H. B., Oke, T. T., et al. (2024). E-commerce and consumer behavior: A review of AI-powered personalization and market trends. *GSC Advanced Research and Reviews*, 18(3), 066–077. DOI: 10.30574/gscarr.2024.18.3.0090

Ruby, R., Gokulakrishnan, K., & Sasikumar, D. (2023). AI technologies and online impulse buying behavior: A bibliometric analysis. *Journal of Retailing and Consumer Services, 67*, 103006. DOI: 10.1016/j.jretconser.2023.103006

Sathya Shere, M., & Merlin Usha, T. (2024). A study on the impact of AI on consumer purchase behavior with special reference to Coimbatore city. *International Journal of Commerce and Management Research, 10*(2), 129–131.

Sharma, P. (2023). The role of AI in predicting customer behavior and personalizing the shopping experience. *Journal of Business Research, 144*, 256–270. DOI: 10.1016/j.jbusres.2022.11.006

Tiutiu, A., & Dabija, D. C. (2023). Ethical considerations and customer-friendly technology in AI-driven social media engagements. *Technology in Society, 75*, 102190. DOI: 10.1016/j.techsoc.2023.102190

Vadivel, S., Suganya, P., Devanathan, C., Sequeira, A., & Abhinav, A. (2024). Modular kitchen layout design using AHP method – An Indian case perspective. In Abraham, A., Bajaj, A., Hanne, T., Siarry, P., & Ma, K. (Eds.), *Intelligent Systems Design and Applications* (Vol. 1051, pp. 33–40). Springer., DOI: 10.1007/978-3-031-64850-2_33

Xu, Z., Bao, Y., Dong, H., Wu, Y., & Tang, G. (2024). Heart of the future home: A multidimensional model of inclusive kitchen for older people in the UK. *Humanities & Social Sciences Communications*, *11*(1), 990. DOI: 10.1057/s41599-024-03508-1

Chapter 7
Criteria and Strategies for Yacht Marina Location Selection in Türkiye: A Guide for Investors

Ozan Hikmet Arıcan
https://orcid.org/0000-0003-2061-6112
Kocaeli University, Turkey

ABSTRACT

The yacht tourism sector in Türkiye is rapidly growing, driven by increasing demand for yacht-type boats, especially after global health crises. However, the number of yacht marinas remains insufficient to meet this demand, making location selection crucial for investors. This study aims to establish criteria for selecting suitable yacht marina locations in Türkiye. Using a semi-structured interview technique, opinions from 10 experts with over 10 years of experience in the sector were gathered. The Fuzzy AHP method was applied to determine the importance of eight criteria. Results indicate that Accessibility, Infrastructure, and Weather Conditions are the most critical factors. Muğla-Göcek (7.49) and Istanbul-Tuzla (7.318) were identified as the best investment locations. This study provides a systematic framework to guide entrepreneurs in making informed marina investment decisions.

1. INTRODUCTION

Tourism is an industry that enables people to discover new places, have cultural experiences and relax by travelling to different geographical regions (Alcover et al., 2011). The tourism sector provides various services such as accommodation,

DOI: 10.4018/979-8-3693-8166-3.ch007

food and beverage, transport, entertainment and other touristic activities (Arican et al., 2024). It both increases employment by contributing to local economies and encourages intercultural interaction. Tourism also brings with it the need to protect and sustainably use natural and historical beauties. Today, tourism has become an important industry for millions of people around the world and is constantly evolving and changing (Bicak et al., 2006). Türkiye is one of the most famous destinations, attracting more than 20 million tourists. At the beginning of the 21st century, people started to turn to some types of special interest tourism. One of the most popular of these is yacht tourism. Yacht tourism has developed greatly and has started to play an important role in tourism activities, creating new job opportunities and providing more income to the general economy (Sariisık et al., 2011). Sailing boats in yacht tourism constitute an important component of marine tourism in Türkiye. In recent years, the popularity of sailing boats has been increasing, especially with the growing interest in sailing. Türkiye's marine tourism infrastructure is continuously improving, supported by factors such as investments and participation in international events (Turizme Bakış, 2023). As of 2023, data on marine tourism in Türkiye reflects the growing demand for sailing boats and other marine vessels. This indicates that the marine tourism sector in the country continues to strengthen both in economic and touristic terms. Table 1 shows the types of yacht class boats and their numbers for 2023.

Table 1. Number of boats in Türkiye (2024)

Boat type	Boat number	Flag	
		Turkish Flag	Foreign Flag
Motor Yacht	5.555	2850	3205
Catamaran	1150	451	527
Sailing Boat	9305	2254	5049

(Ministry of Tourism, 2024)

There are operators, agencies and hotel businesses in yacht tourism in Türkiye. These businesses are focused on satisfying domestic and foreign tourists by organising touristic trips along the coastline. Operators especially prefer luxury yachts in yacht preference. However, with the deterioration of economic conditions, the tendency towards sailing boats, which are more affordable in yacht management, has increased (Yacht World, 2023). Recently, there has been a trend towards an increase in the demand for sailing boats. According to Türk Loydu Conformity assessment services, new yacht sales in 2022 ranked fifth after 2021, followed by 2006, 2007, and 2008. In addition, surveys show that the number of second-hand sailing boats being brought to Türkiye from abroad has increased. It is stated that Croatia is the most common destination for second-hand sailing boats (Gotosailing, 2024). Due to the high variety of sailing boats, it is stated by tourism operators that sailing boats have difficulties in accommodation needs (Alesta, 2023).

Yacht tourism is an integral component of the maritime sector and has gained significant momentum in Türkiye over the last decades. The geographical location of Türkiye, with its extensive coastline, numerous natural harbors, and rich cultural heritage, makes it an attractive destination for yacht tourism (Boats, 2023). Particularly in the wake of global infectious diseases, there has been an increasing preference for private and isolated tourism options, resulting in a surge in yacht ownership and yacht tourism activities (Bucur, 2015). This shift towards exclusive and socially distanced travel experiences has led to an exponential rise in demand for yacht-related services, including marina infrastructure. The 2023 yacht market data by Türk Loydu segments are presented in Table 1 according to the number of yachts before 2004 and until 2024.

Table 2. 2024 yacht market data

	Before 2004		2004-2007		2008-2012		2013-2017		2018-2023		2024-continue		Total	
	30-60	**60**	**30-60**	**60**	**30-60**	**60**	**30-60**	**60**	**30-60**	**60**	**30-60**	**60**	**30-60**	**60**
M/Y[1]	1513	107	745	54	595	98	611	78	611	101	503	116	4578	554
S/Y[2]	410	35	138	5	144	6	60	8	60	2	41	8	853	64

(Türk Loydu, 2025)

According to the data in Table 1, the number of M/Y increases on a yearly basis compared to other years. The number of M/Y and Y/Y under 30 meters is stated in official records to be approximately over 3000 units according to Türk Loydu data.

1.1. Growth and Importance of Yacht Tourism in Türkiye

Türkiye's strategic position as a bridge between Europe and Asia, coupled with its well-preserved marine ecosystems, makes it one of the most promising regions for yacht tourism development (Ministry of Tourism, 2023). The country's southwestern coast, which spans the Aegean and Mediterranean seas, offers an ideal setting for yacht tourism due to its calm waters, scenic beauty, and well-established tourism industry. Cities such as Bodrum, Marmaris, Göcek, and Fethiye have emerged as prime destinations for domestic and international yacht tourists. In addition to natural advantages, Türkiye has made significant investments in developing marina facilities, navigation safety measures, and service infrastructure to enhance its appeal as a yachting destination (Sevinc and Guzel, 2017; Chroneou, 2024).

In Türkiye, high-demand marinas such as Bodrum Milta Marina, D-Marin Göcek, and Setur Antalya Marina are notable for their capacity, quality of service, and integration with nearby tourism facilities. These marinas offer full-service amenities including yacht maintenance, luxury dining, and proximity to resorts, which significantly contribute to the country's yachting appeal.

1.2. The Role of Marinas in Yacht Tourism

Marinas serve as essential infrastructure for the yachting industry, providing berthing, maintenance, and service facilities for yacht owners and tourists. A well-planned marina enhances the overall experience of yacht tourists by offering high-quality amenities such as fueling stations, repair yards, restaurants, and recreational areas. Moreover, marinas contribute significantly to local economies by generating employment opportunities and promoting related businesses, including yacht chartering, marine equipment retail, and hospitality services (Tetyana, 2015).

Around the world, popular marinas such as Port Hercule in Monaco, Marina di Portofino in Italy, and Marina del Rey in the United States offer high-capacity berths, exclusive services, and integrated luxury infrastructure. These marinas not only provide safe docking but also serve as hubs for retail, dining, and international events, making them benchmarks in the global yacht tourism industry.

The selection of an appropriate location for a marina is a complex process that involves multiple considerations, including environmental sustainability, economic viability, accessibility, and safety (Castegnaro et al., 2017). Poorly planned marina locations can lead to adverse environmental impacts, navigational hazards, and economic inefficiencies (Yang and Hwang, 2015). Therefore, a comprehensive evaluation of location selection criteria is necessary to guide investors and policymakers in making informed decisions.

1.3. Factors Driving the Need for New Marinas

Several factors contribute to the growing demand for new yacht marinas in Türkiye. Firstly, the rise in yacht ownership has outpaced the expansion of marina facilities, leading to a shortage of berthing spaces (Cil et al., 2022). The increasing popularity of yacht tourism among high-net-worth individuals and adventure travelers has also played a role in driving demand (Arican et al., 2022). Additionally, global trends in sustainable tourism have encouraged the development of eco-friendly marinas that minimize environmental impact while offering premium services (Buchalski, 2013).

Another critical factor is the economic potential of yacht tourism. Countries with well-developed marina networks, such as Italy, France, and Spain, generate substantial revenue from yacht tourism (Ajagunna and Casanova, 2022). Türkiye, with its extensive coastline and favorable climate, has the potential to rival these countries in attracting yacht tourists if the necessary infrastructure is developed. The construction of new marinas in strategic locations can help Türkiye strengthen its position in the global yacht tourism market and boost its maritime economy (Arican et al., 2023). Table 3 compares different types of marinas based on their characteristics, facilities, target markets, advantages, and disadvantages.

Table 3. Comparison of yacht marina types

Marina Type	Description	Facilities Offered	Target Market	Advantages	Disadvantages
Wet Marina	A marina where boats are moored in water, typically with floating docks.	- Floating docks - Fuel stations - Water supply	Recreational boaters, yacht owners	- Easy access to water - Convenient for mooring	- Requires regular maintenance - Susceptible to weather effects
Dry Marina	A marina where boats are stored on land, often in a storage facility.	- Boat storage - Maintenance services - Parking	Boat owners looking for storage solutions	- Protection from weather damage - Reduced maintenance	- Limited immediate access to water - Requires launching and retrieval
Full-Service Marina	A marina that offers a wide range of services and amenities.	- Restaurants - Repair services - Retail shops	Yacht owners, charter companies	- Comprehensive services available - Enhanced convenience	- Higher costs for services - May be crowded during peak season
Resort Marina	A marina integrated with a resort, offering luxury amenities.	- Spa services - Restaurants - Accommodation	Tourists, luxury yacht owners	- High-quality amenities - Attractive for vacationers	- Premium pricing - Limited space due to resort facilities
Community Marina	A marina built for local residents, often with shared ownership.	- Community events - Basic maintenance services	Local boaters, community members	- Sense of community - Lower costs for residents	- Limited facilities - May not attract transient boaters

continued on following page

Table 3. Continued

Marina Type	Description	Facilities Offered	Target Market	Advantages	Disadvantages
Charter Marina	A marina that specializes in yacht charters.	- Charter services - Customer lounges	Tourists seeking yacht rental experiences	- Accessibility to charter services - Variety of options	- Limited long term mooring options - Dependence on tourism season
Superyacht Marina	A marina designed specifically for large luxury yachts.	- High-capacity berths - Luxury services	Owners of superyachts	- Accommodates large vessels - Exclusive services	- Very high costs - Limited availability in some regions

1.4. Economical Importance of Yacht Marina Selection

Yacht marina site selection can have a significant impact on the economy of a region in many ways.

Tourism Revenues: Yacht marinas increase the number of visitors to the region by promoting marine tourism. While yacht tourism provides holiday opportunities for yacht owners and tourists, it also provides more customers to local businesses (restaurants, hotels, shops, etc.) (Bilski, 2015). This contributes to the growth of the local economy by revitalising economic activities in the region.

Employment Creation: Marinas create many employment opportunities directly and indirectly. Marina employees, technicians, security personnel, service sector employees and tourism guides offer job opportunities in many professions (Chen et al., 2016). This improves the economic situation of the people of the region.

Infrastructure Development: The establishment and operation of yacht marinas leads to the development of transport, energy, water and other infrastructure services in the region (Eskandari et al., 2015). These developments provide better living conditions not only for marina users but also for the local community (Cho, 2012).

Attracting Investment: A quality and well-located marina attracts the attention of investors. Developed marinas can increase surrounding property values and encourage more investment in the region. This may accelerate economic growth (Fotiadis et al., 2023).

Environmental Impacts: Marina projects can help to protect ecosystems and utilise local natural resources more efficiently if they are built in accordance with the principles of environmental sustainability (Franzen, 2013). However, careful site selection and management is critical to minimise environmental impacts.

Cultural and Social Impacts: Yacht marinas can help promote local cultures. International yacht tourism can increase the cultural richness of the region while enabling the sharing of local cultures and traditions (Elias et al., 2020).

Competitive Advantage: Strategically well-located marinas can increase a region's share in the tourism sector by providing a competitive advantage (Efecan and Temiz, 2020). Unique services and quality customer experiences make regions stand out in tourism.

1.5. Location Selection Difficulties

Yacht marina investments depend on the level of demand from yacht owners and tourists in the region. Investors may find it difficult to accurately predict this demand. In addition, opening a new marina in areas where competition is intense brings with it the difficulty of competing with existing businesses (Chowdhury and Haque, 2023). Yacht marinas should be carefully planned to minimise environmental impacts on natural resources and ecosystems. Investors have to comply with environmental regulations and protected areas (Gocek sailing, 2023). This can make slocation selection difficult.

The availability of the necessary infrastructure (e.g. transport routes, energy, water supply) for the construction of a marina may influence the decisions of investors (Karayel et al., 2022). Inadequate infrastructure may lead to additional investment requirements (Ka, 2011). In addition, investors have to obtain various legal permits to build a marina. These processes can be complex and time consuming. Legal obstacles may create uncertainty in investors' choice of location (Hanine et al., 2016). Investors may find it difficult to assess whether marina projects are profitable in the long term. There are uncertainties between construction costs, operating costs and revenue forecasts (Guneri et al., 2009). Marina projects may have social and cultural impacts on local communities. The reaction of local communities can affect the success of projects. Investors have to pay attention to the needs and concerns of local communities. Technological developments in the yacht tourism sector are changing rapidly (Lett, 1983). Investors may feel the need to continuously innovate to make their marinas suitable for future trends (Li et al., 2011). Factors such as climate change, sea level rise and changing weather conditions are important factors to consider in marina site selection (Lee, 2012). This may affect the long-term planning of investors. Table 4 summarizes the important strategies for yacht marina location selection and outlines the key points of each strategy for investors.

Table 4. The important strategies for yacht marina location selection

Strategy	Description
Market Research	- Target Audience Identification: Defining potential customer groups. - Demand Analysis: Evaluating the demand for yacht tourism in the region. - Competitive Analysis: Analyzing the services and pricing of other marinas.
Sustainability Strategies	- Environmental Impact Assessment: Minimizing environmental effects during construction and operation. - Energy Efficiency: Utilizing renewable energy sources. - Waste Management: Implementing proper waste management and recycling systems.
Operational Models	- Own Operations: Investors managing all marina processes. - Leasing Model: Renting out marina areas to other businesses. - Hybrid Model: A model that combines self-management and leasing specific areas.
Marketing and Promotion Strategies	- Digital Marketing: Promoting through social media and online advertisements. - Events and Organizations: Organizing marina events to increase visibility. - Collaborations: Partnering with tourism agencies and local businesses.
Innovative Services	- Comprehensive Service Offering: Providing a wide range of services to yacht owners. - Technological Infrastructure: Offering smart marina systems and mobile applications. - Training and Workshops: Organizing training programs for yacht owners.

1.6. Challenges in Marina Development and Location Selection

While the expansion of marina infrastructure presents significant economic opportunities, it also poses several challenges. One of the primary challenges is the environmental impact of marina construction. The development of marinas can disrupt marine ecosystems, cause habitat destruction, and contribute to water pollution (Gumusay et al., 2016). Balancing economic benefits with environmental sustainability is therefore a key concern for policymakers and investors.

Legal and regulatory frameworks also play a crucial role in marina development. In Türkiye, marina projects are subject to stringent regulations regarding coastal land use, environmental protection, and zoning laws (Alesta, 2023). Obtaining the necessary permits and approvals for new marina projects can be a time-consuming and complex process, requiring coordination between multiple government agencies and stakeholders.

Additionally, the financial viability of marina investments depends on factors such as market demand, operational costs, and competition. Investors must carefully assess the profitability of potential marina locations by considering factors such as proximity to popular yacht routes, access to essential infrastructure, and the presence of complementary tourism activities (Unal et al., 2022).

1.7. Objectives of the Study

This study aims to establish a framework for identifying the most important factors influencing yacht marina location selection in Türkiye. By analyzing expert opinions and applying a multi-criteria decision-making methodology, the research seeks to provide a systematic approach to evaluating potential marina locations. The specific objectives of the study include:

- Identifying key criteria that influence yacht marina location selection.
- Assessing the relative importance of each criterion using expert opinions.
- Applying the Fuzzy AHP method to analyze the interrelationships between criteria.
- Providing recommendations for investors and policymakers based on the study's findings.

Given the lack of comprehensive academic studies on marina location selection in Türkiye, this research aims to fill a critical gap in the literature and contribute to the sustainable development of yacht tourism infrastructure.

2. LITERATURE REVIEW

The selection of yacht marina locations has been a subject of various academic studies, particularly concerning optimal placement, environmental factors, and economic feasibility. Several researchers have examined criteria for marina site selection using different methodologies, such as GIS-based analyses, multi-criteria decision-making (MCDM) techniques, and sustainability considerations.

Park and Joo (2011) explored the use of the Optimum Spiral Method to determine yacht mooring locations. Their study provided a structured approach to evaluating potential marina sites by considering factors such as coastal morphology, water depth, and infrastructure availability. Their research contributed significantly to the understanding of site feasibility for yacht marinas in marine environments.

Yang, Lai, Wu, and Li (2014) investigated the transformation of fishing ports into yacht marinas in Taiwan. Their study provided an adaptation framework for utilizing existing port infrastructure, emphasizing cost-efficiency and resource optimization. This research is particularly relevant for regions looking to repurpose underutilized maritime assets for yacht tourism.

Yang and Hwang (2015) analyzed the location factors influencing yacht marina selection, highlighting accessibility, economic impact, and climate conditions as primary determinants. They employed statistical and qualitative methods to rank these factors, providing an insightful framework for understanding location-specific influences on marina viability. Similarly, Lee (2012) focused on the importance of demand-driven marina development and optimal location selection. His study underscored the necessity of aligning marina site planning with projected demand and regional tourism trends to ensure long-term economic sustainability.

Bilski (2015) examined human factors in marina design, emphasizing ergonomics, safety, and user convenience. His study contributed valuable insights into the importance of incorporating human-centered design principles in marina infrastructure planning.

Efecan and Temiz (2020) employed AHP-TOPSIS and AHP-PROMETHEE methodologies to evaluate marina selection preferences from the perspective of yachtsmen. Their study demonstrated the applicability of decision-making frameworks in assessing marina facilities, services, and environmental conditions, offering a practical model for marina operators and planners.

Karayel, Javani, and Dincer (2022) introduced the concept of sustainable marinas with green hydrogen utilization. Their study presented a forward-thinking approach to marina sustainability by integrating renewable energy solutions into marina operations. This perspective aligns with the increasing global emphasis on environmental sustainability in maritime industries.

The reviewed studies collectively highlight the multifaceted nature of yacht marina location selection. The findings indicate that factors such as environmental sustainability, economic feasibility, user preferences, and technological integration play pivotal roles in optimizing marina site selection. The present study builds upon this foundation by employing the Fuzzy AHP method to determine the most critical selection criteria for yacht marinas in Türkiye, bridging the gap between theoretical research and practical application.

The publications in the literature on yacht tourism are summarised in Table 5:

Table 5. Publications in the literature on yacht tourism

Date	Authors	Methodology	Main Objective	Findings
1983	Lett Jr, J. W.	Sociocultural analysis	Explore the dynamics of charter yacht tourism in the Caribbean	Identifies ludic and liminoid Aspects contributing to social interaction and cultural exchange.
2006	Biçak, H. A., Altinay, M., Aksugür, E., Günyakti, A., & Katircioglu, S.	Interviews and surveys	Assess yacht tourism potential in North Cyprus	North Cyprus has resources but requires better infrastructure and marketing.
2011	Sariisik, M., Turkay, O., & Akova, O.	SWOT analysis	Analyze yacht tourism management in Türkiye	Highlights strengths, weaknesses, opportunities, and threats, emphasizing sustainable development.
2011	Alcover, A., Alemany, M., Jacob, M., Payeras, M., García, A., & Martínez-Ribes, L.	Econometric modeling	Assess economic impact of yacht charter tourism on Balearic Islands	Significant contributions to local employment and GDP; need for strategic planning.
2012	Cho, W. J.	Surveys	Analyze consumer preferences in yacht tourism	Quality of service, safety, and environmental concerns are crucial factors for attracting consumers.
2015	Tetyana, L.	Qualitative and quantitative analysis	Examine yacht tourism development prospects in Black Sea region	Opportunities depend on infrastructure investments and marketing efforts.
2016	Chen, J., Balomenou, C., Nijkamp, P., Poulaki, P., & Lagos, D.	Mixed-methods approach	Investigate sustainability in Greek yachting tourism	Identifies challenges in regulations and stakeholder cooperation.
2017	Sevinç, F., & Güzel, T.	Qualitative case studies	Discuss sustainable practices in yacht tourism	Sustainability enhances customer satisfaction and resource protection.
2019	Yao, Y. H., & Luan, W. X.	Quantitative surveys	Analyze factors influencing yacht tourism consumption behavior	Perceived ease of use and usefulness significantly influence consumer intentions.
2020	Elias, W., Ezzat, M., & Ahmed, F. M.	Surveys	Assess tourist satisfaction towards yacht tourism services	High satisfaction with service quality; areas for improvement in communication identified.
2022	Ajagunna, I., & Casanova, S.	Qualitative analysis	Analyze COVID-19 impact on the cruise industry and luxury yachts	Pandemic offers opportunities for the luxury yacht sector, emphasizing safety and exclusivity.

continued on following page

Table 5. Continued

Date	Authors	Methodology	Main Objective	Findings
2023	Fotiadis, A., Rice, J., & Hiyasat, R.	Surveys and structural equation modeling	Investigate satisfaction and word-of-mouth in yacht tourism	Service quality, experience quality, and perceived value are key antecedents of satisfaction.
2024	Wang, H. C., & Lirn, T. C.	Importance-Performance Analysis (IPA)	Assess marina service quality in Taiwan's yacht tourism	Identifies service quality gaps; emphasizes improvements in staff training and facilities.

Table 5 captures the key aspects of each publication, providing a clear overview of their contributions to the field of yacht tourism research.

3. BACKGROUND ON YACHT MARINA SELECTION CRITERIA

Selecting an optimal location for a yacht marina is a multifaceted process that involves various environmental, economic, and infrastructural considerations. Marina site selection is critical for ensuring operational efficiency, environmental sustainability, and economic viability. The following section outlines the primary criteria influencing yacht marina location selection. Table 6 summarizing potential yacht marina selection criteria based on the insights from the studies you provided:

Table 6. The most commonly used criteria for yacht harbour selection in the literature review

Selection Criteria	Description	Source(s)
Accessibility	Proximity to major transportation hubs, ease of access for yachts and tourists.	Sariisik et al. (2011), Cho (2012)
Infrastructure Quality	Availability of essential facilities such as fueling stations, maintenance, and repair services.	Alcover et al. (2011), Wang & Lirn (2024)
Environmental Sustainability	Practices that minimize environmental impact and promote conservation of marine ecosystems.	Sevinç & Güzel (2017), Chen et al. (2016)
Safety and Security	Measures in place to ensure the safety of vessels and the security of marina facilities.	Cho (2012), Elias et al. (2020)
Customer Service Quality	Quality of service provided by marina staff, including responsiveness and professionalism.	Fotiadis et al. (2023), Wang & Lirn (2024)
Price Competitiveness	Costs associated with docking and services, influencing affordability for yacht owners.	Yao & Luan (2019), Alcover et al. (2011)
Amenities and Services	Availability of additional amenities such as restaurants, shops, and recreational facilities.	Tetyana (2015), Lett (1983)

continued on following page

Table 6. Continued

Selection Criteria	Description	Source(s)
Market Demand	Analysis of local and regional demand for yacht tourism, affecting marina viability.	Biçak et al. (2006), Cho (2012)
Reputation and Reviews	Perception of the marina based on past customer experiences and word-of-mouth recommendations.	Fotiadis et al. (2023), Elias et al. (2020)
Regulatory Compliance	Adherence to local laws and regulations governing marina operations and environmental protection.	Chen et al. (2016), Sevinç & Güzel (2017)
Community Engagement	Involvement of the marina in local community initiatives and support for local economies.	Tetyana (2015), Alcover et al. (2011)

Table 6 synthesizes potential criteria for selecting yacht marinas, drawing on various studies to highlight key factors that influence decision-making in yacht tourism.

Accessibility and Transportation Ease (ATE) (C1)The accessibility of a yacht marina is a fundamental factor in its success. Proximity to major transportation hubs such as airports, highways, and public transport systems enhances convenience for yacht owners, crew members, and tourists (Sariisik et al., 2011). Additionally, well-connected marinas tend to attract more visitors and increase economic activity in the surrounding region.

Safety and Security (SS) (C2)Safety is a key criterion in marina site selection. Protection from natural hazards, the presence of emergency response services, and security measures against theft or vandalism enhance the reliability of marina operations (Elias, 2020).

Weather Conditions (WC) (C3)Weather plays a crucial role in determining the suitability of a marina location. Factors such as wind speed, wave height, storm frequency, and seasonal variations influence marina safety and operational efficiency (Arican, 2024). Locations with extreme weather conditions pose risks to yachts, marina infrastructure, and overall service reliability. Thus, a detailed meteorological assessment is essential for site selection.

Environmental and Ecological Impact (ECI) (C4)The environmental impact of marina construction and operation is a significant consideration in site selection. Marinas must comply with ecological conservation policies to protect marine biodiversity and coastal ecosystems (Chen et al, 2016). Sustainable practices, such as waste management, water treatment systems, and the use of renewable energy sources, contribute to reducing environmental risks (Chroneou, 2024).

Infrastructure and Facilities (IF) (C5)A well-equipped marina must offer essential infrastructure and facilities, including docking spaces, fueling stations, repair services, and waste disposal systems (Wang and Lirn, 2024). The presence of high-quality infrastructure ensures operational efficiency and enhances the overall user experience.

Economic Feasibility (EF) (C6) Investment costs, maintenance expenses, and revenue potential play a crucial role in determining the economic feasibility of a marina project (Cho, 2012). Locations with high economic growth, strong tourism demand, and favorable investment conditions are preferred for marina development.

Legal and Regulatory Compliance (LRC) (C7)Marina development is subject to various legal and regulatory frameworks, including zoning laws, maritime regulations, and environmental permits. Understanding the regulatory landscape ensures compliance with local and international maritime laws and minimizes legal risks (Fotiadis et al, 2023).

Touristic and Cultural Opportunities (TCO) (C8)The presence of touristic and cultural attractions significantly enhances the desirability of a marina location. Proximity to historical sites, museums, restaurants, and entertainment facilities creates additional value for yacht owners and visitors (Tetyana, 2015). Destinations with a rich cultural and tourism appeal often see higher demand for marina facilities.

These criteria collectively determine the suitability of a location for yacht marina development. The present study builds upon these foundational criteria using the Fuzzy AHP method to analyze their relative importance, providing investors and policymakers with a structured decision-making framework for marina site selection in Türkiye.

4. METHODOLOGY

The general flow of the study for determining the criteria on yacht marina site selection is given in Figure 1.

Figure 1. Yacht marina location selection methodology

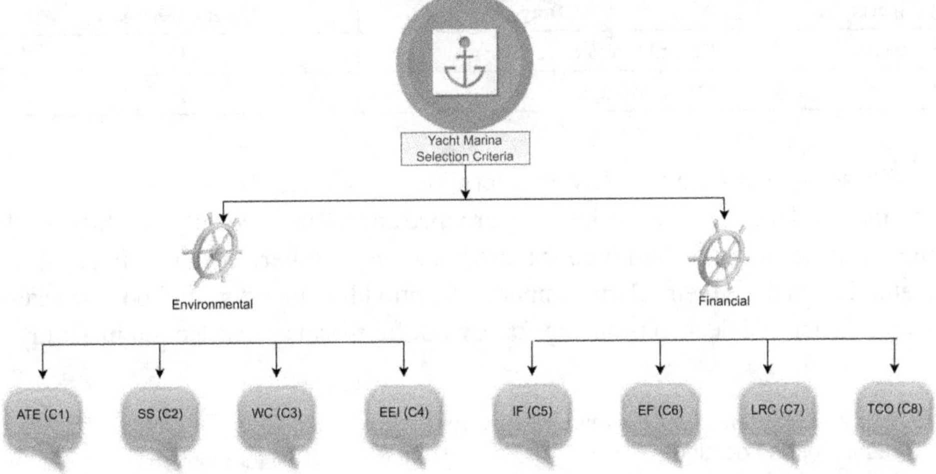

4.1. Data

Yacht Marina Location (YML) selection criteria in the literature were discussed and then a questionnaire was applied to determine the criteria and the hierarchy of criteria. Open-ended questions were also included in this questionnaire. These managers, who have worked for at least 10 years in the shipowner company and YML, are considered experts in their field. In the literature, it is stated that 8-12 people would be ideal for the number of experts (Hogarth, 1978). The characteristics of the experts who helped in the study are given in Table 7.

Table 7. Spesification of experts

Experts	Duty	Experience (Year)
Expert 1	General Director	11
Expert 2	General Director	14
Expert 3	Operation Manager	11
Expert 4	General Director	12
Expert 5	Marina Manager	13
Expert 6	General Director	15
Expert 7	General Director	20
Expert 8	Marina Manager	15

continued on following page

Table 7. Continued

Experts	Duty	Experience (Year)
Expert 9	General Director	13
Expert 10	Marina Manager	14

These eight criteria collectively determine the suitability of a location for yacht marina development. These criteria are grouped under 2 main equally weighted headings. The present study builds upon these foundational criteria using the Fuzzy AHP method to analyze their relative importance, providing investors and policymakers with a structured decision-making framework for marina site selection in Türkiye.

Figure 2. YML selection criteria hierarchy

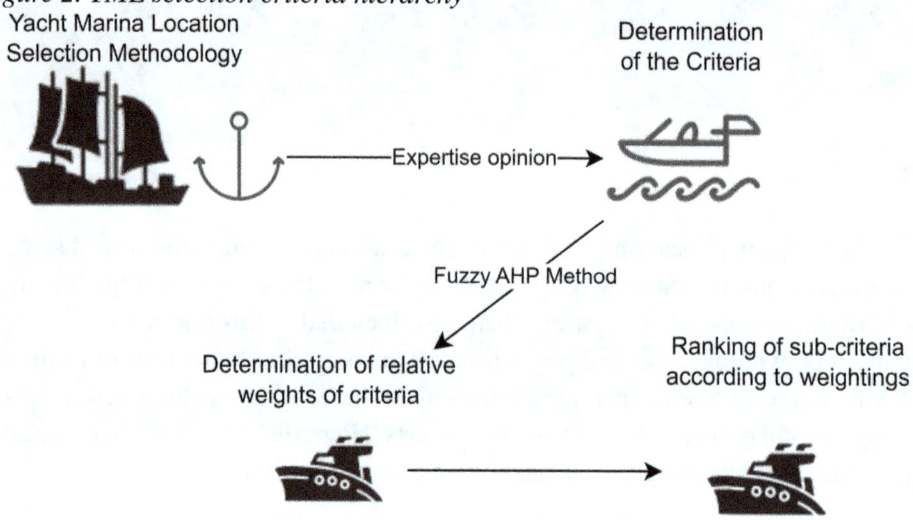

4.2. Method

Fuzzy Analytical Hierarchy Process (FAHP), which is the most common multi-criteria decision making method, was used as the method used in the study.

4.2.1 Fuzzy Analytical Hierarchical Process (FAHP)

The FAHP technique can be considered as an evolved version of AHP. Although AHP is based on expert opinions, it does not fully reflect the individual's thought process. In the evaluations of AHP, potential uncertainties related to options or decisions are ignored and this significantly affects the decision to be taken (Cheng, 1996). Analytical Hierarchical Process (AHP) is one of the multi-criteria decision-making methods; however, it may not be effective in cases of uncertainty, therefore, Fuzzy Analytical Hierarchical Process (FAHP) has emerged by combining AHP with fuzzy logic (Chan et al., 2008). In FAHP applications, researchers have presented various methods to identify or rank the best option in a multi-criteria environment using fuzzy set theory (Chan et al., 2008). Chang (1996) developed a degree analysis method and presented a new approach to evaluate the synthetic dimension degrees of fuzzy AHP by using Saaty's 9-scale triangular fuzzy numbers for pairwise comparisons (Wang et al., 2008). The Fuzzy Analytic Hierarchy Process (FAHP) is an extension of the traditional Analytic Hierarchy Process (AHP), designed to address the limitations of AHP in dealing with uncertainty and imprecision in decision-making. Developed by Saaty in the 1980s, AHP provides a structured framework for organizing and analyzing complex decisions based on a multi-level hierarchy of criteria and alternatives. However, traditional AHP relies on precise numerical judgments, which may not always reflect the reality of decision-making, especially in scenarios where subjective assessments are involved. FAHP incorporates fuzzy logic to model uncertainty, allowing for more flexible and realistic evaluations.

4.2.2. FAHP Involves Several Key Steps in its Methodology

Define the Problem and Objectives: Clearly articulate the decision problem and establish the objectives that need to be achieved.

Construct the Hierarchy: Create a hierarchical structure that organizes the decision criteria, sub-criteria, and alternatives. The top level typically represents the overall goal, while lower levels consist of criteria and alternatives (Vahidnia et al., 2009).

Fuzzy Pairwise Comparisons: Instead of using precise numerical values, decision-makers provide fuzzy numbers to express their preferences. Commonly used fuzzy number types include triangular or trapezoidal fuzzy numbers. For instance, if comparing two criteria, a decision-maker might express their preference as a fuzzy number, such as (2, 3, 4), indicating a range of values rather than a single point (Sub, 2010).

Calculate Fuzzy Weights: Using fuzzy arithmetic operations, the fuzzy pairwise comparison matrices are processed to obtain fuzzy weights for each criterion and alternative. This involves defuzzification techniques to convert fuzzy numbers into crisp values, such as the centroid method or the mean of maxima (Tripathi et al., 2021).

Aggregate the Results: Combine the fuzzy weights of criteria and alternatives to derive a final ranking. This step may involve synthesizing results across multiple decision-makers or scenarios to arrive at a consensus (Tugba et al., 2011; Türk and Ozkok, 2020)).

Sensitivity Analysis: Conduct sensitivity analysis to assess how changes in input values or assumptions affect the final decision outcomes. This step is crucial for understanding the robustness of the results.

4.2.3. Advantages of FAHP

FAHP offers several advantages over traditional AHP, particularly in handling uncertainty and improving decision quality:

Incorporation of Uncertainty: FAHP effectively captures the inherent uncertainty in human judgment by allowing decision-makers to express their preferences as fuzzy numbers (Sengul et al., 2012). This flexibility enhances the accuracy and realism of assessments, particularly in complex decision-making environments.

Improved Decision Quality: By accounting for the vagueness and imprecision associated with subjective evaluations, FAHP helps decision-makers arrive at more reliable conclusions (Ahmed and Kilic, 2019). The fuzzy framework facilitates a nuanced understanding of preferences, leading to better-informed decisions.

Enhanced Communication: FAHP allows for a more intuitive communication of preferences among stakeholders. Decision-makers can express their judgments in linguistic terms (e.g., "slightly more important," "much more important"), which are then translated into fuzzy numbers. This improves the engagement of stakeholders in the decision-making process (Akkaya et al., 2015).

Flexibility in Preference Representation: FAHP accommodates various types of fuzzy numbers, enabling decision-makers to represent their preferences in a manner that aligns with their understanding and experience (Akman and Alkan, 2006). This flexibility enhances the applicability of the method across diverse domains. Fuzzification of saaty's scale shown in table 8.

Table 8. Fuzzification of saaty's scale

Saaty Scale	Definition	Fuzzy Triangular Scale
1	Equally important	(1, 1, 1)
3	Weakly important	(2, 3, 4)
5	Fairly important	(4, 5, 6)

continued on following page

Table 8. Continued

Saaty Scale	Definition	Fuzzy Triangular Scale
7	Strongly important	(6, 7, 8)
9	Absolutely important	(9, 9, 9)

(Soltani and Marandi, 2011)\

In this study, Chang's rank analysis method was used to determine the criteria weights for sailing boat selection, the steps of this method are as follows (Chang, 1996):

Step 1: The value of the fuzzy synthetic order with respect to criterion i is defined as follows:

$$S_i = \sum_{j=1}^{m} M_{g_i}^{j} \otimes \left[\sum_{i=1}^{n}\sum_{j=1}^{m} M_{g_i}^{j}\right]^{-1} \quad (1)$$

Here, $\sum_{j=1}^{m} M_{g_i}^{j}$ the fuzzy addition operation in formula (2) is applied to the m level analysis equation to make the equation of,

$$\sum_{j=1}^{m} M_{g_i}^{j} = \left(\sum_{j=1}^{m} l_j, \sum_{j=1}^{m} m_j, \sum_{j=1}^{m} u_j\right) \quad (2)$$

Ve $\left(\sum_{i=1}^{n}\sum_{j=1}^{m} M_{g_i}^{j}\right)^{-1}$,$M_{g_i}^{j}$ (j= 1,2, .., m) to give the fuzzy addition of the equation, the operation in formula (3) is performed

$$\sum_{i=1}^{n}\sum_{j=1}^{m} M_{g_i}^{j} = \left(\sum_{i=1}^{n} l_i, \sum_{i=1}^{n} m_i, \sum_{i=1}^{n} u_i\right) \quad (3)$$

and the tes operation of the vector in the formula is calculated according to formula (4) below.

$$\left[\sum_{i=1}^{n}\sum_{j=1}^{m} M_{g_i}^{j}\right]^{-1} = \left(\frac{1}{\sum_{i=1}^{n} u_i}, \frac{1}{\sum_{i=1}^{n} m_i}, \frac{1}{\sum_{i=1}^{n} l_i}\right) \quad (4)$$

Step 2: The likelihood level of M2 ≥ M1 is defined as in formula (5).

$$V(M_2 \geq M_1) = \sup_{y \geq x} \min\left(\mu_{M_1}(x), \mu_{M_2}(y)\right) \quad (5)$$

It is also defined by the following formula.

$$V(M_2 \geq M_1) = hgt(M_1 \cap M_2) = \mu_{M_2}(d)$$

$$= \begin{cases} 1, & \text{if } m_2 \geq m_1, \\ 0, & \text{if } l_1 \geq u_2, \\ \dfrac{l_1 - u_2}{(m_2 - u_2) - (m_1 - l_1)} & otherwise, \end{cases} \tag{6}$$

The upper level intersection region is as shown in Figure 3 with the y-axis of D.

Figure 3. Intersection between m1 and m2 (Chang, 1996)

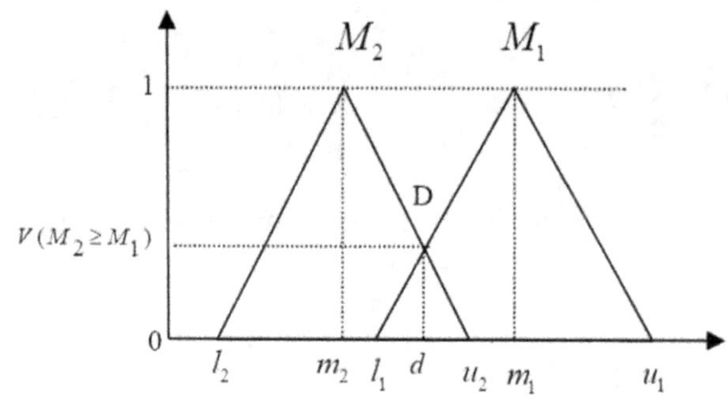

In order to be able to compare points M1 and M2, both V(M2 ≥ M1) and V(M1 ≥ M2) values must exist.

Step 3: The probability degree of a concave fuzzy number being greater than k concave fuzzy numbers Mi (i=1, 2, ..., k) is specified as in formula (7).

$$V(M \geq M_1, M_2, ..., M_k) = V[(M \geq M_1) \text{ and } (M \geq M_2) \text{ and ... and } (M \geq M_k)], \\ = \min V(M \geq M_i), i = 1, 2, 3, ..., k. \tag{7}$$

Assumming that is

$$d'(A_i) = \min V(S_i \geq S_k), k = 1, 2, ..., n;\ k \neq i \tag{8}$$

In the next step, the weight vector is defined as in formula (9):

$$W' = (d'(A_1), d'(A_2), ..., d'(A_n))^T \tag{9}$$

In the formula A_i (i=1, 2, ..., n) indicates as many values as n.

4: Normalised weight vector

$$W= (d(A_1), d(A_2), ..., d(A_n))^T \quad (10)$$

W in formula (10) stands for a non-fuzzy number.

Table 9 summarizing the articles related to location selection by Fuzzy AHP method, focusing on their authors, methodologies, objectives, and key findings. Table 9 summarizes the main aspects of each article, providing a clear overview of the methodologies and findings related to location selection.

Table 9. Location selection studies

Authors	Year	Methodology	Objective	Key Findings
Kaboli, A., Aryanezhad, M. B., Shahanaghi, K., & Niroomand, I.	2007	Fuzzy AHP	Develop a new method for plant location selection	The fuzzy AHP approach effectively handles uncertainty and provides reliable location selection.
Ertuğrul, İ., & Karakaşoğlu, N.	2008	Fuzzy AHP and Fuzzy TOPSIS	Compare Fuzzy AHP and Fuzzy TOPSIS for facility location selection	Fuzzy AHP provides more accurate and flexible decision-making compared to traditional methods.
Vahidnia, M. H., Alesheikh, A. A., & Alimohammadi, A.	2009	Fuzzy AHP	Select hospital sites	Fuzzy AHP enhances the decision-making process by incorporating subjective judgments.
Guneri, A. F., Cengiz, M., & Seker, S.	2009	Fuzzy ANP	Shipyard location selection	Fuzzy ANP enhances multi-criteria decision-making by incorporating expert opinions.
Saracoglu, B. O., Insel, M., & Helvacioglu, I. H.	2009	Identification of key location criteria	New shipyard site selection	Defines the most critical factors influencing shipyard location decisions.
Tuğba Turğut, B., Taş, G., Herekoğlu, A., Tozan, H., & Vayvay, O.	2011	Fuzzy AHP	Develop a decision support system for disaster center location selection	The study demonstrates the effectiveness of fuzzy AHP in identifying optimal locations for disaster management.
Ka, B.	2011	Fuzzy AHP and ELECTRE	Select dry port locations in China	The combination of fuzzy AHP and ELECTRE enhances location selection by considering various criteria.
Li, F., Shi, X., & Hu, H.	2011	AP clustering	Dry port location selection in Southwest China	AP clustering efficiently classifies potential locations based on cargo demand and connectivity.

continued on following page

Table 9. Continued

Authors	Year	Methodology	Objective	Key Findings
Hanine, M., Boutkhoum, O., Tikniouine, A., & Agouti, T.	2016	Fuzzy AHP and Fuzzy TODIM	Compare fuzzy AHP and fuzzy TODIM for landfill location selection	Both methods effectively support landfill location decisions, but fuzzy AHP is preferred for its simplicity.
Eskandari, M., Homaee, M., Mahmoodi, S., Pazira, E., & Van Genuchten, M. T.	2015	Land classification and optimization	Landfill site selection	Optimizing site selection by integrating environmental and geographic factors.
Guler, D., & Yomralioglu, T.	2020	AHP and Fuzzy AHP with GIS	Identify suitable locations for electric vehicle fast charging stations	GIS combined with fuzzy AHP provides a comprehensive analysis for selecting optimal charging station locations.
Türk, A., & Özkök, M.	2020	Fuzzy AHP and TOPSIS	Shipyard location selection	The combined approach provides an effective ranking of potential shipyard locations.
Tripathi, A. K., Agrawal, S., & Gupta, R. D.	2021	GIS-based AHP and Fuzzy AHP	Hospital site selection in Prayagraj City, India	Fuzzy AHP provides better decision support by integrating geographic and subjective criteria.
Cil, İ., Arisoy, F., Özgürbüz, E., Yunus Cil, A., & Kılınç, H.	2022	AHP and PROMETHEE	Indoor positioning technology selection at SEDEF Shipyard	A hybrid approach optimizes the selection of indoor positioning systems in shipyards.
Chowdhury, M. M. H., & Haque Munim, Z.	2023	Fuzzy AHP-BWM-PROMETHEE	Dry port location selection	A hybrid approach improves location decisions by integrating multiple MCDM techniques.

5. FINDINGS

5.1. Results of calculation of criterion weights

In the context of selecting a site for a yacht marina, the initial step entailed the comparison of the environmental sub-criteria. The weights were determined through the utilisation of Chang's rank analysis technique, as outlined in the method section. The comparison matrix of the criteria is presented in Table 10.

Table 10. Pairwise comparison matrix of sub-criteria of the group titled environmental

	C1			C2			C3			C4		
	l	**m**	**u**	**l**	**m**	**u**	**l**	**m**	**u**	**l**	**m**	**u**
C1	1	1	1	1	2	3	1	2	3	1	3	4
C2	1/3	1/2	1	1	1	1	1/2	1/3	1/4	4	5	6
C3	1/3	1/2	1	4	3	2	1	1	1	1	2	3
C4	1/4	1/3	1	1/6	1/5	1/4	1/3	1/2	1	1	1	1

The normalised weights of the data obtained after the pairwise comparison matrix of the sub-criteria under the environmental main heading with the help of the formula specified in step 4 are given in Table 11.

Table 11. Normalised version of the sub-criteria (environmental)

				Mean	**Normalise**
C1	0,172	0,408	0,737	0,439	0,396
C2	0,155	0,210	0,333	0,233	0,210
C3	0,184	0,289	0,471	0,315	0,284
C4	0,059	0,094	0,213	0,122	0,110
Sum				1,109	1,00

As demonstrated in Table 6, the experts' comparison revealed that C1 sub-criteria ATE obtained the highest value of 0.396. The second criterion was WC C3 with a numerical value of 0.284, followed by C2 SS with a numerical value of 0.21 and EEI with a numerical value of 0.19.

The expression of the sub-criteria of the main criterion of Financial with triadic fuzzy numbers, which is the linguistic expression translation, was taken as the average of the values given by the experts and written in the form of the pairwise comparison matrix in Table 12.

Table 12. Pairwise comparison matrix of the sub-criteria of the main criterion financial

	C5			**C6**			**C7**			**C8**		
	l	**m**	**u**	**l**	**m**	**u**	**l**	**m**	**u**	**l**	**m**	**u**
C5	1	1	1	1	2	3	1	1	1	1	3	4
C6	1/3	1/2	1	1	1	1	1/2	1/3	1/4	1	1	1
C7	1	1	1	4	3	2	1	1	1	1	2	3
C8	1/4	1/3	1	1	1	1	1/3	1/2	1	1	1	1

The data pertaining to the pairwise comparison matrix of the four sub-criteria of the financial main criterion, along with the weights of the normalised version of the fuzzy numbers, is presented in Table 13, with the formula specified in step 4 of the FAHP.

Table 13. Normalised version of the sub-criteria of the financial main criterion

	l	*m*	*u*	**Mean**	**Normalise**
C5	0,157	0,299	0,445	0,300	0,390
C6	0,095	0,102	0,125	0,107	0,150
C7	0,207	0,261	0,357	0,275	0,255
C8	0,083	0,111	0,174	0,123	0,205
Sum				1,036	1

As illustrated in Table 8, C5, one of the sub-criteria of the primary financial criterion, exhibits the maximum value of 0.39. C7 sub-criterion, C8 sub-criterion, and C6 sub-criterion demonstrate numerical values of 0.255, 0.255, and 0.15, respectively.

The ranking of the overall weights of the sub-criteria is given in Table 14.

Table 14. Importance weights of sub-criteria and general ranking according to importance weights

Criteria	**Main Vriteria weight**	**Sub-criteria weight**	**Sub vriteria importance weight**	**Rank**
C1	0,50	0,396	0,198	1
C5	0,50	0,390	0,190	2
C3	0,50	0,284	0,142	3
C7	0,50	0,255	0,127	4
C2	0,50	0,210	0,105	5

continued on following page

Table 14. Continued

Criteria	Main Vriteria weight	Sub-criteria weight	Sub vriteria importance weight	Rank
C8	0,50	0,205	0,102	6
C6	0,50	0,150	0,075	7
C4	0,50	0,110	0,055	8

An analysis of the importance ranking of the sub-criteria is presented in Table 7. It is evident that C1 ATE has been ranked first with a numerical value of 0.198 according to the importance weight of the sub-criteria. The C5 IF sub-criteria has been ranked second with a numerical value of 0.195 according to the importance weight. The C3 WC has been ranked third with a numerical value of 0.142. The C7 LRC sub-criterion was ranked fourth with a value of 0.127 in terms of importance weight, while the C2 SS sub-criterion was determined as the fifth most important criterion according to the importance weight calculation of all sub-criteria. Finally, the C4 (EEI) sub-criterion ranked last among the sub-criteria with 0.11.

5.2. Ranking of Alternative Locations

The characteristics of the 5 locations identified by the experts are given in Table 15.

Table 15. Comparison of marina locations based on selection criteria

Criteria	Muğla-Göcek	Istanbul-Tuzla	Antalya-Kaş	İzmir-Çeşme	Mersin-Taşucu
Accessibility & Transportation (C1)	****	*****	***	****	**
Infrastructure & Facilities (C5)	****	*****	***	****	**
Weather Conditions (C3)	****	**	*****	***	**
Legal & Regulatory Compliance (C7)	***	****	***	***	*****
Safety & Security (C2)	****	****	***	***	***
Touristic & Cultural Opportunities (C8)	*****	***	****	****	**
Economic Feasibility (C6)	****	***	***	***	****
Environmental & Ecological Impact (C4)	****	**	***	***	***

The ranking of these marina locations according to the criteria using the Fuzzy AHP method is given in Table 16.

Table 16. Marina location selection rank

Rank	Marina Location	Fuzzy AHP Score
1	Muğla - Göcek	7.490
2	Istanbul - Tuzla	7.318
3	Antalya - Kaş	7.190
4	Izmir - Çeşme	7.126
5	Mersin - Taşucu	6.578

6. DISCUSSION

The importance of various criteria used in selecting yacht marinas, along with their rankings. Here's an analysis of these criteria: C1 (Weight: 0.198): This criterion is considered the most significant in the selection process, indicating that it plays a crucial role in determining the overall effectiveness and satisfaction associated with the marina. C5 (Weight: 0.190): Ranked second, this criterion also carries considerable weight. Its importance is close to C1, suggesting that both should be balanced to ensure a successful marina choice. C3 (Weight: 0.142): Coming in third, this criterion is important as well. Its specifics can greatly influence the overall decision-making strategy for marina selection. C7 (Weight: 0.127): This criterion, while slightly less significant, still holds relevance in the selection process and should be taken into account for a well-rounded decision. C2 (Weight: 0.105): In fifth place, this criterion has moderate importance. It is worth considering, but it does not hold the top priority compared to others. C8 (Weight: 0.102): Although this criterion ranks sixth and carries less importance, it shouldn't be ignored entirely during the selection process. C6 (Weight: 0.075): This criterion ranks seventh, making it less critical. However, it can still be relevant in specific contexts. C4 (Weight: 0.055): As the least important criterion, this factor is generally the least significant in the selection process but may still affect certain marina characteristics. The table 7 highlights which criteria should be prioritized when selecting yacht marinas. The emphasis on the top three criteria suggests that a strategic and careful approach is essential for making an informed decision. Balancing these criteria will be key to achieving success in the selection process.

Among the alternative locations, Muğla-Göcek ranks first with the highest Fuzzy AHP score (7.490). This result aligns with its well-developed infrastructure, favorable weather conditions, and strong touristic potential. Istanbul-Tuzla follows closely, benefiting from its superior transportation connectivity and regulatory compliance.

The lower rankings of Mersin-Taşucu and Izmir-Çeşme suggest that although these locations offer some advantages, their relative weaknesses in accessibility, infrastructure, and economic feasibility impacted their overall scores. These findings provide valuable insights for investors and policymakers aiming to establish sustainable and commercially viable marina locations.

Although both Muğla-Göcek and İzmir-Çeşme are located in the Aegean region, their evaluation scores vary due to differences in infrastructure, accessibility, and seasonal tourist preferences. Göcek benefits from a more secluded and naturally protected bay, along with proximity to luxury accommodation and consistent demand from international yacht charters. On the other hand, Çeşme's marina, while well-developed, caters more to seasonal domestic tourism and faces more constraints related to accessibility and environmental concerns.

Using the Fuzzy AHP method, the selected locations were ranked based on their suitability for marina development. The rankings reflected the importance of accessibility and infrastructure, consistent with existing literature. The prioritization of these criteria suggests that convenience for yacht owners and well-developed amenities play crucial roles in marina sustainability.

6.1. Comparison with Previous Studies

Several studies, including those by Park & Joo (2011) and Yang & Hwang (2015), emphasize accessibility and transportation ease as primary factors in marina selection. These studies align with the present analysis, where accessibility ranks highest among the criteria. Similarly, infrastructure and facilities emerge as critical determinants in both previous research and the current study, reinforcing the significance of well-developed amenities for marina sustainability.

A noteworthy methodological difference arises in the weighting of environmental and ecological impacts. While Gumusay et al. (2016) and Karayel et al. (2022) prioritize environmental sustainability in marina selection, the present study ranks it lower, indicating a more commercially driven decision-making approach. This contrast suggests that, in some regions, economic viability outweighs ecological considerations, whereas in others, environmental protection plays a more dominant role.

The findings also highlight discrepancies in the role of touristic and cultural opportunities. Efecan & Temiz (2020) and Lee (2012) identify these factors as secondary considerations, aligning with the present study's ranking. However, Yang et al. (2014) suggest that integrating marinas with tourism development strategies enhances long-term profitability, implying that location-specific characteristics may alter their relative importance.

Legal and regulatory compliance emerges as another point of divergence. Bilski (2015) examines human factors in marina design and underscores regulatory frameworks as essential for operational efficiency. The present study assigns a moderate weight to this factor, acknowledging its relevance but positioning it below infrastructure and economic feasibility.

7. CONCLUSION

The selection of yacht marinas is a complex process influenced by multiple criteria, each varying in significance based on location-specific characteristics and stakeholder priorities. The insights gained from this study can guide investors and policymakers in making informed decisions that prioritize accessibility, infrastructure, and economic viability while balancing environmental and cultural considerations. Future research should continue to explore these dynamics, particularly in light of evolving market demands and sustainability considerations in the marina industry.

These findings are critical for investors and policymakers aiming to establish sustainable and commercially viable marina locations. The Fuzzy AHP method used in this analysis effectively ranked the locations based on their suitability for marina development, reflecting the importance of accessibility and infrastructure as key determinants of marina sustainability.

Conduct longitudinal studies to analyze the long-term impacts of marina development on local economies, tourism, and environmental sustainability. This approach could provide insights into how selected criteria evolve over time and their effects on marina success. Further research could focus on conducting comprehensive environmental impact assessments (EIAs) for proposed marina sites. Understanding the ecological implications of marina development can help balance economic benefits with environmental protection. Conduct comparative studies of marina selection criteria and success factors across different geographical regions. This can help identify best practices and tailor strategies to specific local conditions and market demands.

The most significant output of the study is the identification of selection criteria for yacht marinas and the prioritization of these criteria based on their importance. This output serves as a strategic guide for investors and policymakers. In summary, the key outputs of the study are as follows:

- **Importance of Criteria:** The criteria identified in the study highlight the most critical factors to consider in the marina selection process. Specifically, high-weight values for accessibility, infrastructure, and service quality indicate that these factors are vital for the success of a marina.

- **Fuzzy AHP Method:** The use of the Fuzzy AHP method provides a more robust assessment by considering uncertainties in complex decision-making processes. This approach enhances the understanding of relationships among various criteria.
- **Strategic Approaches to Site Selection:** The study reveals specific regions (e.g., Muğla-Göcek and Istanbul-Tuzla) as the most suitable locations for marina development. This finding offers insights for investors and developers about where to find more opportunities.
- **Sustainability and Economic Impact:** The study provides important information on how marina selection criteria relate to economic sustainability and environmental impacts. It emphasizes that investments should focus not only on economic gains but also on environmental protection and the benefits to local communities.
- **Contribution to the Literature:** The study fills gaps in the existing literature by aligning with previous research on marina selection criteria and making significant contributions to the body of knowledge in this field.

These outputs offer practical insights for investors, managers, and policymakers planning to develop yacht marinas. Additionally, they support more informed and sustainable decision-making processes in marina management and development.

REFERENCES

Ahmed, F., & Kilic, K. (2019). Fuzzy Analytic Hierarchy Process: A performance analysis of various algorithms. *Fuzzy Sets and Systems*, *362*, 110–128. DOI: 10.1016/j.fss.2018.08.009

Ajagunna, I., & Casanova, S. (2022). An analysis of the post-COVID-19 cruise industry: Could this be a new possibility for the luxury yacht sector in the Caribbean? *Worldwide Hospitality and Tourism Themes*, *14*(2), 115–123. DOI: 10.1108/WHATT-12-2021-0158

Akkaya, G., Turanoğlu, B., & Öztaş, S. (2015). An integrated fuzzy AHP and fuzzy MOORA approach to the problem of industrial engineering sector choosing. *Expert Systems with Applications*, *42*(24), 9565–9573. DOI: 10.1016/j.eswa.2015.07.061

Akman, G., & Alkan, A. (2006). Tedarik Zinciri Yönetiminde Bulanık AHP yöntemi kullanılarak tedarikçilerin performansının ölçülmesi: Otomotiv Yan Sanayiinde bir uygulama. İstanbul Ticaret Üniversitesi Fen Bilimleri Dergisi [Measuring Supplier Performance Using Fuzzy AHP Method in Supply Chain Management: An Application in Automotive Sub-Industry. Istanbul Commerce University Journal of Science], 5(9), 23-46.

Alcover, A., Alemany, M., Jacob, M., Payeras, M., García, A., & Martínez-Ribes, L. (2011). The economic impact of yacht charter tourism on the Balearic economy. *Tourism Economics*, *17*(3), 625–638. DOI: 10.5367/te.2011.0045

Alesta, F. (2023). Yelkenli Tekne Markaları ve Modelleri. https://www.alestaferro.com/post/yelkenli-tekne-markalari-ve-modelleri#viewer-a4pee, Access date: 11.12.2023.

Arıcan, O. H. (2024). Yat Turizm Şirketleri Için Yelkenli Tekne Seçimi Kriterlerinin Belirlenmesİ. *Dokuz Eylül Üniversitesi Denizcilik Fakültesi Dergisi* [Determination of Sailing Boat Selection Criteria for Yacht Tourism Companies. Dokuz Eylül University Maritime Faculty Journal*]*, *16*(1), 22–50. DOI: 10.18613/deudfd.1422201

Arıcan, O. H., Arslan, O., Ünal, A., & Kaya Özbağ, G. (2024). Developing a Comprehensive Yacht Captain Selection Model for Enhancing Competitiveness in Yacht Tourism: A Fuzzy AHP Approach. *Journal for Maritime Research*, *21*(3).

Arıcan, O. H., Arslan, O., & Unal, A. U. (2023). The importance of CATZOC in passage planning and prioritization of strategies for safe navigation. *Marine Science and Technology Bulletin*, *12*(4), 445–458. DOI: 10.33714/masteb.1333432

Arıcan, O. H., Unal, A., Arslan, O., & Bamyacı, M. (2022). A Dry Cargo Coaster Tonnage Selection Model for Shipping Companies in Türkiye. *Kent Akademisi*, *15*(4), 1651–1669. DOI: 10.35674/kent.1017076

Bakış, T. (2023). Yat Turizmi nedir ve yat turizm istatistikleri [What is Yacht Tourism and yacht tourism statistics]. https://www.turizmebakis.com/yat-turizmi/ , Access date: 20.12.2023.

Biçak, H. A., Altinay, M., Aksugür, E., Günyakti, A., & Katircioglu, S. (2006). Could yacht tourism be an alternative tourism potential in North Cyprus? *Tourism in Marine Environments*, *3*(1), 49–57. DOI: 10.3727/154427306779380284

Bilski, M. (2015). Selected human factors in marina design. *Procedia Manufacturing*, *3*, 1646–1653. DOI: 10.1016/j.promfg.2015.07.482

Boats (2023). Sailing boats: sailboat types, rigs, uses and definitions. https://uk.boats.com/on-the-water/sailing-boats-sailboat-types-rigs-uses-definitions/, Access date: 21.12.2023.

Buchalski, Z. (2013). Selection Of Sailing Boats Configuration For Various User Groups. *Information Systems Architecture and Technology*, 43.

Bucur, B. (2015). Conceptual Design. A Case Study: Sailing Boat. *Journal Of Industrial Design And Engineering Graphics*, *10*, 21.

Castegnaro, S., Gomiero, C., Battisti, C., Poli, M., Basile, M., Barucco, P., Pizzarello, U., Quaresimin, M., & Lazzaretto, A. (2017). A bio-composite racing sailboat: Materials selection, design, manufacturing and sailing. *Ocean Engineering*, *133*, 142–150. DOI: 10.1016/j.oceaneng.2017.01.017

Chan, F. T., Kumar, N., Tiwari, M. K., Lau, H. C., & Choy, K. (2008). Global supplier selection: A fuzzy-AHP approach. *International Journal of Production Research*, *46*(14), 3825–3857. DOI: 10.1080/00207540600787200

Chang, D.-Y. (1996). Applications of the Extent Analysis Method on Fuzzy AHP. *European Journal of Operational Research*, *95*(3), 649–655. DOI: 10.1016/0377-2217(95)00300-2

Chen, J., Balomenou, C., Nijkamp, P., Poulaki, P., & Lagos, D. (2016). *The sustainability of yachting tourism: a case study on Greece.*

Cheng, C. H. (1996). Evaluating naval tactical missile systems by fuzzy AHP based on the grade value of membership function. *European Journal of Operational Research*, *96*(2), 343–350. DOI: 10.1016/S0377-2217(96)00026-4

Cho, W. J. (2012). Analyses of consumer preferences and perceptions regarding activation of yacht tourism industry. *Journal of Navigation and Port Research, 36*(5), 401–407. DOI: 10.5394/KINPR.2012.36.5.401

Chowdhury, M. M. H., & Haque Munim, Z. (2023). Dry port location selection using a fuzzy AHP-BWM-PROMETHEE approach. *Maritime Economics & Logistics, 25*(2), 301–329. DOI: 10.1057/s41278-022-00230-0

Chroneou, C. (2024). *Development of marinas in Greece* (Master's thesis, Πανεπιστήμιο Πειραιώς).

Cil, İ., Arisoy, F., Özgürbüz, E., Yunus Cil, A., & Kılınç, H. (2022). Indoor Positioning Technology Selection Using a Combined AHP and PROMETHEE Method at SEDEF Shipyard. *Journal of ETA Maritime Science, 10*(2), 108–123. DOI: 10.4274/jems.2022.47550

Design, B. (2024). Sailing boats' Stability, STIX and Old Ratios https://www.boatdesign.net/forums/attachments/stability/9806d1161681331-sailing-boats-stability-stix-old-ratios-stix-formula-r3.xls, Access date: 02.01.2024.

Efecan, V., & Temiz, İ. (2020). Marina Selection Of Yachtsmen Using AHP-TOPSIS And AHP-PROMETHEE. *Mersin University Journal of Maritime Faculty*, 2(1), 14-24.

Elias, W., Ezzat, M., & Ahmed, F. M. (2020). Assessing the tourists satisfaction towards yacht tourism services in the red sea coast, Egypt. *Minia Journal of Tourism and Hospitality Research MJTHR, 9*(1), 157–170. DOI: 10.21608/mjthr.2020.139593

Ertuğrul, İ., & Karakaşoğlu, N. (2008). Comparison of fuzzy AHP and fuzzy TOPSIS methods for facility location selection. *International Journal of Advanced Manufacturing Technology, 39*(7-8), 783–795. DOI: 10.1007/s00170-007-1249-8

Eskandari, M., Homaee, M., Mahmoodi, S., Pazira, E., & Van Genuchten, M. T. (2015). Optimizing landfill site selection by using land classification maps. *Environmental Science and Pollution Research International, 22*(10), 7754–7765. DOI: 10.1007/s11356-015-4182-7 PMID: 25666474

Fotiadis, A., Rice, J., & Hiyasat, R. (2023). Antecedents of yacht tourism participants' satisfaction and word-of-mouth intention. *Worldwide Hospitality and Tourism Themes, 15*(4), 349–361. DOI: 10.1108/WHATT-03-2023-0042

Franzen, I. (2013). A Refinement of the Method Used to Determine the Balance of a Sailing Vessel During the Design Phase, with Application to Sail Design and Subsequent Sail Selection and Sailing Operations. *In SNAME Chesapeake Sailing Yacht Symposium* (p. D021S003R001). SNAME. DOI: 10.5957/CSYS-2013-007

Gotosailing, (2024). Hırvatistan'da Tekne Tatili Yapmak İçin 10 Neden. https://gotosailing.com/tr/hirvatistan-da-tekne-tatili-yapmak-icin-10-neden, Access date: 23.12.2023.

Guler, D., & Yomralioglu, T. (2020). Suitable location selection for the electric vehicle fast charging station with AHP and fuzzy AHP methods using GIS. *Annals of GIS*, *26*(2), 169–189. DOI: 10.1080/19475683.2020.1737226

Guneri, A. F., Cengiz, M., & Seker, S. (2009). A fuzzy ANP approach to shipyard location selection. *Expert Systems with Applications*, *36*(4), 7992–7999. DOI: 10.1016/j.eswa.2008.10.059

Hanine, M., Boutkhoum, O., Tikniouine, A., & Agouti, T. (2016). Comparison of fuzzy AHP and fuzzy TODIM methods for landfill location selection. *SpringerPlus*, *5*(1), 1–30. DOI: 10.1186/s40064-016-2131-7 PMID: 27186465

Hogarth Robin, M. (1978). A note on aggregating opinions. *Organizational Behavior and Human Performance*, *21*(1), 40–46. DOI: 10.1016/0030-5073(78)90037-5

Ka, B. (2011). Application of fuzzy AHP and ELECTRE to China dry port location selection. *The Asian Journal of Shipping and Logistics*, *27*(2), 331–353. DOI: 10.1016/S2092-5212(11)80015-5

Kaboli, A., Aryanezhad, M. B., Shahanaghi, K., & Niroomand, I. (2007, October). A new method for plant location selection problem: a fuzzy-AHP approach. In *2007 IEEE International Conference on Systems, Man and Cybernetics* (pp. 582-586). IEEE. DOI: 10.1109/ICSMC.2007.4413890

Karayel, G. K., Javani, N., & Dincer, I. (2022). Sustainable marina concept with green hydrogen utilization: A case study. *Sustainable Energy Technologies and Assessments*, *54*, 102900. DOI: 10.1016/j.seta.2022.102900

Lee, J. H. (2012). Marina Development on the Importance of Optimum Demand and Location Selection Study. *Journal of the Korean society of marine environment & safety*, 18(5), 406-415.

Lett, J. W.Jr. (1983). Ludic and liminoid aspects of charter yacht tourism in the Caribbean. *Annals of Tourism Research*, *10*(1), 35–56. DOI: 10.1016/0160-7383(83)90114-7

Li, F., Shi, X., & Hu, H. (2011). Location selection of dry port based on AP clustering-the case of southwest China. *Journal of System and Management Sciences*, *1*(5).

Linker, R. (2023). Yacht in Türkiye Market Overview. 2023-2027. https://www.reportlinker.com/market-report, Access date: 01.01.2024.

Loydu, T. (2023). Yatlar. https://www.linkedin.com/pulse/segmentlerine-g%C3%B6re-2023-yat-pazar%C4%B1-verileri-turk-loydu/?originalSubdomain=tr, Access date: 11.12.2023.

Park, S. H., & Joo, K. S. (2011). The study On An Yacht Moorings Establishment Location Analysis Using Optimum Spiral Method. *Journal of the Korean Society of Marine Environment & Safety*, *17*(4), 323–329. DOI: 10.7837/kosomes.2011.17.4.323

Saracoglu, B. O., Insel, M., & Helvacioglu, I. H. (2009). Identification of location selection criteria for new building shipyards. *Marine Technology and SNAME News*, *46*(01), 34–44. DOI: 10.5957/mtsn.2009.46.1.34

Sariisik, M., Turkay, O., & Akova, O. (2011). How to manage yacht tourism in Türkiye: A swot analysis and related strategies. *Procedia: Social and Behavioral Sciences*, *24*, 1014–1025. DOI: 10.1016/j.sbspro.2011.09.041

Sengul, Ü., Eren, M., & Shıraz, S. E. (2012). Bulanik ahp île belediyelerin toplu taşima araç seçimi. *Erciyes Üniversitesi İktisadi ve İdari Bilimler Fakültesi Dergisi*, [Municipalities' public transport vehicle selection with fuzzy AHP. Erciyes University Faculty of Economics and Administrative Sciences Journal*]*, *40*, 143–165.

Sevinç, F., & Güzel, T. (2017). Sustainable yacht tourism practices. *Management & Marketing Journal*, 15(1).

T.C. Kültür ve Turizm Bakanlığı. (2023). Deniz Turizmi Tesisleri ve Araçları İstatistikleri. https://yigm.ktb.gov.tr/TR-201146/deniz-turizmi-tesisleri-ve-araclari-istatistikleri.html, Access date: 12.02.2024.

T.C. Kültür ve Turizm Bakanlığı (TCKTB). (2024). Turizm İstatistik Raporları. https://www.ktb.gov.tr/genel/searchhotelgenel.aspx?lang=tr, Access date: 22.11.2023.

Tetyana, L. (2015). Prospects of Yacht Tourism Development in the Black Sea Region of Ukraine. Ovidius University Annals, *Series Economic Sciences*, 15(1).

Tripathi, A. K., Agrawal, S., & Gupta, R. D. (2021). Comparison of GIS-based AHP and fuzzy AHP methods for hospital site selection: A case study for Prayagraj City, India. *GeoJournal*, 1–22. PMID: 34075269

Tuğba Turğut, B., Taş, G., Herekoğlu, A., Tozan, H., & Vayvay, O. (2011). A fuzzy AHP based decision support system for disaster center location selection and a case study for Istanbul. *Disaster Prevention and Management*, *20*(5), 499–520. DOI: 10.1108/09653561111178943

Türk, A., & Özkök, M. (2020). Shipyard location selection based on fuzzy AHP and TOPSIS. *Journal of Intelligent & Fuzzy Systems*, *39*(3), 4557–4576. DOI: 10.3233/JIFS-200522

Unal, A. U., Arslan, O., & Arıcan, O. H. (2022). Türkiye'de Ro-Ro taşımacılığının önemi ve geleceği hakkında örnek bir çalışma. *Denizcilik Araştırmaları Dergisi: Amfora*, *1*(1), 60–79.

Vahidnia, M. H., Alesheikh, A. A., & Alimohammadi, A. (2009). Hospital site selection using fuzzy AHP and its derivatives. *Journal of Environmental Management*, *90*(10), 3048–3056. DOI: 10.1016/j.jenvman.2009.04.010 PMID: 19477577

Wang, H. C., & Lirn, T. C. (2024). Enhancement of Marina Service Quality of Yacht Tourism in Taiwan: A Euclidean Distance of Importance-Performance Analysis. *SAGE Open*, *14*(4), 21582440241281634. DOI: 10.1177/21582440241281634

Wang, Y. M., Luo, Y., & Hua, Z. (2008). On the extent analysis method for fuzzy AHP and its applications. *European Journal of Operational Research*, *186*(2), 735–747. DOI: 10.1016/j.ejor.2007.01.050

Wang, Y. M., Luo, Y., & Hua, Z. (2008). On the extent analysis method for fuzzy AHP and its applications. *European Journal of Operational Research*, *186*(2), 735–747. DOI: 10.1016/j.ejor.2007.01.050

World, Y. (2023). Luxury Yachts, Superyachts, Advice & Trends. https://www.yachtworld.com/research/, Access date: 25.12.2023.

WTTC. (2023). Destination 2030 WTTC & JLL assess global cities' tourism readiness. https://research.wttc.org/destination-2030-jll-wttc-report?_gl=1*16mvw3q*_ga*MjExOTI0ODE2NS4xNzA3NzY0MTI1*_ga_JM5GLX6V1W*MTcwNzc2NDEyNC4xLjEuMTcwNzc2NDQxMy4wLjAuMA, Access date: 12.02.2024.

Yang, C. M., Lai, C. C., Wu, L. J., & Li, J. J. (2014). Assessing fishing port locations for adaption into yacht marinas in Taiwan. *Journal of Marine Science and Technology*, *22*(5), 10.

Yang, J. C., & Hwang, K. S. (2015). Study of the Location Factors of Yacht Marina and an Analysis of the Significance. *Journal of the Korea Academia-Industrial Cooperation Society*, *16*(1), 235–245. DOI: 10.5762/KAIS.2015.16.1.235

Yang, J. C., & Hwang, K. S. (2015). Study of the Location Factors of Yacht Marina and an Analysis of the Significance. *Journal of the Korea Academia-Industrial Cooperation Society*, *16*(1), 235–245. DOI: 10.5762/KAIS.2015.16.1.235

Yao, Y. H., & Luan, W. X. (2019). Factors influencing yacht tourism consumption behavior based on the TAM-IDT model.

ENDNOTES

1 M/Y: Motor Yacht

2 S/Y: Sailing Yacht

Chapter 8
Mapping the Nexus Rule of Law's Influence on Good Governance:
A Bibliometric Exploration

Widia Astuti
Muhammadiyah University of Makassar, Indonesia

Asra Yanti
Muhammadiyah University of Makassar, Indonesia

Muhammad Younus
https://orcid.org/0000-0001-9654-1546
Muhammadiyah University of Yogyakarta, Indonesia

Aqmal Reza Amri
Muhammadiyah University of Makassar, Indonesia

Andi Luhur Prianto
Muhammadiyah University of Makassar, Indonesia

Ahmad Harakan
Muhammadiyah University of Makassar, Indonesia

Achmad Nurmandi
Muhammadiyah University of Yogyakarta, Indonesia

Fatmawati A. Mappasere
Muhammadiyah University of Makassar, Indonesia

Ihyani Malik
Muhammadiyah University of Makassar, Indonesia

Haerana Haerana
https://orcid.org/0000-0002-0502-0532
Muhammadiyah University of Makassar, Indonesia

ABSTRACT

The purpose of this study is to spread knowledge regarding how Indonesia's good governance will be impacted by the rule of law in 2021. Following that, we have determined the effects of the Rule of Law on Indonesian residents. Citizenry and the

DOI: 10.4018/979-8-3693-8166-3.ch008

alterations to their mental processes toward the rule of law. "Qualitative research" is the methodology employed by the researchers working in this field. The World Bank website, Dimension AI, and Google Scholar provided the research's data, which was then presented descriptively. This paper's research helps us understand how a robust legal system might promote effective governance in a system or society. Moreover, how the government can effectively and transparently carry out the rule of law, this paper will only cover the extent to which each aspect of the change is explained in detail; it will also examine potential solutions to problems raised by the public and how best to put them into practice; and lastly, it will discuss the beneficial effects that the change in the laws has had on good governance.

1. INTRODUCTION

1.1 Background

Administrative law is an important aspect of the legal system and public government because it regulates the complex relationship between the state and its citizens. (Hirsch et al., 2022). Administrative Law consists of rules, principles, and procedural frameworks that shape the dynamics of administrative actions and decision-making. (O. Russo, 2023). Over time, the study of State Administrative Law has evolved to reflect changes in the government landscape, legal challenges, and societal demands. (Muhammad & Husen, 2019). For example, in Malaysia, additional regulations function as an important part of the legal system, complementing the legislative functions of the Parliament and the State Assembly.(Nugroho & Rahardjo, 2023). This helps ease the burden on legislative institutions in dealing with the details of laws and obtaining expert views on specific issues.(Susanti, 2022)

In the context of decision-making assisted by technology, principles of administrative law have been implemented to address the potential replacement of certain jobs by robots or technology(Budiarrianto & Sebayang, 2021). The emergence of Global Administrative Law has also become a topic of interest, as it explores potential sources and suitability of global regulatory frameworks(Hukum et al., 2023). In Singapore, the evolution of administrative law has been shaped by the context and system of unique laws in the country(Vallejo, 2021). European Standardization Organization (ESO) and Harmonized European standards are also subject to the principles of administrative law, considering public nature and its legal impact(Dinata, 2022). In Russia, the subject of law and administrative proceedings is a complex, multifaceted legal phenomenon that includes a variety of relationships and social issues, such as public administration, administrative and legal regulations, and police law(Szadok-Bratuń, 2021)

In Canada, administrative law principles have been applied to fracking hydraulics, with courts adopting administrative and privileged principles and expert institution regulations.(Shaheen et al., 2019). Overall, administrative law plays an important role in shaping the dynamics of administrative action and decision-making in various legal systems and countries.(Zdyb, 2019). Its evolution reflects the changing governance landscape governance, legal challenges, and societal demands, ensuring that the relationship between the state and its citizens remains well-governed and balanced (Lee, 2021).

1.2 Problem Formulation

Currently, Indonesia is in a chaotic condition, in a state of crisis in various fields, including the legal field.(Mumpuni & Kusumawati, 2021). Laws that are expected to provide justice for society turned out to be the opposite.(Muhammad & Husen, 2019). The effectiveness of law enforcement only applies to small communities committing petty crimes.(Delmana, 2019). Meanwhile, perpetrators of major crimes such as corruption, collusion, and nepotism (KKN), which is commonly called white-collar crime, are hard to touch. In this case, people really need courage, especially law enforcement officers, to make deep breakthroughs to resolve the case.(Nugroho & Rahardjo, 2023).

The laws that apply in society have differences between social classes. A community with upward social stratification clearly receives different treatment than a society that does have downward social stratification.(Triwahyuni, 2020). People whose families have a higher position or position have special treatment or honor, which is different from people who come from ordinary or ordinary family backgrounds and do not have a position in society.(Trofimova, 2020). This means that here is the position. In the applicable law, there is an indication that the treatment for violators of the law injustice occurs to law enforcement officers. The law is sharp down, and the law is blunt and above; this phenomenon occurs in almost all areas of the country in Indonesia.(Karunia et al., 2022).

Laws are basically made to create order and peace in society.(Govindaraju et al., 2023). Therefore, a legal system must operate like a law. The series of social organs must complement each other and have a high awareness of applicable law. The paradigm that views law as a system has dominated the thinking of the majority of legal circles, both theorists and among its practitioners, since the birth of the modern state in the 17th century until today, namely, a paradigm that considers law as an order(Priyo Sembodo et al., 2022). Indonesia, which, in fact, is a rule-of-law country, means everything that relates to violations of law or disobedience to existing legal regulations gets strict sanctions for the perpetrators.(Bërdufi & Nezha, 2023). It is recommended that anyone alive as a citizen of society living on this mother earth create order socially well, namely by upholding applicable laws. The law must be enforced without any favoritism in legal cases.(Sakti Koeswanto et al., 2023)

In Weber's view, law is an order that is coercive because the establishment of the legal order (different from other social orders and norms that are not law) is supported entirely by the coercive power of the state. Weber differentiated various legal systems on the basis of substantive and formal rationality. Weber said that there is substantive rationality when it is substantial. The law does consist of general rules in the abstract, which are ready to be deduced for use in punishing various concrete cases. On the other hand, the law is said to have no substantive rationality if every case is resolved on the basis of a unique political or ethical policy in its order(Rao, 2021). Maybe even resolved emotionally, which cannot refer to general rules at all that objectively exist. On the other hand, the law can be said to have rationality formal (irrational) if the law is only obtained through inspiration or through whispers whispered ideas that are said to be accepted by charismatic leaders so that the truth and its feasibility cannot be tested objectively(Mcneill, n.d.)

Governance is a broad concept with high complexity in its main pillars. Kaufmann (2010) defines government as a set of traditions and institutions that can be used for exercising the power of authority, where the provisions of good governance lead to improvements in institutions related to political stability, absence of terrorism and violence, formulation and proficiency implementation of government policies, better regulatory mechanisms, reduction of corruption and ensuring the supremacy of law that can be recognized as high-quality governance. The institutional framework consists of legal rules and norms that constrain the behavior of policymakers. (Muhammad & Husen, 2019). Legal rules and norms, too, must ensure that government actions do not damage but rather support the functioning of growth economics (Witkowska & Kucheryavaya, 2021).

1.3 Research Objective

The primary objective of this research is to explore the intricate relationship between the rule of law and good governance, aiming to illuminate how a robust legal framework can foster effective governance practices within various contexts. This study seeks to identify specific mechanisms through which adherence to the rule of law enhances accountability, transparency, and public participation, thereby contributing to more equitable governance. Additionally, the research aims to assess the impact of legal compliance on organizational performance, examining both the advantages and challenges that arise in implementing governance strategies grounded in the rule of law. Furthermore, the research intends to provide actionable insights for policymakers and governance practitioners by delineating best practices that promote the rule of law within governance structures.

By doing so, the study aims to inform strategies that can be adopted across different sectors and regions to advance good governance efficiently. This will involve a comprehensive analysis of existing literature and empirical data, with the goal of uncovering gaps in the current understanding of the topic and highlighting areas that require further exploration. Ultimately, the research aspires to contribute to the broader discourse on governance by offering evidence-based recommendations that emphasize the importance of legal frameworks in achieving sustainable development goals and promoting societal welfare. In doing so, it seeks to advocate for the integration of legal principles into governance practices, ensuring that they are not only theoretically sound but also practically applicable in real-world settings.

2. LITERATURE REVIEW

2.1 Defining Public Governance

According to (Gal, 2020) Governance is a set of rules, processes, and behaviors that influence how power is exercised, how decisions are made, how citizens and stakeholders are involved, and how responsibility is attributed between them. Governance refers to the mechanisms, processes, and institutions through which citizens and groups articulate their interests, exercise their legal rights and obligations, and mediate differences between them. (Maryam, 2016). According to other researchers, governance is the traditions and institutions through which power is exercised.(Siljanovska & Shalevska, 2019). This includes policy and decision-making processes as well as mechanisms for involving citizens and other societal groups.(Valerio et al., 2014)

The growth rate of research publications on good governance has indeed increased rapidly since 2011 until now. Several factors that encourage increased publication of good governance research include: Increasingly aware of the fundamental role of good governance in public sector reform and achieving sustainable development goals. Support and funding for governance research from international donor institutions such as the IMF, World Bank, and UN is increasing. Globalization and accelerated knowledge transfer facilitate the diffusion of good governance concepts and policies. Increased availability of governance indicator data since 1996 through Worldwide Governance Indicators. The development of sophisticated quantitative methods makes it easier for empirical research to measure the impact of good governance policies. The development of multi- and inter-disciplinary research to understand the complexity of governance.

According to researchers(Edralin & Pastrana, 2020), the factor driving the increase in good governance research publications is the strengthening consensus that good governance is a prerequisite for administrative efficiency, economic growth, and poverty alleviation. Good governance is becoming an increasingly stringent requirement for international donors and financial institutions to provide aid and loans.(Khodakivskyi, 2021). There are also those who argue that the driving factor for increasing good governance research publications is increasing awareness about corruption and encouraging public sector reform through the application of good governance principles.(Edralin & Pastrana, 2020)

2.2 Explaining Good Public Governance

According to Setyowati (2015), in her journal entitled "Implementation of Good Governance Principles in Public Services," good government must fulfill the following principles: Information Disclosure. The government must be transparent and provide the widest possible information to the public regarding policies and the use of public resources. Public Accountability. The government must be able to account for its performance and decisions to the community. Community empowerment. The government needs to encourage community participation and aspirations in decision-making so that community needs can be accommodated.

Winarna (2018), in her journal entitled "Application of Good Governance Principles in Bureaucratic Reform," also mentions the characteristics of good government, namely: Responsive. The government must be responsive and quickly handle complaints, problems, and community needs. Fair. The government serves all citizens without discrimination and fulfills their civil rights. Efficient and Effective. The government uses the minimum possible resources to achieve the best results. Accountable. The government is responsible for its decisions and performance. Transparent. The government provides information that is open to public scrutiny.

2.3 Defining the Implementation of Rule of Law

Legal rules are a set of regulations, norms, and restrictions made by an authorized body. They are binding and coercive, with the aim of regulating human behavior in social and state life.(Tima et al., 2021). According to Permata (2020), in his journal "Legal Politics of Values-Based Regional Regulations Pancasila," legal rules are binding provisions made by authorized institutions to regulate interactions between members of society. Meanwhile, Sugianto (2021), in his journal "The Influence of Legal Rules on Adolescent Behavior," defines legal rules as a set of written regulations that are generally binding and enforced by relevant institutions to minimize social deviation. The aim of legal rules is to regulate human behavior in society, create order, justice, and legal certainty, protect public interests, and solve social problems in society.(Firmantoro, 2022). There are two forms of legal rules, namely, written and unwritten.(Serohin, 2022). Written forms such as laws, government regulations, and others. Unwritten forms, such as the customs of a particular society(Fredericks & Bradfield, 2023).

2.4 Implementation of Rule of Law in Indonesia

The concept of the "rule of law" relates to the importance of justice and the law. The primary foundation for public life and governance in a state of law is the law.(Tursin & Ahmad, 2000). Everybody must be treated equally and fairly when the law is applied, without exception. Indonesia is a state of law that upholds democratic values. This is reaffirmed in Article 1, paragraph (3) of the 1945 Constitution of the Republic of Indonesia (UUD NRI, 1945), which declares Indonesia to be a state of law.(Busthami, 2017). In recent times, there have been advancements in the application of the rule of law in Indonesia. This has been characterized by strengthening democratic institutions, raising public understanding of the law, and enhancing the caliber of law enforcement personnel.(Akmal et al., 2021).

However, there are still a number of obstacles to the adoption of the rule of law in Indonesia, including corruption. One of the main issues preventing Indonesia from implementing the rule of law is still corruption. Corruption may be detrimental to society and impede progress.(Saputra & Firmansyah, 2023)—regulations' inefficiency. The governance space needs to be effectively regulated by the laws in place. Sometimes, extant regulations conflict, are imprecise, or fail to address demands(Baral & Heinen, 2020)—the caliber of police enforcement personnel. Law enforcement personnel still need to be put up to par. There are instances when law enforcement officials act in an unprofessional manner and lack the bravery to confront corrupt officials—insufficient involvement of the community. The public's involvement in oversight of government operations needs to be higher. Sometimes, people need to be more active in their oversight of government operations and recognize the value of the rule of law(Hukum et al., 2023).

These obstacles must be addressed if Indonesia is to strengthen the application of the rule of law there. Among these initiatives is the bolstering of the fight against corruption.(Abreu et al., 2022). The fight against corruption needs to be taken seriously and persistently. Implement regulatory change. It is necessary to make improvements to the current regulations in order to make them more efficient and relevant. They are raising the standard of law enforcement personnel. Law enforcement personnel need to be properly qualified and equipped. Boost involvement in the community.(Ayu et al., 2019). Encouragement is required for the general public to take part in monitoring government operations.

Table 1. Taxonomy of research data

Papers	Summarized Abstract	Results
Intellectual Dynamics of Good Governance Studies: A Bibliometric Analysis	- Bibliometric analysis of good governance research publications from 1984 to 2020. - Increase in the growth rate of good governance literature since 2011.	Increase in the growth rate of good governance literature since 2011. - The United States, the United Kingdom, and Indonesia are top contributors.
Rule of law approach to the alleviation of poverty: An analysis on human rights dimension of governance	- The rule of law is essential for poverty alleviation and equitable opportunities. - Emphasis on the human rights dimension of governance and legal empowerment.	- The paper argues that poverty is formed by society itself. - The paper emphasizes the importance of the rule of law and human rights for poverty alleviation.
The Importance of the Rule of Law in Governance	- Paper analyzes governance and the role of law in a constructive manner. - Explores how the rule of law affects governance, especially in developing countries.	- The paper provides a constructive understanding of the rule of law and governance. - The paper examines the impact of the rule of law on governance, particularly in the developing world.
Good Governance, Rights, and State: Quo Vadis Administrative Law?	- Good governance emphasizes openness, transparency, and accountability in state activities. - The concept of governance ensures inclusion and respect for fundamental rights.	- The paper discusses the concept of good governance and its importance in assessing the lawfulness of human rights interference with the activities of the state. - The paper highlights the principles of good governance, such as participation, transparency, accountability, and the rule of law.
Good Governance and The Rule Of Law	- Good governance is essential for both public and private sectors. - The rule of law is crucial for ensuring good governance.	
Good Governance: An Analytical Study	- Importance of good governance and methods/tools to assess it - Impacts of governance on development outcomes in developing countries	- The paper highlights the importance of good governance. - The paper discusses the impacts of governance work on development outcomes.
Good governance and rule of law	- Good governance is essential for both public and private sectors. - The rule of law is crucial for ensuring good governance.	- The rule of law is essential for good governance. - Abuse of power and corruption undermines the rule of law and good governance.
The rule of law, governance, and development	- The rule of law is linked to better development outcomes - Different approaches to the rule of law promotion explored in case studies	- Positive relationship between the rule of law and development outcomes - Mixed approaches and results in the rule of law promotion

continued on following page

Table 1. Continued

Papers	Summarized Abstract	Results
Impact of the Rule of Law as a Fundamental Public Governance Principle on Administrative Law Interpretation in the Czech Republic	- The paper analyzes the use of the rule of law in administrative law interpretation in the Czech Republic. - The courts in the Czech Republic have moved from formalistic interpretation to interpretation through values, including the rule of law.	- The paper analyzes the use of the rule of law principle in interpreting administrative law provisions in the Czech Republic. - The courts in the Czech Republic have moved from purely linguistic interpretation to interpretation through values, including the rule of law.
Political Modernisation: The Rule of Law Perspective on Good Governance	- The paper explores the meaning and reference of "good governance" and its relation to the rule of law. - It presents an inquiry into the rule of law I and the rule of law II and validates these concepts using data from the World Bank Governance project.	- The paper presents an inquiry into the rule of law I and the rule of law II. - Data from the World Bank Governance project is used to validate these concepts.

3. RESEARCH METHOD

3.1 Types of Research

Since the goal of this article is to comprehend how the rule of law affects good governance, the qualitative research method is suitable for this kind of research topic. With the help of this method, we can gain a deep understanding of the intricate social phenomenon and conduct an in-depth investigation of the theme that incorporates unbiased viewpoints and experiences.

3.2 Research Locations

Our article's study was conducted using scholarly journals and the World Bank website as sources. However, according to our analysis, academic publications have emerged as a top source of knowledge and data, including in-depth evaluations of expert research. Data relating to Academic Journals were obtained from many online database sources, including Scopus, Google Scholar, Dimension AI, and others. The data underwent peer review to ensure accuracy and dependability.

3.3 Data Collection Techniques

As researchers, in order to collect data, we conducted a literature review, which enabled us to compile the body of current knowledge. We were effective in understanding the data because of the information that was gathered. We identified the holes in the research and the crucial information for our brainstorming. We started by defining the parameters of our study in order to conduct a literature review; specifically, this involved identifying the keywords we would use to look for information pertaining to the article's issue, such as "good governance," "rule of law," etc. We also restricted the scope of our search to papers released in the previous five years. We first checked to make sure the collected publications were related to our article; then, we quickly perused their abstracts

Figure 1. Filters and keywords used for research (Dimension AI)

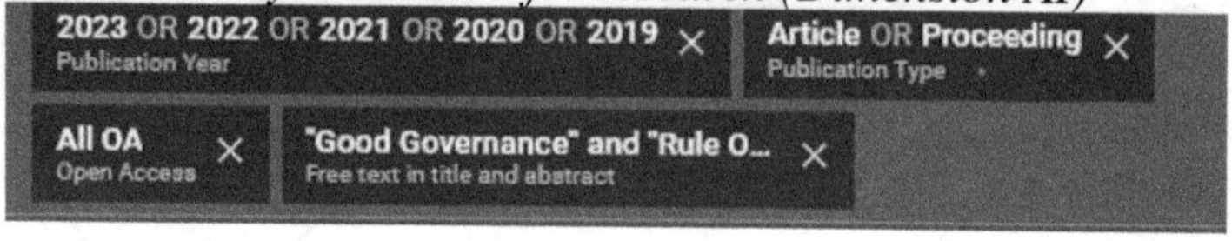

3.4 Data Analysis Techniques

VOSViewer is a great desktop program for bibliometric analysis and visualization of research data. To begin the analysis, we first imported the research data into the VOSViewer program in RIS format. Once the data was imported successfully, we conducted a bibliometric analysis to determine which themes were most influential. The ability to create maps with VOSViewer allowed us to determine which themes were most influential.

Figure 2. Density visualization of research (Created By Author)

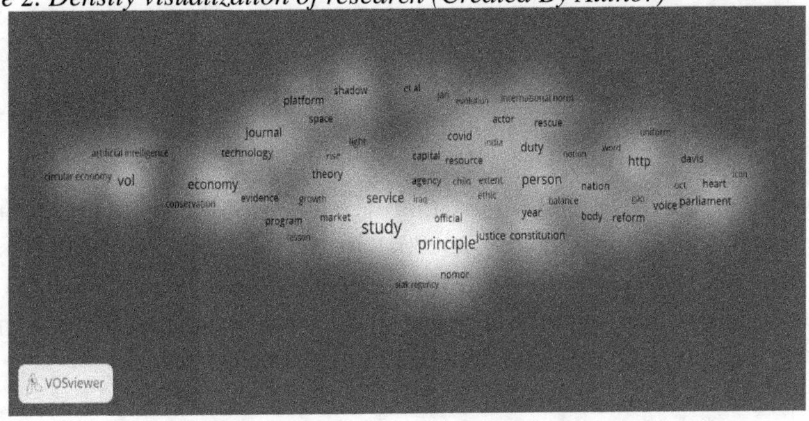

Figure 2 shows the research themes in addressing the rule of law in good governance. There are various related research themes, but only a few are relatively recent and consistently discussed, namely Principle, Study, and Service. Principles are something that researchers prioritize the most. This is because principles in governance such as transparency, accountability, and participation are able to create good governance that can support better governance and also play an important role in directing the organization or entity in a good and sustainable direction. It is expected to improve the quality of public services that are poor in the eyes of the public by applying basic principles such as legal certainty, accountability, transparency, fairness, professionalism, and democracy(Maryam, 2016). Meanwhile, the theme of research related to the study is that by studying the government, it can also find out the rule of law from best practices that exist in other countries in creating governance by comparing governance in other countries(Busthami, 2017). Studies in this field aim to smooth national development to achieve national goals(Akmal et al., 2021). The final theme is service, where service is very important to the rule of law in good governance, as well as with good services useful for meeting the needs or interests of the community(Saputra & Firmansyah, 2023).

4. RESULT AND DISCUSSION

4.1. Result

4.1.1 Document Publication by Years

Figure 3 presents a timeline illustrating the publication of findings on the impact of the rule of law on governance from 2018 to 2023. In 2018, no documents were published, and in 2019, there was a surge in publications, which amounted to 60 documents from 0 documents. In 2020 and 2021, the number of published documents increased by only ten each year, namely 70 and 80 documents.

Figure 3. Publication of Dokumen by years (Dimension AI)

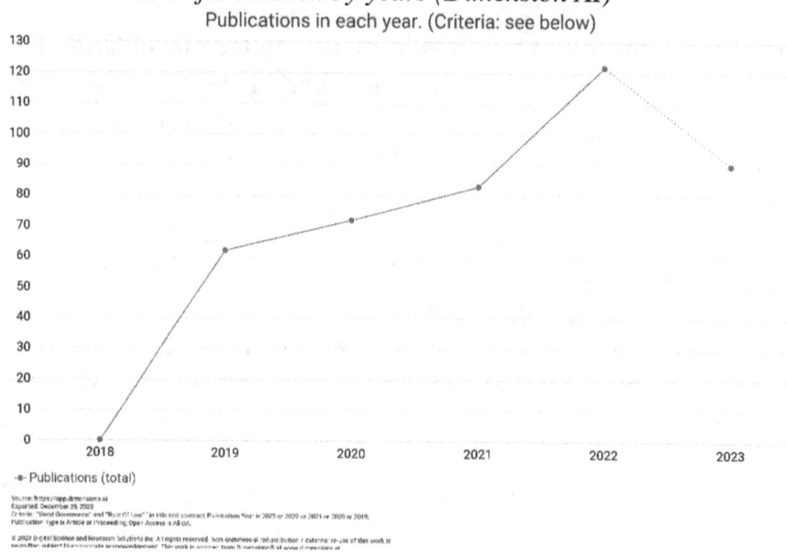

Then, there was a spike in 2022, where the published documents amounted to 120 from 80 documents in the previous year. However, there was a decrease of 30 documents in 2023, where only 90 documents were published from 120 documents in the previous year. From this, it can be concluded that 2019-2022 is a starting point year to achieve and maintain progress.

4.1.2 Document Publication by Subject Area

The graph from 2019, 2020, 2021, 2022, and 2023 is shown in Figure 4. Out of all the organizations that contribute to publications on the subject of good governance and the rule of law, Human Society is the most influential, with 210 articles. With 187 publications published, Law and Legal Studies holds second place in terms of quantity of publications. Next, with 57 publications, commerce and management tourism are among the top three most often published categories. Economics holds the fourth spot, with 22 publications available. With 17 documents, it holds sixth place in information and computing science.

Figure 4. Publication by subject area (Dimension AI)

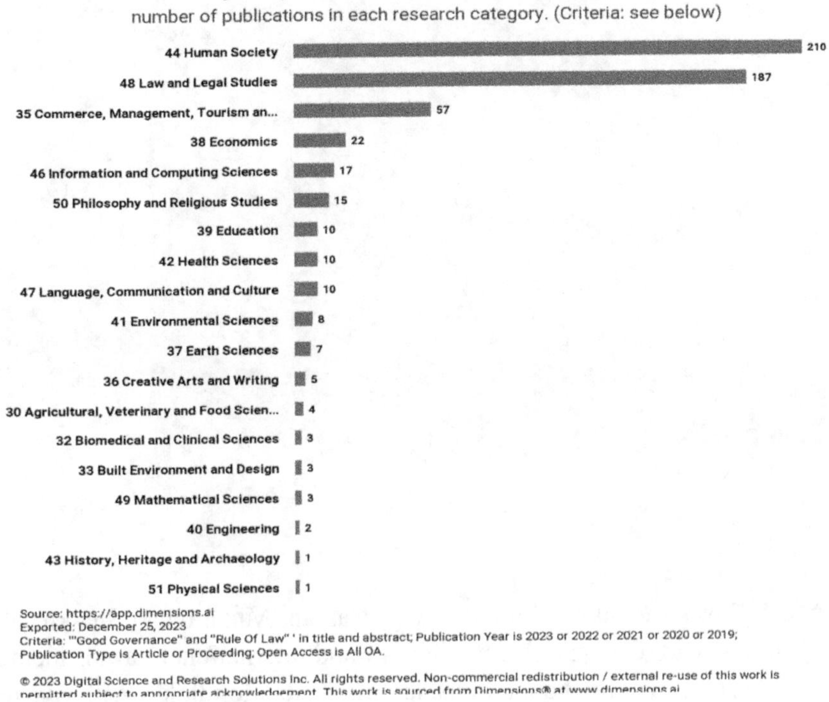

Furthermore, philosophy and religious studies, in the sixth position, produced 15 documents, continued in the seventh position, namely education, healthy science, and language communication and culture; the publications produced by each of the three fields were the same, totaling ten publications, then in the aspects of environmental science and earth science had one difference, totaling 8 and 7 publications, as well as aspects between creative arts and writing and agricultural veterinary and food science which had one difference, namely five and four publications. In addition, aspects of biomedical and clinical science, built environment and design, and mathematical science produced the same publications with three publications. She was followed by aspects of engineering with two publications. Finally, in terms of aspects of history, heritage, archaeology, and physical science, only 1 document has been published related to this subject.

4.1.3 Documents Publication by Author

Figure 5. Publication by author (Dimension AI)

Figure 5 shows the authors' relationship. Hassan, Muhammad Shaikh, of the BRAC University for Comparative Public Law and International Law, is identified by one publication, five total quotations, and five quotation links. With five quote connections, five total quotations, and one publication, Naher, Nahitun of the BRAC University of Bangladesh is indicated with a red cluster. One publication, five total quotations, and five quotation links can be found for Adam, Alayne Mary of McGill University in Canada. Five quotation links, five total quotations, and one publication are provided by Hoque, Roksana of BRAC University. Then, Balabanova, Dina Chavdarova, of the London School of Hygiene & Tropical Medicine, with one publication, five quotation links, and five quotes overall, all highlighted in red. Based on the information provided, it can be deduced that the image above depicts a single cluster, six researchers, fifteen quote linkages, fifteen total quotations, and one group.

4.2 Discussion

4.2.1 Network Visualisation

Using VOSViewer for network visualization, overlay, and density, the network between topics in 324 documents obtained from the Dimensions AI database was bibliometrically performed. A bibliometric network consists of nodes and edges. Nodes can be publication circles, journals, or keywords, while edges show the relationship between nodes, indicating the relationship between two nodes. In addition, distance represents the strength of the relationship; the correlation between nodes becomes more significant the closer the distance between nodes.

When talking about how the rule of law affects good governance, it is important to take legal compliance, accountability, and openness into account. Good governance greatly depends on legal compliance. It has a direct bearing on the management, supervision, and governance of an organization and is related to compliance with relevant rules and laws. On the other side, an essential component of good governance is stakeholder involvement and participation. Involving stakeholders in the decision-making process makes it more inclusive and guarantees that a range of interests and points of view are taken into account. The influence of the rule of law in good governance is depicted in the following VOS viewer analysis findings, which provide a visual representation of the keyword network.

Figure 6. Network visualization or research (Created by Author)

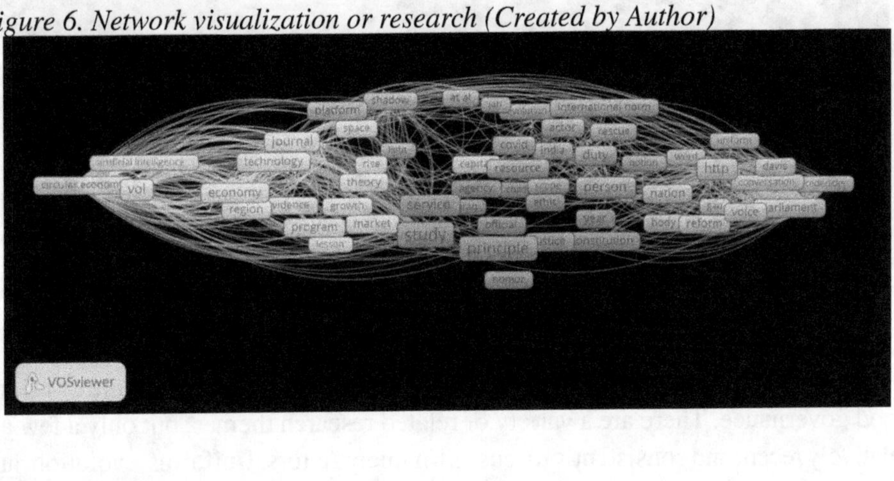

Image labels indicate frequently occurring terms or keywords, and clustering is used to understand bibliometric clustering. On the other hand, image mapping is used to gain additional understanding of the bibliometric network. Commonly used terms or keywords are displayed within each circle. The diameter of the circle indicates the number of papers and publications associated with the phrase or keyword in the document title.

Study, Principle, and Service are the largest nodes, as can be seen in the figure above, where each hue is organized into six groups according to the correspondence between the keywords and their illustrations. The first rank is occupied by study, which has 36832 link strength and 455 total occurrences. With 316 occurrences and 9133 link strength, Principle took second place. Service, with 156 occurrences and 15276 overall strength, came in third. Furthermore, in terms of good governance, the nodes with the lowest frequency in order are artificial intelligence (16 occurrences and 6994 link strength), followed by Gap (14 occurrences and 2578 link strength).

4.2.2 Overlay Visualisation

The theme mapping on the impact of the rule of law in good governance aims to identify and analyze various topics and research focuses related to the impact of the rule of law in good governance. It is expected that this mapping will reveal various issues and innovations that researchers propose to understand and address challenges in the impact of the rule of law in good governance.

Figure 7. Overlay visualization of research (Created by Author)

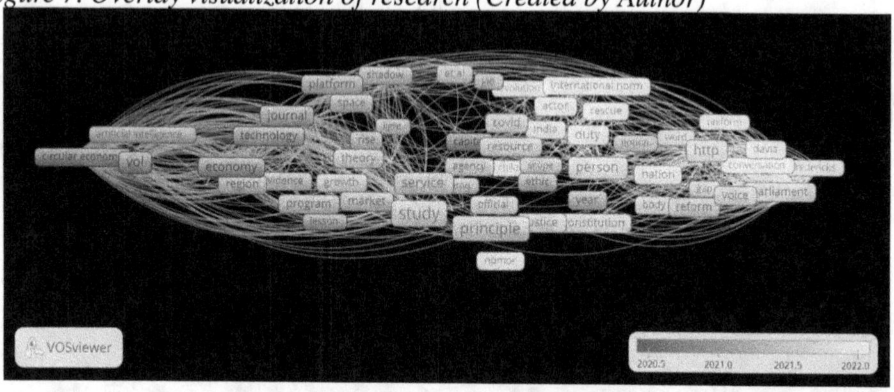

Figure 7 shows the research themes that address the impact of the rule of law on good governance. There are a variety of related research themes, but only a few are relatively recent and consistently discussed, namely Actors, Uniforms, evolution, and international norms. Actors is a longstanding research theme, and the most recently published in 2022 is Actors in the Context of the Rule of Law in Good Governance. Research in this area focuses on Stakeholder Awareness Raising, Transparency and Accountability, and Advocacy for Sustainable Legal Change. Meanwhile, the research theme on Uniforms is becoming increasingly important because the uniform that every employee in governance wears shows order in good governance. The next theme, evolution, highlights the importance of change, which is designed to guide organizational and individual behavior and ensure that good governance is effectively implemented. The final theme, international norms, creates a framework that can influence and shape good governance practices at the global level. The impact of the rule of law on good governance is often closely linked to the engagement and application of international norms.

The discussion of the four research themes, namely Actors, Uniform, Evolution, and international norms, have a significant relationship; actors are the main figures or actors of the rule of law in good governance and can have a significant positive impact. Through the actors in the governance, we can know the duties and functions of each in good governance. In addition, good actors can build public pressure to increase accountability and transparency in business and government practices. With this increased awareness, organizations and governments may feel compelled to strengthen oversight systems, improve policies, and ensure compliance with the rule of law. On the other hand, uniform good governance can reflect good and orderly governance in a country.

International conventions and norms carry broader implications in the context of good governance. Convention implementation can motivate countries and organizations to adopt good governance principles proactively and result in more substantial legal changes. International norms can establish recognized global standards, creating the basis for global adherence to good governance principles. International conventions and norms can lead to harmonization and increased consistency in governance practices at the global level, reducing barriers and supporting effective implementation of the rule of law in the context of good governance.

4.3 Discussion from World Governance Indicator

Figure 8 displays the Rule of Law indicator score from the World Bank's Worldwide Governance Indicators (WGI). Rule of Law is one of the dimensions of governance measured by the WGI in a percentage range of 0-100.

The graph below shows a comparison of the development of Indonesia and Australia's Rule of Law scores from 1996 to 2020. In 1996, Indonesia's Rule of Law score was 36.18. Then there was a decline in 1998 to 27.50. In 2000, it rose again to 30.85. Then the score fell again in 2002 to 21.39. Then, there was a gradual upward trend until it reached the highest score of 44.71 in 2014, although it decreased slightly to 39.52 in 2016. Then, there was stability in the rule of law score in governance in Indonesia from 2017 until 2022. This indicates that the quality of the rule of law, law enforcement, and equal access to justice in Indonesia continues to improve. However, the achievement of 45.28 still needs to reach the ideal standard of 100.

This means there is still much homework for Indonesia to do to strengthen the rule of law and achieve good governance.

Figure 8. Rule of law indicator score (World Bank Website)

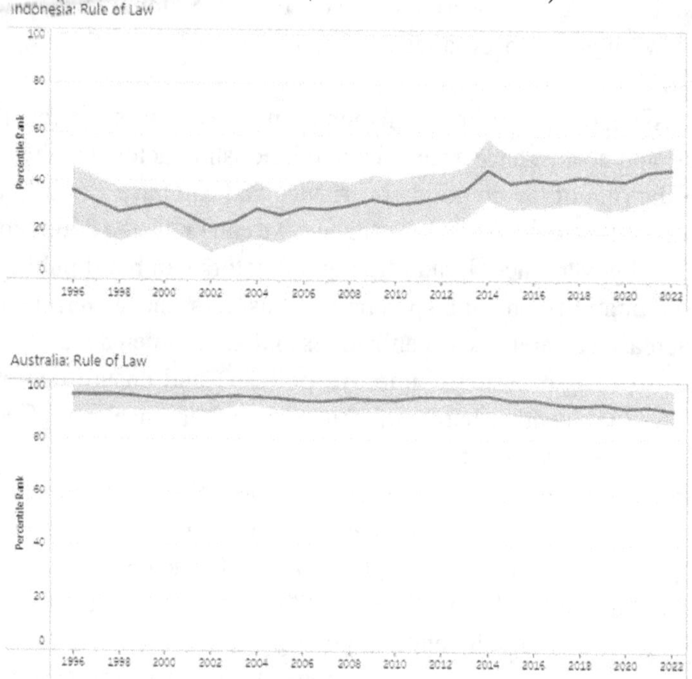

Meanwhile, from 1996 to 2022, Australia has a stable score, namely the initial score in 1996, which is 96.482, although it has slightly decreased the score in 2022 to 91.038. Australia's score is ideal, which indicates that Australia has implemented the rule of law well in its governance compared to Indonesia, which still needs improvement. However, Australia can be an example of applying the rule of law in governance if it wants to create good governance in a country.

Overall, this figure provides an empirical picture of the development of the rule of law in Indonesia and Australia based on objective data from the World Bank's WGI. This data is useful for tracking Indonesia's progress in realizing credible and accountable governance.

Figure 9. Map visualisation of WGI (World Bank Website)

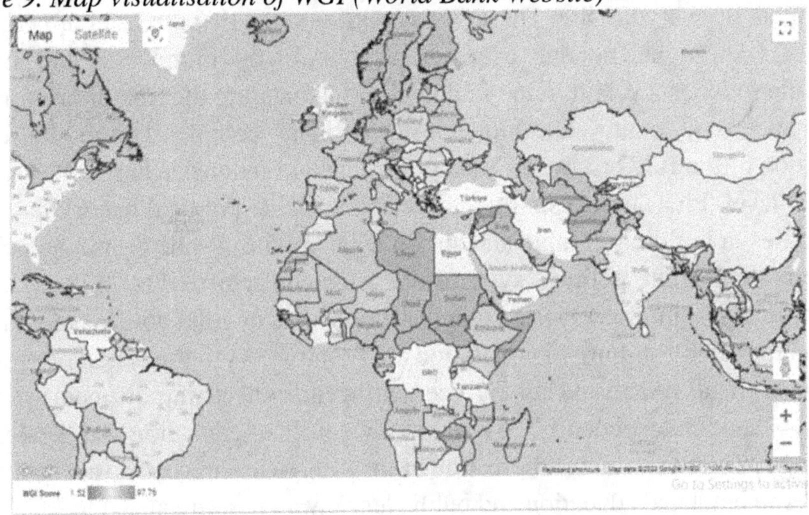

Figure 9 presents a visualization of the map of Rule of Law rankings and scores around the world based on the World Bank's World Governance Indicators (WGI) 2020 data. The map is categorized into quartiles, which divide countries into seven groups based on their Rule of Law score ranking, which can be classified into different colors, namely bright green, light green, yellow, light orange, bright orange, and red colors. The greener the color indicates, the better the application of the rule of law in the country; conversely, the red color indicates that the application of the rule of law in the country is not going well. It can be seen that there are only a few countries that have good applications of the rule of law, such as Finland, Sweden, and Germany. Followed in the second-best position are Poland, Spain, and Italy, then in the third position with a moderate application of the rule of law are China, Saudi Arabia, and Indonesia, while countries with poor levels of application of the rule of law, such as Somalia, Libya, and Afghanistan. Then, in the last position, the countries without any rules of application of law in governance are Yemen, Iran, and Turkey. Where this is due to the Governments in Yemen, Iran, and Turkey tend to be authoritarian, thus not providing space for public participation in the decision-making process.

It can be seen from the visualization of the figure above that the country Denmark is ranked number one in the world in terms of law and order with a score of 0.89 for compliance with the rule of law is a country with a score of 0.87 on compliance with the rule of law. Having the same score as Denmark, Norway is also the leading country in terms of following law and order and adherence to the law. Finland comes in second place, scoring around 0.87 on compliance with the rule of law. The country emphasizes that the rule of law is not just a common phrase but an essential component of everyday life. These two countries show that the level of peace and security is determined not only by geography but also by commitment and policies.

While Indonesia is still in the middle of implementing the rule of law for good governance in a country like Finland, due to many complex factors, the implementation of the rule of law for good governance in Indonesia has yet to reach an optimal level. First, Indonesia's dynamic and unstable political history has led to difficulties in building a stable and strong legal culture. While providing political freedom, democratic political systems are often characterized by shifting leaders and political instability, which can hinder the success of good governance. In addition, an intractable culture of corruption also contributes to the denial of progress. Indonesia's legal system and law enforcement agencies need improvement to operate effectively and independently. Given that low levels of education and legal understanding can hinder public participation in ensuring transparency and accountability in government, legal education and public legal awareness are also important focus in efforts to improve the application of the rule of law.

4.4 Future Directions

The study highlights several future directions for research and practical implementation regarding the intersection of the rule of law and good governance. One critical area for future research lies in exploring the efficacy of anti-corruption measures and their impact on governance outcomes. By examining various anti-corruption strategies within the Indonesian context, researchers can identify best practices that can be replicated in similar environments, thereby enhancing the overall efficacy of governance structures. Additionally, there is a pressing need for initiatives aimed at improving public legal education and awareness. Enhancing legal literacy among citizens can significantly bolster public participation in governance processes, ensuring accountability and transparency. Future studies may focus on how such educational programs can equip citizens with the knowledge necessary to actively engage in legal and governance affairs.

Moreover, a comparative analysis of governance models from other countries that successfully integrate the rule of law could yield valuable insights. By examining successful practices abroad, Indonesia can adopt innovative strategies tailored to its unique socio-political landscape, ultimately leading towards improved governance quality. Lastly, attention should be given to addressing structural barriers that inhibit the effective application of the rule of law, such as corruption and political interference in law enforcement. Future research should aim to develop frameworks that foster greater independence and integrity in legal institutions, thus ensuring that the rule of law genuinely enhances governance for all citizens. Investing in these areas will not only contribute to academic discourse but will also provide actionable insights that can help forge a path toward more effective governance practices rooted in the rule of law.

4.5 Recommendations

Based on the findings of the study, several key recommendations emerge to enhance the relationship between the rule of law and good governance in Indonesia. Firstly, it is essential to strengthen anti-corruption frameworks within governmental institutions. This involves not only tightening legislations to combat corrupt practices but also ensuring that those laws are enforced without bias or favoritism. Establishing independent bodies to oversee these efforts can promote greater accountability and transparency in governance. Secondly, enhancing community engagement in governance processes is crucial. The government should actively encourage public participation through consultations and feedback mechanisms, ensuring that citizens have a voice in decision-making. Programs aimed at increasing public awareness of the rule of law and citizens' rights will empower individuals to demand accountability and participate meaningfully in governance.

Additionally, reforming the education system to include a greater focus on legal studies and civic education is recommended. By integrating these subjects into school curricula, future generations will develop a stronger understanding of their rights and responsibilities, fostering a culture of legal compliance and respect for democratic principles. Furthermore, improving the capacity and integrity of law enforcement agencies must be prioritized. Training programs that focus on ethical practices, professional standards, and community relations can help transform police forces into more reliable and trustworthy entities. This will, in turn, reinforce public confidence in the legal system and its ability to uphold the rule of law. Lastly, consistent monitoring and evaluation of governance initiatives should be implemented to assess progress and identify areas for improvement continuously. By adopting this reflective practice, policymakers can make informed decisions that adapt to changing societal needs and challenges, ultimately leading to a more effective and resilient governance framework grounded in the rule of law.

4.6 Theoretical Implications

The findings of this study carry significant theoretical implications for the fields of governance, law, and public administration. Firstly, the intricate relationship between the rule of law and good governance underscores the necessity for a multidimensional framework that integrates legal, social, and ethical perspectives. Scholars must consider how legal frameworks not only regulate behavior but also shape citizen and state interactions, thus influencing the quality of governance outcomes. This study reinforces the notion that the rule of law is not merely about enforcing regulations but also about fostering a culture of accountability and transparency, which is essential for good governance. Moreover, the study contributes to the theoretical discourse on governance by emphasizing the role of public participation. It challenges traditional top-down approaches that often overlook the importance of engaging citizens in governance processes. This reinforces the theoretical understanding that good governance requires inclusivity and the active involvement of stakeholders. Researchers are encouraged to explore models of participatory governance that empower citizens and enhance their role in legal frameworks.

Additionally, the findings highlight the need for a robust theoretical model that addresses the impact of corruption on governance. By examining the theoretical mechanisms through which corruption undermines the rule of law, scholars can develop more comprehensive theories that tackle systemic challenges in governance. This aspect prompts further research into the dynamics of regulatory frameworks and their effectiveness in curbing corrupt practices. Finally, the study suggests a need for interdisciplinary approaches in governance research. The interplay between legal principles, societal values, and institutional effectiveness proposes that scholars from various disciplines—such as political science, sociology, and law—come together to build a more holistic understanding of how the rule of law can enhance good governance. This collaborative perspective may yield innovative solutions that address both theoretical and practical challenges in this field, ultimately contributing to the advancement of governance scholarship.

4.7 Practical Implications

The practical implications of this study are critical for policymakers and governance practitioners aiming to enhance the rule of law in their jurisdictions. One primary takeaway is the urgent need to establish and strengthen anti-corruption measures within government institutions. Implementing comprehensive regulatory frameworks and independent oversight bodies can significantly deter corrupt practices, thereby reinforcing public trust in governance. By prioritizing transparency and accountability in all governance processes, stakeholders can work towards creating a more equitable environment for all citizens. Furthermore, the findings emphasize the importance of active community engagement in governance. Practitioners should cultivate platforms for public participation, such as town hall meetings and feedback mechanisms, which invite citizens to voice their concerns and contribute to the decision-making process. This approach not only empowers citizens but also ensures that governance initiatives are reflective of the community's needs and values, thereby making policies more effective and widely accepted.

Moreover, enhancing legal education and public awareness is essential for fostering a culture of compliance and respect for the law. Practical initiatives, such as community workshops and outreach programs, can demystify legal frameworks and inform citizens of their rights and responsibilities. Empowering individuals with legal knowledge can lead to increased public participation in governance processes and a stronger collective demand for accountability from public officials. Additionally, improving the capacity and integrity of law enforcement agencies must be a priority. Practical training programs focused on ethics, professionalism, and community engagement can help transform police forces into reliable entities that uphold the rule of law. Building strong relationships between law enforcement and communities fosters a sense of security and encourages collaboration in preventing crime and promoting justice. Lastly, consistent monitoring and evaluation of governance practices are vital for achieving long-term improvements. Policymakers should implement metrics to assess the effectiveness of governance initiatives continuously. This adaptive approach allows for the identification of best practices and the adjustment of strategies to meet evolving challenges, ultimately leading to a more effective and resilient governance framework grounded in the rule of law.

4.8 Managerial Implications

The managerial implications derived from this study underscore the critical role that leaders and managers play in fostering a culture of good governance rooted in the rule of law. First and foremost, managers must adopt a proactive stance on compliance and ethical standards within their organizations. This requires the establishment of clear guidelines and policies that promote integrity and accountability at all levels. By doing so, managers can create an environment where ethical behavior is not only expected but rewarded, thereby reducing opportunities for misconduct and enhancing overall organizational performance. Moreover, effective communication is essential in implementing governance strategies. Managers should prioritize transparent communication channels that allow for open dialogue with employees and stakeholders. Encouraging feedback and suggestions can lead to innovative solutions and improvements in governance practices. By actively listening to the input of team members, managers can demonstrate their commitment to fostering a participatory approach that values diverse perspectives, ultimately enhancing organizational cohesion and morale.

Training and development also represent a crucial component of managerial responsibilities in promoting good governance. Managers should invest in ongoing training programs that equip employees with the necessary skills and knowledge to navigate the legal landscape and understand the importance of the rule of law. This investment not only empowers employees but also reinforces the organization's commitment to lawful and ethical conduct, which can enhance public trust and stakeholder confidence. Additionally, performance metrics should be integrated into governance strategies to measure adherence to ethical practices and the overall effectiveness of governance initiatives. Managers should establish key performance indicators (KPIs) that reflect both legal compliance and organizational values. Regularly reviewing these metrics can help identify areas for improvement and allow managers to make data-driven decisions that align with the principles of good governance. Lastly, cultivating a culture of accountability is essential for effective managerial leadership. Managers should model accountability through their actions and decision-making, holding themselves and their teams responsible for outcomes. By fostering a culture where mistakes are acknowledged and lessons are learned rather than hidden, managers can promote a more resilient and adaptable organization that is better equipped to uphold the rule of law and navigate the complexities of governance challenges.

5. CONCLUSION

To sum up, this study has shed light on good governance in a useful way. We have added to the corpus of information already available on good governance by conducting a thorough analysis of the rule of law. The ramifications of our research encompass pertinent domains or uses of the Rule of Law, emphasizing the advantages and difficulties associated with good governance. However, our research has shown several aspects that are crucial to acknowledge the possible constraints, like diplomatic immunity, postponed justice, and the wealthy and well-connected minority. In order to expand on our basis and deepen our understanding of good governance, future research should include criminal justice reform, anti-corruption and transparent government, and access to justice. In summary, this study highlights the need for more research and careful discussion in the field of the rule of law in order to promote developments that would benefit the pertinent parties and communities.

REFERENCES

Abreu, M., Soares, I., & Silva, S. (2022). Governance quality and environmental policy on emergent, resource-rich economies: The case of Brazil. *Energy Reports, 8*, 70–75. DOI: 10.1016/j.egyr.2022.01.041

Adula, M., Birbirsa, Z. A., & Kant, S. (2023). The effect of interpersonal, problem solving and technical training skills on performance of Ethiopia textile industry: Continuance, normative and affective commitment as mediators. *Cogent Business & Management, 10*(3), 2286672. Advance online publication. DOI: 10.1080/23311975.2023.2286672

Akmal, D. U., Sultan, U., & Tirtayasa, A. (2021). Politik reformasi hukum. *Pembentukan system [LEGAL REFORM POLITICS. SYSTEM FORMATION],8*, 21–35.

Ayu, A., Niswaty, R., Darwis, M., & Arhas, S. H. (2019). Applying the principles of good governance in the efforts of guiding out-of-school children at social service offices at Takalar Regency. *Jurnal Office, 5*(2), 51–58. DOI: 10.26858/jo.v5i2.11821

Baral, N., & Heinen, J. T. (2020). Regulatory Compliance of Community-Based Conservation Organizations: Empirical Evidence from Annapurna Conservation Area, Nepal. *Sustainability (Basel), 12*(22), 9420. DOI: 10.3390/su12229420

Bërdufi, N., & Nezha, K. (2023). Understanding Civilian Participation and its Implications: A Case Study on the Inclusion of Syria's Civilian Population in the Context of Violence. *Interdisciplinary Journal of Research and Development, 10*(2), 68. DOI: 10.56345/ijrdv10n209

Budiarrianto, D., & Sebayang, A. F. (2021). Penerapan Prinsip-Prinsip Good Governance terhadap Pelayanan Publik Desa Rahayu Kecamatan Margaasih Kabupaten Bandung. *Bandung Conference Series: Economics Studies, 1*(1), 33–40. DOI: 10.29313/bcses.v1i1.49

Busthami, D. (2017). *Kekuasaan Kehakiman Dalam Perspektif Negara Hukum. 4.*

Delmana, L. P. (2019). Pengaruh Penerapan Good Governance Dalam E-Purcashing Terhadap Pencegahan Korupsi [The Influence of Good Governance Implementation in E-Purchasing on Corruption Prevention]. *Jurnal Ilmu Pemerintahan Widya Praja [Journal of Government Science Widya Praja], 45*(1), 47–62. DOI: 10.33701/jipwp.v45i1.241

Dinata, A. W. (2022). Legal Implications Of Non-Compliance With The Decision Of The State Administrative Court In Terms Of The Implementation Of Regional Autonomy And The Unitary State. *Jurnal Hukum Peratun, 4*(1), 1–30. DOI: 10.25216/peratun.412021.1-30

Edralin, D., & Pastrana, R. (2020). Nexus between Sustainable Business Practices and the Quest for Peace. *Bedan Research Journal, 5*(1), 1–58. DOI: 10.58870/berj.v5i1.11

Firmantoro, K. (2022). Negligence Of Customs and Excise in the Implementation of Judicial Decisions on Audit Result Disputes that Can Cause Country Loss and Business Actors (A Study On Court Decision No. 46/Pk/Tun/2011 Which Has Not Been Done By Customs And Excise. *International Journal of Business, Economics, and Social Development, 3*(2), 76–87. DOI: 10.46336/ijbesd.v3i2.248

Fredericks, B., & Bradfield, A. (2023). Many Bodies, One Heart. *M/C Journal, 26*(1). DOI: 10.5204/mcj.2908

Gal, J. (2020). Corporate governance of insurers in Germany. German National Report. *Zeitschrift Für Die Gesamte Versicherungswissenschaft, 109*(1), 41–64. DOI: 10.1007/s12297-020-00467-9

Govindaraju, P., Rahman, M. R. A., & Ismail, S. M. (2023). Ekstremisme Ganas Dan Semakan Kehakiman Dalam Kes-Kes Berkaitan Dengannya Dari Perspektif Undang-Undang Tahanan Pencegahan Malaysia : (Violent Extremism and Judicial Review in Related Cases: A Perspective on the Preventive Detention Laws of Malaysia). *UUM Journal of Legal Studies, 14*(1), 297–331. DOI: 10.32890/uumjls2023.14.1.12

Hirsch, B., Schäfer, F.-S., Aristovnik, A., Kovač, P., & Ravšelj, D. (2022). The impact of Digitalized Communication on the effectiveness of Local Administrative Authorities – Findings from Central European Countries in the COVID-19 Crisis. *Journal of Business Economics, 93*(1–2), 173–192. DOI: 10.1007/s11573-022-01110-y PMID: 38013851

Hukum, S., Kurniawati, R., Lubis, A. F., Indrayana, S., & Kurniawan, B. A. (2023). *Rekonstruksi Penelitian Hukum Administrasi Negara melalui Pendekatan Bibliometrik : Sebuah Tinjauan Komprehensif tentang Perkembangan dan Kontribusi Literatur [Reconstruction of State Administrative Law Research through a Bibliometric Approach: A Comprehensive Review of the Development and Contribution of Literature],* 2(01), 20–29. https://doi.org/DOI: 10.58812/shh.v2.i01

Jabo, B., & Kant, S. "Impact of Technical CRM on Ethiopia Bank Human-Computer Interface and Competitive Advantage as Mediators of Performance," 2024 IEEE International Conference on Computing, Power and Communication Technologies (IC2PCT), Greater Noida, India, 2024, pp. 679-682, https://doi.org/DOI: 10.1109/IC2PCT60090.2024.10486237

Kant, S., & Adula, M. (2024). Human-Machine Interaction in the Metaverse in the Context of Ethiopia. In Impact and Potential of Machine Learning in the Metaverse (pp. 196-212). IGI Global. DOI: DOI: 10.4018/979-8-3693-5762-0.ch008

Karunia, R. L., Solihati, K. D., & Wati, N. K. (2022). Implementation of Good Governance Principles in the Land Transportation Management Center. *KnE Social Sciences*, 1253–1269–1253–1269. DOI: 10.18502/kss.v7i9.11014

Khodakivskyi, M. (2021). The formation of Ukraine's legal policy at the present stage. *Yearly Journal of Scientific Articles. Pravova Derzhava*, *32*, 496–505. DOI: 10.33663/0869-2491-2021-32-496-505

Lee, A. (2021). In the Shadow of Platforms. *M/C Journal, 24*(2). DOI: 10.5204/mcj.2750

Muhammad, M., & Husen, L. O. (2019). State Civil Apparatus in Indonesia in the Conception of Welfare State: A Study of Legal Material Law Number 5 Year 2014 on State Civil Apparatus. *Asian Social Science*, *15*(3), 64. DOI: 10.5539/ass.v15n3p64

Mumpuni, N. W. R., & Kusumawati, M. P. (2021). Good governance pengelolaan sampah: Komitmen negara terhadap lingkungan hidup. *Jurnal Cakrawala Hukum*, *12*(1), 79–89. DOI: 10.26905/idjch.v12i1.5725

Nugroho, S. S., & Rahardjo, M. (2023). Penerapan Fungsi Pengawasan Dprd Dalam Mewujudkan Pemerintahan Daerah Yang Baik. *Yustisia Merdeka: Jurnal Ilmiah Hukum*, *9*(1), 59–67. DOI: 10.33319/yume.v9i1.218

Priyo Sembodo, G., Nefi, A., & Fakhriah, E. L. (2022). Urgensi Penerapan Prinsip Business Judgment Rule Dalam Peraturan Pemerintah Nomor 63 Tahun 2019 Tentang Investasi Pemerintah. *Jurnal Poros Hukum Padjadjaran*, *3*(2), 185–208. DOI: 10.23920/jphp.v3i2.789

Rao, S. S. (2021). Police: A Public Safety Institution of Governance. *International Journal for Research in Applied Science and Engineering Technology*, *9*(10), 1351–1353. DOI: 10.22214/ijraset.2021.38593

Russo, O., R. (. (2023). Environmental Rights are a Human Right to a Healthy Environment: A Brief Review. *International Journal of Life Science and Agriculture Research*, *03*(12). Advance online publication. DOI: 10.55677/ijlsar/V02I12Y2023-01

Sakti Koeswanto, E., Riswandi, R., & Redi, A. (2023). Implications of Public Trust Due to Weak Law Enforcement Morality. *Edunity : Kajian Ilmu Sosial Dan Pendidikan, 2*(1), 78–86. DOI: 10.57096/edunity.v1i05.39

Saputra, E. F., & Firmansyah, H. (2023). *Politik Hukum dalam Upaya Pemberantasan Tindak Pidana Korupsi melalui Pembaharuan Pengaturan Tindak Pidana Korupsi sebagai Extraordinary Crime dalam KUHP Nasional. 6*(2), 4493–4504.

Serohin, V. (2022). European governance as an institute of constitutional law of the European Union. The Journal of VN Karazin Kharkiv National University. *Series Law*, (33), 28–43.

Shaheen, Y., Zhiqiang, X., & Zhiqiang, X. (2019). Public Administration in Afghanistan: Challenges and Way Forward. *Open Journal of Social Sciences, 07*(06), 142–160. DOI: 10.4236/jss.2019.76012

Siljanovska, Z., & Shalevska, E. (2019). OECD Principles For Good Corporate Governance And Their Impact On The Process Of Standardization. *Knowledge International Journal, 34*(5), 1491–1497. DOI: 10.35120/kij34051491S

Susanti, A. (2022). Implementation Of The Principles Of Good Governance In Improving Public Services At The Investment Office And One-Stop Integrated Services Of Central Sulawesi Province. *Indonesian Journal of Multidisciplinary Science, 1*(12), 1598–1611. DOI: 10.55324/ijoms.v1i12.243

Szadok-Bratuń, A. (2021). Fullerowski paradygmat (nie)dobrego prawa i jego aktualność „hic et nunc. *Studia Nad Autorytaryzmem i Totalitaryzmem, 43*(2), 295–316. DOI: 10.19195/2300-7249.43.2.19

Tima, T. A., Schneider, P., Chanda, S. K., Mozumder, M. M. H., Hossain, M. M., Begum, A., & Shamsuzzaman, M. (2021). Analyses Implementation Realities of Legal Frameworks for Sustainable Management of Tanguar Haor Fisheries Resources in Bangladesh. *Sustainability (Basel), 13*(16), 8784. DOI: 10.3390/su13168784

Triwahyuni, A. D. (2020). Kewajiban Dan Tanggung Jawab Notaris Sebagai Pejabat Umum. *Acta Comitas, 5*(1), 1. DOI: 10.24843/AC.2020.v05.i01.p01

Trofimova, L. (2020). Problematic points of the quality of qualification assessment of judges. *Law Review of Kyiv University of Law, 2*(2), 198–207. DOI: 10.36695/2219-5521.2.2020.35

Tursin, S. R., & Ahmad, R. (2000). *Konsep Supremasi Hukum, Masyarakat Madani Dan Kaitan Keduanya*. 66–72.

Valerio, A., Parton, B., & Robb, A. (2014). Entrepreneurship Education and Training Programs around the World: Dimensions for Success. In *Entrepreneurship Education and Training Programs around the World: Dimensions for Success*. books.google.com. DOI: 10.1596/978-1-4648-0202-7

Vallejo, R. (2021). *The Private Administrative Law of Technical Standardization.*, *40*(1), 172–229.

Witkowska, M., & Kucheryavaya, E. (2021). The concept of good governance in the eu legislation: analysis in the context of methodology of the civil law research. *Methodological problems of the civil law researches*, *3*(3), 139–162. DOI: 10.33397/2619-0559-2021-3-3-139-162

Zdyb, M. (2019). Prawo do dobrej administracji. Aksjologiczne aspekty dobrej administracji. *Studia Iuridica Lublinensia*, *28*(2), 107. DOI: 10.17951/sil.2019.28.2.107-133

KEY TERMS AND DEFINITIONS

Governance: Governance refers to the processes, structures, and mechanisms through which power and authority are exercised, decisions are made, and stakeholders are held accountable. It involves the systems that manage resources and ensure order and effectiveness within organizations, governments, or communities. Governance emphasizes transparency, participation, and the rule of law in guiding collective action and policy.

Good Governance: The concept refers to the effective and efficient management of resources and affairs in a manner that is transparent, accountable, participatory, and responsive to the needs of society, ensuring equity and the rule of law.

Rule of Law: A principle under which all members of a society, including the government, are equally subject to publicly disclosed legal codes and processes, ensuring fairness, justice, and the protection of rights.

Better Governance: The continuous improvement of governance practices to achieve higher efficiency, accountability, and effectiveness in service delivery and decision-making, emphasizing citizen-centric and results-oriented approaches.

World Governance Indicator (WGI): A composite measure developed by the World Bank, assessing governance quality in countries through six dimensions: voice and accountability, political stability, government effectiveness, regulatory quality, rule of law, and control of corruption.

Chapter 9
Behind the Click: Decoding Legal Frameworks for Clickwrap Agreements With a Lens on Minors in India

Monal
Symbiosis International University, India

Maansi Sinha
Symbiosis Law School, Hyderabad, India

Shalini Singh
Gujarat Maritime University, India

Abhilash Arun Sapre
https://orcid.org/0000-0002-7680-0894
Gujarat National Law University, India

ABSTRACT

Clickwrap agreements represent a type of legal contract that individuals acknowledge by clicking a button or selecting a checkbox to indicate their acceptance of the terms and conditions provided to them. These agreements are frequently encountered during software installations, registration, for services or completing online transactions. Although clickwrap agreements are a simple and seamless experience for people, there can be instances where people, especially minors, may need help comprehending the terms and conditions of the contract. As easy as e-contracts may sound, they are highly complicated. The implications of such agreements on minors raise some serious questions about the enforceability of these contracts as they lack the proper understanding and, more importantly, they lack the legal capacity to consent. The paper provides an overview of clickwrap agreements, which

DOI: 10.4018/979-8-3693-8166-3.ch009

will include their prevalence in the contemporary world the research describes the challenges in ensuring that minors possess the legal capacity to engage in binding contracts such as clickwrap agreements.

1. INTRODUCTION

In the evolving world of technology, which now appears to be a growing trend, soon, many things like internet reaches are going to become age-common among minor segments that require such urges, whereby clickwraps have become integrated parts of lives. Legal provisions on what consisted of the clickwrap agreements have been addressed further. As the digital world continues to change fast, with more than seventy percent of minors aged between 9 and 17 using internet on a daily basis now poses another critical issue regarding the authenticity as well as applicability under law clickwrap agreements that are incorporated in games, social media sites and browsing websites. Since the Indian Contract Act of 1872 was written in a time period that lacked these technological intricacies, there are no specific provisions to address such modern complications until it comes down to a minor level.

a) Consensus ad Idem: The lack of a negotiation room in these contracts, frequently limited to the "I agree" button, may raise the question about the very concept of a "meeting of minds" fundamental for consensus ad Idem(Katarki & Bhat, 2015).
b) Legal Capacity: Reflecting on the landmark case (Mohori Bibee v. Dharmodas Ghose) case to which agreements with minors were not considered enforceable, it becomes a major question whether this principle can be applied to clickwrap agreements. The relevance of pre-existing laws is a matter of concern.
c) Certainty: The problem with clickwrap agreements in the case where contractual liability rests on a party's general understanding is that they are full of minute print. Unfortunately, a minor dealing with terms of service or boilerplate contracts often lacks the necessary understanding to perceive a particular contract's consequences. (Sargent, 2013)

In light of the prevalence of technology in our daily life, clickwrap agreements have become a normal part and parcel for most minors. They need additional specific legal provisions, which meet the peculiarities of clickwrap contracts. Preserving the legality of changes in electronic arts is not only mandatory but an urgent need of the present day. For one thing, in the digital world where technology takes precedence over everything else clarity of law should not be swept under the carpet.

1.1 Literature Review

In 'Evolution of Clickwrap & Browsewrap Contracts,' by Clifford Fisher, the author gives us the definition of clickwrap agreements. The author defines a clickwrap agreement as a contract with a presentation of terms and conditions to the consumer or buyer, in furtherance of which they need to click the I AGREE button if they wish to proceed. The author also gives us insights into Browsewrap agreements. The author mentions that in the Browsewrap agreement, a pseudo-mutual assent is obtained by the web designer from the users in the form of cookies. They make them enter into a contract by just clicking one button and consider the IP address as their signature, thus making the contract legally binding.

In 'The Rights of Private and Publicity for Minors Online: Protecting the Privilege of Disaffirmance in the Digital,' Megan Diffenderfer draws attention to how children become vulnerable victims exploited by marketers and advertisers who seek profit gain from digital platforms. These marketers and advertisers lure children to enter into clickwrap agreements disclosing important information. This book highlights the fact that there is an urgent need to have privacy statutes customized to protect those who heavily rely on the internet. Diffenderfer dives into legal theories, including the infancy doctrine that has historically given minors a right of disaffirmance- cancelling an agreement. The author aims to strengthen the legal structure promoting privacy statutes, which will leave minors more protected from illegal exploitation in virtual space. Thus, the book can be seen as a thorough study of legal approaches to protect minors' rights and privacy against threats related to e-contracts.

R. Shrinika, in the 'Legality of Clickwrap Agreements,' highlights various aspects of legality in clickwrap agreements. The author brings to the attention the elements of a valid contract such as active consent, competency, clear and comprehensible terms and conditions, and most importantly, the "meeting of the minds," i.e., *consensus ad idem,* which are clearly not fulfilled in clickwrap agreements. With time, the internet has become more accessible to minors, i.e., the use of the Internet is increasing, and the age of the users is decreasing. In such a scenario, it is evident that many applications and websites will be accessed by minors who have no knowledge of the terms and conditions of the agreement and their legal implications. Clickwrap agreements do not take into account several significant problems such as misrepresentation, fraud, etc., and most importantly, they fail to take into consideration the age of the user, and therefore, the aspect of 'competency' is completely ignored.

2. THE ANATOMY OF E-CONTRACTS: DEFINITIONS AND CLASSIFICATIONS

E-contracting is defined in the paper 'Survey of E-Contracting Cases: Browsewrap, Clickwrap, and Modified Clickwrap Agreements,' by Deborah Davis Boykin. E-contract is quoted as a method of entering into a contract online. E-contract stores the mutual consent and signature (in the form of IP address) between the user and the web service provider in an electronic format; this gives rise to a mutual obligation between both parties to the contract legally. The most commonly used e-contracts include clickwrap agreements, browsewrap agreements, sign-in wrap agreements, and scroll wrap agreements.

Please provide missing figure by **proofing deadline**.

New files can be uploaded to the proofing system via comment attachment or emailed to **bookproofing@igi-global.com**

2.1 Illustrations

CLICKWRAP AGREEMENT: Imagine that you are signing up for a new streaming service, "StreamOTP." As you create an account, you see a checkbox with the text: "I have read and agree to the *Terms of Service* and *Privacy Policy.*" Below the checkbox, there is a button labeled, "Sign up" which remains disabled until you agree to the terms and conditions. By clicking on the "I agree" button, you enter into a clickwrap agreement.

BROWSEWRAP AGREEMENT: Imagine you visit an e-commerce website, "EasyShop." At the bottom of the homepage, there is a small disclaimer stating: *"By using this website, you agree to our Terms of Service and Privacy Policy."* The words "Terms of Service" and "Privacy Policy" are hyperlinked. Unlike a clickwrap agreement, there is no checkbox or button requiring explicit consent. Instead, simply using the website is considered acceptance of the terms.

SCROLL WRAP AGREEMENT: Imagine you're installing a new mobile app, "Guitar.ly." Before completing the sign-up process, you are presented with a Terms of Service agreement inside a scrollable text box. At the bottom of the box, there is a checkbox with the text: *"I have read and agree to the Terms of Service."* The "Continue" button remains disabled until you scroll to the bottom of the terms and check the box. By forcing users to scroll through the agreement before accepting, this is a Scroll Wrap Agreement, ensuring they have at least been exposed to the terms before agreeing.

SIGN-UP AGREEMENT: Imagine you are creating an account on "FitnessToday," a fitness tracking app. During the sign-up process, you fill in your details and reach the final step, where you see the following text just above the "Create Account" button: *"By clicking 'Create Account,' you acknowledge that you have read and agree to our Terms of Service and Privacy Policy."* The "Create Account" button serves as implicit consent—by clicking it, you automatically accept the terms. This is a Sign-Up Agreement, commonly used in registration forms where agreement to terms is tied directly to account creation.

3. MINOR CLICKS, MAJOR QUESTIONS: NAVIGATING CONSENT AND CAPACITY IN THE DIGITAL FRONTIER

In the digital age, it is ubiquitous for children to use e-devices extensively. They explore a list of various things on several websites. They generally enter e-contracts on e-commerce websites, gaming, and social networking platforms (Pew Internet,2021). These websites enter clickwrap agreements with minors to obtain consent for a better user experience. The minors give away important information, sometimes even misrepresenting their age. In fast-paced online interactions, the issues arising from their overlap with minors' consent and clickwrap agreements warrant critical analysis. However, the implication regarding minors for clickwrap agreements simply by agreeing on some terms and conditions tags that are common in digital transactions remains a complex legal and ethical ground.

Given that there have been no clear rulings on the enforceability of clickwrap agreements with minors in the courts, this question remains rather vague. Mental capacity is also relevant because minors might lack the legal competence to comprehend fully the agreements they are signing. This is intertwined with the doctrine of infancy, which considers minors' lack of aptitude to engage in contracts. Minors are mentally incapable of comprehending the arduous legal language. Consequently, children easily enter contracts whereby they unintentionally deceive about their age and no longer have the right to nullify these arrangements. By doing so, children impose constraints upon themselves by oppressive terms. In this way, minors become easy targets of advertisers and marketers. However, the infancy doctrine in India has not been developed to a level that would help protect children and give them the power of disaffirmance.

The real question is: Can the law implement contracts obtained from a minor who does not know the terms and conditions of the contract? In India, section 11 of the Indian Contract Act of 1872 states, "Every person is competent to contract who is of the age of majority according to the law to which he is subject, and who is of sound mind and is not disqualified from contracting by any law to which he is subject." According to Section 3 of the Indian Majority Act of 1875, a person of or above 18 is an adult, i.e., not a minor. Scholars and practitioners of law are confronted with questions regarding minors' ability to fully understand what they agree upon, as well as ethical obligations for digital service providers in acquiring valid consent.

"Clicking with Caution: Minors and Clickwraps"(Jauhari, 2023)carefully analyses the complex world of minors signing clickwrap agreements, invoking key case laws. Arriving at challenges about enforceability against minors, the article discusses restitution options in case of invalidated contracts. Suggesting directed adjustments it support age verification mechanisms, user-friendly interfaces, and educational programs in order to strengthen the e-contract system. This article balances innovation and protection in offering a nuanced understanding contributing concrete suggestions to fix the drawbacks on issues such as separating minors from executive online activities.

Advertisements can easily lure children to enter such contracts. They can be seduced by the audio-visual effects and agree to terms and conditions against their better judgment (Moses & Baldwin, 2005).Minors do not possess highly developed critical thinking to make such decisions in the Internet sphere. Child psychology says children are much more susceptible to online advertisements than adults. They are more likely to get trapped by marketers and advertisers. This can have an adverse effect on the parents or guardians of the child. All things considered; it can be said that minors do not have an understanding of clickwrap agreements entailing a complex mechanism. Thus, the discussion of mechanisms needs further clarification by considering minors' rights and informed consent. With the development of digital space, knowledge regarding minors' consent towards clickwrap agreements is a crucial tool for finding ethical and proper guidelines in e-business.

4. LEGAL PROTECTIONS FOR MINORS IN CLICKWRAP AGREEMENTS ACROSS JURISDICTIONS

4.1 Hong Kong

Hong Kong takes several precautions for the safety of children on the internet. It is mandatory that the content of a website aimed at children must be child-friendly. The publication of absence articles has been prohibited by the Control of Obscene and Indecent Articles Ordinance (Cap 390). Advertising or promotional activities aimed at minors pertaining to betting, especially, have been strictly prohibited by the Betting Duty Ordinance (Cap 108). The Privacy Commissioner of Hong Kong, Ms. Ada Chung Lai-Ling, in 2020, encouraged the involvement of parents. According to her, the child's vulnerability should be taken into consideration, and age-appropriate approaches should be adopted by the concerned organizations.

4.2 France

The debate on providing safety to children and protecting them from such e-contracts is gaining momentum. One of the most debatable aspects of this is age-verification. Currently, there are technologies that can help in ensuring age-verification, however, they also intrude the privacy of many users. The balance between privacy and the reliability of the age-verification technologies has not been found yet. Although, the European Union (EU) has adopted several regulations to such as the Audiovisual Media Services Directive (AVMSD) and the Digital Servies Act (DSA), none of these address the issue of online child protection.

According to the Commission Nationale de l'Informatique et des Libertés (CNIL), more than half of children in the age group of 10-14 use social networks. The French President has advocated changing the digital age to 15. This step is helpful as by that age, children would be able to comprehend the terms of any e-contract to some extent. The government imposed a fine up to one percent of the platform's global sales if there was a failure to comply with these laws. France has been testing an age verification system since 2023 based on the use of an intermediary to guarantee user privacy and ensure more reliable age verification. When a website requires age verification, a challenge will be sent to the user. This challenge will then be processed by the verification provider, resulting in a group signature. In this process, the authorities will have no information about the websites the user attempts to visit, and the target website will not receive any data from the user, only their group signature. However, the critics argue that this test is not entirely anonymous.

4.3 United States

The American legislature has addressed the requirement of legislation for the regulation of clickwrap agreements entered by minors, as a study in 1998 revealed disturbing numbers (89% of websites collecting minors' data over the internet) without adequate authentication. This raised concerns about the compliance of provisions of legal contracts, which in turn led to the formation of the Children's Online Privacy Protection Act (1998). This act was passed in 1998 but took effect on 21st April 2000. CoPPA helps to regulate websites collecting minors' personal information by mandating parental consent before entering into the clickwrap agreement.

4.4 Russia

An indirect legislation was passed by Russia in 2012 regarding the use of clickwrap agreements by minors over the internet, an amendment was made to the federal law of 29 December 2010(Minors' Protection Law). This protected minors from access to information that was injurious to their health and mental development. Minors' protection law mandates age ratings for online content, a joint account of minors and their parents, restricted access to content labeled as 'prohibited for minors', and guidelines for business-related websites were suggested to protect minors' privacy and security thus protecting their contractual rights and obligations. The act also aimed to improve the previous situation by ordering the websites to delete the minors' data collected before the legislation was passed.

4.5 Judgments From Around the Globe

When the Internet appeared and electronic contracting arose, it transformed business transactions on a global scale. However, the law of contracts—that took centuries to form and was changing with shifts in economics, politics as well as technology but no faster than a tortoise's. In response to this change, there are serious legal implications due the use of traditional principles being applied in an electronic and borderless paper less environment. With the development of Internet and websites, so did online contracts. Scholars argue that wrap agreements were applied to satisfy business requirements in software companies; however, their specific origin is unclear (Hemnes, 1994). Whenever a software delivery on disks movement became identified – disk-based automatism with more words of law than an episode from Law and Order, the courts began to meet challenges evolving out of e-commerce. Even though there were numerous complaints regarding lack of access to the agreement until after completion, rolling contracts drew attention, and as such, courts took a flexible approach towards this problem. Taking interest in Judge Easterbrook and understanding the simple ProCD instead of the full situation, courts allowed rolling contracts, denying concerns that customers could not see the agreement before it was made. Firms sought to make software licensing simple by bundling contracts into a package while using the term "shrink-wrap" for such arrangements (Inc. v. Verio, Inc,2004). The wording comes from "the shrink-wrap plastic wrapping to seal inside of software boxes." (Hotmail Corp. v. Van Money Pie Inc,1998)·Shrink-wrap licensing is closely linked with click-wrap licenses. It is similar to a shrinkwrap license, which the user owns after downloading or buying the product.

A prominent case is ***ProCD, Inc. v Zeidenberg***, where the Seventh Circuit upheld a shrinkwrap license agreement as valid in 1996 One license that managed to stay relevant is the shrinkwrap license, which was dubbed as "A Licensing agreement or other terms and conditions of a contractual nature readable only after unwrapping product" because it is named for plastic wrappers on consumer software. The clickwrap license bears a striking resemblance to shrink wrap in nature. Following its download or purchase, the license and terms are given upon installation of the software represented on a computer monitor. In the process of installation, they have to be read and consented by a user. There is a peculiar case of three contracts including reseller agreement, purchase order particular to one transaction under consideration and clickwrap license contract agreed upon by LAN at installation stage when software should be assured that court observed its interpretative value in context. Thus, in the absence of a reseller agreement or purchase order clickwrap license terms would step up to fill the void. The court refused to award specific performance in that the software developed by Netscout was not unique. Arguments moved to the limitation of liability clause which fell under clickwrap contract, citing Section 2-204 and section 2-37 (i.Lan Sys., Inc. v. Netscout Serv. Level Corp,2002). The reasoning of the court interpreting Section 2-204 revolved around LAN's assent through a click on "I agree" and made it enforceable. While Section 2-207 was the most important question, it implicitly and explicitly asks whether LAN accepted clickwrap license by clicking "I agree" button. The court proceeded to the analysis of two seminal cases concerning rolling terms within software transactions. The comparisons of cases dealing with contract formation – on issuance or receipt by purchaser, viewing the license agreement and rejection to return option for software found in box. That is, if the purchase order can be seen as a contract, then section

2-207 requires effective consent if the contract is signed after you read and are able to examine it. The court ruled that even if Section 2-207 applied, i.LAN implicitly accepted the clickwrap license agreement since the additional terms were not significant.

In other cases such as ***Feldman v. Google*** (Feldman v. Google, Inc., 513 F. Supp. 2d,2007) offer a clear path in this respect by being in favor of the use to clickwrap agreements. One significant guideline from Froeldman states that the agreement is not procedurally unconscionable in the case of a sophisticated purchaser, who was under no pressure to agree, could understand each term and its consequence and would have had the opportunity to reject, which might mean any disadvantage. This creates an overall structure where the user is supposed to view and consent, as it may happen in practice that users do not understand all terms to which they agree.

Clickwrap agreements, recognized in courts since 1968, ***Hotmail C Appendix Corp. v Van Money Pie Inc.*** (Hotmail Corp. v. Van Money Pie Inc.,1998) court cases are broadly developed and used by that time. The employment of clickwrap has remained a dynamic development, which is supported by more than just several legal guidelines meant for its implementation and practice.

Judicial precedents can help immensely in analysing the legal standpoint with respect to the clickwrap agreements and minors. In the ***People v. Direct Revenue LLC*** case (N.Y. Misc. LEXIS 2195,2008), the consumer entered a clickwrap agreement without reading the terms and conditions of the contract. The court held that when one enters a contract, they are bound by the terms even if they did not read it. Similarly, in the case of ***A.V. v. iParadigms, LLC*** (544 F. Supp. 2d 473 (E.D. Va. 2008)., students submitting papers to Turnitin clicked "I agree" to its terms, including archiving papers. Despite disclaimers, the court found the click binding. Turnitin's liability was limited per agreement. The court's decision aligned with precedents, affirming the binding nature of click agreements. The court held that: "Plaintiffs cannot use the infancy defense to void their contractual obligations while retaining the benefits of the contract"(iParadigms, 544 F. Supp. 2d at 481). In India, such contracts are enforceable, too as it is a basic contract law. Although the judgment in the case of an adult can be considered valid, some relaxation can be given in the case of minors. Since they do not have the mental capacity to comprehend such procedures and terms of the agreement, the infancy doctrine should be strengthened and applied in India. The law can be very simple, there is no rocket science, once it is found that a minor has entered a clickwrap agreement, the contract can be made void without the minor retaining any kind of benefits of the contract . As it was held in the suit brought against Apple, ***Scott v. Apple Inc.*** (Scott v. Apple Inc., 1:23-cv-00475, (D.D.C.,2008) which asserts that contracts for in-app purchases were voidable since they were formed with minors. Furthermore, it claims that Apple violated the California Consumers Legal Remedies Act by portraying in-app games as "free," with the intention of encouraging minors to make purchases. The litigation is still ongoing and offers a considerable financial risk to Apple, perhaps resulting in substantial legal bills and damages (In re Apple In-App Purchase Litigation, 855 F. Supp. 2d 1030,2008). Another important case is that of ***Feldman v. Google*** (513 F.Supp.2d 229 (E.D. Pa. 2007), a suit against Google AdWords due to click fraud happened when users maliciously clicked ads with no genuine interest in the advertisement, harming the advertiser financially. Feldman argued that fraudulent clicks should not be charged by Google because the company was being paid for every click on their ads. This brought into question Google's liability to control-click scams and the justice of its rating process. Moreover, the case revealed the importance of a forum selection clause in an agreement between Feldman and Google. This clause governed the process of settling disputes between parties; it thus shows that contractual terms greatly affected determining legal rights and mechanisms for dispute resolution. Therefore, the case they discuss weaves together issues based on fraud prevention, billing integrity, and contracts in relation to online advertising services. If this case is applied to minors, then it can be said that the power of disaffirmance would play an important role in protecting them. Minors may enter clickwrap agreements with complex terms and conditions; if they do not have the power of disaffirmance, it may cause tremendous pecuniary loss to their guardians or parents.

Specht v. Netscape (306 F.3d 17 (2d Cir. 2002) was a case where individuals sued the company known as Netscape regarding what they viewed as breach of their privacy owing to an application called Smart Download which was developed by this very same firm. The more they used the program, the less their sensitive personal data was sent to Netscape. Joining Smart Download meant the people accepted certain rules by which (by pre-burring arbitration instead of law), Netscape said. They noted that when a person imports the software by clicking on "Download", s/he accepted these Terms of Service. However, the court asserted that it is not just at a literal and proverbial click of a button. Agreements should be clearly and transparent in terms. Here, in the case of that arena, there was a statement regarding the legality of such an agreement. One could argue that it isn't clear because those important terms weren't shown directly near "Download" button. But it wasn't enough to push people into clicking a button which did not mean their consent with all the rules. The court held that the people were not bound lawfully by those provisions because they signified too vaguely. ***Bragg v. Linden Research*** (487 F. Supp. 2d 593 (E.D.Penn. 2007)., Inc., in short, was a dispute between Linden and Mr. Bragg – the plaintiff of this game Second Life actionable conduct causes or materially contributes to the lapse of time litigant is seeking relief relating to tort claim case that took place in 2008 pleaded during trial; summons can result from either In fact, second life can be also referred to an internet community that is populated by avatars and with the help of which players see a wide range of things from purchasing virtual lands to real money. Linden confiscated virtual land that Mr. Bragg bought in Second Life, saying he did so accept a loophole while buying the virtual parcel of land. His account was also frozen with all of his virtual belongings blocked. When Mr. Bragg sued Linden, they had to sort out this issue by mediation and not in a court of law because that would lead trivialize the country's ordinary justice system. On the other hand, Mr. Bragg justified that the arbitration clause was unfair. The court sided with Mr. Bragg stating that the arbitration clause is unreasonable because it was contained in "take it or leave it". In other words, Mr. Bragg had simply no way to avoid the deal terms – playing Second Life was not optional for him – and Linden was unquestionably much stronger in that bargaining situation. Essentially, Mr. Bragg only had no remedies if he didn't support the conditions, and such terms were equals as unfair to him based on his court opinion. This case raises concerns about how even adults could miss a seemingly minor technical detail. It prompts questions about how minors, with potentially less experience and understanding, might navigate similar situations. Simply put, minors have no mental capacity to understand such Terms and Conditions, no power of disaffirmance to protect themselves from the boundation of such agreements, and no protection of law. This can prove to be very detrimental for the coming age as AI and other forms of technology continue to advance.

On the other hand, there are some cases the judgments of which can be used in cases of minors as well. These judgments can be applied in India too. ***Sgouros v. Trans Union Corp*** 15-1371 (7th Cir. 2016) notes that many courts in the country have acknowledged some other form of acceptance is valid through clicking on a button or checking off box as agreement to accept a contract. The court further notes that such agreements are acceptable; 'provided the design and lingo of the site gives users a reasonable notice that consent will have effectuated by an act of clicking.' By way of instance, terms displayed using hyperlink rather than directly onto screen may necessitate clearer prompt directing user read them. This approach has the potential to assist the minors and prevent any kind of loss or damage to the parents or guardians. (***Nicosia v. Amazon*** 834 F.3d 220 (2d Cir. Aug. 24, 2016) is one of the popular cases in law that discusses how users should be led to read contract terms that appear on webpages. Court noted that whether the users notice other contract terms on a webpage depends upon how information of such additional contract is placed and made easily understandable. A webpage full of information, buttons and links would seem to be unlikely where a normal person goes through the contact terms. In addition, when the link to terms is placed in a component of the webpage however users do not have typical tendency to look at such a spot, courts will not accept those regulations. In addition, courts look for the use of words on an onscreen message in determining whether users are understandably communicated to what they have agreed. Since language is not clear in the aspect of making an agreement, judges may choose a direction that they will not force to fix any terms. Basically, the case establishes that terms of contract posted on web should be easy to see, clear and easy to understand; that they expressly specify that users are entering into an agreement with the website. Otherwise, the courts might not be able to impose them. For minors, specifically, the terms of the contract must be easy to see and should be written in plain and simple language.

The Google Chromebook case involves children's data protection with complaints that Google broke privacy law when it gathered and stored the personal information of students without getting the permission of parents using its Chromebooks and G Suite for Education services. The problem started in 2019 when a worried parent from Helsingor Municipality filed a complaint, contending that the school did not take sufficient measures to safeguard their child's personal data when they used these digital tools in class. In September 2021, the Danish Data Protection Authority (DPA) held that Helsingor Municipality had not sufficiently evaluated the risks involved in employing Google Chromebooks in schools, specifically regarding children's personal data. Accordingly, an injunction was issued requiring the Municipality to perform a complete risk assessment of the data processing operations involved in the deployment of Google Chromebooks and Workspace. In a further ruling in July 2022, the DPA acted even further by issuing a ban against the processing of personal data within the Municipality. The ban would be enforced until the Municipality furnished enough documentation to establish that their activities in processing data were in conformity with the rules of the GDPR.

In its recent ruling on January 30, 2024 the DPA analyzed whether the Municipality had put the legal basis in place for processing children's personal data with Google,as stipulated in the data processing agreements and connected commercial agreements. The DPA determined that there was no adequate legal justification for the subject data processing activities. As such, the DPA instructed Helsingor Municipality to either implement a legal basis for processing personal information or discontinue the use of Google Chromebooks. In addition, the Municipality was directed to comply with the injunction by August 24, 2024.

These precedents can help start the conversation about clickwrap agreements and minors in India. The fact that there are no cases pertaining to the same in India shows how unaware people are and highlights the need for provisions for the same.

5. UNDERSTANDING CLICKWRAP AGREEMENTS: A SURVEY ON MINORS' VIEWPOINT

5.1 Data Collected

No. of Responses: 108

Table 1.

S.NO.	QUESTIONS	CHARTS
1.	What is your age?	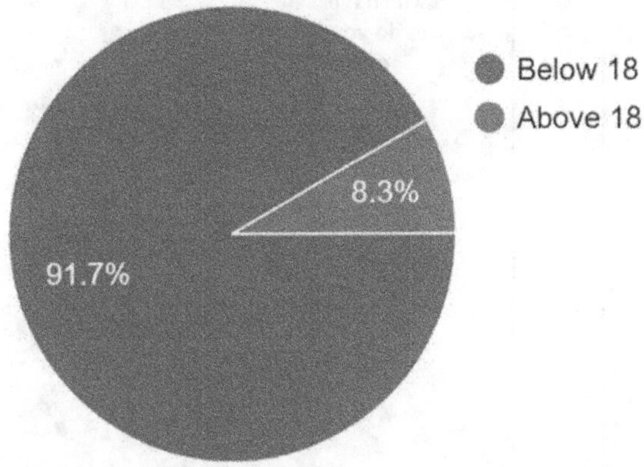
2.	How often do you encounter clickwra agreements when using online services creating accounts?	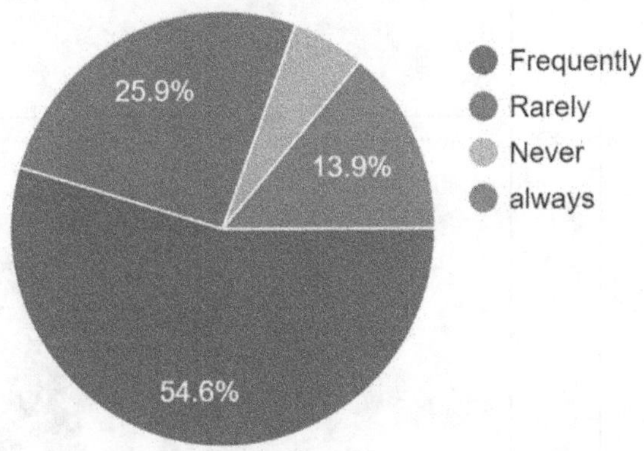

continued on following page

Table 1. Continued

<table>
<tr><th>S.NO.</th><th>QUESTIONS</th><th>CHARTS</th></tr>
<tr><td>3.</td><td>On which types o services do you mo: clickwrap</td><td>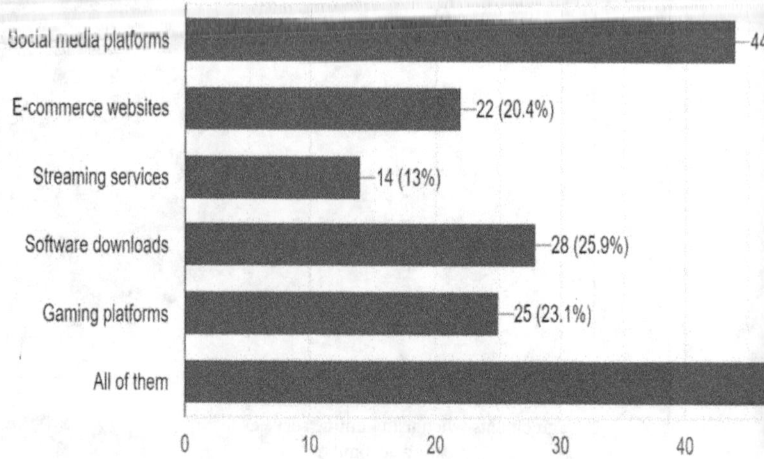
</td></tr>
<tr><td>4.</td><td>According to you are are the clickwra agreements legally binding?</td><td>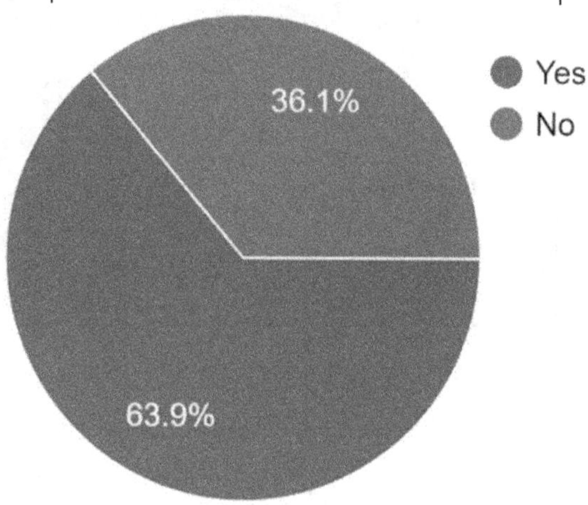
</td></tr>
</table>

continued on following page

Table 1. Continued

S.NO.	QUESTIONS	CHARTS
5.	Have you ever encountered a situation w a minor agreed to a clickwrap agreeme online?	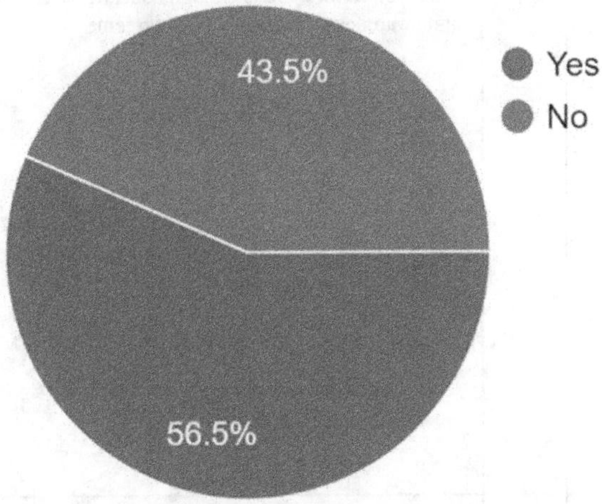
6.	If yes, what platform or service was involved, and what were the consequences, if any?	Games, Robolox a gaming platform, educational guidance platforms, gaming, e-commerce, mobile games, online platform, online site, shopping websites.
7.	Is there an authentic verification proce for identification of age present on eve platform featuring clickwrap agreemen	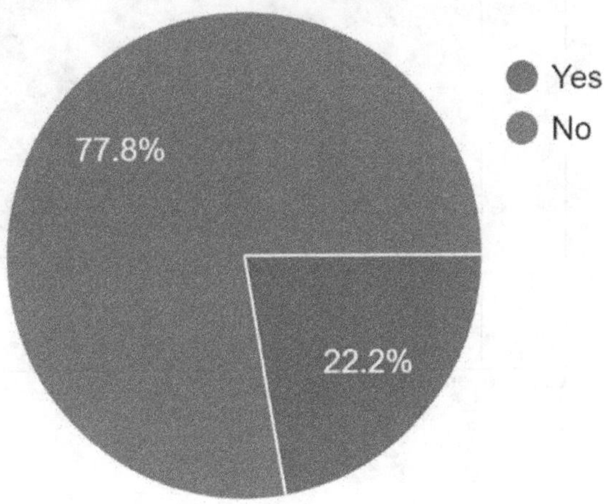

continued on following page

Table 1. Continued

S.NO.	QUESTIONS	CHARTS
8.	Do you think there is enough educatic and awareness about clickwrap agreeme especially among minors?	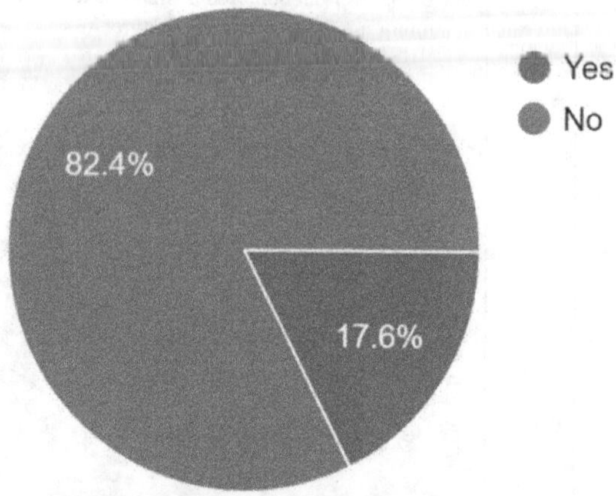
9.	Do you think online platforms shoul implement more robust age verificatic measures to ensure that minors are nc agreeing to terms meant for adults?	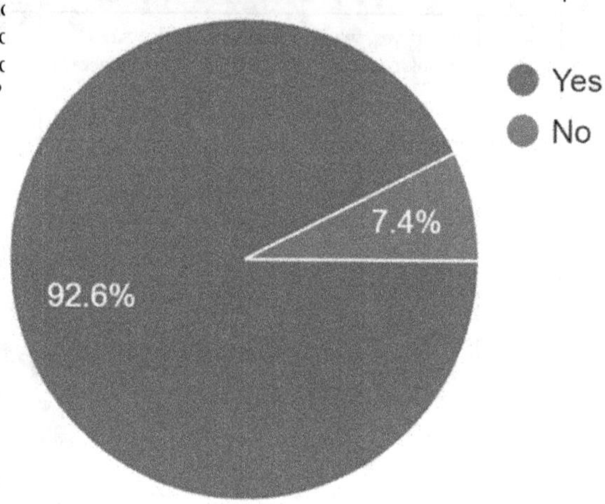

continued on following page

Table 1. Continued

S.NO.	QUESTIONS	CHARTS
10.	Are you able to understand the terms a conditions mentioned in such agreeme (specifically minors)?	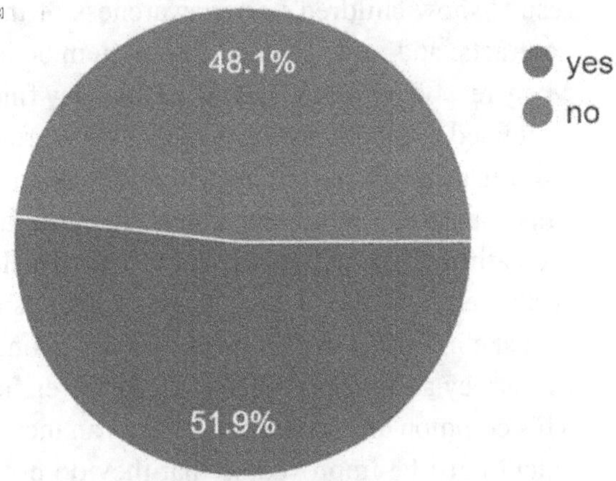
11.	Do you think the age of users influenc their ability to understand clickwrap agreements?	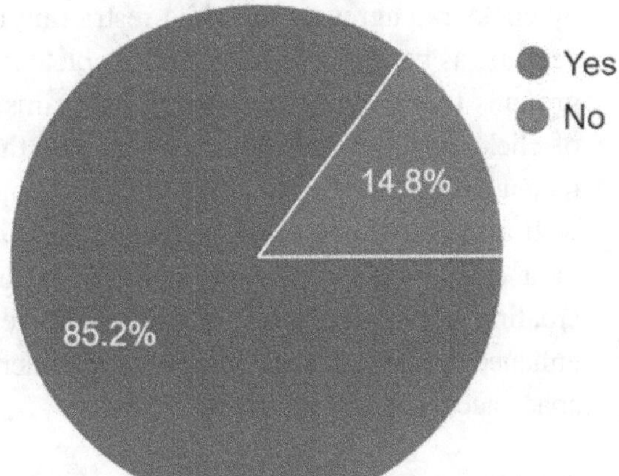

5.2 Empirical Observation on Click-Wrap Agreements in the Case of Minors

The survey is a comprehensive study of minors' interactions with clickwrap agreements in the virtual world, offering valuable perspectives on their understanding, conduct and implications to online security. With almost all the respondents below the age of 18, it becomes easier to identify the digital contract affected population. The statistics reveal that all the kids in online experience commonly come with clickwrap agreements where almost every one of them is often facing this on a daily basis. As can be seen from these agreements, they are mostly met on social media and gaming sites, which clearly demonstrates their popularity, particularly among the younger generation. Even though clickwrap agreements are quite popular, the survey results show children's poor awareness of the legal consequences of signing such contracts, and more than 63.9% of them believe it to be a legally binding contract. Many respondents (48.1%) noted that they find it difficult to comprehend provisions contained in clickwrap agreements which reveals a low level of awareness on their part regarding digital rights and duties. Many people (85.2%) consider age to be an important factor in understanding the terms and conditions of online contracts thus indicating on the mental capacity. This conclusion highlights the pressing need for further education and awareness campaigns targeted at minors, empowering them to make informed decisions in the face of online resources. Considering this issue, the survey addresses the lack of an age verification mechanism (agreed by 77.8%). This common understanding reflects an increasing awareness that children's online safety must be improved so that they do not get hurt so much. Strengthening age verification systems is one of the important measures to resolve some issues raised by clickwrap agreements while restricting risks associated with children's online activity, as believed by 92.6% of people. Given survey results, there are sufficient grounds to cooperate on holistic programs to address problems created because of click developments. This may include the introduction of regulatory measures meant to enhance transparency and accountability in online consent processes, as well as undertaking awareness initiatives on enhancing minors understanding of their digital rights and legal obligations. In addition, further initiatives towards creating and implementing advanced age-verification technology can significantly enhance online safety mechanisms for underage consumers allowing a safer digital space accessible by all users.

5.3 Empirical Data From Secondary Sources

- According to the National Commission for Protection of Child Rights in India 2021, 30.2% of the children between the age group of 8-18 years use e-devices. The Edtech companies collects extensive data personal information on children. Therefore, it raises concerns on how these data is collected, stored, and shared.
- 85% of the surveyed apps had accessed at least one "dangerous permission," or permission for collecting highly sensitive data. The misuse of this data can prove to be very detrimental to the children.
- It was reported, in 2023, that the EU regulator had imposed a staggering amount of fine of 345 million euros on a video sharing app for failing to adequately verify parental consent.

The findings reveal that clickwrap contracts are widely in use by adolescents and the lack of knowledge concerning their legal implications poses a cause for concern. Additionally, it highlights the importance of enhanced learning and awareness practices as well as age verification systems needed to safeguard children's rights and welfare in cyberspace. Policymakers, industry stakeholders, and educators can use these data to develop comprehensive policies to foster digital literacy where minors are protected from dangers while creating an inclusive online environment.

6. CONCLUSION

6.1 Advantages and Disadvantages of Clickwrap Agreements

The advantages of Clickwrap agreements are as follows:

- Clickwrap agreements are user-friendly, and easy to implement because it does not require exhaustive paperwork as they obtain and store the signature and consent digitally within seconds.
- Clickwrap agreements have seamless integration, enabling their incorporation into websites, apps, social media web apps, etc.
- Clickwrap agreements are secure for minors in various cases, due to the parental verification of their consent before they click on the I AGREE button on the website.
- Clickwrap agreements create a legal shield for digital business owners, as these agreements ensure user consent in relation to the terms and conditions applicable.
- Click Wrap agreements are customizable and can be tailored in accordance with the services and interests of the user.

Disadvantages of clickwrap agreements are as follows:

- The legal enforceability of clickwrap agreements is ambiguous in the case of minors as the court of law depends on the facts of the case and the frequency of use by the minor to decide the enforceability of such a contract. Thus creating a high risk for web designers in case of any legal conflict.
- Absence of mental capacity to understand the terms and conditions of clickwrap agreement in case of minors, before entering into a pseudo-contract due to the consent fatigue effect.

- Lack of legitimate verification of age and parental consent, as there is no authenticated way to establish checks and balances related to the credentials of the user.
- The terms and conditions may include complex terminologies to mask any unfair trade practice that the minor may not understand and consent to.
- The website owner gets access to the user's private information through the recent development of the 'accept cookies' feature. Thus, clickwrap agreements can lead to security problems in the case of malicious sites.

6.2 Recommendations

From our research on this topic, it has become clear that there are several loopholes in the framing, execution, and exercise of the law pertaining to clickwrap agreements and minors. Powers of disaffirmation is an area that needs to be explored more by law experts in terms of minors entering clickwrap agreements. It can be granted to minors to prevent the losses parents and guardians face. Infancy doctrine can be explored more in the field of contract law. It is important to understand children's mental capacity level while making laws and giving judgments. There is a clear need for more provisions for clickwrap agreements and minors. The Government should also work towards preventing misrepresentation of minors as adults on the Internet. An application can be designed which can be installed in mobile phones that will help in keeping track of the minor's activities on the device and prevent them from entering into such heavily binding e-contracts by cutting off access. Higher standards of self-identification and age verification can be created to ensure more safety and security for children. For this, India can borrow provisions from the US' Children's Online Privacy Protection Act, 1998. AI can also be used to trace the entry of minors on a website or application. Like France, a fine can also be imposed if there is non-compliance with the laws. More structured provisions can be made to create a standard and ensure uniformity in such procedures. This can further enhance the age-verification process. Websites can help minors make their IDs on family accounts with parental consent. Governmental regulation on such gaming websites, advertisements, and social networking sites can prevent children from getting lured by the audio-visual effects and binding themselves in complex legal terms and conditions. These sites can also provide a clear age-related disclaimer in straightforward language. Specific authorized sites can also make use of Aadhar cards and PAN cards. 'Digital Literacy' (Warschauer & Ware, 2008) can be promoted in schools via workshops, seminars, etc., which would help them learn about the intricacies of clickwrap agreements. It has been observed that no solid judgment. has been given with respect to minors and clickwrap agreements (Moses & Baldwin, 2005).Therefore, it is needless to say that judicial review can be a helping hand for the legislature. These are some of the recommendations that might be helpful for bringing a better mechanism for e-contracts like clickwrap agreements.

6.3 Conclusion

Over 50% of India's population are active users of the internet (The Hindu,2023). In addition, according to a national survey (2022), six out of ten youngsters spend three hours daily on the social media and other gaming platforms (The times of India,2023). And the numbers are expected to increase. This shows that the number of minors entering clickwrap agreements, intentionally or unintentionally, is also increasing. The aspect of minors entering contracts cannot be covered in just one section of a statute. As time evolves and new technological evolutions are being made, the protection of minors from the monstrous terms and conditions of certain clickwrap agreements becomes crucial. It is asserted by more than 75% of people in the survey conducted (data mentioned in Chapter 5) that the age of the user entering into a clickwrap agreement plays an important role in understanding the terms and conditions, bringing up the issue of the mental capacity of minors in understanding these terms. There is clearly a need for proper measures. There is a lack of proper judgments in this regard. No judge has given an opaque judgment on this issue. To prevent a minor from getting entangled in such clickwrap agreements, it is crucial that the judiciary gives solid judgment on these issues. More than 50% of the people believe the clickwrap agreements to be legally binding (data from point 4 in Chapter 5). The legislature also needs to take initiative and make new laws or upgrade the old ones to shield the minors from certain capricious clickwrap agreements.

While the online websites heavily rely on clickwrap agreements, the minors' ability to comprehend the terms and conditions remain questionable which is why the infancy doctrine needs to be given support. It is evident from the survey conducted for the purpose of this paper that more than 48.1% of users who were minors(91.7%) face difficulty in interpreting the terms and conditions on virtual platforms Although, the doctrine is complained of by many, it can still act as a saviour for not only the minors but also for their parents and guardians. Many of the arguments against retaining the infancy defense fail to consider the practical reality of the unlevel playing field between children and major corporations (Slade', 2011) Even if the infancy law doctrine was used as the proverbial sword—by that rare teenager who is even aware that such a doctrine exists to harm the unsuspecting businessman, equitable relief is available. The anti- groups fail to understand that these minors are up against some of the most powerful corporations in the world and therefore, their protection becomes our primary duty. In conclusion, awareness needs to spread, especially among the adults, in order for them to take the initiative, as also believed by more than 82.4% of people from the survey conducted, as mentioned in chapter 5 of this paper. Educational institutions can play a major role in spreading this information. As the internet increasingly integrates into the lives of minors, it becomes essential for them to understand both the advantages and disadvantages it offers. Also, the presence of a robust age verification process is necessary to prevent minors from entering clickwrap agreements that are not suitable for them. More than 77% of users believe that there is a lack of an authentic age verification process on virtual platforms, and 92.6% of users suggest a need for such a robust mechanism in this technologically developing world. Lastly, protecting the rights of minors and informed consent in digital transactions is an endeavor that requires multiple stakeholders, including policymakers, providers of digital services, lawyers, and the society at large, to be deliberate on it. With the digital sphere scrupulously changing, it is important to keep working towards creating ethical standards and legal instruments ensuring minor interest protection and rights performance in a virtual world.

REFERENCES

A.V. v. iParadigms, LLC, 544 F. Supp. 2d 473 (E.D. Va. 2008).

A.V. v. iParadigms, LLC, No. 401325/06, 2008 N.Y. Misc. LEXIS 2195 (Sup. Ct. Mar. 12, 2008).

Cone, L., & Lai, S. S. (2024). Infrastructural dependency in the datafied welfare state: The case of Google Chromebooks. *Learning, Media and Technology*, •••, 1–17.

Dalton, B., & Proctor, C. P. (2008). The changing landscape of text and comprehension in the age of new literacies. In Coiro, J., Knobel, M., Lankshear, C., & Leu, D. J. (Eds.), *Handbook of research on new literacies* (pp. 297–324). Routledge.

DeJohn v. The. TV Corp. Int'l, 487 F. Supp. 2d 593 (E.D. Pa. 2007).

Feldman v. Google, Inc., 513 F. Supp. 2d 229 (E.D. Pa. 2007).

Fisher, C., Calderson, S. J., Mougin, J., & Radford, M. J. (2021). Evolution of clickwrap & browsewrap contracts. *Rutgers Computer & Technology Law Journal*, *48*, 147–178.

Goryachev, I. (2018). *Draft guidelines for safety and development of minors on the internet*.

Griffin, C. N. (2023). Contracting as class. *Brigham Young University Law Review*, *48*(4), 1185–1254.

Hemnes, T. M. S. (1994). Restraints on alienation, equitable servitudes, and the feudal nature of computer software licensing. *Denver University Law Review*, *71*, 577–599.

Hotmail Corp. v. Van Money Pie Inc., No. C98-20064 JW, 1998 U.S. Dist. LEXIS 10729 (N.D. Cal. Apr. 16, 1998). i.Lan Systems, Inc. v. Netscout Service Level Corp., 183 F. Supp. 2d 328 (D. Mass. 2002).

In re Apple In-App Purchase Litigation, 855 F. Supp. 2d 1030 (N.D. Cal. 2012).

Indian Contract Act, § 11, No. 9, Acts of Parliament (1872).

Indian Contract Act, No. 9, Acts of Parliament (1872).

Indian Majority Act, § 3, No. 9, Acts of Parliament (1875).

Jauhari, S. (2023, April 25). India: Though click-wraps are legal, can minors enter click-wraps? Mondaq. https://www.mondaq.com/india/it-and-internet/1305896/though-click-wraps-are-legal-can-minors-enter-click-wraps-

Kar, R. B., & Yu, X. (2024). The contractual death and rebirth of privacy. *SSRN*, •••, 38. DOI: 10.2139/ssrn.4939708

Katarki, S., & Bhat, A. (2015, March 11). India: Happily 'click' after – The real story of e-contracts. Mondaq. https://www.mondaq.com/india/contracts-and-commercial-law/380692/happily-click-after--the-real-story-of-e-contracts

Meyer v. Uber Technologies, Inc., 834 F.3d 220 (2d Cir. 2016).

Mohori Bibee v. Dharmodas Ghose, (1903) LR 30 IA 114.

Moses, L. J., & Baldwin, D. A. (2005). What can the study of cognitive development reveal about children's ability to appreciate and cope with advertising? *Journal of Public Policy & Marketing*, *24*(2), 186–201. DOI: 10.1509/jppm.2005.24.2.186

National Advisory Council for Online Safety. (2021). Report of a national survey of children, their parents and adults regarding online safety. NACOS, 19.

Online contracting and e-commerce under Hong Kong law. (2020).

Parra, A. (2024). Coping with COPPA: Exploring alternatives to the Children's Online Privacy Protection Act. *Indiana Journal of Law and Social Equality*, *12*(2), 193–208.

Pew Internet. (2012). Trend data (teens): Online activities total. https://pewinternet.org/Static-Pages/Trend-Data-%28Teens%29/Online-Activites-Total.aspx

Phillips, D. E. (2009). *The software license unveiled: How legislation by license controls software access*. Oxford University Press. DOI: 10.1093/oso/9780195341874.001.0001

ProCD, Inc. v. Zeidenberg, 86 F.3d 1447 (7th Cir. 1996).

Rana, V., Gandhi, A., & Sharma, I. (2024). Safeguarding children's data under DPDP.

Redondo Maíllo, J. L., & Álvaro Alonso, I. M. (2024). Protection of minors and online age verification: The case of France.

Register.com, Inc. v. Verio, Inc., 356 F.3d 393 (2d Cir. 2004).

Sargent, M. A. (2013). Misplaced misrepresentations: Why misrepresentation-of-age statutes must be reinterpreted as they apply to children's online contracts. *Michigan Law Review*, *112*(2), 312–338. https://www.jstor.org/stable/23816936

Scott v. Apple Inc., 1:23-cv-00475 (D.D.C.).

Sgouros v. TransUnion Corp., No. 15-1371 (7th Cir. 2016).

Shrinika, R. (2023). Legality of clickwrap agreements. *Indian Journal of Law & Legal Research*, *5*(1), 1–12.

Slade, V. (2011). The infancy defense in the modern contract age: A useful vestige. *Seattle University Law Review*, *34*, 613–640.

Specht v. Netscape Communications Corp., 306 F.3d 17 (2d Cir. 2002).

The Hindu. (2023, May 4). Over 50% Indians are active internet users now; base to reach 900 million by 2025: Report. https://www.thehindu.com/news/national/over-50-indians-are-active-internet-users-now-base-to-reach-900-million-by-2025-report/article66809522.ece

Times of India. (2023, September 23). 60% children spend 3 hours a day on social media: Study. https://timesofindia.indiatimes.com/articleshow/103878956.cms

Warschauer, M., & Ware, P. (2008). Learning, change, and power: Competing frames of technology. In Coiro, J., Knobel, M., Lankshear, C., & Leu, D. J. (Eds.), *Handbook of research on new literacies* (pp. 215–240). Routledge.

Compilation of References

A.V. v. iParadigms, LLC, 544 F. Supp. 2d 473 (E.D. Va. 2008).

A.V. v. iParadigms, LLC, No. 401325/06, 2008 N.Y. Misc. LEXIS 2195 (Sup. Ct. Mar. 12, 2008).

Aaker, D. A. (2014). Brand equity: Perspectives on consumer-based brand equity. *Journal of Marketing*, *58*(1), 1–27.

Aaker, D. A., & Biel, A. L. (1993). *Brand equity and advertising: Advertising's role in building strong brands*. Lawrence Erlbaum Associates.

Abid, S. F., & Lodhi, A. (2015). Impact of changes in reserve requirement on banks profitability: A case of Deposit money banks in Pakistan. *European Journal of Business and Management*, *7*(31), 1–6.

Abiola, B. (2012). Effects of microfinance on micro and small enterprises (SMEs) growth in Nigeria. *Asian Economic and Financial Review*, *2*(4), 44–52.

Abreu, M., Soares, I., & Silva, S. (2022). Governance quality and environmental policy on emergent, resource-rich economies: The case of Brazil. *Energy Reports*, *8*, 70–75. DOI: 10.1016/j.egyr.2022.01.041

Acemoglu, D., & Restrepo, P. (2020). The Race Between Man and Machine: Implications of Technology for Growth, Factor Shares, and Employment. *The American Economic Review*, *108*(6), 1488–1542. DOI: 10.1257/aer.20160696

Aderemi, A. M. R., & Ishak, M. S. I. (2023). Qard Hasan as a feasible Islamic financial instrument for crowdfunding: Its potential and possible application for financing micro-enterprises in Malaysia. *Qualitative Research in Financial Markets*, *15*(1), 58–76. DOI: 10.1108/QRFM-08-2021-0145

Adula, M., Birbirsa, Z. A., & Kant, S. (2023). The effect of interpersonal, problem solving and technical training skills on performance of Ethiopia textile industry: Continuance, normative and affective commitment as mediators. *Cogent Business & Management*, *10*(3), 2286672. Advance online publication. DOI 10.1080/23311975.2023.2286672

Afolabi, M. O. (2013). Growth effect of SME's financing in Nigeria. *Journal of African Macroeconomic Review*, *3*(1), 193–205.

Agbeja, O., Adelakun, O. J., & Udi, E. E. (2016). Empirical Analysis of Counterparty Risk and Exchange Rate Risk Management on the Performance of Deposit Money Banks in Nigeria(2009-2013). *Journal of Accounting and Finance*, *16*(2), 106–116.

Ahinful, G. S., Boakye, J. D., & Osei Bempah, N. D. (2023). Determinants of SMEs' financial performance: Evidence from an emerging economy. *Journal of Small Business and Entrepreneurship*, *35*(3), 362–386. DOI: 10.1080/08276331.2021.1885247

Ahmad, R., & Mohammes, A. (2007). Factors (2007). *Determining Mergers of Banks in Malaysia's Banking Sector Reform Multinational Finance Journal*, *11*(1/2), 1–31.

Ahmed, F., & Kilic, K. (2019). Fuzzy Analytic Hierarchy Process: A performance analysis of various algorithms. *Fuzzy Sets and Systems*, *362*, 110–128. DOI: 10.1016/j.fss.2018.08.009

Ahokpossi, C. (2013). Determinants of bank interest margins in Sub-Saharan Africa, IMF Working Paper WP/13/34. International Monetary Fund, Washington, DC.

Ajagunna, I., & Casanova, S. (2022). An analysis of the post-COVID-19 cruise industry: Could this be a new possibility for the luxury yacht sector in the Caribbean? *Worldwide Hospitality and Tourism Themes*, *14*(2), 115–123. DOI: 10.1108/WHATT-12-2021-0158

Ajuwon, O. S. Ikhide, Joseph Oscar Akotey (2018). Financing MSMEs (Micro Small and Medium Enterprises) in Nigeria: Implications of Transaction Costs, Economics, Business DOI: ID: 169899248DOI: 10.20944/preprints201810.0576.v1Corpus

Ajzen, I. (1991). The theory of planned behavior. *Organizational Behavior and Human Decision Processes*, *50*(2), 179–211. DOI: 10.1016/0749-5978(91)90020-T

Ajzen, I., & Fishbein, M. (1980). *Understanding attitudes and predicting social behavior*. Prentice Hall.

Akkaya, G., Turanoğlu, B., & Öztaş, S. (2015). An integrated fuzzy AHP and fuzzy MOORA approach to the problem of industrial engineering sector choosing. *Expert Systems with Applications*, *42*(24), 9565–9573. DOI: 10.1016/j.eswa.2015.07.061

Akmal, D. U., Sultan, U., & Tirtayasa, A. (2021). Politik reformasi hukum. *Pembentukan system [LEGAL REFORM POLITICS. SYSTEM FORMATION],8*, 21–35.

Akman, G., & Alkan, A. (2006). Tedarik Zinciri Yönetiminde Bulanık AHP yöntemi kullanılarak tedarikçilerin performansının ölçülmesi: Otomotiv Yan Sanayiinde bir uygulama. İstanbul Ticaret Üniversitesi Fen Bilimleri Dergisi [Measuring Supplier Performance Using Fuzzy AHP Method in Supply Chain Management: An Application in Automotive Sub-Industry. Istanbul Commerce University Journal of Science], 5(9), 23-46.

Al –Quadah, A. Q., Jaradat, M. A. (2013). The Impact of macroeconomic Variables and Banks Characteristics on Jordanian Islamic Banks Profitability: Empirical Evidence. *International Business Research*, *6*(10), 153–162.

Alcover, A., Alemany, M., Jacob, M., Payeras, M., García, A., & Martínez-Ribes, L. (2011). The economic impact of yacht charter tourism on the Balearic economy. *Tourism Economics*, *17*(3), 625–638. DOI: 10.5367/te.2011.0045

Alesta, F. (2023). Yelkenli Tekne Markaları ve Modelleri. https://www.alestaferro.com/post/yelkenli-tekne-markalari-ve-modelleri#viewer-a4pee, Access date: 11.12.2023.

Almansour, B. Y., & Arabyat, Y. A. (2017). Investment decision making among Gulf investors: Behavioural finance perspective. *International Journal of Management Studies*, *24*(1), 1. DOI: 10.32890/ijms.24.1.2017.10476

Alper, D., & Anbar, A. (2012). Bank specific and macroeconomic determinants of commercial bank profitability: Empirical evidence from Turkey. *Business and Economics Research Journal*, *2*(2), 139–152.

AL-Shboul, M. D. A. (. (2024). Artificial intelligence drivers' influence on willingness to embrace the capital in human form supply chain in manufacturing corporates: An empirical investigation from developing countries–a mediation model. *Industrial Management & Data Systems*, *124*(10), 2919–2938. DOI: 10.1108/IMDS-12-2023-0977

Alsudani, M. Q., Jaber, M. M., Ali, M. H., Abd, S. K., Alkhayyat, A., Kareem, Z. H., & Mohhan, A. R. (2023). RETRACTED ARTICLE: Smart logistics with IoT-based enterprise management system using international market place manufacturing. *Journal of Combinatorial Optimization*, *45*(2), 57. DOI: 10.1007/s10878-022-00977-5

Ananda, R. A., & Syahyuni, D. (2024). Factors influencing consumer purchasing decisions in the modular kitchen market. *Journal of Consumer Behaviour*, *15*(3), 45–52.

Ángeles López-Cabarcos, M., Pérez-Pico, A. M., Vázquez Rodríguez, P., & López Perez, M. L. (2020). Investor sentiment in the theoretical field of behavioural finance. *Economic Research -. Ekonomska Istrazivanja*, *33*(1), 2101–2228. DOI: 10.1080/1331677X.2018.1559748

Ani, N. C., & Özarı, Ç. (n.d.). Behavioral finance: Investors' psychology. In *Behavioral Finance* (pp. 1-15).

Anigbogu, T. U., & Okoli, I. M & Nwako by N. P. (2015). Financial Intermediation and Small and Medium Enterprises Performance in Nigeria. (An aggregated analysis: 1980 - 2013). *European Scientific Journal*, *1*(28), 257–272.

Annofe, S. (2005). Assessing the Impact of Exchange Rate Risk on Performance of Financial Institutions. *Journal of Economic and Development Studies*, *5*(2), 8–2.

Apache Software Foundation. "Apache Jena." https://jena.apache.org/

Arıcan, O. H. (2024). Yat Turizm Şirketleri Için Yelkenli Tekne Seçimi Kriterlerinin Belirlenmesİ. *Dokuz Eylül Üniversitesi Denizcilik Fakültesi Dergisi* [Determination of Sailing Boat Selection Criteria for Yacht Tourism Companies. Dokuz Eylül University Maritime Faculty Journal*]*, *16*(1), 22–50. DOI: 10.18613/deudfd.1422201

Arıcan, O. H., Arslan, O., & Unal, A. U. (2023). The importance of CATZOC in passage planning and prioritization of strategies for safe navigation. *Marine Science and Technology Bulletin*, *12*(4), 445–458. DOI: 10.33714/masteb.1333432

Arıcan, O. H., Arslan, O., Ünal, A., & Kaya Özbağ, G. (2024). Developing a Comprehensive Yacht Captain Selection Model for Enhancing Competitiveness in Yacht Tourism: A Fuzzy AHP Approach. *Journal for Maritime Research*, *21*(3).

Arıcan, O. H., Unal, A., Arslan, O., & Bamyacı, M. (2022). A Dry Cargo Coaster Tonnage Selection Model for Shipping Companies in Türkiye. *Kent Akademisi*, *15*(4), 1651–1669. DOI: 10.35674/kent.1017076

Armijos-Orellana, A., González, M., Maldonado-Matute, J., & Guerrero, P. (2023). Un acercamiento teórico a la economía digital. *Estudios de la Gestión*, 14, 78-90. https://revistas.uasb.edu.ec/index.php/eg/article/download/4116/3999/16300

Arnould, E. J., & Thompson, C. J. (2005). Consumer culture theory (CCT): Twenty years of research. *The Journal of Consumer Research*, *31*(4), 868–882. DOI: 10.1086/426626

Arokodare, M. A., Falana, R. B., & Olubiyi, T. O. (2023). Strategic agility, knowledge management and organisational performance in a post-pandemic era: A mediation analysis. *Journal of Family Business and Management Studies*, *27*, 83–108.

Ashraf, M. H., Triki, A., & Yalcin, M. G. (2024). Logistics digitalization and the third-party logistics blue-collar employees sustainability: The function of paradoxical leader team conduct. *International Journal of Logistics Management*. Advance online publication. DOI: 10.1108/IJLM-03-2024-0194

Ashuro, T. (2025). Mediating Role of MSE Competitiveness. *Eco-Logistics and Sustainable Supply Chain Innovations*, 39.

Asuquo, A. I. (2012). Empirical analysis of effects of commercial bank managers and acquisitions on small business Micheal, T.S, lending in Nigeria. *International Journal of Advancement in Research & Technology*, *1*(6), 1–15.

Athey, S. (2017). Beyond prediction: Using big data for policy problems. *Science*, *355*(6324), 483–485. DOI: 10.1126/science.aal4321 PMID: 28154050

Attah, R. U., Garba, B. M. P., Gil-Ozoudeh, I., & Iwuanyanwu, O. (2024). Competitive domains for digital transformation across logistics and energy industrys: Bridging technology with corporate strategy. *Open Access Res J Sci Technol, 12*(02), 070-80.

Attah, R. U., Ogunsola, O. Y., & Garba, B. M. P. (2023). Revolutionizing logistics with artificial intelligence: Breakthroughs in digitalization of supply chain, analytics, and logistics excellence. *Iconic Investigation and Engineering Journals*, *6*(12), 1471–1493.

Auer, S., ... (2007). "DBpedia: A Nucleus for a Web of Open Data." *The Semantic Web* (ISWC 2007), pp. 722-735.

Autor, D., Dorn, D., Katz, L., Patterson, C., & Van Reenen, J. (2020). The Fall of the Labor Share and the Rise of Superstar Firms. *The Quarterly Journal of Economics*, *135*(2), 645–709. DOI: 10.1093/qje/qjaa004

AWS. (2023). *¿Qué es la transformación digital?* Recuperado de https://aws.amazon.com/es/what-is/digital-transformation/

Ayu, A., Niswaty, R., Darwis, M., & Arhas, S. H. (2019). Applying the principles of good governance in the efforts of guiding out-of-school children at social service offices at Takalar Regency. *Jurnal Office*, *5*(2), 51–58. DOI: 10.26858/jo.v5i2.11821

Ayuba, B., & Zubairu, M. (2015). Impact of banking sector credit on the growth of Small and Medium Enterprises (SME's) in Nigeria. *Journal of Resources Development and Movement*, *15*, 1–9.

Baker, M., Bloom, N., & Davis, S. J. (2020). Measuring economic policy uncertainty. *The Quarterly Journal of Economics*, *131*(4), 1593–1636. DOI: 10.1093/qje/qjw024

Bakış, T. (2023). Yat Turizmi nedir ve yat turizm istatistikleri [What is Yacht Tourism and yacht tourism statistics]. https://www.turizmebakis.com/yat-turizmi/ , Access date: 20.12.2023.

Bakri, M., Krisjanous, J., & Richard, J. E. (2020). Decoding service brand image through user-generated images. *Journal of Services Marketing*, *34*(4), 429–442. DOI: 10.1108/JSM-11-2018-0341

Baldwin, R. (2016). *The great convergence: Information technology and the new globalization*. Harvard University Press., DOI: 10.2307/j.ctv24w655w

Baral, N., & Heinen, J. T. (2020). Regulatory Compliance of Community-Based Conservation Organizations: Empirical Evidence from Annapurna Conservation Area, Nepal. *Sustainability (Basel)*, *12*(22), 9420. DOI: 10.3390/su12229420

Barber, B. M., Huang, X., Odean, T., & Schwarz, C. (2021). Attention induced trading and returns: Evidence from Robinhood users. *The Journal of Finance*, *76*(3), 1171–1216.

Batra, R., Lehmann, D. R., & Singh, D. (1993). *The brand personality component of brand goodwill: Some antecedents and consequences*. Brand Equity and Advertising.

Bazeley, P., & Jackson, K. (2013). *Qualitative data analysis with NVivo* (2nd ed.). SAGE Publications.

Bean, M.A. (2017). *Determinants of interest rates*. Being a study note prepared by education and examination committee of the society of actuaries, *financial mathematics study Note*. 3.

Bërdufi, N., & Nezha, K. (2023). Understanding Civilian Participation and its Implications: A Case Study on the Inclusion of Syria's Civilian Population in the Context of Violence. *Interdisciplinary Journal of Research and Development*, *10*(2), 68. DOI: 10.56345/ijrdv10n209

Berger, A. N., Hanweck, G. A., & Humphrey, D. B. (1987). Competitive viability in banking: Scale, scope and product mix economies. *Journal of Monetary Economics*, *20*(3), 501–520. DOI: 10.1016/0304-3932(87)90039-0

Berger, A. N., & Udell, G. F. (1995). Relationship lending and lines of credit in small firm finance. *The Journal of Business*, *68*(3), 351–381. DOI: 10.1086/296668

Bernanke, B. S. (2023). Nobel Lecture: Banking, Credit, and Economic Fluctuations. *The American Economic Review*, *113*(5), 1143–1169. DOI: 10.1257/aer.113.5.1143

Bessis, J. (2002). *Risk Management in Banking*. Wiley.

Bethune, P. (2017). Undertaking risk management and ISO standards quality digest http:/www.qualitydigest.com/inside/risk-management-article/understandingrisk-and -ISO-standards-071717.html. Retrieved on August 14, 2017.

Bharadwaj, A., El Sawy, O. A., Pavlou, P. A., & Venkatraman, N. (2013). Digital business strategy: Toward a next generation of insights. *Management Information Systems Quarterly*, *37*(2), 471–482. DOI: 10.25300/MISQ/2013/37:2.3

Bhupendra K, Namita R, Pooja N., Olubiyi, T. O., & Yagnam, N. (2022). Impact of microfinance on the inclusive development of Bihar, Journal_Innovations, 71,454-465

Biçak, H. A., Altinay, M., Aksugür, E., Günyakti, A., & Katircioglu, S. (2006). Could yacht tourism be an alternative tourism potential in North Cyprus? *Tourism in Marine Environments*, *3*(1), 49–57. DOI: 10.3727/154427306779380284

Bikas, E., Jurevičienė, D., Dubinskas, P., & Novickytė, L. (2013). Behavioural finance: The emergence and development trends. *Procedia: Social and Behavioral Sciences*, *82*, 870–876. DOI: 10.1016/j.sbspro.2013.06.363

Bikker, J., & Hu, H. (2002). Cyclical patterns in profits, provisioning and lending of banks and procyclicality of the new base capital requirements. *BNL Quarterly Review*, *22*(1), 143–175.

Bilski, M. (2015). Selected human factors in marina design. *Procedia Manufacturing*, *3*, 1646–1653. DOI: 10.1016/j.promfg.2015.07.482

Blanco, F., Eaton, B., & Bawden, D. (2001). La información y el conocimiento: factores de producción en la actividad económica. *Revista Base*, 2(1), 186-200. https://www.redalyc.org/pdf/3372/337228632009.pdf

Boats (2023). Sailing boats: sailboat types, rigs, uses and definitions. https://uk .boats.com/on-the-water/sailing-boats-sailboat-types-rigs-uses-definitions/, Access date: 21.12.2023.

Bodenreider, O. (2004). The unified medical language system (UMLS): Integrating biomedical terminology. *Nucleic Acids Research*, *32*(suppl_1), D267–D270.

Borji, B., & Niguse, T. (2025). Competitive Advantage With Mediating Effect. *Innovative Approaches to Managing Conflict and Change in Diverse Work Environments*, 315.

Botsman, R., & Rogers, R. (2010). *What's Mine Is Yours: The Rise of Collaborative Consumption*. HarperBusiness.

Braun, V., & Clarke, V. (2006). Using thematic analysis in psychology. *Qualitative Research in Psychology*, *3*(2), 77–101. DOI: 10.1191/1478088706qp063oa

Brickley, D. (2005). FOAF vocabulary specification. http://rdfweb. org/foaf/

Bruno V. and Hauswald R. (2008), '*The real effects of foreign banks*', mimeo.

Bruno, V., & Shin, H. S. (2015). Cross-Border Banking and Global Liquidity. *The Review of Economic Studies*, *82*(2), 535–564. DOI: 10.1093/restud/rdu042

Brynjolfsson, E., & Hitt, L. M. (2000). Beyond computation: Information technology, organizational transformation, and business performance. *The Journal of Economic Perspectives*, *14*(4), 23–48. DOI: 10.1257/jep.14.4.23

Brynjolfsson, E., & McAfee, A. (2014). *The second machine age: Work, progress, and prosperity in a time of brilliant technologies*. W.W. Norton & Company.

Buchalski, Z. (2013). Selection Of Sailing Boats Configuration For Various User Groups. *Information Systems Architecture and Technology*, 43.

Bucur, B. (2015). Conceptual Design. A Case Study: Sailing Boat. *Journal Of Industrial Design And Engineering Graphics*, *10*, 21.

Budiarrianto, D., & Sebayang, A. F. (2021). Penerapan Prinsip-Prinsip Good Governance terhadap Pelayanan Publik Desa Rahayu Kecamatan Margaasih Kabupaten Bandung. *Bandung Conference Series: Economics Studies*, *1*(1), 33–40. DOI: 10.29313/bcses.v1i1.49

Bukht, R., & Heeks, R. (2017). Defining, Conceptualising and Measuring the Digital Economy (August 3, 2017). *Development Informatics Working Paper no. 68,* Available at SSRN: https://ssrn.com/abstract=3431732 or http://dx.doi.org/DOI: 10.2139/ssrn.3431732

Busthami, D. (2017). *Kekuasaan Kehakiman Dalam Perspektif Negara Hukum. 4.*

Byrne, D. (2022). The Digital Economy and Productivity. *Finance and Economics Discussion Series (FEDS)* DOI: 10.17016/feds.2022.038

Byrne, A., & Utkus, W. S. P. (n.d.). *Understanding how the mind can help or hinder investment success*. Vanguard Investment Counseling & Research.

Castegnaro, S., Gomiero, C., Battisti, C., Poli, M., Basile, M., Barucco, P., Pizzarello, U., Quaresimin, M., & Lazzaretto, A. (2017). A bio-composite racing sailboat: Materials selection, design, manufacturing and sailing. *Ocean Engineering*, *133*, 142–150. DOI: 10.1016/j.oceaneng.2017.01.017

Castells, M. (1996). *The Rise of the Network Society*. Blackwell.

Central Bank of Nigeria (2015), Understanding Monetary Policy Series No. 12. Inflation targeting as a monetary policy framework

CEPAL. (2013). *La economía digital: Un motor para el desarrollo sostenible.* Retrieved from https://www.cepal.org/es/publicaciones/25756-economia-digital-motor-desarrollo-sostenible

Chan, F. T., Kumar, N., Tiwari, M. K., Lau, H. C., & Choy, K. (2008). Global supplier selection: A fuzzy-AHP approach. *International Journal of Production Research, 46*(14), 3825–3857. DOI: 10.1080/00207540600787200

Chang, D.-Y. (1996). Applications of the Extent Analysis Method on Fuzzy AHP. *European Journal of Operational Research, 95*(3), 649–655. DOI: 10.1016/0377-2217(95)00300-2

Chen, J., Balomenou, C., Nijkamp, P., Poulaki, P., & Lagos, D. (2016). *The sustainability of yachting tourism: a case study on Greece.*

Chen, C., Li, X., & Wu, H. (2020). Big data analytics in financial markets: A review. *The Journal of Financial Data Science, 2*(2), 15–27. DOI: 10.3905/jfds.2020.1.035

Cheng, C. H. (1996). Evaluating naval tactical missile systems by fuzzy AHP based on the grade value of membership function. *European Journal of Operational Research, 96*(2), 343–350. DOI: 10.1016/S0377-2217(96)00026-4

Chen, Y., & Lee, J. (2021). Greenwashing and consumer trust: A cross-cultural examination. *Journal of Business Ethics, 174*(3), 567–584. DOI: 10.1007/s10551-021-04924-y

Chesbrough, H. (2006) *Open Innovation: A New Paradigm for Understanding Industrial Innovation. 10th Anniversary Summer Conference on Dynamics of Industry and Innovation: Organizations, Networks and Systems*, Copenhagen, 27-29 June 2005, 1-12. DOI: 10.1093/oso/9780199290727.003.0001

Chesbrough, H. W. (2007). Business Model Innovation: It's Not Just About Technology Anymore. *Strategy and Leadership, 35*(6), 12–17. DOI: 10.1108/10878570710833714

Chimobi, O. P., & Igwe, O. L. (2010). Budget Deficit, Money supply and Inflation in Nigeria. *European. Journal of Economics, Finance and Administrative Science, 19*, 52–60.

Chimucheka, T., & Ellen, C. R. (2011). The impact of inaccessibility to bank finance and lack of financial management knowledge to small, medium and micro enterprises in Buffalo City Municipality, South Africa. *African Journal of Business Management, 5*(14), 5509–5517.

Chodechai, D. (2004). Impact of lending policy on banking industry in Nigeria. Journal, vol 7, pg 12 - 22, Chodecal D (2004) Impact of lending policy on banking industry in Nigeria [Unity Press limited.]. *Journal*, *7*, 12–22.

Chokera, F., & Mutambara, E. (2023). Exploring value addition initiatives among small-to-medium enterprises in the leather sector in emerging economies. *Acta Commercii Independent Research Journal in the Management Sciences*, *23*(1), 1000. DOI: 10.4102/ac.v23i1.1000

Cho, W. J. (2012). Analyses of consumer preferences and perceptions regarding activation of yacht tourism industry. *Journal of Navigation and Port Research*, *36*(5), 401–407. DOI: 10.5394/KINPR.2012.36.5.401

Chowdhury, M. M. H., & Haque Munim, Z. (2023). Dry port location selection using a fuzzy AHP-BWM-PROMETHEE approach. *Maritime Economics & Logistics*, *25*(2), 301–329. DOI: 10.1057/s41278-022-00230-0

Christensen, C. M. (1997). *The innovator's dilemma: When new technologies cause great firms to fail*. Harvard Business Review Press.

Chroneou, C. (2024). *Development of marinas in Greece* (Master's thesis, Πανεπιστήμιο Πειραιώς).

Cil, İ., Arisoy, F., Özgürbüz, E., Yunus Cil, A., & Kılınç, H. (2022). Indoor Positioning Technology Selection Using a Combined AHP and PROMETHEE Method at SEDEF Shipyard. *Journal of ETA Maritime Science*, *10*(2), 108–123. DOI: 10.4274/jems.2022.47550

Coase, R. H. (1937). The nature of the firm. *Economica*, *4*(16), 386–405. DOI: 10.1111/j.1468-0335.1937.tb00002.x

Cohen, M., & Sundararajan, A. (2015). Self-regulation and innovation in the peer-to-peer sharing economy. *University of Chicago Law Review Online*, 82

Cohen, S., de Long, D., & Zysman, J. (2000). *The New Economy: A New Perspective on the Economic Landscape*.

Cone, L., & Lai, S. S. (2024). Infrastructural dependency in the datafied welfare state: The case of Google Chromebooks. *Learning, Media and Technology*, •••, 1–17.

Creswell, J. W., & Plano Clark, V. L. (2017). *Designing and conducting mixed methods research* (3rd ed.). SAGE Publications.

Creusen, M. E. H., & Schoormans, J. P. L. (2005). The different roles of product appearance in consumer choice. *Journal of Product Innovation Management*, *22*(1), 63–81. DOI: 10.1111/j.0737-6782.2005.00103.x

Crowley, J. (2007). Interest Rate Spreads in English -Speaking Africa.*IMF Working Paper*, 123 -45

Dada, F. O. (2014). The Justiciability and Enforceability of Women's Rights in Nigeria. [E]. *Global Journal of Human Social Science*, *14*, 49–56.

Dalton, B., & Proctor, C. P. (2008). The changing landscape of text and comprehension in the age of new literacies. In Coiro, J., Knobel, M., Lankshear, C., & Leu, D. J. (Eds.), *Handbook of research on new literacies* (pp. 297–324). Routledge.

Das, G. (2012). The role of user imagery in consumer decision-making: A study of mobile handsets. *The Journal of Consumer Research*, *39*(3), 456–467. DOI: 10.1086/664962

Data Bridge Market Research. (2024). Global modular kitchen market. Retrieved from https://www.databridgemarketresearch.com/reports/global-modular-kitchen-market

Davenport, T. H., & Beck, J. C. (2001). *The attention economy: Understanding the new currency of business*. Harvard Business Review Press.

Davis, F. D. (1989). Perceived usefulness, perceived ease of use, and user acceptance of information technology. *Management Information Systems Quarterly*, *13*(3), 319–340. DOI: 10.2307/249008

DCMI. "Dublin Core Metadata Initiative." https://dublincore.org/

De Stefano, V. (2016). The rise of the "just-in-time workforce": On-demand work, crowdwork, and labor protection in the gig-economy. *Comparative Labor Law & Policy Journal*, *37*, 471–504.

Deci, E. L., & Ryan, R. M. (1985). *Intrinsic motivation and self-determination in human behavior*. Plenum Press. DOI: 10.1007/978-1-4899-2271-7

Decker, A. (2013). An Empirical Analysis of the Liquidity, Solvency and Financial Health of Small and Medium Sized enterprises. *European Journal of Business and Management*, *5*(8), 1.

DeJohn v. The. TV Corp. Int'l, 487 F. Supp. 2d 593 (E.D. Pa. 2007).

Delmana, L. P. (2019). Pengaruh Penerapan Good Governance Dalam E-Purcashing Terhadap Pencegahan Korupsi [The Influence of Good Governance Implementation in E-Purchasing on Corruption Prevention]. *Jurnal Ilmu Pemerintahan Widya Praja [Journal of Government Science Widya Praja]*, *45*(1), 47–62. DOI: 10.33701/jipwp.v45i1.241

Design, B. (2024). Sailing boats' Stability, STIX and Old Ratios https://www.boatdesign.net/forums/attachments/stability/9806d1161681331-sailing-boats-stability-stix-old-ratios-stix-formula-r3.xls, Access date: 02.01.2024.

Deusto, O. (2017). *Por qué la Economía Digital.* Retrieved from https://www.orkestra.deusto.es/euskadi-economia-digital/2017/por-que-economia-digital.phtml

Dietvorst, B. J., Simmons, J. P., & Massey, C. (2015). Algorithm aversion: People erroneously avoid algorithms after seeing them err. *Journal of Experimental Psychology. General*, *144*(1), 114–126. DOI: 10.1037/xge0000033 PMID: 25401381

Dinata, A. W. (2022). Legal Implications Of Non-Compliance With The Decision Of The State Administrative Court In Terms Of The Implementation Of Regional Autonomy And The Unitary State. *Jurnal Hukum Peratun*, *4*(1), 1–30. DOI: 10.25216/peratun.412021.1-30

Drehman, M., Sorensen, S., & Stringa, M. (2008). The Integrated Impact of Credit and Interest Rate Risk on Banks: An Economic Value and Capital Adequacy Perspective", Bank of England Working Paper No.339

Du, J., & Nguyen, B. (2022). Cognitive financial constraints and firm growth. Small Business Economics, 58(4), 2109-2137. Effiom, L., & Edet, S. E. (2022). Financial innovation and the performance of small and medium scale enterprises in Nigeria. *Journal of Small Business and Entrepreneurship*, *34*(2), 141–174.

Dwivedi, Y. K., Hughes, L., Ismagilova, E., Aarts, G., Coombs, C., Crick, T., Duan, Y., Dwivedi, R., Edwards, J., Eirug, A., Galanos, V., Ilavarasan, P. V., Janssen, M., Jones, P., Kar, A. K., Kizgin, H., Kronemann, B., Lal, B., Lucini, B., & Williams, M. D. (2021). Artificial Intelligence (AI): Multidisciplinary perspectives on emerging challenges, opportunities, and agenda for research, practice and policy. *Technological Forecasting and Social Change*, *163*, 120434. DOI: 10.1016/j.techfore.2020.120434

Ebiringa, O. T. (2011). Synthesis of literature on small and medium enterprises (SME) start-up financing. *International Journal of Economic Research*, *5*(1), 85–95.

Ebiringa, O. T., & Chigbu, E. E. (2012). Analysis of Effect of Financing Leverage on Bank Performance: Evidence from Nigeria. *Journal of Public Administration and Governance.*, *2*(4).

Edralin, D., & Pastrana, R. (2020). Nexus between Sustainable Business Practices and the Quest for Peace. *Bedan Research Journal*, *5*(1), 1–58. DOI: 10.58870/berj.v5i1.11

Efecan, V., & Temiz, İ. (2020). Marina Selection Of Yachtsmen Using AHP-TOPSIS And AHP-PROMETHEE. *Mersin University Journal of Maritime Faculty*, 2(1), 14-24.

Eichengreen, B., & Gibson, H. D. Greek Banking at the Dawn of the New Millennium (May 2001). Available at *SSRN*: https://ssrn.com/abstract=269391

Einav, L., & Levin, J. (2014). Economics in the age of big data. *Science, 346*(6210), 1243089. DOI: 10.1126/science.1243089 PMID: 25378629

Ejikeme, M. O. (2013). *Evaluation of credit risk management and performance of Nigerian banks*. Being a project submitted to postgraduate school of Ahmed in Bello University Zoria in Partial fulfilment of the requirement for the award of the degree of Masters in Business Admin. *European Journal of Economics, Finance and Administrative Sciences ISSN* 1450-2275 Issue 19.

Elias, W., Ezzat, M., & Ahmed, F. M. (2020). Assessing the tourists satisfaction towards yacht tourism services in the red sea coast, Egypt. *Minia Journal of Tourism and Hospitality Research MJTHR, 9*(1), 157–170. DOI: 10.21608/mjthr.2020.139593

Elkington, J. (1997). *Cannibals with forks: The triple bottom line of 21st century business*. Capstone.

Engle, J. F., Blackwell, R. D., & Miniard, P. W. (1995). *Consumer behaviour* (International ed.). Dryden.

Ertuğrul, İ., & Karakaşoğlu, N. (2008). Comparison of fuzzy AHP and fuzzy TOPSIS methods for facility location selection. *International Journal of Advanced Manufacturing Technology, 39*(7-8), 783–795. DOI: 10.1007/s00170-007-1249-8

Eskandari, M., Homaee, M., Mahmoodi, S., Pazira, E., & Van Genuchten, M. T. (2015). Optimizing landfill site selection by using land classification maps. *Environmental Science and Pollution Research International, 22*(10), 7754–7765. DOI: 10.1007/s11356-015-4182-7 PMID: 25666474

European Commission. (2020). *Digital Economy and Society Index 2020*.

Evans, D., & Schmalensee, R. (2016). *Matchmakers: The New Economics of Multisided Platforms*. Harvard Business Review Press.

Fagerström, S. (2008). Behavioural finance: The psychological impact and overconfidence in financial markets. Institutionen för teknik och samhälle. https://urn.kb.se/resolve?urn=urn:nbn:se:his:diva-1326

Fahrizal, I., Santoso, B., & Budiono, A. (2023). Resolving Work Engagement: How Leadership and Total Rewards Influence Employee Work Engagement Through the Mediating Function of Service Climate in Supply Chain and Logistic Company in Indonesia. *Jurnal Pamator: Jurnal Ilmiah Universitas Trunojoyo, 16*(2), 328–349. DOI: 10.21107/pamator.v16i2.19791

Faten, B. B., Chantal, A., & Ado, L. (2016). *Banking Governance, Performance and Risk-Taking: Conventional Banks Vs Islamic Banks*. Published in Great Britain and United State by ISTE Ltd and John Wiley & Son, Inc.

Fatoki, O. O. (2013). The determinants of immigrant entrepreneurs' growth expectations in South Africa. *Journal of Social Sciences, 37*(3), 209–216. DOI: 10.1080/09718923.2013.11893219

Feldman v. Google, Inc., 513 F. Supp. 2d 229 (E.D. Pa. 2007).

Firat, D., & Fettahoğlu, S. (2011). Investors' purchasing behaviour via a behavioural finance approach. *International Journal of Business and Management, 6*(7), 153–160. DOI: 10.5539/ijbm.v6n7p153

Firmantoro, K. (2022). Negligence Of Customs and Excise in the Implementation of Judicial Decisions on Audit Result Disputes that Can Cause Country Loss and Business Actors (A Study On Court Decision No. 46/Pk/Tun/2011 Which Has Not Been Done By Customs And Excise. *International Journal of Business, Economics, and Social Development, 3*(2), 76–87. DOI: 10.46336/ijbesd.v3i2.248

Fisher, C., Calderson, S. J., Mougin, J., & Radford, M. J. (2021). Evolution of clickwrap & browsewrap contracts. *Rutgers Computer & Technology Law Journal, 48*, 147–178.

Fiske, D. W. (1971). *Measuring the concepts of personality*. Aldine.

Fogaat, M., Sharma, S., & Meena, D. R. P. (2022). Behavioral finance psychology: A review paper. *Journal of Contemporary Issues in Business and Government, 28*(4), 4.

Fotiadis, A., Rice, J., & Hiyasat, R. (2023). Antecedents of yacht tourism participants' satisfaction and word-of-mouth intention. *Worldwide Hospitality and Tourism Themes, 15*(4), 349–361. DOI: 10.1108/WHATT-03-2023-0042

Franzen, I. (2013). A Refinement of the Method Used to Determine the Balance of a Sailing Vessel During the Design Phase, with Application to Sail Design and Subsequent Sail Selection and Sailing Operations. *In SNAME Chesapeake Sailing Yacht Symposium* (p. D021S003R001). SNAME. DOI: 10.5957/CSYS-2013-007

Fredericks, B., & Bradfield, A. (2023). Many Bodies, One Heart. *M/C Journal, 26*(1). DOI: 10.5204/mcj.2908

Gal, J. (2020). Corporate governance of insurers in Germany. German National Report. *Zeitschrift Für Die Gesamte Versicherungswissenschaft, 109*(1), 41–64. DOI: 10.1007/s12297-020-00467-9

Garvin, D. A. (1984). What does product quality really mean? *Sloan Management Review, 26*(1), 25–43.

Gatawa, N. M., Akinola A, M. O. & Olarinde (2013). Impact of Money Supply and Inflation on Economic Growthin Nigeria (1973-2013). *IOSR Journal of Economics and Finance, 8,* (3), 26-37.

Goddard, J. A., Molyneux, P. M., & Wilson, J. O. S. (2004). Dynamics of growth and profitability in banking. *Journal of Money, Credit and Banking, 36*(6), 1069–1090. DOI: 10.1353/mcb.2005.0015

Gogia, E. H., Shao, Z., & Akhter, A. R. (2024). Resolving Success: Exploring the Influence of Human Resource Competence on Job Sustainability in Pakistan's Engineering Industry. *Engineering. Technology & Applied Science Investigation, 14*(3), 14754–14759.

Gokal, V., & Hanif, S. (2004). *Relationship between Inflation and Economic Growth. Working Paper, Economics Department Reserve Bank of Fiji Suva Fiji, 2004/04.* Retrieved from https://rbf.gov.fj/docs/2004_04_wp.pdf

Goldsmith, R., Kim, D., Flynn, L., & Kim, W. (2005). Price sensitivity and innovativeness for fashion among Korean consumers. *The Journal of Social Psychology, 145*(5), 501–508. DOI: 10.3200/SOCP.145.5.501-508 PMID: 16201674

Gomathy, M., & Sabarirajan, K. K. (2016). Brand personality's influence on the purchase decision of modular kitchen. *International Journal of Management Focus, 6*(4), 12–17.

Gomathy, M., & Sabarirajan, K. K. (2017a). Influence of product features on consumer purchase decisions in the modular kitchen market. *Journal of Consumer Marketing, 34*(5), 432–440. DOI: 10.1108/JCM-02-2017-2078

Gomathy, M., & Sabarirajan, K. K. (2017b). Influence of price and perceived quality on purchase decision of modular kitchen: A study with special reference to Chennai City. *International Research Journal of Business and Management, 6*(4), 45–52.

Gomathy, M., & Sabarirajan, K. K. (2017c). Role of product design in consumers' purchase decision of modular kitchen in Chennai City. *International Journal of Global Business Management and Research, 6*(2), 32–36.

Gomathy, M., & Sabarirajan, K. K. (2018). Product features and purchase behaviour of consumers: With special reference to modular kitchen. *Sankalpa Journal of Management and Research, 8*(1), 72–77.

Gomber, P., Koch, J.-A., & Siering, M. (2017). Digital finance and fintech: Current research and future research directions. *Journal of Business Economics*, *87*(5), 537–580. DOI: 10.1007/s11573-017-0852-x

Gomes, S., Lopes, J., & Ferreira, L. The impact of the digital economy on economic growth: The case of OECD countries. *RAM Revista de Administração Mackenzie* https://doi.org/DOI: 10.1590/1678-6971/eRAMD220029.en

Goos, M., Manning, A., & Salomons, A. (2014). Explaining job polarization: Routine-biased technological change and offshoring. *The American Economic Review*, *104*(8), 2509–2526. DOI: 10.1257/aer.104.8.2509

Gormley, C., & Tong, Z. (2015). *Elasticsearch: The Definitive Guide*. O'Reilly Media.

Goryachev, I. (2018). *Draft guidelines for safety and development of minors on the internet*.

Gotosailing, (2024). Hırvatistan'da Tekne Tatili Yapmak İçin 10 Neden. https://gotosailing.com/tr/hirvatistan-da-tekne-tatili-yapmak-icin-10-neden, Access date: 23.12.2023.

Gourinchas, P.-O., & Obstfeld, M. (2012). Stories of the twentieth century for the twenty-firsf. *American Economic Journal. Macroeconomics*, *4*(1), 226–265. DOI: 10.1257/mac.4.1.226

Govindaraju, P., Rahman, M. R. A., & Ismail, S. M. (2023). Ekstremisme Ganas Dan Semakan Kehakiman Dalam Kes-Kes Berkaitan Dengannya Dari Perspektif Undang-Undang Tahanan Pencegahan Malaysia : (Violent Extremism and Judicial Review in Related Cases: A Perspective on the Preventive Detention Laws of Malaysia). *UUM Journal of Legal Studies*, *14*(1), 297–331. DOI: 10.32890/uumjls2023.14.1.12

Granovetter, M. (1973). The Strength of Weak Ties. *American Journal of Sociology*, *78*(6), 1360–1380. DOI: 10.1086/225469

Griffin, C. N. (2023). Contracting as class. *Brigham Young University Law Review*, *48*(4), 1185–1254.

Guizzardi, G. (2005). "Ontological Foundations for Structural Conceptual Models." Ph.D. thesis, University of Twente.

Guler, D., & Yomralioglu, T. (2020). Suitable location selection for the electric vehicle fast charging station with AHP and fuzzy AHP methods using GIS. *Annals of GIS*, *26*(2), 169–189. DOI: 10.1080/19475683.2020.1737226

Guneri, A. F., Cengiz, M., & Seker, S. (2009). A fuzzy ANP approach to shipyard location selection. *Expert Systems with Applications*, *36*(4), 7992–7999. DOI: 10.1016/j.eswa.2008.10.059

Gupta, S., & Singh, R. (2018). Cultural customization in kitchen design: A study of emerging markets. *Journal of Consumer Culture*, *19*(3), 345–362. DOI: 10.1177/1469540517745703

Guzavicius, A., Vilkė, R., & Barkauskas, V. (2014). Behavioural finance: Corporate social responsibility approach. *Procedia: Social and Behavioral Sciences*, *156*, 518–523. DOI: 10.1016/j.sbspro.2014.11.232

Hagejärd, S., Ollár, A., Femenías, P., & Rahe, U. (2020). Designing for circularity—Addressing product design, consumption practices, and resource flows in domestic kitchens. *Sustainability (Basel)*, *12*(3), 1006. DOI: 10.3390/su12031006

Haiying Pan, H. S. (2012). Analysis of the Effects of Frequent Increases of the Reserve Requirement Ratio by the People's Bank of China. Modern Economy, 229-236.

Hanine, M., Boutkhoum, O., Tikniouine, A., & Agouti, T. (2016). Comparison of fuzzy AHP and fuzzy TODIM methods for landfill location selection. *SpringerPlus*, *5*(1), 1–30. DOI: 10.1186/s40064-016-2131-7 PMID: 27186465

Heath, T., & Bizer, C. (2011). *Linked data: Evolving the web into a global data space*. Morgan & Claypool Publishers.

Hemnes, T. M. S. (1994). Restraints on alienation, equitable servitudes, and the feudal nature of computer software licensing. *Denver University Law Review*, *71*, 577–599.

Hess, T., Matt, C., Benlian, A., & Wiesböck, F. (2016). Options for formulating a digital transformation strategy. *MIS Quarterly Executive*, *15*(2), 123–139.

Hirsch, B., Schäfer, F.-S., Aristovnik, A., Kovač, P., & Ravšelj, D. (2022). The impact of Digitalized Communication on the effectiveness of Local Administrative Authorities – Findings from Central European Countries in the COVID-19 Crisis. *Journal of Business Economics*, *93*(1–2), 173–192. DOI: 10.1007/s11573-022-01110-y PMID: 38013851

Hogarth Robin, M. (1978). A note on aggregating opinions. *Organizational Behavior and Human Performance*, *21*(1), 40–46. DOI: 10.1016/0030-5073(78)90037-5

Holland, J. H. (1995). *Hidden Order: How Adaptation Builds Complexity*. Addison-Wesley.

Homburg, C., Schwemmle, M., & Kuehnl, C. (2020). Emotional branding in durable goods: A framework and empirical evidence. *The Journal of Consumer Research, 47*(4), 535–558. DOI: 10.1093/jcr/ucaa030

Horrocks, I., et al. (2004). "SWRL: A Semantic Web Rule Language Combining OWL and RuleML."

Hossain, M. B., Rahman, M. U., Čater, T., & Vasa, L. (2024). Determinants of SMEs' competitive entrepreneurial innovative digitalization: examining the mediation function of capital in human form. *European Journal of Investigation Management*.

Hotmail Corp. v. Van Money Pie Inc., No. C98-20064 JW, 1998 U.S. Dist. LEXIS 10729 (N.D. Cal. Apr. 16, 1998). i.Lan Systems, Inc. v. Netscout Service Level Corp., 183 F. Supp. 2d 328 (D. Mass. 2002).

Hoyer, W. D., & MacInnis, D. J. (2010). *Consumer behavior* (5th ed.). South-Western Cengage Learning.

Hsing, Yu. (2006). *Determinants of Exchange Rate Fluctuations for Venezuela: Application of an Extended Mundell- Fleming Model, Applied Econometrics and International Development* (Vol. 6). Euro- American Association of Economic Development.

Huang, T. L., & Liao, S. (2017). Augmented reality in home design: Enhancing consumer engagement. *Computers in Human Behavior, 75*, 1–10. DOI: 10.1016/j.chb.2017.05.006

HubSpot. (2023). *Qué es la transformación digital: características, proceso y ejemplos*. Recuperado de https://blog.hubspot.es/sales/transformacion-digital

Hukum, S., Kurniawati, R., Lubis, A. F., Indrayana, S., & Kurniawan, B. A. (2023). *Rekonstruksi Penelitian Hukum Administrasi Negara melalui Pendekatan Bibliometrik : Sebuah Tinjauan Komprehensif tentang Perkembangan dan Kontribusi Literatur [Reconstruction of State Administrative Law Research through a Bibliometric Approach: A Comprehensive Review of the Development and Contribution of Literature], 2*(01), 20–29. https://doi.org/DOI: 10.58812/shh.v2.i01

Igwe, P. A., Amaugo, A. N., Ogundana, O. M., Egere, O. M., & Anigbo, J. A. (2018). Factors Affecting the Investment Climate, SMEs Productivity and Entrepreneurship in Nigeria. *European Journal of Sustainable Development, 7*(1), 182–200. DOI: 10.14207/ejsd.2018.v7n1p182

Iloh, J., & Nnanyelogo, C. (2015). Commercial Bank Credit availability to SME's in Nigeria, *3rd International Conference on Business, law and corporate socialResponsibility.* Held in Bali Indonesia. May 5 – 6.

Imed Drine & ChristopherRault. (2003). Long-Run Determinants of the Real Exchange Rate for MENA Countries. *Journal of International Advances in Economics Research, 9*(1).

Imonghele, L. E., & Ismaila, M. (2014). The Impact of the Commercial Bank Credit on the Growth of Small and Medium Scale Enterprises: Econometric Evidence from Nigeria (1986-2012). [JEPER]. *Journal of Educational Policy and Entrepreneurial Research, 1*(2), 251–262.

In re Apple In-App Purchase Litigation, 855 F. Supp. 2d 1030 (N.D. Cal. 2012).

Indian Contract Act, § 11, No. 9, Acts of Parliament (1872).

Indian Contract Act, No. 9, Acts of Parliament (1872).

Indian Majority Act, § 3, No. 9, Acts of Parliament (1875).

Jabo, B., & Kant, S. "Impact of Technical CRM on Ethiopia Bank Human-Computer Interface and Competitive Advantage as Mediators of Performance," 2024 IEEE International Conference on Computing, Power and Communication Technologies (IC2PCT), Greater Noida, India, 2024, pp. 679-682, https://doi.org/DOI: 10.1109/IC2PCT60090.2024.10486237

Jacobides, M. G., Cennamo, C., & Gawer, A. (2018). Towards a theory of ecosystems. *Strategic Management Journal, 39*(8), 2255–2276. DOI: 10.1002/smj.2904

Jauhari, S. (2023, April 25). India: Though click-wraps are legal, can minors enter click-wraps? Mondaq. https://www.mondaq.com/india/it-and-internet/1305896/though-click-wraps-are-legal-can-minors-enter-click-wraps-

Joo, B. A., & Durri, K. (2015). Comprehensive review of literature on behavioural finance. *Indian Journal of Commerce and Management Studies, 6*(2), 2.

Joshi, Y., & Rahman, Z. (2015). Price sensitivity and consumer behavior in the luxury market: A study of consumer perceptions. *Journal of Retailing and Consumer Services, 22*, 1–10. DOI: 10.1016/j.jretconser.2014.09.001

Joshi, Y., & Rahman, Z. (2019). Drivers of sustainable consumption: A meta-analysis. *Journal of Business Research, 98*, 64–77. DOI: 10.1016/j.jbusres.2019.01.030

Justin, I. I. (2014). Evaluation of survival strategies of small and medium enterprises in Benue State, Nigeria.*InternationalJournal of Academic Research in Accounting. Finance and Management Sciences, 4*(2), 255–263.

Ka, B. (2011). Application of fuzzy AHP and ELECTRE to China dry port location selection. *The Asian Journal of Shipping and Logistics*, *27*(2), 331–353. DOI: 10.1016/S2092-5212(11)80015-5

Kaboli, A., Aryanezhad, M. B., Shahanaghi, K., & Niroomand, I. (2007, October). A new method for plant location selection problem: a fuzzy-AHP approach. In *2007 IEEE International Conference on Systems, Man and Cybernetics* (pp. 582-586). IEEE. DOI: 10.1109/ICSMC.2007.4413890

Kahneman, D., & Tversky, A. (1979). Prospect theory: An analysis of decision under risk. *Econometrica*, *47*(2), 263–291. DOI: 10.2307/1914185

Kant, S., & Adula, M. (2024). Human-Machine Interaction in the Metaverse in the Context of Ethiopia. In Impact and Potential of Machine Learning in the Metaverse (pp. 196-212). IGI Global. DOI: DOI: 10.4018/979-8-3693-5762-0.ch008

Kant, S., & Degefa, T. T. (2025). Public Administration 5.0 Effect on Super Smart Society by Mediation of Digital Governance in Horn of Africa. In *Public Governance Practices in the Age of AI* (pp. 201-222). IGI Global Scientific Publishing.

Kant, S., Niguse, T., Terefe, A., & Adula, M. (2025). Upskilling Workforces for New Competencies by the Mediating Role of Life Skills in HRM 5.0 for the Hospitality Industry. In *Humanizing the Hyperconnected Workplace* (pp. 137-164). IGI Global Scientific Publishing.

Kant, S., Adula, M., & Alemu, G. M. (2025). Effect of Green Supply Chain Management Practice on Firm Performance With Mediation of Green Innovation in Ethiopia. In *Eco-Logistics and Sustainable Supply Chain Innovations* (pp. 61–84). IGI Global Scientific Publishing.

Karayel, G. K., Javani, N., & Dincer, I. (2022). Sustainable marina concept with green hydrogen utilization: A case study. *Sustainable Energy Technologies and Assessments*, *54*, 102900. DOI: 10.1016/j.seta.2022.102900

Kar, R. B., & Yu, X. (2024). The contractual death and rebirth of privacy. *SSRN*, •••, 38. DOI: 10.2139/ssrn.4939708

Karras, G. (1994). Macroeconomics Effects of Budget Deficit: Further International Evidence. *Journal of International Money and Finance*, *13*(2), 190–210. DOI: 10.1016/0261-5606(94)90015-9

Karunia, R. L., Solihati, K. D., & Wati, N. K. (2022). Implementation of Good Governance Principles in the Land Transportation Management Center. *KnE Social Sciences*, 1253–1269–1253–1269. DOI: 10.18502/kss.v7i9.11014

Kässi, O., & Lehdonvirta, V. (2020). Digital labor and the pandemic: The case of platform work. *Socio-economic Review*, *18*(4), 1001–1025.

Katarki, S., & Bhat, A. (2015, March 11). India: Happily 'click' after – The real story of e-contracts. Mondaq. https://www.mondaq.com/india/contracts-and-commercial-law/380692/happily-click-after--the-real-story-of-e-contracts

Kenney, M., & Zysman, J. (2016). The rise of the platform economy. *Issues in Science and Technology*, *32*(3), 61–69.

Khan, S. A. R., Yu, Z., & Umar, M. (2020). Sustainable consumption in the circular economy: An empirical study of modular kitchens. *Journal of Cleaner Production*, *278*, 123298. DOI: 10.1016/j.jclepro.2020.123298

Khodakivskyi, M. (2021). The formation of Ukraine's legal policy at the present stage. *Yearly Journal of Scientific Articles. Pravova Derzhava*, *32*, 496–505. DOI: 10.33663/0869-2491-2021-32-496-505

Kimani, J. (2013). *Assessment of Effects of Monetary Policies on Lending Behaviour of Commercial Banks in Kenya*. Kenyatta University.

Kim, K. A., & Nofsinger, J. R. (2022). *Behavioral finance* (3rd ed.). Routledge.

Kogut, B., & Zander, U. (1992). Knowledge of the firm, combinative capabilities, and the replication of technology. *Organization Science*, *3*(3), 383–397. DOI: 10.1287/orsc.3.3.383

Konstantinidis, A., Katarachia, A., Borovas, G., & Voutsa, E. (n.d.). From efficient market hypothesis to behavioural finance: Can behavioural finance be the new dominant model for investing?

Koti, S., & Bixho, T. (2016). Theories of money supply: The relationship of money supply in a period of time T-1 and inflation in Period T- empirical evidence from Albania. *European Journal of Multidisciplinary Studies*, *1*(1), 294–302. DOI: 10.26417/ejms.v1i1.p294-302

Kotler, P. (1997). *Marketing Management*. Prentice Hall.

Kotler, P. (2016). *Marketing management* (15th ed.). Pearson Education.

Kotter, J. P. (1996). *Leading Change*. Harvard Business Review Press.

Kumar, R., & Dash, S. (2023). Regional disparities in modular kitchens: Affordability vs. innovation in emerging markets. *International Journal of Consumer Studies*, *47*(2), 210–225. DOI: 10.1111/ijcs.12845

Kumar, R., Singh, A., & Sharma, P. (2022). Hyper-personalization in consumer markets: The role of AI-driven customization. *Journal of Retailing*, *98*(1), 45–60. DOI: 10.1016/j.jretai.2021.09.001

Kumar, S., & Goyal, N. (2015). Behavioural biases in investment decision making: A systematic literature review. *Qualitative Research in Financial Markets*, *7*(1), 88–108. DOI: 10.1108/QRFM-07-2014-0022

LARKC Large Knowledge ColliderBojars, U.. (2010). LarKC: A Platform for Scalable Reasoning on the Web. *Semantic Web Journal*, *1*(2), 89–96.

Latour, B. (2005). *Reassembling the social: An introduction to actor-network-theory*. Oxford University Press. DOI: 10.1093/oso/9780199256044.001.0001

Lee, A. (2021). In the Shadow of Platforms. *M/C Journal*, *24*(2). DOI: 10.5204/mcj.2750

Lee, J. H. (2012). Marina Development on the Importance of Optimum Demand and Location Selection Study. *Journal of the Korean society of marine environment & safety*, 18(5), 406-415.

Leogrande, A. (2024). Integrating ESG Principles into Smart Logistics: Toward Sustainable Supply Chains.

Lett, J. W.Jr. (1983). Ludic and liminoid aspects of charter yacht tourism in the Caribbean. *Annals of Tourism Research*, *10*(1), 35–56. DOI: 10.1016/0160-7383(83)90114-7

Li, F., Shi, X., & Hu, H. (2011). Location selection of dry port based on AP clustering-the case of southwest China. *Journal of System and Management Sciences*, *1*(5).

Li, J., Zhang, Z., & Yu, Y. (2021). Artificial intelligence in behavioural finance: A bibliometric review and future research agenda. *Finance Research Letters*, *39*, 101645. DOI: 10.1016/j.frl.2020.101645

Li, K., Kim, D. J., Lang, K. R., Kauffman, R. J., & Naldi, M. (2020). How should we understand the digital economy in Asia? Critical assessment and research agenda. *Electronic Commerce Research and Applications*, *44*, 101004. DOI: 10.1016/j.elerap.2020.101004 PMID: 32922241

Linker, R. (2023). Yacht in Türkiye Market Overview. 2023-2027. https://www.reportlinker.com/market-report, Access date: 01.01.2024.

Liwawo, T. N., Ayalew, B. B., Kero, C. A., & Kant, S. (2025). Effect of Open Innovation on Competitive Advantage With Mediating Effect of Human Capital: Evidence From SMEs, Ethiopia. In *Open Innovation Strategies for Effective Competitive Advantage* (pp. 99–122). IGI Global Scientific Publishing. DOI: 10.4018/979-8-3693-9266-9.ch004

Loydu, T. (2023). Yatlar. https://www.linkedin.com/pulse/segmentlerine-g%C3%B6re-2023-yat-pazar%C4%B1-verileri-turk-loydu/?originalSubdomain=tr, Access date: 11.12.2023.

Malede, M. (2014). Determinants of Deposit money banks' Lending: Evidence from Ethiopian Deposit money banks. *European Journal of Business and Management, 6*(20), 109=117. *Management, 3*(2), 108–117.

Malik, K., Kant, S., Kaswan, K. S., Dhatterwal, J. S., & Panwar, A. (2025). Blockchain-Enabled Edge Computing for Cognitive IoT. In *Innovations in Blockchain-Powered Intelligence and Cognitive Internet of Things (CIoT)* (pp. 113–134). IGI Global Scientific Publishing.

Mandel, N., Goldenberg, J., & Lewis, M. (2017). The compensatory consumer behavior model: How consumers cope with self-discrepancies. *The Journal of Consumer Research, 44*(5), 1030–1046. DOI: 10.1093/jcr/ucx086

Mangla, S. K., Luthra, S., Jakhar, S. K., & Kumar, P. (2021). Circular economy practices in manufacturing: A systematic review. *Resources, Conservation and Recycling, 170*, 105569. DOI: 10.1016/j.resconrec.2021.105569

Margherio, C. (1998). *The Emerging Digital Economy*. U.S. Department of Commerce.

Memon, N. A., Shah, G. M., & Warsi, F. (2023). Resolving the major to customer loyalty in pakistan's e-logistics industry: A quantitative survey analysis. *Journal of Entrepreneurship and Corporate Venturing, 3*(1).

Mesenbourg, T. L. (2001). *Measuring the Digital Economy*. U.S. Bureau of the Census.

Meyer v. Uber Technologies, Inc., 834 F.3d 220 (2d Cir. 2016).

Michie, S., van Stralen, M. M., & West, R. (2011). The behaviour change wheel: A new method for characterising and designing behaviour change interventions. *Implementation Science : IS, 6*(1), 42. DOI: 10.1186/1748-5908-6-42 PMID: 21513547

Miller, G. A. (1995). WordNet: A Lexical Database for English. *Communications of the ACM, 38*(11), 39–41. DOI: 10.1145/219717.219748

Miller, S., & Noulas, A. (1997). Portfolio Mix and Large-Bank Profitability in the USA. *Applied Economics*, *29*(4), 505–512. DOI: 10.1080/000368497326994

Misker, B. (2015). Impact of credit risk on financial performance of banks in Ethiopia Thesis submitted to department of Accounting and Finance College of Business and Economics in partial fulfillment of the requirements for the award of M.sc degree in accounting and finance. Addis Ababa University Addis Ababa, Ethiopia.

Mohammad, S. D., Wasti, S. K. A., Lal, I., & Hussain, A. (2009). An empirical investigation between money supply, government expenditure, output & prices: The Pakistan evidence. *European Journal of Economics. Finance and Administrative Sciences*, *17*, 60–68.

Mohori Bibee v. Dharmodas Ghose, (1903) LR 30 IA 114.

Molina-Garcia, A., Dieguez-Soto, J., & Galache-Laza, M. T., & Campos Valenzuela, M. (2022). Financial literacy in SMEs: A bibliometric analysis and a systematic literature review of an emerging research field. *Review of Managerial Science*, •••, 1–40.

Montier, J. (2007). *Behavioural investing: A practitioner's guide to applying behavioural finance*. John Wiley & Sons. DOI: 10.1002/9781118673430

Moses, L. J., & Baldwin, D. A. (2005). What can the study of cognitive development reveal about children's ability to appreciate and cope with advertising? *Journal of Public Policy & Marketing*, *24*(2), 186–201. DOI: 10.1509/jppm.2005.24.2.186

Muhammad, M., & Husen, L. O. (2019). State Civil Apparatus in Indonesia in the Conception of Welfare State: A Study of Legal Material Law Number 5 Year 2014 on State Civil Apparatus. *Asian Social Science*, *15*(3), 64. DOI: 10.5539/ass.v15n3p64

Muhammad, N. M. N. (2009). Behavioral finance vs traditional finance: A review. *Journal of Behavioral Economics and Finance*, *2*, 1–7.

Mumford, E. (2006). The story of sociotechnical design: Reflections on its successes, failures and potential. *Information Systems Journal*, *16*(4), 317–342. DOI: 10.1111/j.1365-2575.2006.00221.x

Mumpuni, N. W. R., & Kusumawati, M. P. (2021). Good governance pengelolaan sampah: Komitmen negara terhadap lingkungan hidup. *Jurnal Cakrawala Hukum*, *12*(1), 79–89. DOI: 10.26905/idjch.v12i1.5725

Muradoglu, G., & Harvey, N. (2012). Behavioural finance: The role of psychological factors in financial decisions. *Review of Behavioral Finance*, *4*(2), 68–80. DOI: 10.1108/19405971211284862

Musen, M. A. (2015). The Protégé Project: A Look Back and a Look Forward. *AI Matters, 1*(4), 4–12. DOI: 10.1145/2757001.2757003 PMID: 27239556

Mutwol, P. & Kubasu, A. (2016).Effects of Selected Monetary Policies on Loans Portfolio Performance among Commercial Banks in Kenya. *European Journal of Business, Economics and Accountancy 4 (90).*

National Advisory Council for Online Safety. (2021). Report of a national survey of children, their parents and adults regarding online safety. NACOS, 19.

Niguse, T., Borji, B., Amentie, C., & Kant, S. (2025). Effect of Organization Readiness on Competitive Advantage With Mediating Effect of Human Capital: A Case of SMEs, Ethiopia. In *Organizational Readiness and Research: Security, Management, and Decision Making* (pp. 25-52). IGI Global Scientific Publishing.

Niguse, T., Kant, S., & Adula, M. (2025). Mediation Effect of Customer Loyalty in Relationship Between Market Orientation, Entrepreneurial Orientation, and Firm Performance in Ethiopia. In *Leveraging AI for Effective Digital Relationship Marketing* (pp. 419–458). IGI Global.

North, D. C. (1990). *Institutions, Institutional Change and Economic Performance.* Cambridge University Press. DOI: 10.1017/CBO9780511808678

Noy, N. F., ... (2009). "BioPortal: Ontologies and Integrated Data Resources at the Click of a Mouse." *Nucleic Acids Research*, 37(Web Server issue), W170-W173. Ontotext. "GraphDB – Semantic Graph Database." https://www.ontotext.com/products/graphdb/

Nugroho, S. S., & Rahardjo, M. (2023). Penerapan Fungsi Pengawasan Dprd Dalam Mewujudkan Pemerintahan Daerah Yang Baik. *Yustisia Merdeka: Jurnal Ilmiah Hukum, 9*(1), 59–67. DOI: 10.33319/yume.v9i1.218

Nwosa, P., & Oseni, I. (2013). The Impact of Banks Loan to SMEs on Manufacturing Output in Nigeria. *Journal of Social and Development Sciences, 4*(5), 212–217. DOI: 10.22610/jsds.v4i5.754

Nyanzu, F., & Quaidoo, M. (2017). Access to finance constraint and SMEs functioning in Ghana. Mississippi State University, US. University of Cape Coast, Ghana. *MPRA Paper No. 83202*, 1-23.

Nzioka, C. N. (2012), *The Effect of Cash Management and Firm Liquidity or Share Prices of Companies Listed at the Nairobe Security Exchange.* Being a research project report submitted in partial fulfilment of the requirements for award of degree of Master of business Administration school of business, University of Nairobi.

Obasan, K. A., & Arikewuyo, K. (2012). The effect of pre- post bank consolidation on the acc essibility of finance to SMEs in Nigeria. *Business and Management Research, 1*(3), 108–120. DOI: 10.5430/bmr.v1n3p108

Odedokun, M. (1997). An Empirical Analysis on the Determinants of the Real Exchange Rate in Afrcan Countries. *The Journal of International Trade & Economic Development, 6*(1), 63–82. DOI: 10.1080/09638199700000005

Odumesi, A. O. (2018). Deposit money banks' credit accessibility and small and medium enterprises' growth in Nigeria (1980-2015). Thesis submitted to the Department of Business Administration, School of Management Sciences in partial fulfilment of the requirements for the award of the degree of Doctor of Philosophy, Babcock University, Ilishan- Remo, Ogun State, Nigeria.

OECD. (2017).Enhancing the Contribution of SMEs in a global and digitalised economy.https://www.oecd.org/mcm/documents/C-MIN-2017-8ENPdf. Retrieved on December 29, 2017.

OIT/Cinterfor. (2020). *Digitalización en las organizaciones*. Recuperado de https://www.oitcinterfor.org/digitalizacion/digitalizacion-organizaciones

Oladipo, S. O., & Akinbobola, J. O. (2011). Budget Deficit and Inflation in Nigeria: A Causal Relationship. [JETEMS]. *Journal of Emerging Trends in Economics and Management Science, 2*(1), 1–8.

Olubiyi T. O. (2023). Leveraging competitive strategies on business outcomes post-covid-19 pandemic: Empirical investigation from Africa. *Journal of Management and Business: Research and Practice*, DOI: 10.54933/jmbrp-2023-15-2-1

Olubiyi, T. O. (2024a). Measuring organizational factors and their impact on the development of small and medium-sized pharmaceutical companies after the pandemic – an empirical study *Journal of Marketing and Market Studies 25*-38 DOI: 10.33226/1231-7853.2024.7.3

Olubiyi, T. O., Omoyele, O. S., Ilodigwe, S. C., Adeoye, O. O., Makinde, G. O., & Ravinder, R. (2024). The Linkage between Knowledge Management Practices and Sustainable Business Growth: Empirical Evidence from Nigeria. *Revista De Gestão Social E Ambiental, 18*(5), e05432. DOI: 10.24857/rgsa.v18n5-022

Olubiyi, O. T., Lawal, A. T., & Adeoye, O. O. (2022). Succession planning and family business continuity: Perspectives from Lagos State, Nigeria. *Organization and Human Capital Development, 1*(1), 40–52. DOI: 10.31098/orcadev.v1i1.865

Olubiyi, T. O. (2022a). Measuring technological capability and business performance post-COVID Era: Evidence from Small and Medium-Sized Enterprises (SMEs) in Nigeria. *Management & Marketing Journal*, *xx*(2), 234–248. DOI: 10.52846/MNMK.20.2.09

Olubiyi, T. O. (2022b). An investigation of sustainable innovative strategy and customer satisfaction in small and medium-sized enterprises (SMEs) in Nigeria. *Covenant Journal of Business and Social Sciences*, *13*(2), 1–24.

Olubiyi, T. O. (2024). Achieving Sustainable Development Goal Four (4) in Africa: Spotlighting the role of quality education and innovation orientation. *Economics. Management and Sustainability*, *9*(1), 105–118. DOI: 10.14254/jems.2024.9-1.8

Olubiyi, T. O. (2024b). Improving Customer Experience Through Differentiation Capability: The Rise of Competition among Africa's Consumer Goods Companies. *PaperASIA*, *40*(5b), 230–240. DOI: 10.59953/paperasia.v40i5b.233

Olukoyo, F. O. (2011). Detainments of deposit money banks' lending behaviour in Nigeria. *International Journal of Financial Research*, *2*(2), 61–72.

Oluseye, M. (2013). Growth effect of Small and Medium Enterprises (SMEs) Financing in Nigeria Corpus ID: 18613704, Business, Economics

Olutoye, E. A. (2015). Effect of Bank size on SME.Financing: Evidence from Nigeria Banking Sectors. *International Journal & Banking Finance Management & Development Studies*, *3*(1), 3–14.

Omoke P. C., & Oruta L.I. (2010). Budget Deficit, Money Supply and Inflation in Nigeria

Online contracting and e-commerce under Hong Kong law. (2020).

Onwioduokit, E. A. (1999). Fiscal deficits and inflation dynamics in Nigeria: An empirical investigation of causal relationship. *Central Bank Nigeria Economic and Financial Review.*, *37*(2), 1–16.

OpenLink Software. "Virtuoso Universal Server." https://virtuoso.openlinksw.com/

Oprean, C., & Tanasescu, C. (2014). Effects of behavioural finance on emerging capital markets. *Procedia Economics and Finance*, *15*, 1710–1716. DOI: 10.1016/S2212-5671(14)00645-5

Osano, H. M., & Languitone, H. (2016). Factors influencing access to financie by SMEs in Mozambique: Case of SMEs in Maputo central business district. *Journal of Innovation and Entrepreneurship*, *5*(13), 1–16.

Parker, G. G., Van Alstyne, M. W., & Choudary, S. P. (2016). *Platform revolution: How networked markets are transforming the economy and how to make them work for you*. W.W. Norton & Company.

Park, S. H., & Joo, K. S. (2011). The study On An Yacht Moorings Establishment Location Analysis Using Optimum Spiral Method. *Journal of the Korean Society of Marine Environment & Safety*, *17*(4), 323–329. DOI: 10.7837/kosomes.2011.17.4.323

Parra, A. (2024). Coping with COPPA: Exploring alternatives to the Children's Online Privacy Protection Act. *Indiana Journal of Law and Social Equality*, *12*(2), 193–208.

Pérez, A., & Guzmán, M. (2015). Los estudios organizacionales como programa de investigación. *Revista Latinoamericana de Estudios Organizacionales*, 2(1), 1-20. https://www.scielo.cl/scielo.php?pid=S0717-554X2015000200001&script=sci_arttext

Pew Internet. (2012). Trend data (teens): Online activities total. https://pewinternet.org/Static-Pages/Trend-Data-%28Teens%29/Online-Activites-Total.aspx

Phillips, D. E. (2009). *The software license unveiled: How legislation by license controls software access*. Oxford University Press. DOI: 10.1093/oso/9780195341874.001.0001

PowerData. (2023). *Transformación digital: Qué es y su importancia*. Recuperado de https://www.powerdata.es/transformacion-digital

Priyo Sembodo, G., Nefi, A., & Fakhriah, E. L. (2022). Urgensi Penerapan Prinsip Business Judgment Rule Dalam Peraturan Pemerintah Nomor 63 Tahun 2019 Tentang Investasi Pemerintah. *Jurnal Poros Hukum Padjadjaran*, *3*(2), 185–208. DOI: 10.23920/jphp.v3i2.789

ProCD, Inc. v. Zeidenberg, 86 F.3d 1447 (7th Cir. 1996).

Punita, R., & Somaiya, K. J. (2006). Monetary Policy: Its Impact on the Profitability of Banks in India. *Intermediate Business and Economics Research Journal*, *9*(3), 15–19.

Putnam, R. D. (2000). *Bowling Alone: The Collapse and Revival of American Community*. Simon & Schuster.

Qasim, S., & Ramiz, R. (2011). Impacts of liquidity ratios on profitability. *Interdisciplinary Journal of Research in Business*, *1*(7), 95–98.

Raissi, N., & Missaoui, S. (2015). Role of investor sentiment in financial markets: An explanation by behavioural finance approach. *International Journal of Accounting and Finance, 5*(4), 362–401. DOI: 10.1504/IJAF.2015.076182

Rana, V., Gandhi, A., & Sharma, I. (2024). Safeguarding children's data under DPDP.

Rao, S. S. (2021). Police: A Public Safety Institution of Governance. *International Journal for Research in Applied Science and Engineering Technology, 9*(10), 1351–1353. DOI: 10.22214/ijraset.2021.38593

Redhead, K. (2008). *Personal finance and investments: A behavioural finance perspective*. Routledge., DOI: 10.4324/9780203895634

Redondo Maíllo, J. L., & Álvaro Alonso, I. M. (2024). Protection of minors and online age verification: The case of France.

Register.com, Inc. v. Verio, Inc., 356 F.3d 393 (2d Cir. 2004).

Rochet, J. C., & Tirole, J. (2003). Platform competition in two-sided markets. *Journal of the European Economic Association, 1*(4), 990–1029. DOI: 10.1162/154247603322493212

Rogers, E. M. (1962). *Diffusion of innovations*. Free Press.

Russo, O., R. (. (2023). Environmental Rights are a Human Right to a Healthy Environment: A Brief Review. *International Journal of Life Science and Agriculture Research, 03*(12). Advance online publication. DOI: 10.55677/ijlsar/V02I12Y2023-01

Sakti Koeswanto, E., Riswandi, R., & Redi, A. (2023). Implications of Public Trust Due to Weak Law Enforcement Morality. *Edunity : Kajian Ilmu Sosial Dan Pendidikan, 2*(1), 78–86. DOI: 10.57096/edunity.v1i05.39

Samad, A. (2015). Determinants Bank Profitability: Empirical Evidence from Bangladesh Commercial Banks. *International Journal of Financial Research, 6*(3), 173–179. DOI: 10.5430/ijfr.v6n3p173

Sankar, J. G., & Kant, S. (2025). Assessing Consumer Trust and Perception in Online Food Marketplaces. In *Innovative Trends Shaping Food Marketing and Consumption* (pp. 375–394). IGI Global Scientific Publishing. DOI: 10.4018/979-8-3693-8542-5.ch015

SAP. (2023). *¿Qué es la Transformación Digital? | Importancia y Beneficios*. Recuperado de https://www.sap.com/latinamerica/insights/what-is-digital-transformation .html

Saputra, E. F., & Firmansyah, H. (2023). *Politik Hukum dalam Upaya Pemberantasan Tindak Pidana Korupsi melalui Pembaharuan Pengaturan Tindak Pidana Korupsi sebagai Extraordinary Crime dalam KUHP Nasional. 6*(2), 4493–4504.

Saracoglu, B. O., Insel, M., & Helvacioglu, I. H. (2009). Identification of location selection criteria for new building shipyards. *Marine Technology and SNAME News, 46*(01), 34–44. DOI: 10.5957/mtsn.2009.46.1.34

Sargent, M. A. (2013). Misplaced misrepresentations: Why misrepresentation-of-age statutes must be reinterpreted as they apply to children's online contracts. *Michigan Law Review, 112*(2), 312–338. https://www.jstor.org/stable/23816936

Sariisik, M., Turkay, O., & Akova, O. (2011). How to manage yacht tourism in Türkiye: A swot analysis and related strategies. *Procedia: Social and Behavioral Sciences, 24*, 1014–1025. DOI: 10.1016/j.sbspro.2011.09.041

Scott v. Apple Inc., 1:23-cv-00475 (D.D.C.).

Sengul, Ü., Eren, M., & Shıraz, S. E. (2012). Bulanik ahp île belediyelerîn toplu taşima araç seçîmî. *Erciyes Üniversitesi İktisadi ve İdari Bilimler Fakültesi Dergisi*, [Municipalities' public transport vehicle selection with fuzzy AHP. Erciyes University Faculty of Economics and Administrative Sciences Journal*], 40*, 143–165.

Serohin, V. (2022). European governance as an institute of constitutional law of the European Union. The Journal of VN Karazin Kharkiv National University. *Series Law*, (33), 28–43.

Sethi, A., & Nagrecha, M. (2013). The impact of user imagery on consumer behavior: A study of television purchases among MBA students. *International Journal of Marketing Studies, 5*(4), 1–10. DOI: 10.5539/ijms.v5n4p1

Sevinç, F., & Güzel, T. (2017). Sustainable yacht tourism practices. *Management & Marketing Journal*, 15(1).

Sgouros v. TransUnion Corp., No. 15-1371 (7th Cir. 2016).

Shaheen, Y., Zhiqiang, X., & Zhiqiang, X. (2019). Public Administration in Afghanistan: Challenges and Way Forward. *Open Journal of Social Sciences, 07*(06), 142–160. DOI: 10.4236/jss.2019.76012

Shahid, M., Aftab, F., Latif, K., & Mahmood, Z. (2018). Behavioral finance, investors' psychology and investment decision making in capital markets: An evidence through ethnography and semi-structured interviews. *Journal of Economic Psychology, 2*, 14–37.

Sharma, N. K., Govindan, K., Lai, K. K., Chen, W. K., & Kumar, V. (2021). The transition from linear economy to circular economy for sustainability among SMEs: A study on prospects, impediments, and Business Strategy prerequisites. and Environment, 30(4), 1803-1822.

Shiller, R. J. (2019). *Narrative economics: How stories go viral and drive major economic events*. Princeton University Press.

shopping-on-society-information-technology-essay.php?vref=1

Shrinika, R. (2023). Legality of clickwrap agreements. *Indian Journal of Law & Legal Research*, *5*(1), 1–12.

Sieglin, V. (2014). Economía de conocimiento y culturas organizacionales en la academia. *Ciencia UANL*, 17(69), 45-60. https://cienciauanl.uanl.mx/?p=2590

Siljanovska, Z., & Shalevska, E. (2019). OECD Principles For Good Corporate Governance And Their Impact On The Process Of Standardization. *Knowledge International Journal*, *34*(5), 1491–1497. DOI: 10.35120/kij34051491S

Singhal, A. (2012). *Introducing the Knowledge Graph: Things, Not Strings*. Google Official Blog.

Singh, S., & Yadav, S. S. (2021). Behavioural finance. In Singh, S., & Yadav, S. S. (Eds.), *Security Analysis and Portfolio Management: A Primer* (pp. 51–77). Springer., DOI: 10.1007/978-981-16-2520-6_2

Slade, V. (2011). The infancy defense in the modern contract age: A useful vestige. *Seattle University Law Review*, *34*, 613–640.

Soludo, C. (2004) *Consolidation of the Nigeria Banking to meet the Developmental Challenges of 21st century.*

Song, S., Shi, X., Song, G., & Huq, F. A. (2021). Associationing digitalization and capital in human form to shape supply chain combination in omni-channel retailing. *Industrial Management & Data Systems*, *121*(11), 2298–2317. DOI: 10.1108/IMDS-09-2020-0526

Specht v. Netscape Communications Corp., 306 F.3d 17 (2d Cir. 2002).

Srnicek, N. (2016). *Platform Capitalism*. Polity Press.

Srnicek, N. (2017). *Platform capitalism*. Polity Press.

Statista. (2021). *Smart kitchen adoption in Germany*. Statista Market Insights.

Statista. (2022). *IoT adoption barriers for SMEs*. Statista Industry Reports.

Statman, M. (2019). *Behavioral finance: The second generation.* CFA Institute Research Foundation.

Suchanek, F., Kasneci, G., & Weikum, G. (2007). "YAGO. A Core of Semantic Knowledge." *Proceedings of WWW 2007.*

Suleimenova, G., Sadvokassova, A., Rakinsheva, B., & Nurmaganbetov, A. (2018). SMES development and corruption: Case of Kazakhstan. *Business: Theory and Practice, 19*(1), 1–8. DOI: 10.3846/btp.2018.01

Sundararajan, A. (2016). *The sharing economy: The end of employment and the rise of crowd-based capitalism.* MIT Press., DOI: 10.7551/mitpress/10425.001.0001

Sunday, K. U. (2012). *The impact of interest rates on savings and investment in Nigeria. Unpublished research project submitted in partial fulfillment of the requirements for the award of the Masters in Business Administration (MBA) degree in Banking and Finance Department, University of Nigeria.* Campus.

Susanti, A. (2022). Implementation Of The Principles Of Good Governance In Improving Public Services At The Investment Office And One-Stop Integrated Services Of Central Sulawesi Province. *Indonesian Journal of Multidisciplinary Science, 1*(12), 1598–1611. DOI: 10.55324/ijoms.v1i12.243

Sweeney, J. C., & Soutar, G. N. (2001). Consumer perceived value: The development of a multiple item scale. *Journal of Retailing, 77*(2), 203–220. DOI: 10.1016/S0022-4359(01)00041-0

Szadok-Bratuń, A. (2021). Fullerowski paradygmat (nie)dobrego prawa i jego aktualność „hic et nunc. *Studia Nad Autorytaryzmem i Totalitaryzmem, 43*(2), 295–316. DOI: 10.19195/2300-7249.43.2.19

T.C. Kültür ve Turizm Bakanlığı (TCKTB). (2024). Turizm İstatistik Raporları. https://www.ktb.gov.tr/genel/searchhotelgenel.aspx?lang=tr, Access date: 22.11.2023.

T.C. Kültür ve Turizm Bakanlığı. (2023). Deniz Turizmi Tesisleri ve Araçları İstatistikleri. https://yigm.ktb.gov.tr/TR-201146/deniz-turizmi-tesisleri-ve-araclari-istatistikleri.html, Access date: 12.02.2024.

Taiwo, J. N., & Faloun, T. O. (2016). SMEs Financing and its effects on Nigeria Economic growth. *European Journal of Business. Economic and Accountancy, 4*(4), 1–18.

Taiwo, O., & Adesola, O. A. (2013). Exchange Rate Volatility and Bank Performance in Nigeria. *Asian Economic and Financial Review, 3*, 178–185.

Tapscott, D. (1996). *The Digital Economy: Promise and Peril in the Age of Networked Intelligence*. McGraw-Hill.

Tapscott, D. (2016). *Blockchain Revolution: How the Technology Behind Bitcoin is Changing Money, Business, and the World*. Penguin.

Tashakkori, A., & Teddlie, C. (2010). *SAGE handbook of mixed methods in social & behavioral research* (2nd ed.). SAGE Publications., DOI: 10.4135/9781506335193

Tetyana, L. (2015). Prospects of Yacht Tourism Development in the Black Sea Region of Ukraine. Ovidius University Annals, *Series Economic Sciences*, 15(1).

Thaler, R. H. (2015). *Misbehaving: The making of behavioral economics*. W. W. Norton & Company.

The Hindu. (2023, May 4). Over 50% Indians are active internet users now; base to reach 900 million by 2025: Report. https://www.thehindu.com/news/national/over-50-indians-are-active-internet-users-now-base-to-reach-900-million-by-2025-report/article66809522.ece

Tima, T. A., Schneider, P., Chanda, S. K., Mozumder, M. M. H., Hossain, M. M., Begum, A., & Shamsuzzaman, M. (2021). Analyses Implementation Realities of Legal Frameworks for Sustainable Management of Tanguar Haor Fisheries Resources in Bangladesh. *Sustainability (Basel)*, *13*(16), 8784. DOI: 10.3390/su13168784

Times of India. (2023, September 23). 60% children spend 3 hours a day on social media: Study. https://timesofindia.indiatimes.com/articleshow/103878956.cms

Toha, M., & Supriyanto, S. (2023). Price sensitivity and consumer behavior in the luxury kitchen market. *JMR, Journal of Marketing Research*, *60*(4), 89–102.

TopQuadrant. “TopBraid Enterprise Data Governance Solutions.”

Tripathi, A. K., Agrawal, S., & Gupta, R. D. (2021). Comparison of GIS-based AHP and fuzzy AHP methods for hospital site selection: A case study for Prayagraj City, India. *GeoJournal*, 1–22. PMID: 34075269

Triwahyuni, A. D. (2020). Kewajiban Dan Tanggung Jawab Notaris Sebagai Pejabat Umum. *Acta Comitas*, *5*(1), 1. DOI: 10.24843/AC.2020.v05.i01.p01

Trofimova, L. (2020). Problematic points of the quality of qualification assessment of judges. *Law Review of Kyiv University of Law*, *2*(2), 198–207. DOI: 10.36695/2219-5521.2.2020.35

Tuğba Turğut, B., Taş, G., Herekoğlu, A., Tozan, H., & Vayvay, O. (2011). A fuzzy AHP based decision support system for disaster center location selection and a case study for Istanbul. *Disaster Prevention and Management, 20*(5), 499–520. DOI: 10.1108/09653561111178943

Türk, A., & Özkök, M. (2020). Shipyard location selection based on fuzzy AHP and TOPSIS. *Journal of Intelligent & Fuzzy Systems, 39*(3), 4557–4576. DOI: 10.3233/JIFS-200522

Tursin, S. R., & Ahmad, R. (2000). *Konsep Supremasi Hukum, Masyarakat Madani Dan Kaitan Keduanya*. 66–72.

UASB. (2020). Un acercamiento teórico a la economía digital. Recuperado de https://revistas.uasb.edu.ec/index.php/eg/article/download/4116/3999/16300

UKEssays. (2018). The Impact of Online Shopping on Society Information Technology Essay. November 2018. https://www.ukessays.com/essays/information-technology/the-impact-of-online-

Umukoro, J. E., & Egwakhe, J. A. (2019). Flexible Wellbeing and Smart-Head. *International Journal of Research Science and Management, 6*(12), 103–118.

Unal, A. U., Arslan, O., & Arıcan, O. H. (2022). Türkiye'de Ro-Ro taşımacılığının önemi ve geleceği hakkında örnek bir çalışma. *Denizcilik Araştırmaları Dergisi: Amfora, 1*(1), 60–79.

Vahidnia, M. H., Alesheikh, A. A., & Alimohammadi, A. (2009). Hospital site selection using fuzzy AHP and its derivatives. *Journal of Environmental Management, 90*(10), 3048–3056. DOI: 10.1016/j.jenvman.2009.04.010 PMID: 19477577

Valerio, A., Parton, B., & Robb, A. (2014). Entrepreneurship Education and Training Programs around the World: Dimensions for Success. In *Entrepreneurship Education and Training Programs around the World: Dimensions for Success*. books.google.com. DOI: 10.1596/978-1-4648-0202-7

Vallejo, R. (2021). *The Private Administrative Law of Technical Standardization., 40*(1), 172–229.

Vargo, S. L., & Lusch, R. F. (2004). Evolving to a new dominant logic for marketing. *Journal of Marketing, 68*(1), 1–17. DOI: 10.1509/jmkg.68.1.1.24036

Vasiulis Ferreira Rodrigues, N., De Camargo Fiorini, P., Piato, É. L., Lopes de Sousa Jabbour, A. B., & Chiappetta Jabbour, C. J. (2024). Resources and proficiencies for logistics 4.0 and sustainable value creation: A investigation of logistics service providers in an emerging market. *International Journal of Logistics Management*. Advance online publication. DOI: 10.1108/IJLM-11-2023-0471

Venkatapathy, D. R., & Sultana, A. H. (2016). Behavioural finance: Heuristics in investment decisions. *International Journal of Management Research*, *1*, 1–10.

Verma, A., & Agarwal, R. (2024). Emotional branding and its impact on consumer loyalty. *Journal of Brand Management*, *31*(1), 67–79.

Virigineni, M., & Rao, M. B. (2017). Contemporary developments in behavioural finance. *International Journal of Economics and Financial Issues*, *7*(1), 1.

W3C. "RDF Schema 1.1." https://www.w3.org/TR/rdf-schema/

W3C. "Resource Description Framework (RDF)." https://www.w3.org/RDF/

W3C. "SKOS Simple Knowledge Organization System Reference."

Wang, X., & Qi, M. (2024). A Study of the Impact of Digital Transformation on the Risk Level of Commercial Banks. Proceedings of the 2024 3rd International Conference on Artificial Intelligence, Internet and Digital Economy (ICAID 2024)., DOI: 10.2991/978-94-6463-490-7_29

Wang, H. C., & Lirn, T. C. (2024). Enhancement of Marina Service Quality of Yacht Tourism in Taiwan: A Euclidean Distance of Importance-Performance Analysis. *SAGE Open*, *14*(4), 21582440241281634. DOI: 10.1177/21582440241281634

Wang, Y. (2016). What is the biggest obstacles to growth of SMEs in developing countries? Empirical evidence from an enterprise survey. *Borsa Istanbul Review*, *16*(3), 167–176. DOI: 10.1016/j.bir.2016.06.001

Wang, Y. M., Luo, Y., & Hua, Z. (2008). On the extent analysis method for fuzzy AHP and its applications. *European Journal of Operational Research*, *186*(2), 735–747. DOI: 10.1016/j.ejor.2007.01.050

Watson Knowledge Studio, I. B. M. IBM. "Watson Knowledge Studio." https://www.ibm.com/cloud/watson-knowledge-studio

Williamson, O. E. (1981). The economics of organization: The transaction cost approach. *American Journal of Sociology*, *87*(3), 548–577. DOI: 10.1086/227496

Witkowska, M., & Kucheryavaya, E. (2021). The concept of good governance in the eu legislation: analysis in the context of methodology of the civil law research. *Methodological problems of the civil law researches*, *3*(3), 139–162. DOI: 10.33397/2619-0559-2021-3-3-139-162

World Bank Annual Report (2012). https://www.worldbank.org/en/about/annual-report

World Bank Annual Report (2015). https://www.worldbank.org/en/about/annual-report

World, Y. (2023). Luxury Yachts, Superyachts, Advice & Trends. https://www.yachtworld.com/research/, Access date: 25.12.2023.

WTTC. (2023). Destination 2030 WTTC & JLL assess global cities' tourism readiness. https://research.wttc.org/destination-2030-jll-wttc-report?_gl=1*16mvw3q*_ga*MjExOTI0ODE2NS4xNzA3NzY0MTI1*_ga_JM5GLX6V1W*MTcwNzc2NDEyNC4xLjEuMTcwNzc2NDQxMy4wLjAuMA, Access date: 12.02.2024.

Wu, T. (2017). *The attention merchants: The epic scramble to get inside our heads*. Vintage.

Xie, D., Wei, W., & Li, Y. A General Theory of Digital Economy: The World after Turing (July 1, 2023).http://dx.doi.org/DOI: 10.2139/ssrn.4531884

Yang, C. M., Lai, C. C., Wu, L. J., & Li, J. J. (2014). Assessing fishing port locations for adaption into yacht marinas in Taiwan. *Journal of Marine Science and Technology*, *22*(5), 10.

Yang, J. C., & Hwang, K. S. (2015). Study of the Location Factors of Yacht Marina and an Analysis of the Significance. *Journal of the Korea Academia-Industrial Cooperation Society*, *16*(1), 235–245. DOI: 10.5762/KAIS.2015.16.1.235

Yao, Y. H., & Luan, W. X. (2019). Factors influencing yacht tourism consumption behavior based on the TAM-IDT model.

Yin, R. K. (2017). *Case study research: Design and methods* (6th ed.). SAGE Publications.

Yoo, Y., Boland, R. J.Jr, Lyytinen, K., & Majchrzak, A. (2012). Organizing for innovation in the digitized world. *Organization Science*, *23*(5), 1398–1408. DOI: 10.1287/orsc.1120.0771

Yu, Y., & Sung, T.-J. (2023). Consumer preferences for smart kitchen appliances: A value-based approach. *International Journal of Consumer Studies*, *47*(2), 123–135.

Zammuto, R. F., Griffith, T. L., Majchrzak, A., Dougherty, D. J., & Faraj, S. (2007). Information technology and the changing fabric of organization. *Organization Science, 18*(5), 749–762. DOI: 10.1287/orsc.1070.0307

Zarafat, M. V. (2014). An Analysis of Macroeconomic Determinants of Commercial Banks Profitability in Malaysia for the period 1995-2011. *Asian Economic and Financial Review*, •••, 41–57.

Zdyb, M. (2019). Prawo do dobrej administracji. Aksjologiczne aspekty dobrej administracji. *Studia Iuridica Lublinensia, 28*(2), 107. DOI: 10.17951/sil.2019.28.2.107-133

Zhang, Chao. (2021). An empirical study on the impact of digital economy development on the upgrading and optimization of industrial structure. E3S Web of Conferences. 275. 01046. . DOI: 10.1051/e3sconf/202127501046

Zhang, Y., & Chen, J. (2018). Big data analytics in behavioural finance: A systematic review. *Technological Forecasting and Social Change, 136*, 78–90. DOI: 10.1016/j.techfore.2018.06.016

Zuboff, S. (2019). *The age of surveillance capitalism: The fight for a human future at the new frontier of power*. PublicAffairs.

About the Contributors

Ford Lumban Gaol is currently Associate Professor Informatics Engineering and Information System, Bina Nusantara University. He is the Head Department of Doctor of Computer Science Bina Nusantara University and Research Interest Group Leader "Advance System in Computational Intelligence & Knowledge Engineering (IntelSys). Dr Ford Lumban Gaol is the President of IEEE Indonesia Section Computer Society and also the IAIAI South East Asia Region Director. Dr Ford was the Vice Chair of IEEE Indonesia section and former Chair of the ACM Indonesia.

|**Allayarov Piratdin** is an associate professor of Mathematical methods in Economics Department at Tashkent State University of Economics in Uzbekistan. He graduated a Bachelor's degree in Finance from Karakalpak State University and a Master's degree in Accounting from the Karakalpak State University. He obtained Ph.D. in Economics at Hunan University in China. He participated as a local consultant in projects of international organizations such as the World Bank, UN Development Program. His primary research is in international trade and economics. He published more than 20 papers in local and international journals.

Elena Maslyukova is an associate professor of Economics and the acting head of the Economic Cybernetics Department at Southern Federal University (Russia). She received her Ph.D. from Southern Federal University (Russia). Her current research projects focus on Mathematical and Quantitative Methods, Econometric and Statistical Methods and Methodology, Data Collection and Data Estimation Methodology. Prof. Maslyukova acts as a reviewer for many scientific journals and presents her work at international conferences and other venues.

***

Usharani Bhimavarapu is working as an Assistant Professor in the Computer Science and Engineering Department at Koneru Lakshmaiah Education Foundation at Vaddeswaram, Andhra Pradesh, India. She has been teaching from last 14 years with emphasis on Data Mining, Machine Learning, and Data Structure. She communicated more than 40 research papers in SCI, SCIE, Scopus indexed Journals. She has authored 12 books in programming languages like CPP, Java, Python, HTML,CSS and so on. Dr. Jude D. Hemanth received his B.E degree in ECE from Bharathiar University in 2002, M.E degree in communication systems from Anna University in 2006 and Ph.D. from Karunya University in 2013. His research areas include Computational Intelligence and Image processing. He has authored more than 230 research papers in reputed SCIE indexed International Journals and Scopus indexed International Conferences. His Cumulative Impact Factor is more than 350. He has published 37 edited books with reputed publishers such as Elsevier, Springer and IET.

Fatmawati A. Mappasere completed his education as a bachelor of Anthropology at the Faculty of Social and Political Sciences, Hasanuddin University in 1990. He completed his Master's degree in 1996 in Environmental Planning and Administration at Hasanuddin University. Doctoral Education was completed at Negero University Makassar in 2014 in the scientific field of Public Administration. He has served as a lecturer since 1992 at the University of Muhammadiyah Makassar. In 2009 he had the opportunity to participate in the Sandwich Program from DIKTI to the University of Southern Queensland, Australia. As a lecturer, in addition to performing duties as a teacher, the author is active in conducting research and community service. Some research and service are funded by internal grants from universities and those funded by the Ministry of Research, Technology and Higher Education. In 2015, in partnership with the Makassar City Government and JICA (Japan International Cooperation Agency), Junior Expert assisted 25 elementary schools as a pilot project “School Waste Bank” in Makassar City. The result of this activity gave birth to a book entitled “School Waste Bank Movement”. Some of the research results that have also been contained in the form of books, including entitled: Partnership Model in Public; Partnership-Based Community Empowerment in Waste Management.

PKowo Solomon is a Professor of Business Administration at Global Humanistic University Curacao; Facilitator and Examiner at National Open University of Nigeria (NOUN); Academic Leader at Accredited Agency Curacao (AAC); Visiting Professor at UCM University Trnava Slovak Republic; Research Scholar and Associate at America Research Center in Sofia Bulgaria. His research interest are

Human Resources, Entrepreneurship, Strategic Mgt, International Business, SMEs, and Organizational Behavior.

Ahmad Harakan is an Associate Professor at the Department of Government Studies, Faculty of Social and Political Sciences, Universitas Muhammadiyah Makassar, Indonesia. His research interests are on Paradiplomacy, Security and Defense Issues, Political Economy, Southeast Asia Issues and published in many international journal and Book Chapter. He is currently the Head of Department of Government Studies, Faculty of Social and Political Sciences, Universitas Muhammadiyah Makassar, Indonesia. He is also the Editor-in-Chief of Journal of Contemporary Governance and Public Policy, and the Guest Editor of International Journal of Sustainable Society.

Andi Luhur Prianto currently Associate Professor at the Department of Government Studies, Universitas Muhammadiyah Makassar, Indonesia. Also served as Research Fellow at Universitat Bremen, Germany. Andi does research in politics, governance, public policy, urban environmental politics, and sustainable development.

Ihyani Malik was born in Ujung Pandang on May 15, 1971 and now resides in Makassar City, South Sulawesi. The author completed his S1 education in the Department of State Administration at the University of Muhammadiyah Makassar in 1994. The author then continued his S2 education at Hasanuddin University and successfully completed his studies in 2004. The author's last education was in 2014 by completing a doctoral program in Public Administration at Makassar State University. The author has expertise in the field of Public Administration and is one of the lecturers in the State Administration Study Program. The writer also temporarily serves as the Dean of the Faculty of Social and Political Sciences at the University of Muhammadiyah Makassar. To realize a career as a professional lecturer, the author is also active as a researcher in his field of expertise. Some of the research that has been carried out is funded by internal universities and also the Ministry of Research, Technology and Higher Education. In addition to research, the author is also active in writing journals and books in the hope of making a positive contribution to this much-loved nation and country. The author is also active in off-campus activities and serves in various capacities as the Chairman of the Aisyiyah Community Unismuh Makassar for the 2021-2026 period and the Board of the Dean's Forum of the Faculty of Social and Political Sciences of Muhammadiyah Aisyiyah Higher Education.

Achmad Nurmandi is a Professor at the Department of Government Affairs and Administration, Jusuf Kalla School of Government, Universitas Muhammadiyah

Yogyakarta, Indonesia. His research interests are on e-government, urban governance and strategic management in the public sector and published in many international journal and Book Chapter, such as International Journal of Public Sector Management, Transforming Government: People, Policy and Process, Jamba Journal of Disaster Studies, Asian Review of Political Science, Journal of Human Behavior in the Social Environment, Public Policy and Administration, Global Encyclopedia of Public Administration, Public Policy, and Governance, Springer. He is currently the Secretary of the Asia Pacific Society for Public Affairs (APSPA). He is also the Editor-in-Chief of Jurnal Studi Pemerintahan (Journal of Government and Politics) and a Guest Editor of International Journal of Public Sector Performance Management and International Journal of Sustainable Society.

Abolaji Odumesi is a seasoned banker with over twenty years of experience in the finance industry. He retired as Regional Operations Coordinator of Wema Bank Plc, Abeokuta Region, one of Nigeria's leading financial institutions. After retiring from Wema Bank, he worked as Chief Operating Officer (COO) of Ababmop Ventures Limited for over five years before floating Gabis Investment Company Limited (G.I.C.L); a company that is into financial intermediary which commenced operations in 2022. He is the Founding Managing Director/Chief Executive Officer of the company as he brings his wealth of experience and expertise to the role. ChIldhood and FamilyAbolaji was born in Bariga, Lagos State, Nigeria on 8th February, 1964 to late Mr and Mrs. Afolabi Odumesi from Ikenne Remo in Ikenne Local Government Area of Ogun State. He grew up with a Sibling - Oladele Odumesi, a retired civil servant.He studied Economics from Ahmadu Bello University (ABU) Zaria, where he obtained a Bachelor of Science in 1989. Afterwards, he studied and received a Master of Science degree in Economics from University of Jos, Plateau State in 1991. After retiring from Wema Bank in 2010, he attended Babcock University, Ilishan in Ogun State, where he obtained a PhD degree in Business Administration (Entrepreneurship) in 2018. CareerDuring his early career, Odumesi worked as a Credit Analyst in Ventures Finance and Procurement Limited from 1991-1993 before joining Wema Bank Plc as a Risk Management Officer, Customer Service Team Lead, Operations Manager, Business Manager, Training Manager at Wema Learning Management Centre, Head-SME and Capital Market Department and Regional Operations Cordinator, Ogun Region of Wema Bank Plc.Odumesi has to his credit many Articles published in both local and International Journals, coupled with his participation in many academic seminars and conferences. He belongs to some professional bodies such as National Institute of Marketing (NIM), Association of Management and Social Sciences Research of Nigeria and National Institute of Credit Administration.

Timi Olubiyi is an Entrepreneurship and Small Business Management expert with a Ph.D in Business Administration. A Babcock University Business School Affiliated Scholar and senior government official. He is a prolific investment coach, business engineer, Chartered Member of the Chartered Institute for Securities & Investment (CISI), and a financial literacy specialist.

Dilyora Pakhritdinovna Khashimova was born on June 29, 1972 in Tashkent. In 1989, she entered the Faculty of Economic Cybernetics (now the Faculty of Digital Economy) of Tashkent State University of Economics and graduated with honors in 1994. In 1995-1996, she began her career as a junior research fellow at the Tashkent Institute of Communications and Electrotechnical Engineering (now the Tashkent University of Information Technologies). Since 1996, she has been working as an assistant at the Department of Economic Informatics and Information Technology of Tashkent State University of Economics. From 2004 to 2022, she has been working as a senior lecturer at the Department of Digital Economy and Information Technology of Tashkent State University of Economics. Currently, she is working as the Deputy Dean of the Faculty of Digital Economy of Tashkent State University of Economics. In 2004, she graduated from the Uzbek-American Academy with a grant from the USAID Foundation and received an MBA degree. In 2011, he was awarded the "20th Anniversary of Independence of the Republic of Uzbekistan" badge. He teaches courses in the subjects "Information and Communication Technologies and Systems in the Economy", "Instrumental Tools for Processing Economic Data", "Programming Technologies", "Practical Software Packages for Business Analytics". He has published a textbook as a sole author and several textbooks and manuals as a co-author. He is the author of a number of educational, methodological and scientific works. He has prepared and published more than 50 scientific articles and theses devoted to the problems of applying information and communication technologies in various sectors of the economy.

Kali Charan Rath is presently working as Associate Professor, Department of Mechanical Engineering, GIET University, Gunupur, Odisha, India. He has more than 19yrs of experience in academic and research .He awarded with Ph.D. degree by National Institute of Technology, Jamshedpur, India, year 2013, in the area of CAD/CAM. He guided more than 20 M.Tech students as project supervisor and scholars received their degree. Recently he is supervising 3 Ph.D scholar work. He attended more than 300 webinars during pandemic time. He presented his research work in various national and International conferences. His work is not only published in various reputed journals but also published as book chapters by reputed publishers. He attended a bunch of FDP and STTP programme conducted by reputed organizations.He is the Ambassador of:Bentham Science

Publication ; SPSC- support to Sustainable Development Goals, Global Brand Ambassador 21STDIGISKILLZ, NIGERIA ; Ambasador of "Management and Strategy Institute"; Advisor of "Mendeley Advisor Community"- Elsevier. He is the member of IEI, CSI, ISTE, IAENG, ISRD,IFERP, Member of "All India Council for Technical Skill Development" and also the member of "National Institute For Technical Training & Skill Development". He is also acting as Mendeley Advisor community (Elsevier) . Received more than 40 certificates with knowledge from research academy- Elsevier, after completion of various research modules. Three Certificate of Excellence received for successfully completed every module within Going through peer review, from research academy- Elsevier. He delivered his research talk in various FDP, STTP, AICTE ATAL academy, National and International Conferences as a keynote speaker. He also received various awards from different national and International communities for his excellence contribution of knowledge to the society. He has one international patent (granted) . One Indian patent published and waiting for examination for grant. Accredited professional certificate on (a) ISO 9001 Quality Management System Associate,(b)Foundation of Business and Entrepreneurship, (c) Lean Foundations Professional certification (LFPC), (d)"Focus on peer Review", Nature Master classes (Springer Nature), (e) "The Fundamental of Digital Marketing", Google Digital Garage, (f) Six Sigma Yellow belt His research field: Robotics and Automation; Smart Manufacturing System; IOT applications,Product design, Modeling and Simulation;CAD/CAM/ CIM ; Finite Element Analysis, Design thinking and Innovation etc.. He likes people to share the knowledge and work in collaborative manner.

Aqmal Reza Amri is a lecturer at the Department of Government Studies, Universitas Muhammadiyah Makassar. He also serves as a co-editor of the Journal of Contemporary Governance and Public Policy. Additionally, he is a researcher at the Center for Research on Society and Humanity in Indonesia with research areas encompassing political science and governance, with a focus on topics such as ethics, migrant labor, studies of civil society, and indigenous studies.

Manjari Sharma is an Associate Professor at CHRIST University, Pune Lavasa Campus, India, with over 15 years of extensive academic experience across multiple universities in Asia, including the Maldives, Malaysia, Sri Lanka, Myanmar, and Dubai. She specializes in Finance, Managerial Economics, Financial Management, Securities Analysis, Portfolio Management, and Operations Management. Dr. Sharma is recognized for her innovative pedagogical methods, focusing on experiential learning, case-based teaching, and technology-driven education. She actively integrates real-world business applications into her courses, ensuring students develop practical skills alongside theoretical knowledge. Her dedication to enhancing learning experiences has led her to design industry-oriented programs and collaborative research projects that bridge the gap between academia and professional practice. An accomplished researcher and author, Dr. Sharma has published extensively in the areas of behavioral finance, AI in education, financial analytics, and innovative teaching methodologies. She has co-authored several books, including "Innovative Pedagogy: A Beginner's Guide to Modern Teaching Strategies", and her research has contributed to advancing financial literacy, digital transformation in education, and investment behavior analysis. Beyond teaching and research, Dr. Sharma is actively involved in global academic collaborations, serving as a key coordinator for international immersion programs. She has led initiatives such as the Global Immersion Program in Texas, USA, and the Indian Cultural Immersion Program in Ladakh, fostering cross-cultural learning experiences. Additionally, she has been instrumental in establishing academic partnerships with universities in the USA, New Zealand, and other international institutions, enhancing opportunities for student and faculty exchanges. A strong advocate for capacity-building programs, she has organized international conferences and faculty development workshops, focusing on emerging trends in finance, business analytics, and higher education pedagogy. She is also involved in research projects on the National Education Policy (NEP) 2020, sustainable business practices, and the role of AI in financial decision-making. Dr. Manjari Sharma's passion for mentoring students and young researchers is evident in her collaborative approach to academic leadership. She continuously works towards bridging the gap between academia and industry, ensuring that her students are equipped with critical thinking, financial acumen, and strategic decision-making skills for global careers.

C.V. Suresh Babu is a pioneer in content development. A true entrepreneur, he founded Anniyappa Publications, a company that is highly active in publishing books related to Computer Science and Management. Dr. C.V. Suresh Babu has also ventured into SB Institute, a center for knowledge transfer. He holds a Ph.D. in Engineering Education from the National Institute of Technical Teachers Training & Research in Chennai, along with seven master's degrees in various disciplines such as Engineering, Computer Applications, Management, Commerce, Economics, Psychology, Law, and Education. Additionally, he has UGC-NET/SET qualifications in the fields of Computer Science, Management, Commerce, and Education. Currently, Dr. C.V. Suresh Babu is a Professor in the Department of Information Technology at the School of Computing Science, Hindustan Institute of Technology and Science (Hindustan University) in Padur, Chennai, Tamil Nadu, India.

Omar C. Vargas-Gonzàlez is a professor, research assistant and former Head of Computer Systems Department at Tecnológico Nacional de México Campus

Ciudad Guzmán, professor at Telematic Engineering at Centro Universitario del Sur Universidad de Guadalajara with a master degree in Computer Systems. Has been trained in Innovation and Multidisciplinary Entrepreneurship at Arizona State University (2018) and a Generation of Ecosystems of Innovation, Entrepreneurship and Sustainability for Jalisco course by Harvard University T.H. Chan School of Health. At present conduct research on diverse fields such as Entrepreneurship, Economy, Statistics, Mathematics and Information and Computer Sciences. Has collaborated in the publication of many scientific articles and conducted diverse Innovation and Technological Development projects.

Muhammad Younus graduated in 2019 from the Karachi Institute of Economics and Technology University in Karachi, Pakistan, and got a Bachelor's degree in Computer Science. The four-year undergraduate program in Computer Science formed the basis of Younus's perseverance towards achieving an in-depth knowledge in the field. After graduation, Younus worked for the past few years as a business IT analyst in the product and research development of a logistics startup in Pakistan called TPL Logistics. They aim to Digitize Logistics Operations in Pakistan from the First Mile to the Last Mile.

Index

N

P

Q

R

S

T

W

Y

www.ingramcontent.com/pod-product-compliance
Lightning Source LLC
LaVergne TN
LVHW061541290926
849162LV00004B/870